Programmed Learning Materials

ARTES LATINAE

LATIN: LEVEL ONE, BOOK TWO

by Waldo E. Sweet

BOLCHAZY-CARDUCCI PUBLISHERS
1000 Brown Street, Wauconda, Illinois 60084

Formerly published by Encyclopaedia Britannica Educational Corporation

In using this book, the student should follow the procedure and techniques described in Unit One of *Latin: Level One, Book One*. There he will also find an explanation of the symbols employed in the Program.

Copyright © 1991
Bolchazy-Carducci Publishers, Inc.

ISBN 0-86516-292-1

Original Copyright © 1966
Encyclopaedia Britannica Educational Corporation.

Reprint 1998

All rights reserved. This work may not be transmitted by television or other devices or processed nor copied, recast, transformed, adapted or utilized in any manner, in whole or in part, without a license. For information regarding a license, write Bolchazy-Carducci Publishers, Inc.

Printed in the United States of America
by United Graphics

Bolchazy-Carducci Publishers, Inc.
1000 Brown Street, Wauconda, Illinois 60084
http://www.bolchazy.com

TABLE OF CONTENTS

Unit 16 Plural of neuters; Basic Sentences 45-48

Unit 17 The {-s -s est} construction; Basic Sentences 49-56; word formation; **hic** and **ille**

Unit 18 Past participles; word formation; Basic Sentences 57-61

Unit 19 Ordinal numerals 1-10; adverbs; vocative; subordinate clauses; Basic Sentences 62-68

Unit 20 Dative singular; Basic Sentences 69-72

Unit 21 Dative plural; special verbs with the dative; Basic Sentences 73-78

Unit 22 Genitive singular; Basic Sentences 79-89

Unit 23 Genitive plural; Basic Sentences 90-97; Basic Sentence review; explanation of noun system

Unit 24 Infinitives; 1st and 2nd person singular of 2nd Conjugation; Basic Sentences 98-104

Unit 25 1st and 2nd person singular of other conjugations; 1st and 2nd person plural of all conjugations; **sum** and **possum**; Basic Sentences 105-114; criss-cross order

Unit 26 Tenses #1 and #3 (Past and Future Incomplete Action); synopses, Basic Sentences 115-123

Unit 27 Prepositions with accusative; Tense #5 (Completed Action in Present Time); principal parts; Basic Sentences 124-136

Unit 28 Tense #4 (Completed Action in Past Time); Basic Sentences 137-138; Readings 1-4

Unit 29 Tense #6 (Completed Action in Future Time); Basic Sentences 139-141; Readings 5-6

Unit 30 Readings 7-12

UNIT SIXTEEN

1. In this Unit we will take up the plural of neuter nouns. You remember that neuter nouns are *always* alike in the ＿＿＿＿＿ and ＿＿＿＿＿ cases.

A: nominative   accusative

2. The signal for the *nominative* plural of neuter nouns is **-a**, as in **vīna**. You therefore know that the *accusative* plural form of **vīnum** must be ＿＿＿.

A: vīna.

3. To remind yourself that the signal for the ambiguous nominative-accusative form on **vīna** is **-a**, rewrite the word; make the signal as a capital letter: ＿＿＿.

A: vīnA.

4-7. Echo your teacher as he transforms these italicized neuter *accusative* forms from singular to plural, that is by changing the **-um** to **-a**. If there is any sentence which you do not understand, ask your classroom teacher for help.

4. Fūr *perīc'lum* metuit → ★ ○ • ○ • Fūr perīc'lA metuit.

5. Jūdex *factum* cognōscit → ★ ○ • ○ • Jūdex factA cognōscit.

6. Fēmina *cōnsilium* capit → ★ ○ • ○ • Fēmina cōnsiliA capit.

7. Medicus *auxilium* vult → ★ ○ • ○ • Medicus auxiliA vult.

TEST INFORMATION

You are responsible for the principal parts of all the verbs which you have had, and you are now expected to be able to give a synopsis or a paradigm of any verb whose principal parts you know.

You will also be asked to produce the synopsis of a verb which you have never seen before, whose principal parts will be given to you.

While you are expected to know all 141 Basic Sentences well enough to produce them when clued by just the first letter, you need know the 12 Readings well enough to produce them with four removals in each line. These removals may or may not be the same as the removals given in the Summary.

FINIS

Verbs:
circueō, circuīre, circuiī (83-85)
crēdō (109-112)
expingō (90)
incipiō (16-17)
requīrō (172-176)
subeō, (69-71)

Adjectives:
alter, altera, alterum (95)
īdem, eadem, idem (128-129)
lūscus-a-um (44)

Miscellaneous:
frūstrā (114-118)   Ō (177)
māne (169-170)   tam (111)

16-2

8. The difference in meaning between **Medicus auxilium vult** and **Medicus auxiliA vult** is that the first means that the doctor wants help, while the second (using the plural) means that he wants s_____ k___s of help.

A: several kinds

9-12. Make the same change in these sentences yourself. Say the entire sentence.

9. Fēmina *cōnsilium* capit → Fēmina _____ capit. √ ★ ○ •

R: Fēmina cōnsiliA capit.

10. Medicus *auxilium* vult → Medicus _____ vult. √ ★ ○ •

R: Medicus auxiliA vult.

11. Jūdex *factum* cognōscit → Jūdex _____ cognōscit. √ ★ ○ •

R: Jūdex factA cognōscit.

12. Fūr *perīc'lum* metuit → Fūr _____'_ metuit. √ ★ ○ •

R: Fūr perīc'lA metuit.

[Give all answers aloud, if possible, particularly if you don't have the use of a tape recorder.]

30-36

VOCABULARY INVENTORY

Proper names:
  Andragorās, Andragorae, m (167)
  Eutrapelus -ī, m (78)
  Fīdentīnus -ī, m (3)
  Hermocratēs, Hermocratis, m (167)
  Faustīnus -ī, m (167)
  Zōilus -ī, m (119)

Nouns:
  Andragorās, Andragorae, m (167)
  Eutrapelus -ī, m (78)
  Hermocratēs, Hermocratis, m (167)
  Zōilus -ī, m (119)
  Lupercus -ī, m (80)
  Fīdentīnus -ī, m (3)
  color, colōris, m (90)
  gena -ae, f (86)
  os, ōris, n (83)
  somnus -ī, m (179-180)
  successus -ūs, m (114-115)
  tōnsor, tōnsōris, m (79)

198.
Dif_____, facilis, jūcund__, ac_____ es id___

Nec tē___ possum viv___ sine ___

R:
Difficilis, facilis, jūcundus, acerbus es idem.
Nec tēcum possum vīvere nec sine tē. (#11)

199.
Lō___ nōbīs___ est, hil____ cēnāvit, et īd___ in____tus mā___ est mort___ Andrāgor___
T__ subī___ mortis caus___, Faustīne, re___is?
In somn___ medi___ vīd____ Hermocrat___.

R:
Lōtus nōbīscum est, hilaris cēnāvit, et īdem inventus māne est mortuus Andragorās.
Tam subitae mortis causam, Faustīne, requīris?
In somnīs medicum vīderat Hermocratēn. (#12)

16-3

13-16. Transform the italicized Second Declension neuter accusative nouns in these new sentences from singular to plural in the same way. Change **-um** to **-A**. [Check *after* you say the answer.]

13. Rēgīna *rēgnum* possidet → R_____ r___A p_____. ✓ ★ ○ •

▼   ▼

R: Rēgīna
rēgnA possidet.

14. Vir *vitium* habet → V__ v____ h_____. ✓ ★ ○ •

▼   ▼

R: Vir vitiA habet.

15. Juvenis *respōnsum* quaerit → J_____ r_____ qu_____. ✓ ★ ○ •

▼   ▼

R: Juvenis
respōnsA quaerit.

16. Amīcus *factum* quaerit → A_____ f____ qu_____. ✓ ★ ○ •

▼   ▼

R: Amīcus
factA quaerit.

17. In the following series, which of these forms are the ambiguous nominative-accusative *neuter plural* with the signal **-A**, like **vitiA**?
muscaØ rēgnA rēgīnaØ perīc'lA auxiliA
formaØ

▼   ▼

A: rēgnA   perīc'lA auxiliA

194.
Qu__ rec____, m___ est, Ō Fīdentīn_,
libellus;
sed ma__ cum recitās, inci__ es__ t____.

▼

R:
Quem recitās, meus est, Ō Fīdentīne,
libellus;
sed male cum recitās, incipit esse tuus. (#7)

195.
Thā___ Quīntus am___ Qu__ Thāida?
Thāida Iusc___
Ūnum ocul__ Thāis nōn ha___; il__ du___.

▼

R:
Thāida Quīntus amat. Quam Thāida.
Thāida luscam.
Ūnum oculum Thāis nōn habet; ille duōs. (#8)

196.
Eutrapelus tōn__ dum circu__ ōr__ Luperc__
expingit__ gen__, al___ barba sub___.

▼

R:
Eutrapelus tōnsor dum circuit ōra Lupercī
expingitque genās, altera barba subit. (#9)

197.
Fr____ ego __ laudō; frūstrā mē, Zōile,
l____s.
Nēmō m__ crēdit, Zōil_; nēmō t____.

▼

R:
Frūstrā ego tē laudō; frūstrā mē, Zōile,
laedis.
Nēmō mihi crēdit, Zōile; nēmō tibi. (#10)

16-4

18. Which of these forms are the nominative singular of First Declension nouns with the signal zero, like **foveaØ**?
sīmiaØ   cōnsiliA   vitiA   muscaØ   factA vīperaØ

A: **sīmiaØ**   **muscaØ**
vīperaØ

19. Which of these forms are the ambiguous nominative-accusative *neuter plural*?
cōnsilia   vitia   aquila   vīta   facta   fēmina ūmbra

A: **cōnsilia vitia**   **facta**

20-23. Echo your teacher as he changes the italicized *subjects* from singular to plural. This transformation involves the same change from **-um** to **-a**, and, of course, the verb changes from singular to plural, too.

20. *Vitium* virum regit → V___A v____ regunt. ★ ○ • ○ •

Cōnf: **VitiA virum regunt.**

21. *Respōnsum* juvenēs adjuvat →
R_____A j_____ adjuvant. ★ ○ • ○ •

Cōnf: **RespōnsA juvenēs adjuvant.**

22. *Vīnum* sapientēs obumbrat → V___ s_____ obumbrant. ★ ○ • ○ •

Cōnf: **VīnA**
sapientēs obumbrant.

SUMMARY

In this Unit you learned the principal parts of a number of verbs. You will probably wish to review these in your Notebook.

You also had six Readings. Following is a review, with four removals in each line.

190. He asks Faustinus, "_____
_____?"

A: Do you seek the cause of such a sudden death?

191. Then the punch line. Andragoras died because _____.

A: in his dreams he had seen Dr. Hermocrates.

192. You will remember that Symmachus visited Martial (along with 100 students) and gave him a fever which he didn't have before; but this Dr. Hermocrates was the kind of physician who could ____ you if you even _____.

A: kill   dreamed that he visited you.

193. Today doctors are sometimes sued for "malpractice," which means that the patient received improper treatment through inexcusable ignorance or neglect. This is a serious charge, of course. Suppose that the family of Andragoras decided to sue Dr. Hermocrates for malpractice, by bringing forth as evidence this poem of Martial. You are Dr. H's lawyer. How could you prove *beyond all doubt* that Martial's evidence is totally worthless?

A: This is the last frame of the course. If you can't figure out the answer, you will just have to wait until *Latin: Level Two.*

Goodbye until we meet again in *Latin: Level Two!*

16-5

23. *Venēnum* taurōs necat → V_____ t_____ necant. ★ ○ • ○ •

Cōnf: VenēnA taurōs necant.

24-27. Change the subjects of these same sentences from singular to plural. Check with the tape.

24. *Vīnum* sapientēs obumbrat → V___ s_____ _____ant. √ ★ ○ •

R: VīnA sapientēs obumbrant.

25. *Venēnum* taurōs necat → V_____ t_____ ___ant. √ ★ ○ •

R: VenēnA taurōs necant.

26. *Vitium* virum regit → V____ v____ ___unt. √ ★ ○ •

R: VitiA virum regunt.

27. *Respōnsum* juvenēs adjuvat → R_____ j_____ _____ant. √ ★ ○ •

R: RespōnsA juvenēs adjuvant.

28-31. Change these italicized subjects from singular to plural in these *new* sentences.

28. *Perīc'lum* rēgīnam vincit → P_____ r_____ v____unt. √ ★ ○ •

R: Perīc'lA rēgīnam vincunt.

---

184. The poem as a whole is arranged as a tricolon. The first sentence (lines 1 & 2) tells us about the exp_____ces of a man named Andragoras.

A: experiences

185. Line three is a qu_____ and line four is the _____ to it.

A: question answer

186. What happened to Andragoras? Well, first of all he _____. [In your own words]

A: went to the baths with Martial and his friends.

187. Secondly he __ed _____ly with them.

A: dined cheerfully

188. And then, lo and behold! This same Andragoras who had been so cheerful the day before _____.

A: was found dead in the morning.

189. In line three Martial asks a question of his friend _____us.

A: Faustinus. (Give the *nominative* form in English.)

30-33

16-6

29. *Dictum* auctōrem obumbrat → D____
a_____ ob____ant. ✓ ★ ○ •

R: DictA auctōrem obumbrant.

30. *Cōnsilium* fūrem irrītat → C_____
f____ ir____ant. ✓ ★ ○ •

R: CōnsiliA fūrem irrītant.

31. *Factum* virum reddit → F____ v____
r____unt. ✓ ★ ○ •

R: FactA virum reddunt.

[If you have any question about the meaning of any of these sentences, get some help from your friends or your teacher.]

32. The statement that neuters are alike in the nominative and accusative cases applies ____ (only to the singular/only to the plural/to both singular and plural).

A: to both singular and plural.

33. "The accusative case of a neuter noun or adjective is *always* like the nominative case; there are no exceptions to this rule." Copy this in your Reference Notebook under Facts About Latin.

34. "Neuter nouns always end in -a in the nominative-accusative plural; there are no exceptions to this rule." Copy under Facts About Latin.

30-32

179. Tam crēdula rēs est amor! Etiam in *somnīs* videt juvenis l____em suam.

R: lūcem

180. He sees the girl even in his s____s.

A: dreams.

Refer once again to the poem.

181. "Andragorās et Hermocratēs sunt virī Graecī. Uter est medicus?" "_____."

R: Hermocratēs est medicus.

182. "Hermocratēn" est forma Graeca, cāsūs accūsātīvī. Forma Latīna hujus nōminis est "Her____em."

R: Hermocratem.

183. "Hermocratēn" est cāsūs _____.

R: accūsātīvī.

35. Echo a new technical term ★ ○ • ○ • phrase.

VCh: "fraze"

36. A group of words which is connected in some way is called a "phrase." **Sub jūdice** is a prep_____al _____.

A: prepositional phrase.

37-40. Echo your teacher as he changes these phrases from singular to plural.

37. sine auxiliō → ★ ○ • ○ •

Cōnf: sine auxiliīs

38. sine perīc'lō → ★ ○ • ○ •

Cōnf: sine perīc'līs

39. sine rēgnō → ★ ○ • ○ •

Cōnf: sine rēgnīs

40. sine respōnsō → ★ ○ • ○ •

Cōnf: sine respōnsīs

41-43. Change these phrases from singular to plural yourself.

41. sine membrō → s___ m_____

R: sine membrīs

---

172. requīrō requīrere requīsīvī requīsītus ★ ○ • ○ •

173. Copy in your Notebook.

174. An English derivative of **requīrō** is "_____."

A: require.

175. However, in this sentence, the word **requīrō** means "ask." "Requīrō" signal "qu___ō."

R: quaerō.

176. Notice that when the prefix **re-** is added, the diphthong **-ae-** of **quaerō** becomes the vowel _____.

A: ī.

Members of a Latin class occasionally find it useful to talk in Latin when others are present.

177. Ō, hoc t__ m____ subīt__ est!

Vīsne mihi nūbere, mea lūx?

R: Ō, hoc tam subitum est!

178. The girl claims to be surprised because the proposal is __ s____ n.

A: so sudden.

42. sine vīnō → s___ v____

R: sine vīnīs

43. sine dictō → s___ d_____

R: sine dictīs

44. Echo the paradigm of a Second Declension neuter noun:

★ ○ •   rēgnum   rēgnA
         rēgnum   rēgnA
         rēgnō   rēgnīs

45. Copy **rēgnum** into your Notebook under "Forms."

46. Observe that before the signals **-a** and **-īs** the characteristic vowel **-o** has d_____ed.

A: disappeared.

47. Using **rēgnum** as a model, write the paradigm of **vitium**; make the **-a** a capital:

R: vitium   vitiA
    vitium   vitiA
    vitiō   vitiīs

48. We have mentioned before the difficulty of "look-alikes." Which of these words are ablative singular like **omnī**?

ēloquentī hilarī asinī elephantī crūdēlī

A: ēloquentī hilarī   crūdēlī

---

169. Sequuntur verba quae in carmine inventa sunt. "*Māne*" est tempus: est prima pars diēī. Hī convīvae ---- (māne/nocte) cēnant.

R: māne

170. Hī equī nōn nocte sed m---- aquam bibunt.

R: nocte

171.

Tam magnus erat.

Quantus erat piscis quem tū āmīsistī?

"Tam magnus" significat "t---tus."

R: tantus.

49. We will now give you practice so that you will be able to distinguish **sīmia** from **perīc'lA**. Although these words both end in the same sound, they ____ (do/do not) have the same signal.

A: do not

50. **Sīmia** is _____ case and _____ number.

A: nominative   singular

51. The signal on **sīmia** which indicates its case and number is the signal ____.

A: zero (∅).

52. **Perīc'lA** is _____ or _____ case and _____ number.

A: nominative   accusative
         plural

53. Write down the words in this list which are the ambiguous nominative-accusative form like **perīc'lA**. Write the signal **-A** in capital letters.
   membra   respōnsa   aqua   musca
   venēna   vitia   rāna

A: membrA   respōnsA
   venēnA   vitiA

54. Write the words which are nominative singular of the First Declension, like **sīmia∅**. Use the signal zero, as in **sīmia∅**.
   rēgna   aquila   cōnsilia   lacrima   vīna   forma

A: aquila∅   lacrima∅   forma∅

---

165. Make the transformation from active to passive to say that the baby was washed by the old lady.

Active
Anus īnfantem lāvit
Passive
Ab anū īnfāns ____us ____.

R: **Ab anū īnfāns lōtus est.**

166. A second point which needs clarification is that the Romans spent a great deal of time every day in luxurious baths. These were a combination of country club, gymnasium, library, recreation center, and swimming pool. In our poem the phrase **Lōtus nōbīscum est** occurs. This does not mean simply that this person took a bath because he was dirty; it means that he and Martial spent several hours

A: at the bath, reading, playing ball, talking, etc.

167. Here is the poem.

Lōtus nōbīscum est, hilaris cēnāvit, et īdem inventus māne est mortuus Andragorās. Tam subitae mortis causam, Faustīne, requīris? In somnīs medicum vīderat Hermocratēn.
(Reading #12)

168. Copy in your Notebook.

16-10

55. Echo the paradigm of a Third Declension neuter noun.

★ ○ • ("family") génus   génerA
                   génus   génerA
                   génere genériBUS

56. Copy in your Notebook the paradigm of **genus**.

57. There is nothing new in Third Declension neuters: the signal for the ambiguous nominative-accusative form is ___.

A: -a.

58. The signal for the ablative plural is like other Third Declension nouns, that is _____.

A: -bus.

59. ★ ○ • ("body") córpus   córporA
                        córpus   córporA
                        córpore corpóriBUS

60. ★ ○ • ("river") flúmen   flúminA
                        flúmen   flúminA
                        flúmine flúminiBUS

61. Write the paradigm of **corpus**. Remember that the **-s** changes to **-r**. _____ _____

A: corpus   corporA
                        corpus   corporA
                        corpore corporiBUS

62-63. Echo your teacher as he changes these Third Declension neuter accusatives from singular to plural, using the **-A** signal.

62. Auctor *opus* laudat → ★ ○ • ○ •

Cōnf: Auctor operA laudat.

30-28

158. Ā Nātūrā datī sunt agrī = F____s have been ____en by ____.

A: Fields have been given by Nature.

159. √ t ____ • ○ ★ •
Fidem servāvī → Ā mē fidēs servāta est.

R: Ā mē fidēs servāta est.

160. Ā mē fidēs servāta est = F____h has b____k____t by ____.

A: Faith has been kept by me.

161. Ars hūmāna aedificāvit urbēs → Arte hūmānā ____ātae sunt u____ • ○ ★ •

R: Arte hūmānā aedificātae sunt urbēs.

162. Arte hūmānā aedificātae sunt urbēs = C____s h____ b____t by h____ sk____.

A: Cities have been built by human skill.

163. Here are the principal parts of the Latin verb meaning "wash."

lavō   lavāre   lāvī   lōtus ★ ○ •

164. Copy in your Notebook.

63. Lupus *flūmen* quaerit → ★ ○ • ○ •

Cōnf: Lupus flūminA quaerit.

64-65. Make the same changes yourself from singular accusative to plural accusative.

64. Auctor *opus* laudat → A_____ o_____ l_____.

R: Auctor operA laudat.

65. Lupus *flūmen* quaerit → L_____ fl_____ qu_____.

R: Lupus flūminA quaerit.

66-67. Change the italicized Third Declension neuter accusatives in these new sentences from singular to plural; use the **-A** ending.

66. Auctor *genus* cernit → A_____ g_____ c_____.

R: Auctor generA cernit.

67. Morsus *corpus* irrītat → M_____ c_____ ir_____.

R: Morsus corporA irrītat.

68-69. Echo your teacher as he changes the following Third Declension neuter nominatives from singular to plural. Notice that the verb also changes.

68. *Corpus* ā medicīs cernitur → ★ ○ • ○ •

Cōnf: Corpora ā medicīs cernuntur.

---

157. Active → Passive transformation
Nātūra dedit agrōs → Ā Nātūrā datī sunt agrī ★ ○ •

the verb **sum**. Here are some examples:
Romans used a two word phrase, consisting of the past participle (like **positus**) and a form of passive endings **-tur** and **-ntur**. Instead the form, **pōnitur**, perfective forms do *not* have the is that while the #2 form **pōnit** has a passive the others. Perhaps the chief thing to point out Reading #12 requires less explanation than even more. (End of Commercial).

Latin: *Level One*, you will enjoy *Latin: Level Two* the Romans lived and thought. If you liked more reading of materials that illustrate how these. There will be less and less drill, more and *Level Two*, where you will read more poems like *Level One*. We hope you will go on with *Latin:*
Here is the last Reading and the end of *Latin:*

A: You (pl) won't be able to live with me.

156. Nec mēcum poteritis vīvere = _____

A: You (pl) were hard and easy to get along with.

155. Difficilēs, facilēs erātis = _____

A: We believed you
(Crēdidimus is #5; the #2 form would be crēdimus.)

154. Tibi crēdidimus = _____

16-12

69. *Genus* ā fēminīs laudātur → ★ ○ • ○ •

Cōnf: Genera ā fēminīs laudantur.

70-71. Make these same changes yourself from singular subject to plural subject. Remember to make the necessary verb changes.

70. *Corpus* ā medicīs cernitur → C_____
ā m_____ _____untur.

R: CorporA
ā medicīs cernuntur.

71. *Genus* ā fēminīs laudātur → G_____ ā
f_____ _____antur.

R: GenerA ā
fēminīs laudantur.

72-73. Change the italicized nominatives in these new sentences from singular to plural.

72. *Opus* ab auctōribus laudātur → Op_____
ab au_____ _____antur.

R: OperA
ab auctōribus laudantur.

73. *Flūmen* ab īnsānō quaeritur → Fl_____
ab īn_____ _____untur.

R: FlūminA
ab īnsānō quaeruntur.

74. Here are the ambiguous nominative-accusative plural forms of all the neuter nouns which you have had so far. Study them.

cōnsiliA membrA venēnA dictA factA
flūminA generA corporA rēspōnsA
operA rēgnA auxiliA vitiA vīnA perīc'lA

30-26

148. Incipiet esse meus = _____
A: It will begin to be mine.

149. Thāida amāverat Quīntus = _____
A: Quīntus had loved Thais.

150. Ūnum oculum Thāis nōn habēbit = _____
A: Thāis won't have one eye.

151. Eutrapelī tōnsor circuit ōra Luperus = _____
A: Lupercus the barber goes around the cheeks of Eutrapelus.

152. Expīnxeritis genās = _____
A: You will have rouged the cheeks.

153. Frūstrā ego tē laedō; frūstrā mē, Zōile, laudās = _____
A: In vain I harm you; in vain, Zōilus, do you praise me.

75. Which of these words are the ambiguous nominative-accusative neuter plural form with the signal -A?

corpora   respōnsa   fēmina
Fortūna   flūmina   līnea

A: corporA   respōnsA
            flūminA

76. Which of these words have the signal zero indicating nominative singular of a First Declension noun?

opera   membra   umbra   vīta
venēna   pecūnia

A: umbraØ   vītaØ
         pecūniaØ

77-78. Echo your teacher as he changes these ablative phrases of neuter nouns from singular to plural.

77. sine opere → ★ ○ • ○ •

Cōnf: sine operibus

78. sine corpore → ★ ○ • ○ •

Cōnf: sine corporibus

79-80. Make this same change yourself from singular to plural.

79. sine opere → ____ o _____ √ ★ ○ •

R: sine operibus

80. sine corpore → ____ c _____ √ ★ ○ •

R: sine corporibus

16-14

81-82. Change these Third Declension ablative phrases from the singular to the plural.

81. sine genere → ____ _____ ✓ ★ ○ •

R: sine generibus

82. sine flūmine → ____ _____ ✓ ★ ○ •

R: sine flūminibus

83-90. Here are Second and Third Declension nouns mixed. Echo your teacher as he transforms them from singular to plural.

83. sine opere → ★ ○ • ○ •

Cōnf: sine operibus

84. sine vitiō → ★ ○ • ○ •

Cōnf: sine vitiīs

85. sine genere → ★ ○ • ○ •

Cōnf: sine generibus

86. sine respōnsō → ★ ○ • ○ •

Cōnf: sine respōnsīs

87. sine vīnō → ★ ○ • ○ •

Cōnf: sine vīnīs

---

135. Martial says in the first line that his friend has a con_____ry nature.

A: contradictory

136. One day he is _____ [In your own words]

A: easy to get along with and pleasant.

137. The next day he will be _____ [In your own words]

A: difficult and unpleasant.

138. Martial tells his friend that _____.

A: he can't live either with him or without him.

139. You were able to guess the meaning of the unknown verb *vivere* from its resemblance to the Latin adjective v___s.

A: vīvus.

140. The flattering adjectives in the first line are the ____ and ____ (1st/2d/3d/4th) words.

A: 2d   3d

141. The unpleasant traits of his friend are described in the ____ and ____ (1st/2d/3d/4th) adjectives.

A: 1st   4th

30-24

88. sine rēgnō → ★ ○ • ○ •

Cōnf: sine rēgnīs

89. sine corpore → ★ ○ • ○ •

Cōnf: sine corporibus

90. sine flūmine → ★ ○ • ○ •

Cōnf: sine flūminibus

91-98. Change these same words from ablative singular to plural. [Speak up!]

91. sine vitiō → _____

R: sine vitiīs

92. sine flūmine → _____

R: sine flūminibus

93. sine opere → _____

R: sine operibus

94. sine corpore → _____

R: sine corporibus

95. sine respōnsō → _____

R: sine respōnsīs

130.

Ecce! Venit ad mē *idem* canis quī herī mē momordit!

Minimē; est alter canis, blandus et amīcus.

Ego errāvī et tū rēctē dīxistī. Est *idem* canis quī tē herī mo——

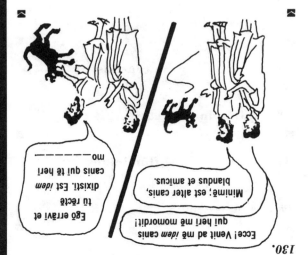

R: momordit.

131. The first man was afraid of the dog be-cause he thought it was the s---- dog who ---- him the day be----.

A: _____ same dog who bit him the day before.

132. Tū īdem es et fortis et ignāvus = ---- , the s---- p------, --- b---- a-- c--------.

A: You, the same person, are both brave and cowardly.

133. ● ○ ★

Difficilis, facilis, jūcundus, acerbus es īdem.
Nec tēcum possum *vīvere* nec sine tē. (Reading #11)

134. Copy in your *Notebook.* Write what the poem is about. You remember that Quōcum is more common than cum quō. With the personal pronoun the Romans never used * cum tē but always ——————.

A: tēcum.

96. sine rēgnō → _ _ _ _ _ _ _ _ _ _ _ _ _ _ _

R: sine rēgnīs

97. sine vīnō → _ _ _ _ _ _ _ _ _ _ _ _ _ _ _

R: sine vīnīs

98. sine genere → _ _ _ _ _ _ _ _ _ _ _ _ _ _ _

R: sine generibus

99-103. Change these ablative phrases from the singular to the plural. Since there are both Second and Third Declension neuters, the endings will be either **-īs** or **-bus**.

99. ex opere → _ _ _ _ _ _ _ _ _ _

R: ex operibus

100. sine factō → _ _ _ _ _ _ _ _ _

R: sine factīs

101. in cōnsiliō → _ _ _ _ _ _ _ _ _

R: in cōnsiliīs

102. ā flūmine → _ _ _ _ _ _ _ _ _ _ _

R: ā flūminibus

103. sine venēnō → _ _ _ _ _ _ _ _ _

R: sine venēnīs

---

124. The reason that both the author's praise of Zoilus and Zoilus' criticism of the author are in vain is that _ [In your own words]

A: no one believes either of them.

125. Give an English translation.

_ _ _ _ _ _ _ _ _ _ _ _ _ _ _ _ Z _ _ _ _ _ _ _ ;
_ _ _ _ _ _ _ _ _ _ _ _ _ _ _ _ Z _ _ _ _ _ _ _ ;
_ .

A: In vain do I praise you; in vain, Zoilus, do you harm me. Nobody believes me, Zoilus; nobody believes you. [Don't expect to have exactly this translation.]

126. The form **nēmō** is a poetical variant of _ _ _ _ _ _ _

A: **nēmō**.

127. ★ ○ • • ○ • **crēdō, crēdere, crēdidī, crēditus**

128. In this next poem there is a new word, an irregular adjective and pronoun. We will ask you to know just the nominative forms at this time.

★ ○ • • ○ • **īdem   eadem   īdem**
             m   f   n

129. From these forms you can see that the **-dem** part is a s _ _ _ _ x.

A: suffix.

16-17

104-111. ★ ●

> Auctor opus laudat. (24)
> Numquam perīc'lum sine perīc' lō vincitur. (25)
> Insānus mediō flūmine quaerit aquam. (32)
> Nēmō sine vitiō est. (26)
> Mēns rēgnum bona possidet. (28)
> Sapientia vīnō obumbrātur. (27)
> Habet suum venēnum blanda ōrātiō. (34)
> Rem nōn spem, factum nōn dictum, quaerit amīcus. (33)

112-130. Change the italicized neuters from singular to plural.

112. **Nēmō** sine *vitiō* est → _____ _____.

R: Nēmō sine vitiīs est.

113. This means, "_____."

A: Nobody exists without faults.

114. **Auctor** *opus* **laudat** → _____ _____.

R: Auctor operA laudat.

115. **Sapientia** *vīnō* **obumbrātur** → _____ _____.

R: Sapientia vīnīs obumbrātur.

117. You trust me = _ _ m___ cr__is.

R: Tū mihi crēdis.

118. I trust you in vain = Fr___ā t___ cr___.

R: Frūstrā ego tibi crēdō.

119. ★ ○ ●

Frūstrā ego tē laudō; frūstrā mē, Zōile, laedis. Nēmō mihi crēdit, Zōile; nēmō tibi. (Reading #10)

120. Copy in your Notebook. Write what you think the poem says.

121. Part of the humor of this poem lies in the fact that the verbs in the first line (**laudō** and **laedis**) look and sound very much alike but are very _____ in meaning.

A: different

122. The author says that he _____s Z_____ in ____, and in ____ does h_____ ____.

A: he praises Zoilus in vain, and in vain does Zoilus harm him.

123. Expand the kernel which has an element missing: Nēmō mihi crēdit, Zōile; nēmō tibi.

A: Nēmō mihi crēdit, Zōile; nēmō tibi crēdit.

30-21

16-18

116. This means, "......................."

A: Wisdom is overshadowed by (different types of) wine.

117. Numquam perīc'lum sine *perīc'lō* vincitur → ....

R: Numquam perīc'lum sine perīc'līs vincitur.

118. Rem nōn spem, *factum* nōn *dictum*, quaerit amīcus → ....

R: Rem nōn spem, factA nōn dictA, quaerit amīcus.

119. This means, "......................."

A: A friend seeks support, not a promise; he seeks deeds not words.

120. Mēns *rēgnum* bona possidet → ......
....

R: Mēns rēgnA bona possidet.

121. This means, "......................."

A: A good mind possesses kingdoms.

122. Mēns rēgna bona possidet is an ambiguous sentence, since the adjective bona could modify either mēns or ......

A: rēgna.

20-30

111. Quī nimis amat saepe nimis crēdit ...... (puellam/puellae).

R: puellae.

112. Hoc verbum "crēdere" capit cāsum ...... (accūsātīvum/datīvum).

R: datīvum.

113. Verba quae quoque cāsum datīvum capiunt sunt "s...īre," "pl...ēre," "n...ēre," "n...ere," et "imp...āre."

R: servīre, placēre, nocēre, nūbere, imperāre.

114. Frūstrā sīgnificat "sine successū." Hic vir asinum *frūstrā* trahit. Hoc est, asinum trahere nōn pot...

R: potest.

115. "Sine successū" sīgnificat "fr......"

R: frūstrā.

116. Egō tibi crēdō = ...

R: I trust you.

123. If **bonA** modifies **rēgnA,** the sentence **Mēns rēgnA bonA possidet** means, "The ____ possesses ____ _____s."

A: The mind possesses good kingdoms.

124. If **bonaØ** modifies **mēnS,** then **MēnS rēgnA bonaØ possidet** means, "A ____ ____ _____s _____s."

A: A good (noble) mind possesses kingdoms.

125. **Habet** *suum venēnum* **blanda ōrātiō** → _____.

R: Habet sua venēna blanda ōrātiō.

126. This means, "_____."

A: Pleasant speech has its own poisons.

127. **Habet sua venēna blanda ōrātiō** is also an ambiguous sentence. If **blandaØ** is feminine gender, nominative singular, it modifies _____.

A: ōrātiōØ.

128. **BlandA** could also be neuter gender, accusative plural. It would then modify _____.

A: venēnA.

129. If **blandA** modifies **venēnA,** the meaning of **Habet sua venēnA blandA ōrātiō** would be, "S_____ has its own _____ _____s."

A: Speech has its own smooth poisons.

106. "Quōrum colōrem mūtāre volēbat Eutrapelus?" "_____ c_____."

R: Genārum colōrem.

107. "Cujus arte mūtābantur colōrēs genārum Luperci?" "Ar_____ _____."

R: Arte Eutrapelī tōnsōris.

108. The next poem was written by a "transplanted Roman" named Buchanan, who lived 1506–1582. He was a famous author, who, although he lived in Scotland, wrote in the _____ language.

A: Latin

109. Haec sunt verba quae inveniēs in proximō carmine. Hāc in pictūrā canis virō *crēdit.* Ergō, hic canis est animal crē_um.

R: crēdulum.

110. Amor est rēs crēdula. Noster juvenis puellae cr__t.

R: crēdit.

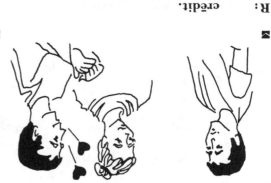

16-20

130. Īnsānus *mediō flūmine* quaerit aquam → _____.

R: Īnsānus mediīs flūminibus quaerit aquam.

131. We hope that by now you have been made *well* aware that **fēmina** is _____ case and _____ number, while **genera** is _____ _____.

A: _____ nominative singular _____ nominative or accusative case and plural number.

132. However, you could *not* tell which of these nouns are like **fēminaØ** and which are like **generA**.

Fāta   puella   pēnsa   causa   sīgna

You cannot tell because _____.
[In your own words]

A: _____ if a person does not know which words are neuter and which ones are First Declension, he cannot tell when he sees the words in isolation.

133. However, if we were to put these words into a context, you would be able to tell. Echo the first half of Basic Sentence 45, which uses one of these words. ★ ○ • ○ • **Dūcunt volentem Fāta.**

134. We picked this sentence because all the words are new. In spite of this fact, however, you can see that the verb is _____.

A: _____ dūcunt.

---

99. An English name for Eutrapelus might be "G_____."

A: Gabby.

Quaestiōnēs et Respōnsa

100. "Quotī temporis sunt circuit,' expingit,' et 'subit'?" "T_____."

R: Temporis secundī.

101. "Hōc in carmine, cujus cāsūs est 'ōra'?" "Est c_____."

R: Est cāsūs accūsātīvī.

102. "Cui Eutrapelus serviēbat?" "_____."

R: Lupercō.

103. "Quae partēs faciēī pingēbantur?" "_____."

R: Genae.

104. "Ā quō genae expingēbantur?" "_____ _____."

R: Ab Eutrapelō tōnsōre.

105. "Dum Eutrapelus nimis nārrat, ex quō locō subibat barba?" "_____ _____ g_____."

R: Ex alterā genā.

16-21

135. The new word **volentem** must be the {__} of the sentence.

A: {-m}

136. Therefore **Fāta** must be the {__} of the sentence.

A: {-s}

137. What tells you whether the subject **Fāta** is singular or plural? _____ [In your own words]

A: It is plural because the verb **dūcunt** is plural.

138. Since **Fāta** is nominative plural, is it a First Declension noun like **vīperaØ** or a Second Declension neuter like **vīnA**? _____

A: Second Declension neuter like **vīnA**.

139. Echo the complete Basic Sentence. ★ ○ • ○ • *Dūcunt volentem FātA, nōlentem trahunt.* (45)

140. The verb in the second kernel is _____.

A: trahunt.

141. The word **nōlentem** is the {__} of the **trahunt** kernel.

A: {-m}

---

94. Et dum Eutrapelus rēs vānās nārrat et nimis sē laudat, in *alterā genā Luperci barba s--it.*

95. Quid significat hoc adjectīvum "alter?" *Si tū duōs libellōs habēs et mihi ūnum ex hīs dās, tū jam habēs ūnum libellum et ego habeō al-------.*

R: alterum.

96. Hoc est, dum Eutrapelus ūnam genam cūrat, subit secunda barba in al---- parte faciēī Luperci.

R: altera

97. Nōndum ad fīnem labōris suī Eutrapelus est, sed jam al----- b----- s---t.

R: altera barba subit.

98. Give an English translation in your own words.

A: While Eutrapelus the barber was going around the face of Luperus and was rouging his cheeks, the beard on the other side started to grow out.

142. Without knowing the meaning of *any* of the words, you can supply the missing element of the second kernel. **Dūcunt volentem FātA, ____ nōlentem trahunt.**

A: **Dūcunt volentem FātA, FātA nōlentem trahunt.**

143. Now we know that the **FātA** (whoever or whatever they are) do the act of **dūcunt** to a **volentem,** and they do the act of _____ to a _____.

A: **trahunt nōlentem.**

144. The first thing which you must do when you see a new sentence is to observe its str_____

A: structure.

Now comes the new vocabulary of this Basic Sentence.

145. Echo your teacher's description of this picture. ★ ○ • ○ • V__ t_____ d_____

Cōnf: **Vir taurum dūcit.**

146. This sentence means that the ___ is l___ing the _____.

A: the man is leading the bull.

---

90. Hāc in pictūrā Eutrapelus tōnsor genās Luperci pingit (vel *expingit*). Vult *colōrem* genārum mūtāre. Lupercus nōn jam pallet sed rub___.

R: rubet.

91. At rubet Lupercus nōn ex nātūrā sed ex arte t____is.

R: tōnsōris.

92. Eutrapelus tōnsor dum barbam cūrat nōn tacet. Multa verba dīcit et celeriter nōn agit. Lupercus vult factum, nōn d_____.

R: dictum.

93. Nōmen "Eutrapelus" est Graecum, significāns "facilis," "ēloquēns," "hilaris." At Lupercus nōn quaerit tōnsōrem ē_____.

R: ēloquentem.

16-23

147. Echo your teacher's description of this picture. ★ ○ • ○ • J_____ c____ tr____.

◢   ◣

Cōnf: Juvenis canem trahit.

148. This sentence means that the _____ ___ is dr___ing the ___.
◢   ◣

A: young man is dragging the dog.

149. ★ ○ ○ D_____ v_____ F___, n_____ tr_____.
◢   ◣

A: Dūcunt volentem FātA, nōlentem trahunt.

150. It now appears that the **FātA** ____ the **volentem** but ____ the **nōlentem**.
◢   ◣

A: lead   drag

151. ★ ○ •   fātum   FātA
                 fātum   FātA
                 fātō   Fātīs
◢   ◣

---

86. Genae sunt partēs faciēī hūmānae quae sub oculīs sunt. Hāc in pictūrā genae sunt membra quae indicantur numerō ____ (prīmō/secundō/tertiō/quārtō).

◣
R: secundō.

◣
87. Sed ōs (numerī singulāris) indicātur numerō _____.

◣
R: quārtō.

88. "Ex quibus partibus faciēī subit bar- ba?" "_____."

◣
R: Ex genīs.

89. "In quā parte faciēī sunt dentēs?" "_____."

◣
R: In ōre.

16-24

152. The singular form of this word means a decree of the gods which cannot be changed. There is a short English derivative of this word, which is "_ _ _ e."

A: fate.

153. In the plural, however, this word **FātA** refers to the three mythological goddesses who decided in advance the course of human lives and even had power over the gods themselves. We have therefore capitalized this word in the plural to show that it is a p_____ noun.

A: personal

154. Pronounce and check. Stoic ✓ ★ ○ •

VCh: "stów-wick"

155. This Basic Sentence is by the Roman philosopher Seneca, who was a Stoic. One of the beliefs of Stoic philosophy was that since the Fates had already determined one's life, the wise man should not resist the Fates but instead should _____. [In your own words]

A: yield to them.

156. Dūcunt volentem Fāta, nōlentem trahunt means that _____. [Use the words **volentem** and **nōlentem,** even if you cannot figure out what they mean yet.]

A: The Fates guide the **volentem** and drag the **nōlentem.**

157. ★ ○ •   volēns   volentēs
               volentem volentēs
("willing person")   volente   volentibus

158. Now see if you can guess the meaning of the unknown word **nōlentem**. **Dūcunt volentem Fāta, nōlentem trahunt** = The ____ ____ the ____ and ____ the ____.

A: The fates guide the willing ("person") and drag the unwilling ("person").

159. Copy this Basic Sentence in your Notebook.

160. On the model of **volēns** ("willing person"), decline **nōlēns** ("unwilling person"). Remember that the macron disappears before **-nt-**.

A: nōlēns   nōlentēs
    nōlentem   nōlentēs
    nōlente   nōlentibus

161. Make sure you understand about the macron. Vowels in Latin are always long before **-ns** and always short before **-nt**. Copy this information in your Notebook under "Facts About Latin."

162. Here follows a list of words which you have never seen. Keeping in mind the rule which we have just given you, write down the words which contain a long vowel, and mark the vowel long. **tensus   placent   placens   patiens   patientem**

A: tēnsus   placēns   patiēns

78. Eutrapelus est tōnsor. Ergō "Eutrapelus tōnsor," significat "Eutrapelus qui _____ est."

R: tōnsor

79. "Tōnsor est qui capillōs cūrat. In hāc pictūrā vir cujus capillōs tōnsor cūrat est Lupercus. Uter est tōnsor, Eutrapelus an Lupercus?" "_____."

R: Eutrapelus est tōnsor.

80. Vir in illā pictūrā cujus capillī ā tōnsōre cūrantur est L_____ nōmine.

R: Lupercus

81. Noster auctor Mārtiālis nōn dīcit, "Dum Eutrapelus tōnsor circuit ōra Lupercī," sed, "Eu_____ t_____ d_____ c_____ ō_____ L_____."

R: Eutrapelus tōnsor dum circuit ōra Lupercī.

82. Hoc est, conjūnctiō **dum** nōn est prīma vōx hujus sententiae sed _____ vōx.

R: tertia

16-26

163. Write down the Basic Sentence from dictation. D_____ v_____ F___, n_____ tr_____. ★ ○ ○ [Listen to the three long vowels.]

R: Dūcunt volentem Fāta, nōlentem trahunt.

164. This sentence means that if you go willingly the Fates will _____, but if you are unwilling, they will _____. [In your own words]

A: help (guide, lead) you,
      make you do it anyhow.

165. This is a principle of _____ philosophy and was written by the Roman philosopher named _____.

A: Stoic
   Seneca.

166. Write the paradigm of **fātum**.

R: fātum   Fāta
      fātum   Fāta
      fātō   Fātīs

167. Does the form **Fāta** have the signal Ø (like **lacrimaØ**) or the signal **-A** (like **rēgnA**)?

A: It has the signal **-A**, like **rēgnA**.

30-12

72. "Barba subit dum Eutrapelus tōnsor duās āctiōnēs agit. Et quās duās āctiōnēs agit?" "Eu_____ t_____ ōra _____ et genās _____."

R: Eutrapelus tōnsor ōra circuit et genās expingit.

73. "Quid Eutrapelus circuit?" "_____."

R: Ōra.

74. "Ōra" est nōmen ____ (masculīni/fēminīni/neutrīus) generis et ____ (singulāris/plūrālis) numerī.

R: neutrīus   plūrālis

75. "Cujus ōra circuit tōnsor Eutrapelus?" "_____ c_____."

R: Luperci ōra circuit.

76. "Et cujus genās expingit?" "_____ _____."

R: Luperci   genās expingit.

77. "Et cujus barba subit dum Eutrapelus ōra circuit et genās expingit?" "_____ b____ t."

R: Luperci   quoque barba subit.

168. Transform **Dūcunt volentem Fāta, nōlentem trahunt** to the passive: D__itur v____s ā F____, n_____ tr__itur.

R: Dūcitur volēns ā Fātīs, nōlēns trahitur.

Question and Answer Drill

169. "Quem dūcunt Fāta?" "_____."

R: Volentem.

170. "Quis ā Fātīs dūcitur?" "_____."

R: Volēns.

171. "Ā quibus volēns dūcitur?" "_ _____."

R: Ā Fātīs.

172. "Quem trahunt Fāta?" "_____."

R: Nōlentem.

173. "Quī nōlentem trahunt?" "_____."

R: Fāta.

174. "Ā quibus nōlēns trahitur?" "_ _____."

R: Ā Fātīs.

175. "Quis ā Fātīs trahitur?" "_____."

R: Nōlēns.

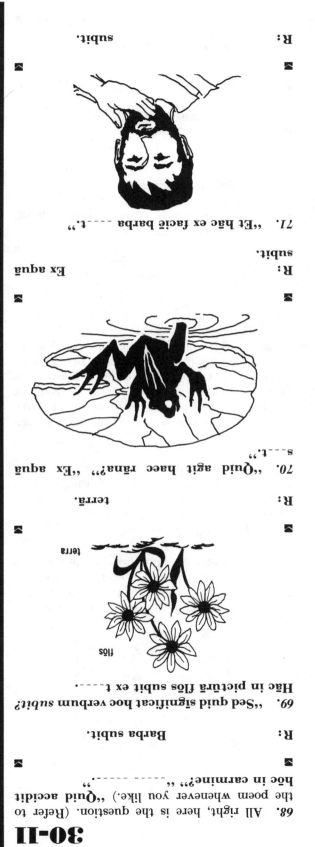

68. All right, here is the question. (Refer to the poem whenever you like.) "Quid accidit hōc in carmine?" "_____ _____."

R: Barba subit.

69. "Sed quid significat hoc verbum subit? Hāc in pictūrā flōs subit ex t_____."

R: terrā.

70. "Quid agit haec rāna?" "Ex aquā s__t."

R: subit.

71. "Et hāc ex faciē barba ____t."

R: subit.

16-28

176. "Quī volentem dūcunt?" "____."

R: Fāta.

177. "Quid agunt Fāta?" "V_____ d_____, n_____ tr_____."

R: Volentem dūcunt, nōlentem trahunt.

178. Although **Fortūna∅** was a single goddess, the **FātA** were three _____.

A: goddesses.

The early Greeks invented numerous stories about the gods and goddesses to explain the natural world. Sometimes the story would try to explain the name of some god. For example, the story that Aphrodite (called **Venus** in Latin) was born from the waves arose from the fact that the first part of her name sounded like the Greek word **aphros,** which means "sea foam."

Although Latin writers used these myths extensively in their writings, they did not believe that the myths were literally true. Some Romans believed in a single God, others believed that there were several gods.

179. The Fates are described by some writers as three old ladies, more powerful even than the gods themselves. One of the Fates spins a thread, the second measures it, and the third one __s it off.

A: cuts

---

61. "Quālis rēs est amor?" "Cr____ r____ est."

R: Crēdula rēs est.

62. In the next poem there are 11 words, nine of them unknown to you. It is therefore obvious that you cannot comprehend the meaning of the poem at once. But even without knowing the dictionary meaning of the words you can see the st_____ l meaning.

A: structural

63. The italicized words are all new. ● ○ ★
Eutrapelus tōnsor dum circuit ōra Lupercī expīngitque genās, altera barba subit. (Reading #9)

64. Copy in your Notebook.

65. You are familiar with the expression **Quid accidit?**, which means "____ is h_____ing?"

A: What is happening?

66. When you are asked **Quid accidit?** about a poem, you are supposed to reply briefly with the most important single fact. In a sentence, this information would usually be contained in the m___ cl_____.

A: main clause.

67. This poem consists of a single sentence. "Quid accidit hōc in carmine?" therefore means that you are to give the ____ _____ of the sentence.

A: main clause

16-29

180. This story is a metaphorical way of saying that when a person is born, the _____ of his life is already _____.

A: length (course, fate) determined (measured).

181. There were several goddesses of Fortune. There was one who looked after women, another that watched over men, and many others. **Fortūna Redux,** for example, was the goddess to whom one prayed on setting out on a journey. The prefix **re-** means "back" and the **-dux** part is connected with the verb **dūcit**. **Fortūna Redux** was therefore the goddess who would ____ one back home.

A: lead (guide)

182. The Fates were used by poets and other writers as symbols of Fortune. Let us substitute the neuter plural **FātA** for the First Declension singular **FortūnaØ** in these Basic Sentences. But first, be sure to remember that the **-a** of **Fortūna** is the _____ _____.

A: characteristic vowel.

183. The **-a** of **Fāta,** on the other hand, is the signal for the _____ or _____ case.

A: nominative accusative

184-186. ★ ●
    Fortūna fortēs metuit, īgnāvōs premit. (41)
    Vītam regit Fortūna, nōn Sapientia. (18)
    Stultī timent Fortūnam, sapientēs ferunt. (42)

30-9

55. Here is the second line; expand the second kernel, supplying the missing elements from what has gone before.

Ūnum oculum Thāis nōn habet; ille duōs _____ ___ _____.

R: Ūnum oculum Thāis nōn habet; ille duōs oculōs nōn habet.

56. That is, Thāis is missing just ___ ___; Quintus is missing b____ s.

A: one eye both eyes.

57. The point of the poem is that _____ [in your words]

A: Love is certainly blind if Quintus (who can see perfectly well) is in love with someone as homely as Thāis.

Quaestiōnēs et Respōnsa

58. "Quid agēbat Quintus?" "_____."

R: Thāidem amābat.
(vel, Thāida)

59. "Quālis puella erat Thāis?" "_____ a___ t___."

R: Lusca erat.

60. "Quālis vidēbātur Quintus quī Thāidem luscam amābat?" "C_____ v_____ r_____."

R: Caecus vidēbātur.

16-30

187-193. Substitute the appropriate form of the neuter plural **Fāta** for the singular **Fortūna** in these sentences.

187. Stultī timent *Fortūnam*, sapientēs ferunt → _____ _____ ___A, _____ _____.

R: Stultī timent FātA, sapientēs ferunt.

188. Vītam *regit Fortūna*, nōn Sapientia → _____ ___unt ____, ___ _____.

R: Vītam regunt Fāta, nōn Sapientia.

189. Fortēs *Fortūna adjuvat* → _____ ____ _____ant.

R: Fortēs Fāta adjuvant.

190. *Fortūna* fortēs *metuit*, īgnāvōs *premit* → ____ _____ ____unt, _____ ____unt.

R: Fāta fortēs metuunt, īgnāvōs premunt.

191. Fortūna is _____ case and _____ number.

A: nominative singular

192. The form **Fāta**, depending on its use in the sentence, may be _____ and is _____ number.

A: nominative or accusative plural

30-8

49. Perhaps *one* student in every class can understand this poem without further help. Is it you this time? If you know you understand the poem (test: did you laugh?), go to frame 57. Otherwise, continue with the program.

50. The first thing to do is to change the Greek form Thāida to a good old honest Roman form: Th___ em Quīntus amat. Quam Th____? Th_____ luscam.

A: Thāidem Quīntus amat. Quam Thāidem? Thāidem luscam.

51. The second sentence (Quam Thāidem?) consists only of the {- -} of the sentence.

A: {-m-}

52. As you have done so many times before, supply the missing parts of the kernel from what has gone before: Quam Thāidem _____ ?

R: Quam Thāidem Quīntus amat?

53. Expand the third sentence: Thāidem luscam _____ ____.

R: Thāidem luscam Quīntus amat.

54. Give back the original line, changing the Roman forms back to Greek forms and removing the added parts of the kernel:

Thāida Quīntus amat. Quam Thāidem Quīntus amat? Thāidem luscam Quīntus amat.

Th___ Qu____ am___. Qu___ Th__ ? l____ ?

R: Thāida Quīntus amat. Quam Thāida? Thāida luscam.

16-31

193. **Fortūna** is _____ case and _____ number.

A: nominative singular

194. Adjectives, too, have neuter plurals. Echo the paradigm of **bonus** gender by gender, first the singular, then the plural. ★ ○ •

```
         Singular
    m        f        n
  bonus    bona     bonum
  bonum    bonam    bonum
  bonō     bonā     bonō

         Plural
    m        f        n
  bonī     bonae    bona
  bonōs    bonās    bona
  bonīs    bonīs    bonīs
```

195. Say the paradigm of **malum vitium**, first in the singular.

```
  ___um    v___um
  -----    ------
  ___ō     ____ō
```

R: malum vitium
    malum vitium
    malō vitiō

196. Now say the plural of **malum vitium**.

```
  ___a     v___A
  ----     -----
  ___īs    ____īs
```

R: mala vitiA
    mala vitiA
    malīs vitiīs

197. It is *much* more difficult when the adjective and noun belong to different declensions and do not rhyme. Repeat these many times after echoing.
★ ○ • magnum opus   magna opera
       magnum opus   magna opera
       magnō opere   magnīs operibus

30-7

New vocabulary for Reading #8.

44. Quī vidēre nōn potest dīcitur caecus esse. Sed quī nōn duōs sed ūnum oculum habet dīcitur esse luscus.

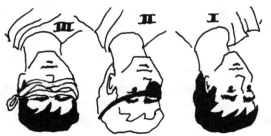

Prīmus homō est ____ (caecus/luscus/sānus).

R: sānus.

45. Secundus homō est _____.

R: luscus.

46. Tertius homō est _____.

R: caecus.

47. ★ ○ ◉
Thāida Quīntus amat. Quam Thāida? Thāida luscam.
Ūnum oculum Thāis nōn habet; ille duōs. (Reading #8)

Latīn poets sometimes used Greek endings for Greek names. In the following poem the form **Thāida** is accusative singular; the Latin form would be **Thāidem**.

48. Copy in your Notebook.

16-32

198. While **malum vitium** contains two words which rhyme, the phrase **magnum opus** does --- ------.

A: not rhyme.

199. On the model of **magnum opus,** say the singular paradigm of **bonum genus.**

    ----- -----
    ----- -----
    ---ō ------

R: bonum genus
       bonum genus
       bonō genere

200. Say the plural of **bonum genus.**

    ---a -----a
    ---a -----a
    ---īs -----ibus

R: bona genera
       bona genera
       bonīs generibus

201. Here are the forms of a Third Declension adjective. Echo, first the masculine-feminine singular, then the neuter singular, and so on.

★ ○ • m&f n m&f n
    hilaris hilare hilarēs hilaria
    hilarem hilare hilarēs hilaria
    hilarī hilarī hilaribus hilaribus

202. Which four of these words are nominative-accusative neuters?

  cane magnum juvene crūdēle forte
         īgnāvum auctōre

A: magnum   crūdēle forte
    īgnāvum

Third Conjugation

33. ★ ○ • **pingō, pingere, pinxī, pictus**

34. ★ ○ • **dīcō, dīcere, dīxī, dictus**

35. ★ ○ • **metuō, metuere, metuī**

36. ★ ○ • **premō, premere, pressī, pressus**

37. Copy these Third Conjugation verbs in your Notebook.

Third Conjugation (-iō)

38. ★ ○ • **sapiō, sapere, sapīvī**

39. ★ ○ • **incipiō, incipere, incēpī, inceptus**

40. Copy these Third Conjugation (-iō) verbs in your Notebook.

Fourth Conjugation

41. ★ ○ • **custōdiō, custōdīre, custōdīvī, custōdītus**

42. ★ ○ • **inveniō, invenīre, invēnī, inventus**

43. Copy these Fourth Conjugation verbs in your Notebook.

16-33

203. Which of these nouns could **hilarī** modify?
lupī cane forte auctōre agnī
fūre asinō muscā

A: cane   auctōre
   fūre asinō muscā

204. Say the singular paradigm of **forte∅ corpus∅**.

```
----∅  -----∅
----∅  -----∅
----ī  -----e
```

R: forte corpus
    forte corpus
    fortī corpore

205. Say the plural of **forte corpus**.

```
----iA  -----A
------  -------
----ibus -----ibus
```

R: fortiA corporA
    fortiA corporA
    fortibus corporibus

Here is the more difficult combination, with noun and adjective in different declensions.

206. ★ ○ •
crūdēle cōnsilium   crūdēliA cōnsiliA
crūdēle cōnsilium   crūdēliA cōnsiliA
crūdēlī cōnsiliō   crūdēlibus cōnsiliīs

207. Say the singular paradigm of **hilare dictum**.

```
-----e  ----um
------  ------
-----ī  ----ō
```

R: hilare dictum
    hilare dictum
    hilarī dictō

---

21. "Cum Fidentīnus recitābat, quālia vidēbantur carmina, mala an bona?" "-----."

R: Mala.

Here follow the principal parts of verbs which you used in the last Unit.

First Conjugation

22. ★ ○ • adjuvō, adjuvāre, adjūvī, adjūtus

23. ★ ○ • negō, negāre, negāvī, negātus

24. ★ ○ • laudō, laudāre, laudāvī, laudātus

25. ★ ○ • cantō, cantāre, cantāvī, cantātus

26. ★ ○ • mūtō, mūtāre, mūtāvī, mūtātus

27. ★ ○ • cūrō, cūrāre, cūrāvī, cūrātus

28. Copy these First Conjugation verbs in your Reference Notebook. [It is enough to write (1) to indicate that this is a regular First Conjugation verb in its principal parts.]

Second Conjugation

29. ★ ○ • palleō, pallēre, palluī

30. ★ ○ • stupeō, stupēre, stupuī

31. ★ ○ • rubeō, rubēre, rubuī

32. Copy these Second Conjugation verbs in your Notebook.

16-34

208. Say the plural paradigm of **hilare dictum**.

```
_____ia  ____A
_____  ____
_____ibus ____īs
```

R: hilariA dictA
          hilariA dictA
          hilaribus dictīs

209. ★ ○ •   ánimalØ   animáliA
               ánimalØ   animáliA
               animálī   animálibus

[This is a hard one; say it several times after echoing.]

210. In the paradigm of the Latin word **animal,** the characteristic vowel is ___ and appears in all cases except the _____ and _____ singular.

A: -i-
                             nominative (sg)
accusative (sg)

211. Write the paradigm of the Latin word for "animal." [Put in the signals Ø and A, as done above.] _____ _____

A: animalØ   animāliA
          animalØ   animāliA
          animālī   animālibus

212-218. ★ ◉
Elephantus nōn capit mūrem. (5)
Lupus nōn mordet lupum. (6)
Cautus metuit foveam lupus. (8)
Parva necat morsū spatiōsum vīpera taurum. (21)
Ā cane nōn magnō saepe tenētur aper. (23)
Aquila nōn capit muscās. (36)
Ex auribus cognōscitur asinus. (43)

30-4

15. The word in the second line which receives special emphasis because it is placed outside its clause is the word _____.

A: male.

16. The new verb **incipiō** is a compound verb, combining the prefix **in-** with the familiar verb _____.

A: **capiō**.

17. However, in the compound the **a** of **capiō** changes to _____.

A: **i**.

18. Remember in this Question and Answer Drill that "mine" refers to what belongs to _____ and "yours" to what belongs to _____.

A: Martial
Fidentīnus.

Quaestiōnēs et Respōnsa

19. "Cujus carmina recitābat Fidentīnus?" "_____ c_____ c_____."

R: Mārtiālis carmina.

20. "Quāliter recitābat Fidentīnus?" "_____."

R: Male.

16-35

219-223. In this sequence you are to substitute the right form of **animal** for the italicized word (or words) in each sentence. First refresh your mind by echoing the paradigm of **animal**.

219. ★ ○ • ○ •

Cōnf: animal animālia
animal animālia
animālī animālibus

220. Elephantus nōn capit *mūrem* →
------------------------------------.

R: Elephantus nōn capit animal.

221. *Lupus* nōn mordet *lupum* → ---------
----------------------------.

R: Animal nōn mordet animal.

222. Ex auribus cognōscitur *asinus* →
-------------------------------.

R: Ex auribus cognōscitur animal.

223. Aquila nōn capit *muscās* → --------
-------------------------.

R. Aquila nōn capit animālia.

In these next two, the word is modified by an adjective. Be sure that the adjective agrees with the neuter word **animal**, although the two words will not rhyme.

224. Ā *cane* nōn *magnō* saepe tenētur aper → Ab ------- nōn ----- saepe tenētur aper.

R: Ab animālī nōn magnō saepe tenētur aper.

---

9. Remove the modifiers of both nouns, leaving just the kernel: -------- est -------- .

A: Libellus est libellus.

10. This means, "A ----- a ----- ."

A: A book is a book.

11. Now we will put back the modifiers: Libellus quem recitās meus est libellus. This means, "The ---- which --- --- ----ing is my book."

A: The book which you are reciting is my book.

12. That is, Fīdentīnus is reciting as his own a book which was wr----- by --------.

A: written by Martial.

13. The second line, also, is missing some forms of the word libellus in three places. Supply them. Sed male cum tū meum ------ un----- recitās, m--s l------s incipit esse tuus.

R: Sed male cum tū meum libellum recitās, meus libellus incipit esse tuus libellus.

14. This means that when Fīdentīnus reads Martial's poems, he reads them so ---ly that one could easily believe that he actually wrote them himself. (If you skipped, did you really know?)

A: badly that [In your own words]

225. In **Ā cane nōn magnō** the adjective **magnō** is _____ gender.

A: masculine

226. In **Ab animālī nōn magnō** the word **magnō** is _____ gender.

A: neuter

227. Again, substitute some form of **animal**. **Parva** necat morsū spatiōsum *vīpera* taurum → P_____ n____ m____ sp_____ an____ t_____.

R: **Parvum necat morsū spatiōsum animal taurum.**

228. This new sentence ____ (is/is not) ambiguous.

A: is

229. Parvum necat morsū spatiōsum animal taurum means either, "_____" or, "_____."

A: A small animal kills a large bull with a bite or, A large animal kills a small bull with a bite.

230. ★ ○ • ○ • *Magna dī cūrant, parva neglegunt.* (46)

231. Copy this sentence in your Answer Pad. If **Magna** is an adjective, draw a line from **magna** to the noun it modifies; if there is no noun which it modifies, then say so.

A: There is no noun for **magna** to modify: it is therefore used as a noun. **Magna** could be nominative feminine singular or neuter nominative or accusative plural.

---

4. First try to understand this poem without any help from the program. If you get the point of the joke, go to frame 14. You can judge yourself here. If you are not *sure* that you understand a joke, you *don't* understand it. [For those who don't get the joke at first, and this will be almost everyone, continue with the program.]

5. The difficulty lies in two areas. First you must remember that Roman authors "published" their works by _____ in public.

A: reading them aloud

6. The second difficulty is that in the first line it is difficult to find the kernel. Let us begin by stripping away the least essential part, which is the name of the person to whom the poem is addressed. This leaves us with the following:

Qu____ re____, m___ est l_____.

A: **Quem recitās, meus est libellus.**

7. The relative pronoun **quem** must refer to something which is _____ gender and _____ number.

A: masculine singular

8. There is only one noun in this sentence which is masculine singular: add it. _____ quem recitās meus est libellus.

A: **Libellus** quem recitās meus est libellus.

16-37

232. In the kernel **Magna dī cūrant**, the word **magna** cannot be nominative singular because the verb **cūrant** is _____ _____.

A: plural number.

233. We must now determine whether **magna** is {-s} or {-m} in the kernel **Magna dī cūrant**. Because **dī** is the {__}, we know that **magna** must be the {__} of the kernel.

A: {-s}
   {-m}

234. The masculine or feminine form of an adjective, when there is no noun for it to modify, is used as a noun itself to indicate a person. Thus **crūdēlis** means "a _____ _____."

A: cruel person.

235. When a neuter adjective has no noun to modify and is used as a noun itself, it refers not to a person but to a non-personal th____.

A: thing.

236. **Magna** therefore means "l____ ____s."

A: large things.

237. If we supply the colorless word "blank" for the two unknown verbs, the sentence **Magna dī cūrant, parva neglegunt** means, "The ____ _____ _____ _____ (but) _____ _____ _____."

A: The gods blank large things (but) blank small things.

238. **Magna** and **parva** are an_____s.

A: antonyms.

UNIT THIRTY

This is the last Unit of *Latin: Level One*. The activities will consist of three types. One will be drill on the principal parts of verbs. The second will be more contrast readings, where little changes are made in the individual sentences of the Readings to improve response to Latin signals. But mostly it will be just Readings.

1. The friend asks if he is l___ to d_____.

[Nōnne sērus ad cēnam vēnī? / Minimē, sērus conviva nōn es; nōs jam cēnāre incipimus.]

A: late to dinner.

2. The host answers, "We are just ---ing to ----."

A: We are just now beginning to dine.

3. ★ ○ ● Quem recitās, meus est, Ō Fīdentīne, libellus; sed male cum recitās, incipit esse tuus. (Reading #7)

You are now familiar with the type of saying in which somebody does one thing to one type of person, but a different sort of thing to another. Here are two examples:

Dūcunt volentem Fāta, nōlentem trahunt.
Fortūna fortēs metuit, īgnāvōs premit.

239. Now guess the meaning of **Magna dī cūrant, parva neglegunt** and write it in your Answer Pad. However, we will not tell you immediately whether your answer is right or not. We will instead explain the meaning of **cūrant** and **neglegunt**. You can see if your guess was correct.

240. "Quid agit hic medicus?" ★ ○ ○
"Hic medicus _____."

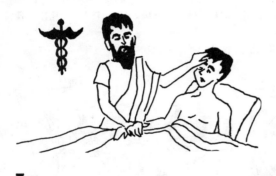

R: Hic medicus aegrum cūrat.

241. "Quid agit hic medicus?" ★ ○ ○
"Hic medicus aegrum _____."

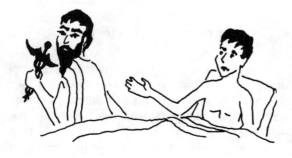

R: Hic medicus aegrum neglegit.

VOCABULARY INVENTORY

Nouns:
aedificium-ī n (206)   rūs, rūris, n (207-208)
carmen,
  carminis, n (160)   Tībur,
hospes,   Tīburis, n (215)
  hospitis, m&f (225) voluntās,
libellus-ī, n (159)   voluntātis, f (44)

Pronouns: quīdam, quaedam, quoddam (117)

Adjectives:
citus-a-um (85)   Tīburtīnus-a-um (217)
meus-a-um (109)   tuus-a-um (109)
nūbilus-a-um (58-65) ūtilis, ūtile (94)
rēctus-a-um (43)

Verbs:
*canto (99)   rubeō (137-138)
*impōnō (212-214)   rumpō (77-84)
laxō (78-82)   stupeō (141-142)
ōscitō (144)   tendō (76-83)
palleō (209-210)   vendō (137-139)

Subordinating Conjunction: dōnec (57)

Coordinating Conjunction: at (92)

Exclamation: ecce! (104)

TEST INFORMATION

You will be expected to write the synopsis of or write the paradigm of any tense, with the principal parts supplied you. You are responsible for the principal parts of all verbs which you had in previous Units, plus those in this Unit, namely **tendō, rumpō, laxō.**

You are responsible for the #2 tense of the irregular verb **volō.**

16-39

242. Magna dī cūrant, parva neglegunt =
The ____ take c___ of _____ _____s (but)
n_____ _____ _____s.

A: The gods take care of large things but neglect small things.

243. Enter this sentence and its meaning in your Notebook.

244. This means that we should not lose our faith in the gods to protect us in important matters just because we have suffered some _____ misfortune.

A: small

245. It also means that we must ourselves take care of the daily routine matters of life but that the important things of our lives, our ultimate destination, have been determined by the _ _ _s.

A: gods (Fates).

246. Sometimes doctors take such good care of their patients that they make them well; the English derivative of the verb **cūrat** in this sense is the word "_____."

A: cure.

247. Transform to the passive:
Magna dī cūrant, parva neglegunt →
M___a ā d__ c__antur, p___a
n_____untur.

R: Magna ā dīs cūrantur, parva neleguntur.

29-48

273.
D__ er__ f__, m____ n____
am___;
t_____ si f___n___ n__bi__, s___ er__.

(140)

R: Dōnec eris fēlix, multōs numerābis amīcōs;
tempora si fuerint nūbila, sōlus eris.

You had three new readings. You should be able to produce these with parts of four words removed in each line, as in the next sequence.

274.
Laudat, am__, c_____ nostr__ mea Rōma
_____llōs,
mē__ sin__ omnēs, man__ omn__ habet.
Ec_! Rubet qui____, p__et, stupet, ōscitat,
__it.
Hoc v____, Nu__ nō__ car___ nostra
placent.   (R #5)

R: Laudat, amat, cantat nostrōs mea Rōma libellōs,
mēque sinūs omnēs, manus omnis habet.
Ecce! Rubet quidam, pallet, stupet, ōscitat, ōdit.
Hoc volo. Nunc nōbis carmina nostra placent.

275. Hospes er__ nos__ sem___, Matho,
Tīburtī__ Hocc em___ Impo___; rūs t___
ven__ tuum.   (R #6)

R: Hospes erās nostrī semper, Matho,
Tīburtīni. Hocc emis. Imposuī; rūs tibi vendō tuum.

248. The word **magna** in the original sentence is in the _____ case, but in the transformation **Magna ā dīs cūrantur, parva negleguntur, magna** is in the _____ case.

A: accusative
            nominative

Question and Answer Drill

249. "Quī magna cūrant?" "_____."

R: Dī.

250. "Quanta ā dīs cūrantur?" "_____."

R: Magna.

251. "Ā quibus magna cūrantur?" "_____."

R: Ā dīs.

252. "Quī parva neglegunt?" "_____."

R: Dī.

253. "Quanta ā dīs negleguntur?" "_____."

R: Parva.

254. "Quid agunt dī?" "_____ _____ sed _____ _____."

R: Magna cūrant sed parva neglegunt.

269. Look over this list of verb forms and pick out those which are #6: **aspiciuntur, metuērunt, cucurrerunt, quaesīverint, poterō, āmīserō, eris, fueris, laxāverās, rīsistī, potuerō.**

A: quaesīverint   fueris   āmīserō   potuerō

270. This #6 form shows that an action was _____ in _____ time.

A: complete in future time.

271. You learned three new Basic Sentences. Write the sentence which expresses a thought something like this: **Quī male cōgitāverit, nōn rēctē aget. Ac_____ rēc_____ n_____ er_____, n_____ r_____ f_____ vol_____.** (139)

R: **Actiō rēcta nōn erit, nisi rēcta fuerit voluntās.**

272. Write the Basic Sentence which this picture suggests:
C_____ r_____ ar_____ s_____ t_____ h_____; at s_____ l_____ c_____ v_____ er_____ ūt_____. (141)

R: **Citō rumpēs arcum, semper sī tēnsum habueris; at sī laxā'ris, cum volēs, erit ūtilis.**

16-41

255. ★ ○ ○ M____ d_ c_____, p____ n_____. [Two macrons]

R: Magna dī cūrant, parva neglegunt.

256. M____ d_ c_____, p____ n_____.

R: Magna dī cūrant, parva neglegunt.

257. ★ ○ • ○ • *Parva levēs capiunt animōs.* (47)

258. Copy this new Basic Sentence in your Answer Pad.

   m&f   n
259. **Levis, leve** is an adjective. If the word **levēs** in this sentence modifies a noun, draw an arrow from it to the word it modifies; if there is no noun which it modifies, then say so.

A: *Parva levēs capiunt animōs.* (arrow from levēs to animōs)

260. You now know that **Parva** is the { _ _ } of the sentence and **levēs animōs** is the { _ _ }.

A: {-s}
                             {-m}.

261. Using the colorless words "some kind of things" for the unknown phrase **levēs animōs**, the sentence **Parva levēs capiunt animōs** means, "_____."

A: Small things catch some kind of things.

29-46

263. **Dērīdēre** in the 2d person singular ("You-one-person"):

R: dērīdēbās   dērīdēs   dērīdēbis
    dērīsistī   dērīseris

——   ——   ——
——   ——

264. **Esse** in the 1st person plural ("We"):

R: erāmus   sumus   erimus
    fuerāmus   fuimus   fuerimus

——   ——   ——
——   ——

265. **Nārrāre** in the 1st person singular ("I"):

R: nārrābam   nārrō   nārrābō
    nārrāveram   nārrāvī   nārrāverō

——   ——   ——
——   ——

266. **Venīre** in the 3d person plural ("They"):

R: veniēbant   veniunt   venient
    vēnerant   vēnērunt   vēnerint

——   ——   ——
——   ——

267. **Facere** in the 2d person plural ("You"):

R: faciēbātis   facitis   faciētis
    fēcerātis   fēcistis   fēcerītis

——   ——   ——
——   ——

SUMMARY

268. In this Unit you learned a new tense, number #__.

A: 6.

16-42

Now for the meaning of **levis** and **animus**.

262. Ask your teacher how large a body this man is carrying. "Qu__t_m cor__s hic ___ fert?" ✓ ★ ○ •

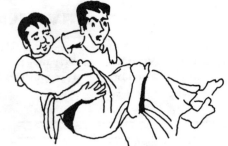

Cōnf: Quantum corpus hic vir fert?

263. Write his answer. ★ ○ ○
"_____ vir fert."

R: Grave corpus hic vir fert.

264. Ask your teacher again how large a body the man is carrying. "Qu_____ c_____ hic ___ f___?" ✓ ★ ○ •

Cōnf: Quantum corpus hic vir fert?

265. Write his answer. ★ ○ ○
"_____ vir fert."

R: Leve corpus hic vir fert.

29-45

257. dērīseris, dērīserās, dērīsistī, dērīdēs, dērīdēbās, dērīdēbis.

---- #1	---- #2	---- #3
---- #4	---- #5	---- #6

R: dērīdēbās #1   dērīdēs #2   dērīdēbis #3
   dēriserās #4   dērīsistī #5   dērīseris #6

258. As in the last two frames, arrange in synopsis order: mīsit, mittēbat, mittet, mīserat, mittit, mīserit.

R: mittēbat #1   mittit #2   mittet #3
   mīserat #4   mīsit #5   mīserit #6

259. facitis, fēcerātis, faciētis, fēceritis, faciēbātis, fēcistis.

R: faciēbātis #1   facitis #2   faciētis #3
   fēcerātis #4   fēcistis #5   fēceritis #6

260. vēnerant, vēnient, vēnerint, veniēbant, veniunt, vēnērunt.

R: veniēbant   veniunt   vēnerunt
   vēnient   vēnerant   vēnerint

261. erāmus, fuerāmus, sumus, fuimus, erimus, fuimus.

R: erāmus   sumus   erimus
   fuerāmus fuimus   fuimus

262. We will now ask you to write the same synopsis which you just practiced. First, mittere in the 3d person singular. [Review if you feel it necessary.]

---- #1	---- #2	---- #3
---- #4	---- #5	---- #6

R: mittēbat   mittit   mittet
   mīserat   mīsit   mīserit

266. **Gravis** and **levis** are antonyms. **Gravis** means "h___y" and **levis** means "l___t."

A: heavy light.

Both of these words have another common meaning which does not refer to weight, but rather to dignity.

267. Ask your teacher what kind of man this is. "Quā__s hic v__ ___?" √ ★ ○ •

Cōnf: **Quālis hic vir est?**

268. Write his answer. ★ ○ ○

R: **Levis hic vir est.**

269. Ask him what kind of man this one is. "Qu____ hic ___ ___?" √ ★ ○ •

Cōnf: **Quālis hic vir est?**

270. ★ ○ ○ "_____ vir est."

R: **Gravis hic vir est.**

---

251. **Hospes erit noster Matho Tīburtīnī** =

A: Our friend Matho will be a guest at our Tivoli farm.

252. **Mārtiālem ōdistī** =

A: You (now) hate Martial.

253. Remember that the verb **ōdī** is found only in the perfective system; **ōdī** means "I have learned to hate; I now hate." Now try this one. **Quendam Mārtiālis ōderat** = _____

A: Martial hated somebody (in the past). [That is, he had learned to hate, therefore he hated.]

254. In the same way, **nōvistis** means, "_____."

A: You (plural) now know.

255. **Edet numquam Gelliam lepus** = _____

A: A rabbit will never eat Gellia (and that seems reasonable).

256. **nārrābō, nārrō, nārrābam, nārrāveram, nārrāverō, nārrāvī.**

In this sequence we will give you forms of verbs in scrambled order. Arrange them in the correct order of the synopsis, that is, #1, #2, #3, etc. Here is the first frame. Later you will write.

---- #1	---- #2	---- #3
---- #4	---- #5	---- #6

R: nārrābam #1   nārrō #2   nārrābō #3
   nārrāveram #4   nārrāvī #5   nārrāverō #6

16-44

271. A **levis vir** is a man who is s___y or fr___lous.

A: silly frivolous.

272. And a **gravis vir** is a man who is s_____s.

A: serious.

273. If we tell you that **animus** means "mind," then **Parva levēs capiunt animōs** means, "_____ _____ cap___e _____ _____."

A: Small things capture frivolous minds.

274. Copy Basic Sentence 47 and its meaning into your Notebook.

275. You may think it is mean of us to illustrate this picture with a silly girl, but if you look up the passage in Ovid you will find that he was telling young men how to make an impression on _____s.

A: girls.

276. ★ ○ • levis animus   levēs animī
           levem animum levēs animōs
           levī animō   levibus animīs

29-43

244. Bella sum (Nōvistī.) = _____

A: I am pretty (You know it.) [Remember that #5 form of this verb means "I *now* know."]

245. Ēderat numquam Gellia leporem = _____

A: Gellia had never eaten a rabbit.

246. Hoc rūs ēmistī = _____

A: You bought this farm.

247. Cantāverat tuōs Rōma libellōs = _____

A: Rome had sung your poems.

248. Libellōs sinūs omnēs habuerint = _____

A: Every fold (pocket) will have held the books.

249. Sed cum tē nimium laudābat Fabulla = _____

A: But when Fabulla praised you too much.

250. Quis poterit enim negāre?" = _____

A: For who will be able to deny it?

277. Transform to the passive:
Parva levēs capiunt animōs →
P___īs l___s ___iuntur an___.

R: **Parvīs levēs capiuntur animī.**

278. In the original sentence **levēs** was
_____ case; in the transformation, **levēs**
has become _____ case.

A: accusative
    nominative

Question and Answer Drill

279. "**Quālēs animōs parva capiunt?**"
"_____."

R: **Levēs.**

280. "**Quanta levēs animōs capiunt?**"
"_____."

R: **Parva.**

281. "**Quālēs animī capiuntur parvīs?**"
"_____."

R: **Levēs.**

282. "**Quantīs animī levēs capiuntur?**"
"_____."

R: **Parvīs.**

---

237. **Martiālī Mathō imposuerat** = _____
  .
A: Matho
    had cheated Martial.

238. **Formōsus septem Mārcus diēbus erit**
  = _____.
A: Marcus will be beautiful in seven days.

239. **Centum tetigī manūs Aquilōne gelā-
tās** = _____.
A: I touched a hundred hands frozen by the
North Wind.

240. **Vēnerint centum Symmachī discipulī**
= _____.
A: A hundred students of Symmachus will have
come.

241. **Centum tetigerat manūs Aquilō gelātās** = _____.
A: The North Wind had touched a hundred
frozen hands.

242. **Rūs mihi vendēs tuum** = _____
  .
A: You will
sell me your farm.

243. **Vōbīs carmina vestra placuerint** =
  _____.
A: Your poems will have pleased you.

The following questions on this same Basic Sentence are not simple substitution or transformation questions. It is, after all, possible to do substitution questions and transformations without understanding the dictionary meaning of the words. This was satisfactory in the beginning, but now we wish to extend you a little bit more. To answer these questions you will have to understand the question and answer according to the sense of the Basic Sentence.

283. "Quālēs virī laude capiuntur?"
"_____."
          (Auxilium sub hāc lineā invenītur.)

▲   ▲

Auxilium: Capiunturne laude virī gravēs an levēs?

▲   ▲

R: Levēs (virī).

284. "Quālis vir laudem vult?" "_____."

▲   ▲

R: Levis (vir).

285. This sentence was written by the same poet who wrote **Parva necat morsū spatiōsum vīpera taurum.** The English name of this poet is _____.
(Auxilium sub hāc lineā est).

▲   ▲

Aux: The name begins with an "O."

▲   ▲

A: Ovid.

286. Pronounce his name in English. Ovid.
√ ★ ○ •

▲   ▲

VCh: "áwe-vid"

---

231. **Sī leporem tibi miserō, dīcam: "......."**

▲   ▲

A: If I send you a rabbit, I will say: "......."

▲   ▲

232. The #6 form **miserō** shows time _____ (before/after) **dīcam.**

▲   ▲

A: before

▲   ▲

233. In our translation, "If I send you a rabbit, I will say," the sending of the rabbit comes _____ (before/after) the speech.

▲   ▲

A: before

▲   ▲

234. Therefore in this sentence, the English "I send a rabbit" is translated by I _____ m_____.

▲   ▲

A: leporem miserō.

▲   ▲

235. In a sentence like, "Because I like you, I send you a rabbit," the expression "I send a rabbit" would be in Latin l_____ m_____.

▲   ▲

A: leporem mittō.

▲   ▲

236. **Hospes eris nostrī Tīburtīnī** = _____.

▲   ▲

A: You will be a guest at our farm at Tivoli.

Do not expect that your translation will be exactly the same as the one given in the answer; consider the sense of what is said. If you are in doubt, ask your teacher whether your answer is correct.

Remember, this is just an exercise; the sentences out of context don't make any real sense.

287. Ovid was quite an expert on love—or so he thought. He wrote poems on how to win and retain the affections of women. He had to marry three times before he found a wife who would stay with him! The emperor Augustus sent him into exile. That's what happens to people who say that girls have _____ minds.

A: frivolous

288. ★ ○ • ○ • *Fāta regunt orbem; certā stant omnia lēge.* (48)

289. You have had each one of these words before. You know that these words ____ (will have the same meanings they had before/may well have different meanings).

A: may well have different meanings.

290. Let us at least try the old familiar meanings and see what happens. **Fāta regunt orbem** = The _____ ____ the _____.

A: The Fates rule the circle.

This translation might make sense if we knew what kind of a circle it was (mushrooms? gods? chairs?). Let us look at the second kernel to see if it gives us any help.

291. In **certā stant omnia lēge** there are two words which you know are adjectives. What are the two adjectives?

A: certā   omnia

292. Copy in your Answer Pad: **Certā stant omnia lēge.**

This sequence consists of Contrast Readings #1 through #6. You will be given sentences *similar* to the Readings but with some changes in nouns or verbs or perhaps both. Be alert! Since there is *no context* to help you, you must react to *all* the signals.

Quaestiōnēs et Respōnsa

225. ★ ○ • hospes   hospitēs
hospitem
hospitēs
hospite   hospitibus
hospiti   hospitibus
hospitis   hospitum

226. ★ ○ • rūs   rūra
        rūs
        rūra
        rūre   (no other plural forms)
        rūrī
        rūris

227. ★ ○ • Mathō
Mathōnem
Mathōne
Mathōnī
Mathōnis

228. "Cujus locī erat Mathō semper hospes?" "R____ Tīburt____."

R: Rūris Tīburtīnī.

229. "Cui Mārtiālis fraudem imposuit?" "Hos____ suō M____."

R: Hospitī suō Mathōnī.

230. "Rūs Tīburtīnum fuit Mārtiālis; cujus jam est?" "_____."

R: Mathōnis.

16-48

293. If **certā** modifies a noun, draw an arrow from it to the noun it modifies; if it does not modify a noun and is used as a noun itself, say so.

A: **Certā stant omnia lēge.** (arrow from certā to omnia)

294. If **omnia** modifies a noun, draw an arrow from it to the noun it modifies; if it does not modify a noun and is used as a noun itself, say so.

A: It is used as a noun itself.

295. Certā stant omnia lēge = ___ th___s ____ under a f__ed ____.

A: All things stand under a fixed law.

296. Fāta regunt orbem; certā stant omnia lēge. Let us return to the problem in the first kernel. What is it which is like a circle and which the Fates rule in such a way that everything stands under a fixed law? It must be the w_____.

A: world.

297. ★ ○ ○ F___ r_____ or___; c____ st___ o____ l___. [Listen for the long vowels and mark them.]

R: Fāta regunt orbem; certā stant omnia lēge.

---

219. Copy Reading #6 in your Notebook. When you have extracted all the information you can from the poem, continue with the program. [Give extra effort to these big steps, since the program will ask you to do these more and more. If you prepare yourself now, you will be ready for them.]

220. _____ The first clause says that _____

A: Matho was always a visitor (guest) at Martial's place at Tibur.

221. The second clause is brief; it says that _____

A: Matho bought the place.

222. Imposuī = _____

A: I have cheated (you).

223. The punctuation mark after **imposuī** shows that an explanation will follow showing in what way Martial cheated Matho. Martial confesses, "_____."

A: I sold you your own farm. (Again, the #2 form shows action in past time.)

224. Wasn't it Martial's farm? Why does he say that it belonged to Matho all along and that therefore he is cheating Matho in selling him the farm? _____ [In your own words]

A: Because Matho lived there all the time anyway and had the use of it without any of the expense.

16-49

298. This means that the ____ ____ the
____; ___ _____ _____ a _____ ___.

A: Fates rule the world; all things stand under a fixed law.

299. Copy Basic Sentence 48 and its meaning in your Notebook.

300. Transform **Fāta regunt orbem** to the passive. A F__ īs r__itur o___s.

R: Ā Fātīs regitur orbis.

301-307. **Fāta regunt orbem; certā stant omnia lēge.** We will have questions and answers on this Basic Sentence and its transformation. Say your answers aloud and write.

301. "Quī orbem regunt?" "_____."

R: Fāta.

302. "Quid ā Fātīs regitur?" "_____."

R: Orbis.

303. "Ā quibus orbis regitur?" "_____ _____."

R: Ā Fātīs.

304. "Quālī lēge stant omnia?" "_____ _____."

R: Certā lēge.

---

215. Quīnta vōx est adjectīvum *Tiburtīnus*. *Tibur* est locus Rōmae proximus. Nōmen *Tiburtīnum*, neutrīus generis, significat "rūs Tiburtīnum." In hāc parte orbis terrārum possidet Martiālis rūs vel ag___ suum.

R: agrum

216. Hoc est meum T_____ num _____ num.

217. Tiburtīnum, -ī, n = a f____ located at _____.

R: Tiburtīnum rūs.

A: a farm located at Tibur (modern Tivoli).

218. Here is Reading #6. ● ○ ★
Hospes erās nostrī semper, Matho, Tiburtīnī.
Hocc emis. Imposuī: rūs tibi vendō tuum. (Hocc is a variant of hoc.)

16-50

305. "Quid Fāta certīs lēgibus regunt?"
"_____."

R: Orbem.

306. "Quālibus lēgibus Fāta orbem regunt?" "_____ _____." (Auxilium sub hāc līneā est.)

Aux: Notice that we have transformed **lēge** from singular to plural.

R: Certīs lēgibus.

307. "Quālēs lēgēs habent Fāta, certās an incertās?" "_____."

R: Certās.

308. The next point of structure is easy because we have a similar construction in English. Echo your teacher as he describes this picture.
★ ○ ● ○ •

Equus currit.

Juvenis equum aspicit.

Cōnf: Juvenis equum currentem aspicit.

309. This sentence means that the _____ ___ ___s the ___ing _____.

A: _____ young man sees the running horse (or "the horse running").

29-37

211. A person who sells things is sometimes called a "v___or."

A: vendor.

212. Quārta vōx est quoque verbum, *impōnere*. Haec anus est praeter ratiōnem īrāta. Quid est causa tantae īrae? Vir quī piscēs vendidit fraudem anuī imp-u-__ ___.

Mihi fraudem imposuistī! Pecūniam meam quaerō!

Rēctē dīcis; egō errāvī.

R: imposuit.

213. You are well aware by now that Latin frequently leaves out parts of the sentence which must be understood by the reader. If you were asked what the man had done you could give a long answer, *Vir fraudem anuī imposuit*, or the shortest answer, which would be just the verb, "*Quid ēgit vir?*" "_____ it."

R: Imposuit.

214. In the context of the picture, *imposuit* means that the ___ ch___ed the ___ out of her _____.

A: _____ man cheated the old lady out of her money.

16-51

310. Write your teacher's description of this picture. ★ ○ ○ J_____ e____ c_____ asp____.

Equī currunt.

R: Juvenis equōs currentēs aspicit.

311. This sentence means that _____.

A: _____ the young man sees the running horses.

312. Write this description. ★ ○ ○ **Lupus** _____ c_____ c____.

R: Lupus agnum currentem capit.

313. He said that _____.

A: _____ the wolf is catching the running lamb.

---

206. Secunda vōx est nōmen *rūs*, neutrīus generis. *Rūs* oppōnitur "urbs." In urbibus sunt multī hominēs, *aedificia*, portīcūs. At rūs habet agrōs, arborēs, animālia. Leporēs ____ (rūs/urbēs) amant.

R: rūs

207. Patria and **rūs** both mean "country," but **patria** means "my country" in the sense of my "n_____ l_____."

A: native land.

208. Rūs, on the other hand, means "the country," as opposed to _____.

A: the city.

209. ★ ● Tertia vōx est verbum *vendere*. Hāc in pictūrā anus piscēs emit. Sed quid agit vir ex quō hōs piscēs anus emit? Anus emit, vir piscēs vendit.

210. At in hāc pictūrā, anus piscēs __ it, vir __ it.

R: vendit _____ emit.

16-52

314-317 Compare these two similar sentences.
Juvenis equum **fortem** aspicit.
Juvenis equum **currentem** aspicit.

314. **Fortem** is an adjective and agrees with **equum** in _____, _____, and _____.

A: number, gender, and case.

315. The **currentem** form of the verb also _____s with **equum** in _____, _____, and _____.

A: agrees number, gender, and case.

316. In other words, **currentem** is the ad_____ive form of the verb **currit**.

A: adjective

317. English verbs have a form ending in "-ing" which makes an adjective out of the verb. For example, a person might say, "The horse ran," and his friend could answer, "Yes, I saw the r_____ horse."

A: running

318. Echo a new technical term. ★ ○ • ○ •
párticiple

VCh: "párt-tiss-sip-pull"

319. The adjective form of the verb that in English ends in "-ing" is called the "present participle." The present participle in the sentence "We saw the sinking ship" is the word "_____."

A: sinking.

320. Latin has a present participle, too. Echo the paradigm of the present participle that means "running." ★ ○ •

Singular	
m&f	n
currēns	currēns
currentem	currēns
currentī	currentī

Plural	
m&f	n
currentēs	currentia
currentēs	currentia
currentibus	currentibus

321. Now study it and note which forms are alike and which are different. If necessary, repeat the paradigm.

322. Write a different description of a picture which you have just seen. Notice that your teacher is now using the neuter noun **animal**.
★ ○ ○ _____.

R: Lupus animal currēns capit.

323. The form **currēns** can be the nominative of the masculine, feminine, and neuter genders. In **Lupus animal currēns capit**, if it modifies **animal**, **currēns** is _____ case.

A: accusative

---

194. servīre
#3 tense ★ ○ •

R: serviam   serviēs   serviet
    serviēmus   serviētis   servient

195. aperīre
#3 tense

R: aperiam   aperiēs   aperiet
    aperiēmus   aperiētis   aperient

196. posse
#3 tense ★ ○ •

R: poterō   poteris   poterit
    poterimus   poteritis   poterunt

197. esse
#3 tense

R: erō   eris   erit
    erimus   eritis   erunt

198. The #4, #5, and #6 tenses are much easier to learn than the first three because the signals are the same for all conjugations. However, in order to form one of these tenses you have to know the _____-ive _____-ive stem of the verb.

A: perfective active stem

199. The signal of the #4 tense is {-erā-}. Conjugate **trahere** in the #4 tense. [If you have forgotten the principal parts of **trahere**, look them up in your Notebook.]

R: traxeram   traxerās   traxerat
    traxerāmus   traxerātis   traxerant

16-54

324. **Lupus animal currēns capit** is an ambiguous sentence. It could mean either that the ----ing ---- is -----ing the ------, *or* that the ---- is -----ing the ----ing ------.

A: running wolf is catching the animal, *or* that the wolf is catching the running animal.

325. Write the singular paradigm of **currēns.**

m&f	n
______	______

(Sub hāc līneā auxilium est.)

Aux:	**c-----s**	**c-----s**
	c------em	**c-----s**
	c------ī	**c------ī**

R:	**currēns**	**currēns**
	currentem	**currēns**
	currentī	**currentī**

326. Write the plural paradigm of **currēns.**

m&f	n
______	______

(Auxilium sub hāc līneā est.)

Aux:	**c------ēs**	**c------ia**
	c------ēs	**c------ia**
	c------ibus	**c------ibus**

R:	**currentēs**	**currentia**
	currentēs	**currentia**
	currentibus	**currentibus**

327-331. Write a description of the next four pictures. Use the correct form of the participle **currēns.**

29-33

187.	**cūrāre**	------	---------
	#3 tense	-------	---------
		-------	--------

R:		**cūrābō**	**cūrābimus**
		cūrābis	**cūrābitis**
		cūrābit	**cūrābunt**

188.	**pallēre**	**pallēbō**	**pallēbimus**
	#3 tense	**pallēbis**	**pallēbitis**
	★ ○ •	**pallēbit**	**pallēbunt**

189.	**timēre**	------	---------
	#3 tense	-------	---------
		-------	--------

R:		**timēbō**	**timēbimus**
		timēbis	**timēbitis**
		timēbit	**timēbunt**

The 3d and 4th Conjugations have the signal {-ē} except in the first person singular.

190.	**quaerere**	**quaeram**	**quaerēmus**
	#3 tense	**quaerēs**	**quaerētis**
	★ ○ •	**quaeret**	**quaerent**

191.	**premere**	------	--------
	#3 tense	------	--------
		------	-------

R:		**premam**	**premēmus**
		premēs	**premētis**
		premet	**prement**

192.	**sapere (-iō)**	**sapiam**	**sapiēmus**
	#3 tense	**sapiēs**	**sapiētis**
	★ ○ •	**sapiet**	**sapient**

193.	**fugere (-iō)**	------	--------
	#3 tense	------	--------
		------	-------

R:		**fugiam**	**fugiēmus**
		fugiēs	**fugiētis**
		fugiet	**fugient**

327. A___ c____ c____nt__ cernit.

R: Anus canem currentem cernit.

328. Ag___ ā v____ c_____ī capit__.

R: Agnus ā vulpe currentī capitur.

329. In the next two frames we will use the word **animal**. Remember that this word is _____ gender.

A: neuter

330. Describe the picture. F__ an____ c_____s metuit.

R: Fūr animal currēns metuit.

---

181. **aspicere (-iō)**
#2 tense
— — — — — — —
— — — — — — —
— — — — — — —

R: aspiciō aspicimus
aspicis aspicitis
aspicit aspiciunt

182. **custōdīre**
#2 tense ★ ○ •
custōdiō custōdīmus
custōdīs custōdītis
custōdit custōdiunt

183. **invenīre**
#2 tense
— — — — — — —
— — — — — — —
— — — — — — —

R: inveniō invenīmus
invenīs invenītis
invenit inveniunt

184. **esse**
#2 tense ★ ○ •
sum sumus
es estis
est sunt

185. **posse**
#2 tense
pos--- pos-----
pot--- pot-----
pot--- pos-----

R: possum possumus
potes potestis
potest possunt

186. **mūtāre**
#3 tense ★ ○ •
mūtābō mūtābimus
mūtābis mūtābitis
mūtābit mūtābunt

There are two kinds of #3 tenses. The 1st and 2d Conjugations have the signal {-b-}.

16-56

331. Describe the picture. **V__ a_____ia c_____ia asp____.**

R: Vir animālia currentia aspicit.

332. Write your teacher's description of this picture. ★ ○ ○ **J_____ m_____ __ gr___ st_____ as_____.**

R: Juvenis medicum in gradū stantem aspicit.

333. This means, "_____."

A: The young man sees the doctor standing on the steps.

334. **Stantem** is the _____ form of the verb **stat.**

A: present participle

The differences between the different conjugations appear more clearly in the #2 tense than in any other. First echo sample verbs in the #2 tense.

174. **laudāre** ★ ○ ● | laudō laudās laudat | laudāmus laudātis laudant

175. **cantāre** #2 tense | ----- ----- | ------- ------- -------
R: | cantō cantās cantat | cantāmus cantātis cantant

176. **stupēre** ★ ○ ● | stupeō stupēs stupet | stupēmus stupētis stupent

177. **rubēre** #2 tense | ----- ----- | ------ ------ ------
R: | rubeō rubēs rubet | rubēmus rubētis rubent

178. **edere** ★ ○ ● | edō edis edit | edimus editis edunt

179. **metuere** #2 tense | ----- ------ | ------- ------- -------
R: | metuō metuis metuit | metuimus metuitis metuunt

180. **capere (-iō)** ★ ○ ● | capiō capis capit | capimus capitis capiunt

335. Echo the paradigm of **stāns**, first the singular, then the plural. ★ ○ •

m&f	n	m&f	n
stāns	stāns	-----ēs	-----ia
-----em	-----	-----ēs	-----ia
-----ī	-----ī	-----ibus	---------

Cōnf:

stāns	stāns	stantēs	stantia
stantem	stāns	stantēs	stantia
stantī	stantī	stantibus	stantibus

336-339. Describe the following four pictures. Use the participle of **stāns**.

336. A___ sub qu____ st__s īnf_____ aud___.

R: Anus sub quercū stāns īnfantem audit.

337. V___ st___ēs l____ metu___.

R: Virī stantēs lupum metuunt.

16-58

338. J_____ s a___ in u____ st____ m vid___.

R: Juvenis anum in umbrā stantem videt.

339. F_____ c___ ēs st_____ vid___.

R: Fēmina canēs stantēs videt.

340. Several of the words which you have been using as adjectives (or as nouns) are actually present participles of verbs. For example, the verb **sapit** means "is wise." The sentence **Vir sapit** means, "The ___ __ ____."

A: The man is wise.

341. The present participle of the verb **sapit** is a word which you learned as a noun in Unit Twelve; it is _____.

A: sapiēns.

342. Write as your teacher says in Latin, "The man is being helped by the wise judge." ★ ○ ○ "_____ vir adjuvātur."

R: Ā sapientī jūdice vir adjuvātur.

Quaestiōnēs et Respōnsa

162. "In quibus locīs positī sunt libellī Martiālis?" "__ s_____."

R: In sinibus.

163. "In quibus scrīpta sunt carmina Martiālis?" "__ l_____."

R: In libellīs.

164. "Quid omnēs Rōmānī cantant et laudant?" "C_____ M_____."

R: Carmina Martiālis.

165. "Quālem virum aspicit Martiālis?" "Virum rubentem, pall___ m, st_____."

R: Virum rubentem, pallentem, stupentem.

166. In this sequence we will review the paradigm of six tenses of the Latin verb. If you do not need this practice, skip to frame 205. The signal for the #1 tense is {-bā-} for all four conjugations. The only way in which the conjugations differ is in the characteristic vowel which comes before the signal {----}.

A: {-bā-}.

167. Say the #1 form of these verbs.

negāre, #1 tense
____ā____   ____ā____
____ā____   ____ā____
____ā____   ____ā____

R: negābam   negābāmus
   negābās   negābātis
   negābat   negābant

343. There is a slight difference here. See if you can spot it. Your teacher will now say, "The young man is being helped by the wise person."
★ ○ ○ "_____ juvenis adjuvātur.

R: Ā sapiente juvenis adjuvātur.

344. When **sapiēns** is used as an adjective, the ablative singular form is _____. However, when **sapiēns** is used as a noun, the ablative singular form is _____.

A: sapientī sapiente.
(There is some variation on this, but the rule will hold good most of the time.)

345. The verb **vult** is irregular. In this Unit you used its present participle as a noun; the word that means "willing person" is _____.

A: volēns.

346. A person is said to be "fluent" when words flow easily from his mouth. This English word is derived from the Latin word **fluēns,** which is the _____ of the verb **fluit.**

A: present participle

347. Most English words which end in "-ent" or "-ant" are derivatives of this Latin participle. For example, the people who are trustees of universities are often called "Regents." The word "regent" is derived from the present participle of the Latin verb _____.

A: regit.

16-60

348. The name "Vincent" is a derivative of a Latin verb; the name therefore means, "The _____ing one."

A: conquering

349. We speak of the "current" of a river. The word "current" is a derivative of the _____ _____ of the Latin verb _____.

A: present participle **currit.**

350. The English derivative of the present participle of **irrītat** is "_____."

A: irritant.

351. You have now learned 48 Basic Sentences. There are several reasons why you should know these sentences thoroughly. In the first place they illustrate the forms which you are learning. For example, **Fortēs Fortūna adjuvat** was used to illustrate the plural of the _____ case.

A: accusative

352. Therefore one use of the Basic Sentences is to have you learn new f___s.

A: forms.

353. Secondly, these Basic Sentences were chosen because the words which are used will occur repeatedly in later parts of the course. The Basic Sentences therefore also teach you v_____ry.

A: vocabulary.

---

147. *Like what?* Think of what has gone before.
He likes _____
[In your own words]

A: the fact that his poems upset this man so.

148. Martial then continues, **Nunc nōbīs carmina nostra placent,** which means, "___ my ____s ___."

A: Now my poems please me (or, "Now our poems please us.").

149. Why is Martial pleased with the fact that this man dislikes the poems so much? _____ [There may be several answers for this.]

A: The **quīdam** may have been somebody like Sabīdius, Symmachus, Diaulus, or Caecilīānus, and they were reading a poem about themselves. Perhaps this certain person was such a poor judge of poetry that Martial would have been insulted if the man had thought they were good. Any other explanations? If you can think of any, write and let me know.

150. We will take the poem line by line, giving an English version of the Latin. **Laudat, amat, cantat nostrōs mea Rōma libellōs** = _____

A: My Rome (the Rome I love) praises, loves, and recites my (our) books.

151. Copy in your Notebook.

152. mēque sinūs omnēs, mē manus omnis habet. = _____

A: All "pockets" hold me, every hand holds me.

153. Copy.

354. Finally, we use these familiar sentences to practice new structures. For example, when you were learning the passive voice you practiced transforming active verbs to the _____ voice.

A: passive

355. When you learned the plural of the five declensions, you suddenly doubled the number of noun forms you knew. We wish to give you lots of practice on these new forms before moving on to anything new. We will do this by means of question and answer drills on the 48 _____ _____.

A: Basic Sentences.

356. First, of course, you must know what the question words mean. We will begin with the paradigms. Echo the word that asks for a personal noun ("Who?"). ★ ○ •

Quis?　Quī?
Quem?　Quōs?
Quō?　Quibus?

Question and Answer Drill

Remember that your answer must be in the same number and case as the question word.
Fortēs Fortūna adjuvat. (40)

357. "Quōs Fortūna adjuvat?" "_____."

R: Fortēs.

358. "Quis fortēs adjuvat?" "_____."

R: Fortūna.

---

141. One English derivative of **stupēre** is "___-pid."

A: stupid.

142. When a person has had an experience which has frozen him into complete inactivity, we say that he has been st___-fied by what he has gone through.

A: stupefied

143. Hic quidam, quī libellum Martiālis tenet, ōscit___.

R: ōscitat.

144. The verb **ōscitāre** means "op__ one's m___."

A: open one's mouth.

145. But *why* is he opening his mouth? He hates the poems of Martial so much that he is about to be _____.

A: sick.

146. In the final line Martial says, **Hoc volō,** which means "_____."

A: I want this (or perhaps better, "I like this").

If you have the Basic Sentence in front of you, this type of simple substitution is almost *too* easy now to benefit you. We will therefore give you questions in which the original sentence has been transformed, as in the following examples.

359. "Ā quō fortēs adjuvantur?" "Ā F_____." (Auxilium hāc sub līneā est.)

Aux: Since **Quō?** is ablative, answer in the ablative with a noun which fits the sense.

R: Ā Fortūnā.

360. The question **Ā quō?** asks for a p_____l noun in the _____ case.

A: personal ablative

361. "Quī ā Fortūnā adjuvantur?" "_____."

R: Fortēs.

362. The word **Fortēs** in answer to **Quī ā Fortūnā adjuvantur?** is _____ case.

A: nominative

363. Fortēs is an ambiguous form. The word fortēs in the sentence **Fortēs Fortūna adjuvat** is _____ case.

A: accusative

---

135. Now for the big question. Remembering what was said in the first two lines, who or what does this man hate? _____.

A: Martial (and Martial's poems)

136. Here is a diagram of the sentence.

Quīdam {rubet, pallet} {stupet, ōscitat} ōdit
        appearance actions   emotions

From this diagram you can see that the first two verbs (**rubet, pallet**) describe this person's physical _____, **stupet** and **ōscitat** describe his _____s, while **ōdit** describes his _____s.

A: appearance actions emotions

137. The verbs describing his appearance (**rubet** and **pallet**) both have English derivatives. There is a precious stone called a "r____."

A: ruby.

138. When a person has had a severe shock his color becomes p____.

A: pale.

139. Therefore when this certain person reads Martial's poems, his color is first ___ and then _____.

A: red pale (white).

140. He turns these colors because he ____s Martial's poems so much.

A: hates

364. While **Quis?** asks for personal nouns, the word **Quid?** ("What?") asks for _____ nouns.

A: non-personal

365. The plural of **Quid?** has the forms **Quae rēs?** and **Quās rēs?** ("What things?") in the plural. **Quae rēs?** asks for a non-personal noun in the nominative case, while **Quās rēs?** asks for a non-personal noun in the _____ case.

A: accusative

366. ★ ○ •   Quid?   Quae rēs?
                Quid?   Quās rēs?
                Quō?   Quibus?

367. Copy in your Reference Notebook under "Forms."

368. We can be more specific in our questions if we wish to. For example, we can ask "What animal?" ★ ○ •

Quod animal?   Quae animālia?
Quod animal?   Quae animālia?
Quō animālī?   Quibus animālibus?

369. Those of you who are observant noticed that the adjective form of the question word in the nominative-accusative singular is not **Quid?** but _____.

A: **Quod?**

370. Finally, we can ask, "What part of the body?" We will receive as answers the words for "hand," "eye," "ear," etc. ★ ○ •

Quod membrum?   Quae membra?
Quod membrum?   Quae membra?
Quō membrō?   Quibus membrīs?

---

128. It is now apparent that the first line is the first member of the tricolon, and that the second and third members are found in the ____ line.

A: next (second)

129. But here we have the tricolon in reverse, because it is the ____ (first/second/third) clause which is as long as the other two.

A: first

130. In the form of verse used in this poem, it is common for the second line (the shorter one) to repeat or add to the information given in the first line. This is true here. The first two lines say in *three* different ways that everybody in the city of ____ is _____.

A: Rome is reading Martial's poems (books).

131. The third line breaks in abruptly with a word that demands your attention. This word is _____.

A: Ecce!

132. "Look!" says Martial, and then he describes what a c_____ p_____ is doing.

A: certain person

133. How many actions is this certain person doing? ____ (1/2/3/4/5/6/7/8)

A: 5

134. Of these five verbs, you know only one: **ōdit**. But this is important: you know that this man ____s something or somebody.

A: hates

16-64

371. In your Notebook copy these Facts About Latin:

1. **Quis** asks for a personal noun.
2. **Quid** asks for a non-personal noun.
3. **Quod animal** asks for an animal.
4. **Quod membrum** asks for a part of the body.

372. The important thing to remember is that you must answer with a word which is the *same case* and *same number* as the question word. You must also note whether a personal noun is required. For example, which is the *one* possible answer for the question "**Quōs auctor laudat?**" "____ (Flūmina/Virum/Fēminae/Asinōs)."

A: **Asinōs.**

373. Let us see why the other answers were wrong. **Flūmina,** being the ambiguous nominative-accusative plural form, was the right number and case, but **Quōs?** asks for a _____ noun. **Flūmina** is a _____ noun.

A: personal
non-personal

374. **Virum** is accusative case, but as an answer for **Quōs?** it is the wrong _____.

A: number.

375. And **Fēminae,** while plural number, is the wrong ____ for **Quōs?**

A: case

376. The only possible answer for **Quem?** in this list is ____ (Sīmiās/Vīnum/Aprum/Vir).

A: **Aprum.**

29-23

121. Copy into your Reference Notebook. [As we discuss this poem, refer to it either by looking back in the program or in your Notebook.]

122. Too often students studying a foreign language think in terms of single words. This is a bad habit. You must think in larger units, for example, a s_____ce.

A: sentence.

123. We will try to teach you to approach this poem not word by word but s_____ by s_____.

A: sentence   sentence.

124. We have mentioned that the Roman authors liked to write in series of three. This poetical device is called a _____.

A: tricolon.

125. The first line of the poem [look at it] is a tricolon because it contains three ____s.

A: verbs

126. The subject of all three verbs is _____ and the object is _____.

A: mea Rōma   nostrōs libellōs.

127. Expand the second line with the missing element: **mēque sinūs omnēs** _____, **mē manus omnis habet.**

R: **mēque sinūs omnēs habent,**
mē manus omnis habet.

We might represent this sentence by this figure.

Laudat,
amat { nostrōs mea Rōma libellōs,
cantat } 1

mēque sinūs omnēs habent ,
2

mē manus omnis habet.
3

377. Notice that you do not even need to see the rest of the sentence to know that the answer to **Quem?** must be a ____ (personal/non-personal) noun in the _____ case and _____ number.

A: personal
accusative
singular

378. The question word **Quid?**, however, is an _____ form.

A: ambiguous

379. Therefore we will have to give you practice in determining whether it asks for the accusative case or the nominative case. To do this without also making you think of the meaning of the words, we will first give you practice by means of symbols. For example, in the question **Quid {-s -t}?** the answer will be a non-personal noun in the _____ case.

A: accusative

380. You know in **Quid {-s -t}?** that the **Quid?** asks for the {-m}, because the sentence already contains an {__}.

A: {-s}.

381. This sequence is purposely a little harder than most of the others. Do not be surprised if your error rate is higher than usual on this section. If you make an error you should ____ (go on immediately to the next frame/study the frame until you know why your answer was wrong).

A: study the frame until you know why your answer was wrong.

---

116. Another way to translate would be to explain and say, "The Romans used to carry small books in the ____ of ____ ____."

A: folds of their clothes.

117. The word **quidam, quaedam, quoddam,** means "a certain person or thing," in the sense of "somebody," or "something." **Heri quidam mēcum manēbat** = Y_____ s_____ re_____ w_____ ____.

A: Yesterday somebody remained with me.

118. **Heri quidam amīcus mēcum manēbat** = Y_____ a c_____ _____ _____ _____ _____ ____.

A: Yesterday a certain friend remained with me.

119. But note carefully that **quidam** means "certain" in the sense of "no special person, just a friend, that's all." On the other hand, **Heri certus amīcus mēcum manēbat** means _____ [In your own words]

A: Yesterday my sure and certain friend (whom I trust) stayed with me.

120. Here is the poem, Reading #5. The third line contains five verbs, four of them unknown to you. Don't be nervous. ✱ ○ ●

**Laudat, amat, cantat nostrōs mea Rōma libellōs,
mēque sinus omnēs, mē manus omnis habet.
Ecce! Rubet quīdam, pallet, stupet, ōscitat, ōdit.
Hoc volo. Nunc nōbīs carmina nostra placent.** (Reading #5)

382. After you know why your answer was wrong you should try to remember the _____ _____.

A: right answer.

383. At first the program makes it almost impossible for you not to do things right. In other words, it makes all students study the way it appears that good students study. But you cannot always study from a program, and in this program you will gradually learn to do things more and more _____.
[In your own words]

A: _____ on your own responsibility.

384. Here is a chance to see if you have learned something about being a good student. If you rush through this next sequence, pay no attention to your errors, and miss these same questions on the test, it would seem that you _____. [In your own words]

A: have not yet learned how to work properly.

385. On the other hand, if in spite of making errors you learn from these mistakes, then it would seem that you _____ _____. [In your own words]

A: _____ are learning to work the way good students do.

CAUTION: Do not rush through this sequence; take enough time to give yourself a chance to figure out the answer.

To break the task down into small divisions, we will have three steps for every question. First we will be sure that you know the meaning of the question word in the particular sentence structure in which it will occur. Then we will give you

---

112. *Sinus est quoque pars corporis. Anus infantem in s____ suō tenet.*

R: sinū

113. *Sinus est quoque locus in quō nāvēs stābant. Haec nāvis in ____ manet.*

R: in sinū

114. A "sine" curve (derived from the Latin *sinus*) is shaped like this: ～～～
The common element in these four examples is that of a c___e of some sort.

A: curve

115. You can see here one of the difficulties of translation. How can we translate into English *Rōmānī libellōs in sinū ferēbant?* One way is to use the *modern* equivalent place where a person could put a small book and say, "The Romans used to carry small books in their _____."

A: pockets.

16-67

the paradigm of the words which will furnish the answer. Finally we will give you the Basic Sentence and ask you to write the answer to a question.

We will take the odd numbered Basic Sentences in this unit, and we will do them in sets of four.

386. The first question is "**Ex quō {-s -tur}?**" Give the *one* answer which will fit. "Ex ____ (ōrātiō/oculīs/manū/vitium)."

A: Ex manū.
(as in the sentence "**Ex manū cognōscitur fūr.**")

387. **Ōrātiō** is not the right answer because it is not in the same case as **Quō?** It is not ablative case but _____.

A: nominative.

388. The ablative of **ōrātiō** is _____.

A: ōrātiōne.

389. And **oculīs** was not the right answer to **Ex quō?** because _____.

A: **oculīs** is not the same number as **quō?**.

390. "**Quālēs auctōrēs {-t -s}?**" "____ (Bonum/Bonī/Bonōs/Bonus)."

R: Bonōs.
(as in "**Bonōs auctōrēs laudat rēgīna.**")

29-20

107. The Romans did the same thing. When Martial wants to tell us how popular his books were, instead of saying, "**Rōma meōs libellōs laudat,**" he says, "**Rōma n_____ libellōs laudat.**"

R: nostrōs

108. "**Estne Caeciliānus vester amīcus?**" "**Certē, est amīcus n__er.**"

R: Certē, est amīcus noster.

109. "**Estne Caeciliānus tuus amīcus?**" "**Certē, meus est am____.**"

R: Certē, meus est amīcus.

110. The Romans had no pockets in their clothes. Ask your teacher where the Romans carried small books. "__ I__ R_____ lib_____ ferēb____?"

R: Quō locō Rōmānī libellōs ferēbant?

111. Write down his answer. ★ ○ ○ __ s____.

R: In sinū.

16-68

391. Although in certain sentences **Quālēs** could get **bonī** as an answer, you knew that in **Quālēs auctōrēs {-t -s}?** the noun **auctōrēs** was accusative case because there already was an {_ _} in the sentence.

A: {-s}

392. "Quae animālia {-ntur}?" "____ (Canis/Taurum/Rānae/Muscās)."

R: Rānae.
(as in "Rānae ā vīperīs capiuntur")

393. "Quid {-s -t}?" "____ (Pecūniam/Datōrem/Vīta/Saccōs)."

R: Pecūniam. (as in "Pecūniam rēgīna dōnat.")

394. Datōrem was not the right answer for **Quid {-s -t}?** because **datōrem** is a _____ noun.

A: personal

395. Saccōs was not the right answer for **Quid {-s -t}?** because **saccōs** is _____ _____.

A: plural number.

We will here give you practice on the paradigms of the nouns with which you will answer the questions on the Basic Sentences. Where the plural of a noun is uncommon (as in **vestis**, which means clothing in general and does not usually have a plural), we have given you only the singular. The number identifies the declension.

29-19

102. "Ex quō recitat Martiālis carmen suum?" "_ l_____."

R: Ex libellō.

103. The verb **vult** is irregular in some of its forms. Learn the #2 tense.

★ ○ ○ ● volō   vult
            vīs   vultis
            volumus volunt

104. The word **Ecce!** does not change form; it is used to call attention to something exciting.

R: Ecce! Illa vipera mē mordēbit!

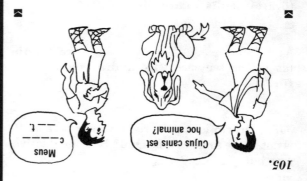

105.

Cujus canis est hoc animal?

Meus c___ t.

R: Meus canis est.

106. Editors and writers frequently use what is called "the editorial 'we.'" That is, instead of saying, "I heard from one of my readers yesterday," they will say, "__ h____ from ____ ____ ____."

A: We heard from one of our readers yesterday.

396. ★ ○ • (3)
vestis
vestem
veste

397. ★ ○ •
    (3)   (3)
hilaris dator   hilarēs datōrēs
hilarem datōrem   hilarēs datōrēs
hilarī datōre   hilaribus datōribus

398. ★ ○ •
         (3)
mūs   mūrēs
mūrem   mūrēs
mūre   mūribus

399. ★ ○ • (3)
vēritās
vēritātem
vēritāte

[A reminder: the single echo indicates the *minimum* number of times you say the paradigm. Most of you will learn faster if you repeat it several times.]

400. Now for the questions on four Basic Sentences. If you need to look back to get the correct form, of course you may do so, but make every effort to _ _ _ _ _ _ _ _ it first.

A: remember (recall, etc.)

401. Vestis virum reddit. (1) "Ex quō cognōscitur vir?" "_____ _____."

R: Ex veste.

402. Hilarem datōrem dīligit Deus. (3) "Quālēs datōrēs dīligit Deus?"
"_____ _____."

R: Hilarēs datōrēs.

---

98. "Quid accidet arcuī quī semper tēnsus erit?" "Hic ar--- c--- r-----tur."

R: Hic arcus citō rumpētur.

Here is the vocabulary for Reading #5.

99. "Cantāre" significat duās rēs. Fēmina in hāc pictūrā cantat. Sed hic auctor opus suum quoque cantat vel rec---t.

R: recitat.

100. Opera quae Marcus Martiālis scrīpsit dīcuntur "*carmina*." Haec carmina scrīpta sunt in *libellīs*. "Nōn amō tē, Sabidī" est carmen Marcī Martiālis. "Nūper erat medicus, nunc est vespillō Diaulus" est quoque c--- n M---------.

libellus

101. "Quid cantat Martiālis ex libellō?" "C------ suum."

R: carmen Martiālis.

R: Carmen suum.

403. **Elephantus nōn capit mūrem.** (5) "Quae animālia ab elephantīs negleguntur?" "_____."

R: Mūrēs.

404. **Vēritās numquam perit.** (7) "Quid sapientēs semper colunt?" "_____."

R: Vēritātem.

405. The transformation in **Hilarem datōrem dīligit Deus** was from singular to plural. Since God loves a cheerful giver, when asked what kinds of givers God loves, you replied in Latin that he loves _____ _____.

A: cheerful givers (in the plural).

406. The form **opus** is the same as ____ (corpus/saltus).

A: **corpus.**

407. The form **hilare** is the same as ____ (lēge/facile).

A: **facile.**

408. Pick the neuter nominative-accusative forms from this list: **equus genus asinus leve aure capillus crūdēle**

A: **genus leve crūdēle**

---

92. "At" significat "sed," at **sī laxā'ris, cum volēs, erit ūtilis** = _____

A: but if you unstring it, it will be useful when you want it.

93. Copy in your Notebook.

94. Although **ūtilis** was a new word, we hoped that you would be able to figure out that it meant "useful," because of the English word "_____."

A: utility (utilize, utilitarian).

95. C---- rum--- ar---, s----- s- tēn---- h------; at s. laxā', c---, v----, er---, ūt----. (141)

R: Citō rumpēs arcum, semper sī tēnsum habueris; at sī laxā'ris, cum volēs, erit ūtilis.

Quaestiōnēs et Respōnsa

96. "Quō tempore rumpētur arcus semper tēnsus?" "_____."

R: Citō.

97. "Quod instrūmentum tū citō rumpēs sī semper tēnsum habueris?" "_____ ego c... r------."

R: Arcum ego citō rumpam.

16-71

You will practice four more questions and answers. If you feel that you do *not* need the practice on the question words and on the paradigms, you may go to frame 423.

409. "Quōs {-t -s}?" "____ (Rānam/Rānās/Oculōs/Vitia)."

R: Rānās. (as in "*Rānās quaerunt vīperae.*")

410. **Oculōs** was not the right answer because **Quōs?** asks for a _____ noun.

A: personal

411. **Rānam** was not the right answer because **Quōs?** asks for the _____ number.

A: plural

412. "Quō {-s -tur}?" "____ (Vitiō/Leō/Imitātiō/Taurō)."

R: Vitiō (as in "*Vitiō juvenis vincitur.*")

413. **Imitātiō** and **leō** are not the answer to **Quō?** because **imitātiō** and **leō** are _____ case.

A: nominative

414. **Taurō** is ablative like **Quō?**, but **Quō?** expects a _____ noun.

A: non-personal

16-72

415. "Quī {-ntur}?" "____(Asinī/Vitia/Ēloquentī/Omnī)."

R. **Asinī.** (as in "**Asinī laudantur.**")

416. **Ēloquentī** and **Omnī** are _____ case and _____ number.

A: ablative singular

417. Although **Quī?** is masculine, it may be answered by a feminine gender noun, since when a person asks "Who?" he does not know what the answer is. A person asking **Quī?** would not know what g_____ the noun would be in the answer.

A: gender

418. "Quī {-ntur}?" "____ (Vīna/Fēminae/Aurēs/Oculī)."

R: **Fēminae.** (as in "**Fēminae laudantur.**")

419-422. Echo the paradigms of the words with which you will answer the next four Basic Sentences.

419. ★ ○ •   (1)
fēmina   fēminae
fēminam fēminās
fēminā   fēminīs

420. ★ ○ •   (2)
īrātus   īrātī
īrātum   īrātōs
īrātō   īrātīs

16-73

421. ★ ○ • (2)

capillus   capillī
capillum   capillōs
capillō   capillīs

422. ★ ○ •

    (2)   (3)
medicus ēloquēns
medicum ēloquentem
medicō ēloquentī
medicī ēloquentēs
medicōs ēloquentēs
medicīs ēloquentibus

(If you feel the need, do more study on these; you might, for example, copy any paradigm which you have not learned.)

Question and Answer Drill

423. Nōn quaerit aeger medicum ēloquentem. (9) "Quī nōn quaeruntur ab aegrīs?" "_____ _____."

R: Medicī ēloquentēs.

424. Etiam capillus ūnus habet umbram suam. (11) "Quō musca obumbrātur?" "_____."

R: Capillō.

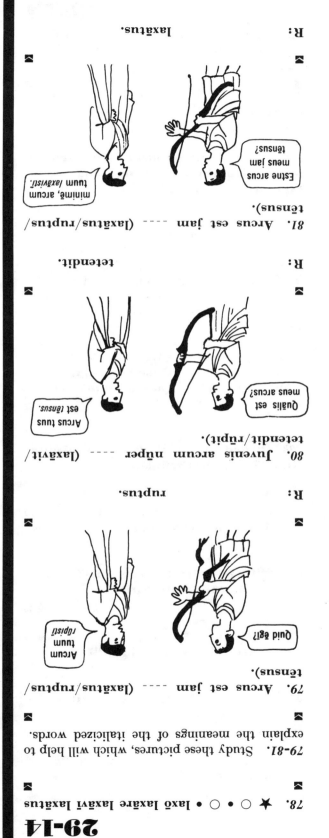

425. Lēx videt īrātum, īrātus lēgem nōn videt. (13) "Quōs lēx semper capit?" "_____."

R: Īrātōs.

426. Vulpēs vult fraudem, lupus agnum, fēmina laudem. (15) "Quī laude saepe capiuntur?" "_____."

R: Fēminae.

[Again, if you do not need practice on question words and paradigms, skip to frame 436.]

427. ★ ○ •
    (3)
Quod animal?   Quae animālia?
Quod animal?   Quae animālia?
Quō animālī?   Quibus animālibus?

428. "Quid {-s -t}?" "____ (Venēnum/Gradibus/Sīmia/Pecūnia)."

R: Venēnum (as in "Venēnum medicus metuit").

429. "Quae animālia {-m -nt}?" "____ (Rānās/Taurum/Asinī/Virī)."

R: Asinī (as in "Asinī flūmen aspiciunt").

430. "Quid {-t}?" "____ (Anus/Vitia/Fraus/Laudem)."

R: Fraus (as in "Fraus numquam perit").

---

73. Dōn— e— fē— m— n
    a—;
    t— n— f— s— e—
    (140)

R: Dōnec eris fēlix, multōs numerābis amīcōs;
tempora sī fuerint nūbila, sōlus eris.

74. Basic Sentence 141 is also two lines long.
★ ○ ○ ○ C— ru— ar—, sem— sī
    tēn— hab—.

R: Citō rumpēs arcum, semper sī tēnsum habueris.
[There are four macrons in this line.]

75. ★ ○ ○ ○ at sī l— ā'r—, c— v—,
    ut— . (141)

R: at sī laxā'ris, cum volēs, erit utilis.

76. ★ ○ • ○ ○ • tendō tendere tetendī tēnsus

77. ★ ○ • ○ ○ • rumpō rumpere rūpī ruptus

16-75

431. "Quae animālia {-s -t}?" "____ (Equī/Taurum/Agnī/Sīmiās).

R: Sīmiās. (as in "Sīmiās īnfāns lavat."). (If there is anything we can't stand, it's dirty monkeys.)

432. ★ ○ • (2)

taurus	taurī
taurum	taurōs
taurō	taurīs

433. ★ ○ • (1)

pecūnia	pecūniae
pecūniam	pecūniās
pecūniā	pecūniīs

434. ★ ○ • (1)

poena	poenae
poenam	poenās
poenā	poenīs

435. ★ ○ • (3)

canis	canēs
canem	canēs
cane	canibus

436. Pecūnia nōn satiat avāritiam sed irrītat. (17) "Quid avāritia vult?" "_____."

R: Pecūniam.

437. Nūlla avāritia sine poenā est. (19) "Quid habet omnis avāritia?" "_____."

R: Poenam.

438. Parva necat morsū spatiōsum vīpera taurum. (21) "Quae animālia vīperās parvās saepe metuunt?" "_____."

R: Taurī.

29-12

68. In each sentence the adjective is separated from its noun by the _____

A: verb.

69. Latin poets frequently emphasize an adjective by separating it from its _____ by a _____

A: noun, verb.

Quaestiōnēs et Respōnsa

70. "Sī rēs incertae fuerint, quantum numerum amīcōrum habēbis, parvum an magnum?" "____ n____ am____ ego h____."

R: Parvum numerum amīcōrum ego habēbō.

71. "Cum Ovidius haec verba scrīpsit, fuitne hilaris an tristis?" "_____."

R: Tristis.

72. Hilaris auctor dē vērīs amīcīs haec verba scrīpsit, "Am____ c____ r. in c____."

R: Amīcus certus in rē incertā cernitur.

16-76

439. Ā cane nōn magnō saepe tenētur aper.
(23) "Quae animālia aprī saepe metuunt?"
"_____."

R: Canēs.

(If you think that you do not need the preliminary drill, go directly to the questions in frame 449. However, do *not* skip this next section if you have been making errors on the question-and-answer part.)

440. For this sequence you need to know two question phrases. **Ā quō?** and **Ā quibus?**. The difference between them is that **Ā quō?** asks for the _____ number, and **Ā quibus?** asks for the _____ _____.

A: singular
   plural number.

441. "Ā quō {-s -tur}?" "____ (Vīnō/Auxiliō/Aure/Ab anū)."

R: Ab anū. (as in "Ab anū īnfāns lavātur").

442. "Ā quibus {-s -tur}?" "____ (Ab anibus/Diēbus/Ā sīmiā/Equī)."

R: Ab anibus. (as in "Ab anibus īnfantēs lavantur").

443. "Quās rēs {-s -t}?" "____ (Oculī/Noctem/Saccōs/Fēminās)."

R: Saccōs. (as in "Saccōs fūr quaerit.")

444. ★ ○ • Quid?   Quae rēs?
              Quid?   Quās rēs?
              Quō?   Quibus?

62. "Herī caelum serēnum erat, sed hodiē est nūbilum. Potestne hoc īnstrūmentum hōrās numerāre sī caelum nūbilum est?"
"------------."

R: Nōn potest.

63. Caelum, sī nōn est serēnum, est nūb---m.

R: nūbilum.

64. Ovid is feeling sorry for himself in exile on the Black Sea and he complains that his friends are all "fair-weather" friends of his prosperous days. ★ ○ ○ ○ ————

R: Dōnec eris fēlix, multōs numerābis amīcōs;
Tempora si fuerint nūbila, sōlus eris.

65. Ovid says, "------------."

A: While you are prosperous, you will number many friends; if the times have been cloudy, you will be alone.

66. Copy this in your Notebook.

67. By arrows connect the adjectives **multōs** and **nūbila** to the nouns they modify.

R: Dōnec eris fēlix, multōs numerābis amīcōs;
Tempora si fuerint nūbila, sōlus eris.

R: Dōnec eris fēlix, multōs numerābis amīcōs,
tempora si fuerint nūbila, sōlus eris.

HORĀS NŌN NUMERŌ NISI SERĒNĀS

16-77

In this next sequence there are two First Declension nouns and two Second Declension neuters. We will give you practice on the paradigm of only one of each kind.

445. ★ ○ • (2)
    perīc'lum   perīc'la
    perīc'lum   perīc'la
    perīc'lō   perīc'līs

446. ★ ○ • (3)
    aúctor   auctórēs
    auctórem   auctórēs
    auctóre   auctóribus

447. ★ ○ • (2)
    vīnum   vīna
    vīnum   vīna
    vīnō   vīnīs

448. ★ ○ • (1)
    rēgína   rēgínae
    rēgínam   rēgínās
    rēgínā   rēgínīs

449. Numquam perīc'lum sine perīc'lō vincitur. (25) "Quās rēs vir fortis perīc'līs vincit?" "_____."

R: Perīc'la.

450. Sapientia vīnō obumbrātur. (27) "Quid virum sapientem saepe vincit?" "_____."

R: Vīnum.

451. Auctor opus laudat. (29) "Ā quibus sua opera laudantur?" "_____ _____."

R: Ab auctōribus.

16-78

452. Et genus et formam Rēgīna Pecūnia dōnat. (31) "Ā quō vītae reguntur?"
"_____ _____ _____."

R: Ā Rēgīnā Pecūniā.

453. "Quālibus ā dictīs {-s -t}?" "____ (Malīs/Malōs/Hilarī/Hilarēs)."

R: Malīs.
(as in "Malīs ā dictīs sapiēns currit").

454. Malīs ā dictīs sapiēns currit = The w___ ___ ___s away ____ ev__ w___s.

A: The wise man runs away from evil words.

455. ★ ○ •   (2)
       amīcus   amīcī
       amīcum   amīcōs
       amīcō   amīcīs

456. ★ ○ •
         (2)   (3)
       pūrus fōns   pūrī fontēs
       pūrum fontem   pūrōs fontēs
       pūrō fonte   pūrīs fontibus

457. ★ ○ •   (2)
       Deus   dī
       Deum   deōs
       Deō   dīs

458. ★ ○ •   (3)
       crūdēlis   crūdēlēs
       crūdēlem   crūdēlēs
       crūdēlī   crūdēlibus

29-9

48. Actiō rēcta nōn erit, nisi rēcta fuerit voluntās. (139) ∨ ★ ○ •

49. Actiō rēcta nōn erit, nisi rēcta fuerit voluntās = The _____ ____ ___ be _____ unl___ the ____ is _____.

A: The action will not be correct unless the wish is correct.

50. Copy this in your Notebook.

51. Because of the form **fuerit** you know that the act of wishing must ____ (precede the action/ occur at the same time as the action/follow the action).

A: precede the action.

52. We know this because the #6 form **fuerit** shows _____ action in _____ time.

A: completed future [Notice, however, how awkward "will have" would sound in this sentence.]

Quaestiōnēs et Respōnsa

53. "Sī voluntās mala fuerit, quālis āctiō erit?" "_____."

R: Mala.

54. "Quāliter aget cuius voluntās rēcta fuerit, rēctē an iniūstē?" "_____."

R: Rēctē.

55. "Quāliter agēs sī tua voluntās rēcta fuerit?" "Egō ____ ag__."

R: Egō rēctē agam.

16-79

459. Rem nōn spem, factum nōn dictum, quaerit amīcus. (33) "Quī et factum et rem quaerunt?" "_____."

R: Amīcī.

460. Ā fonte pūrō pūra dēfluit aqua. (35) "Quālibus ā fontibus dēfluit aqua pūra?" "_____ _____ _____."

R: Pūrīs ā fontibus.

461. Religiō deōs colit, superstitiō violat. (37) "Ā quibus religiō laudātur?" "_____ _____."

R: Ā dīs.

462. Crūdēlis lacrimīs pāscitur, nōn frangitur. (39) "Quōs lacrimae nōn vincunt?" "_____."

R: Crūdēlēs.

463. ★ ○ •
    Quod membrum?   Quae membra?
    Quod membrum?   Quae membra?
    Quō membrō?   Quibus membrīs?
    ("What part of the body?")

464. "Quae membra {-t -s}?" "____ (Capillōs/Oculī/Aurem/Auribus)."

R: Capillōs. (as in "Capillōs cūrat fēmina.")

465. "Quae rēs {-ntur}?" "____ (Sīmiae/Perīc'la/Asinōs/Orbis)."

R: Perīc'la. (as in "Perīc'la nōn semper vincuntur.")

---

44. Ask your teachers what their wish is, and write their answer. "_____."

R: Nostra voluntās est perīc'lum effugere.

45. Listen to your teacher's question and then answer it.

46. Echo this synopsis of esse in the third person singular. ★ ○ •

	Future	Present	Past
Imperfective	erit[3]	est[2]	erat[1]
Perfective	fuerit[6]	fuit[5]	fuerat[4]

R: Certē; vestra āctiō rēcta fuit.

47. As you can see from the preceding diagram, fuerit shows _____ action in _____ time.

A: perfective   future

16-80

466. ★ ○ •   (3)
      fortis   fortēs
      fortem fortēs
      fortī   fortibus

467. ★ ○ •   (3)
      auris   aurēs
      aurem   aurēs
      aure   auribus

468. ★ ○ •   (2)
      fātum   Fāta
      fātum   Fāta
      fātō   Fātīs

469. ★ ○ •
     (3)   (2)
     levis animus   levēs animī
     levem animum levēs animōs
     levī animō   levibus animīs

470. Fortūna fortēs metuit, īgnāvōs premit. (41) "Ā quibus Fortūna vincitur?" "_____ _____."

R: Ā fortibus.

471. Ex auribus cognōscitur asinus. (43) "Quae membra possidet asinus stultus?" "_____."

R: Aurēs.

472. Dūcunt volentem Fāta, nōlentem trahunt. (45) "Ā quibus volentēs adjuvantur?" "_____ _____."

R: Ā Fātīs.

29-7

38. Certā stetērunt omnia lēge = _____ _____.

A: Every-thing has stood under a fixed law.

39. Copy this diagram of the six tenses of the verb in your Reference Notebook.

	Past	Present	Future
Imperfective	aspiciēbās[3]	aspicis[2]	aspiciēs[1]
Perfective	aspexerās[6]	aspexistī[5]	aspexeris[4]

40. Copy this #6 paradigm in your Reference Notebook.

R: fēcerō   fēcerimus
     fēceris   fēceritis
     fēcerit   fēcerint

41. On the model of fēcerō, write the #6 paradigm of habeō. [Remember that you must know the active perfective stem. If you have forgotten the principal parts of habeō, look them up now in your Notebook and learn them.]

R: habuerō   habuerimus
     habueris   habueritis
     habuerit   habuerint

42. ★ ○ ○ Ā‑‑‑ n‑‑‑ er‑‑‑ (139) r‑‑‑ v‑‑‑ r‑‑‑ f‑‑‑ r‑‑‑

R: Āctiō rēcta nōn erit, nisi rēcta fuerit voluntās.

43. Rēctus significat "vērus" vel "bonus." Rēctus oppōnitur "m‑‑‑‑‑."

R: malus.

16-81

473. Parva levēs capiunt animōs. (47)
"Quae rēs parvīs capiuntur?" "_____
_____."

⌇   ⌇

R: Levēs
animī.

On the test for this Unit you will be asked several of these same questions. If you feel you need more practice, we suggest that you go through this sequence again, beginning at frame 356.

SUMMARY

474. The purpose of this Unit was to learn the plural of _____ nouns.

⌇   ⌇

A: neuter

475. *All* the neuter nouns have the *same* signal for the ambiguous nominative-accusative form in the plural: it is {__}.

⌇   ⌇

A: {-a}.

476. Let us see whether you learned these forms thoroughly. Write the paradigm, singular and plural, of **bonum genus**.

_____   _____   _____

⌇   ⌇

A: bonum genus   bona genera
    bonum genus   bona genera
    bonō genere   bonīs generibus

⌇

477. Write the paradigm of **hilare dictum**.

_____   _____   _____

⌇   ⌇

A: hilare dictum   hilaria dicta
    hilare dictum   hilaria dicta
    hilarī dictō   hilaribus dictīs

---

31. Caelō fulget lūna serēnō. "Fulget" est t-------- --------.

⌇

R: temporis secundī.

⌇

32. Caelō fulget lūna serēnō = ---------- ---------------------.

⌇

A: The moon shines in the clear sky.

⌇

33. Rem nōn spem quaesīverat amīcus. "Quaesīverat" est t-------- --------.

⌇

R: temporis quārtī.

⌇

34. Rem nōn spem quaesīverat amīcus = ---------------------------------------.

⌇

A: A friend had sought support and not a promise.

⌇

35. Imposuistī finem et rēbus honestīs. "Imposuistī" est t-------- --------.

⌇

R: temporis quīntī.

⌇

36. Imposuistī finem et rēbus honestīs = ---------------------------------------.

⌇

A: You have put a limit to even honorable endeavors.

⌇

37. Certa stetērunt omnia lēge. "Stetērunt" est t-------- --------.

⌇

R: temporis quīntī.

16-82

478. Until this Unit, all words which ended in -a were like **musca, aquila,** and **Fortūna.** From now on, however, a word ending in **a** might be _____ or _____ case, _____ number, like **Fāta.**

A: nominative   accusative   plural

479. The *main* purpose of this Unit was to teach you to _____.
[In your own words]

A: tell the difference between a form like **muscaØ** and one like **generA.**

480. Pick out the neuter nouns which are the ambiguous nominative-accusative plural form:
perīc'la   vīta   rāna   fovea   rēgna   poena

A: **perīc'la   rēgna**

481. You were given further drill upon recognizing the fact that, while **cane** is ablative case, the form **omne** is the _____ and _____ case.

A: nominative accusative

482. Which of these forms are the nominative-accusative neuter singular?
leōne   pisce   forte   hilare   vulpe   facile

A: **forte   hilare   facile**

483. Third Declension adjectives have the characteristic vowel **-i-** before the neuter plural signal **-a.** The nominative-accusative plural form of **forte** is _____.

A: **fortia.**

---

24. **Parva levēs capient animōs** = _____
A: Small things are going to capture frivolous minds.

25. **Fortēs Fortūna adjūvit. "Adjūvit"** est t_____.
R: **temporis quīnti.** (The principal parts are **adjuvō, adjuvāre, adjūvī, adjūtus.**)

26. **Fortēs Fortūna adjūvit** = _____
A: Fortune has aided the brave.

27. **Mihi praeter omnēs rīdētis, "Rīdētis"** est t_____.
R: **temporis secundī.**

28. **Mihi praeter omnēs rīdētis** = _____
A: You smile upon me beyond all others.

29. **Absentem laesistī, "Laesistī"** est t_____.
R: **temporis quīnti.**

30. **Absentem laesistī** = _____
A: You have injured an absent person.

484. In most Third Declension nouns the characteristic vowel disappears in the neuter nominative-accusative plural, as in **flūmina** and **opera**. The only noun you have had so far which keeps the **-i-** is the word an_____.

A: animal.

485. The nominative-accusative plural of **animal** is _____.

A: animālia.

486. You also learned a new form of the verb. In the sentence **Equus ā fonte dēfluentī currit**, the form **dēfluentī** is the pr____ p_____.

A: present participle.

487. Equus ā fonte dēfluentī currit = The ____ is _____ ____ the _____ .

A: The horse is running from the flowing spring (or "fountain").

488. Finally, you had a question-and-answer drill on your 24 ____ _____s.

A: Basic Sentences.

Be sure that you know the new Basic Sentences. If you wish, study Basic Sentences 45–48 in your Notebook before trying this sequence.

489-492. Say the Basic Sentences which the pictures on the following page illustrate.

---

17. **Cum ēbriō lītigāverīs.** "Lītigāverīs."
est t_____ _____.

R: temporis sextī.

18. **Cum ēbriō lītigāverīs** = _____ _____
_____.

A: You will have quarrelled with a drunken person.

19. **Nōn cēnāverō sine aprō.** "Cēnāverō."
est t_____ _____.

R: temporis sextī.

20. **Nōn cēnāverō sine aprō** = _____ _____ .

A: I will not have dined without a boar.

21. **Fāta regent orbem.** "Regent." est
t_____ _____.

R: temporis tertiī.

22. **Fāta regent orbem** = _____ _____ .

A: Fates are going to rule the world.

23. **Parva levēs capient animōs.** "Capient."
est t_____ _____.

R: temporis tertiī.

489. P____ l____ cap____ an____.

R: Parva levēs capiunt animōs.

490. D____ vol____ F___, nōl____ tr____.

R: Dūcunt volentem Fāta, nōlentem trahunt.

491. F___ reg___ or___; c____ st___ om___ l___.

R: Fāta regunt orbem; certā stant omnia lēge.

11-38. In this sequence you will be given 15 Basic Sentences with some change in the verb. First read and check, then identify the verb form; then translate according to the conventional translations given in the previous frame. Refer to the previous frame when necessary.

11. **Littera scripta mānserit.** "Mānserit" est temporis ____ (prīmī/secundī/tertiī/ quārtī/quīntī/sextī).

R: sextī.

12. Littera scripta mānserit = ____

A: The written letter will have remained.

13. Crūdēlis lacrimīs nōn frangēbātur. "Frangēbātur" est temporis ____

R: prīmī.

14. Crūdēlis lacrimīs frangēbātur = ____

A: The cruel person used to be broken by tears.

15. Mulierēs multīs nōn placent. "Placent" est temp____

R: temporis secundī.

16. Mulierēs multīs nōn placent = ____

A: Women don't please many people. (Surely this is not so!)

492. M___ d_ cū___, p___ neg___.

R: Magna dī cūrant, parva neglegunt.

VOCABULARY INVENTORY

In this Unit you learned two new nouns
  fātum, n (151)   **animus**, m (273)

and a new meaning for
  orbis (296)

Two new adjectives
  levis (265)   **gravis** (263)

Two participles
  volēns (157)   **nōlēns** (160)

And five new verbs
  dūcit (145)   **trahit** (147)
  cūrat (246)   **neglegit** (241)   **sapit** (340)

TEST INFORMATION

For this test you will be asked only questions which occurred in this Unit, except for the usual Basic Sentence review (1–48). Obviously, heavy stress will be placed on the signal {-a} for the neuter nominative-accusative plural. You are not yet responsible for producing the different forms of the irregular adjective **hic, haec, hoc**.

In every test from now on you will be given new sentences, similar to the Basic Sentences, and will be asked to figure out the meaning. There will usually be at least one new word; try to figure out the meaning, as you have been doing in the program.

---

6. **Quod nōn dederit Fortūna nōn ēripiet** =
F_____ w___' t___ a___ wh___ h__ n__ g_____.

7. Notice the contrast with the original Basic Sentence: **Quod nōn dederit Fortūna nōn ēripiet. Quod nōn dedit Fortūna nōn ēripuit.** The original Basic Sentence means
_____.

A: Fortune does not take away what she has not given.

8. In both sentences the relative clause may be translated by "what she has not given." However, when the form was **dedit**, the meaning was ____ (completed/incompleted) action in ____ (past/present/future) time.

A: completed action in present time.

9. When the form was **dederit**, the meaning was ____ action in ____ time.

A: completed future

10. Let us practice the meaning of all six of these tenses. To emphasize the fact that all these tenses have more than one translation in English, in this sequence we will use different translations for the six forms from those used in Unit 28. One exception is #4 which can almost always be translated by "had."

pingēbās (#1) = you used to paint
pingis (#2) = you paint
pingēs (#3) = you are going to paint
pinxerās (#4) = you had painted
pinxistī (#5) = you have painted
pinxeris (#6) = you will have painted

Repeat these forms and their translations until you have learned them.

UNIT SEVENTEEN

17-1

1. So far you have had *three* types of Latin sentences. By far the most common type is that represented by **Vestis virum reddit** (1) or **Fortēs Fortūna adjuvat** (40.) We call this an {_____} type of sentence.

A: {-s -m -t}

2. Most {-s -m -t} sentences can be transformed to {-s -tur} sentences. The passive of **Fortēs Fortūna adjuvat** is F_____ ā For____ adjuvantur.

R: **Fortēs ā Fortūnā adjuvantur.**

3. **Fortēs ā Fortūnā adjuvantur** is an {_____} type of sentence.

A: {-s -tur}
(The answer {-s -ntur} is satisfactory, too.)

4. Transform from an {-s -m -t} sentence to an {-s -tur} sentence. **Vīnum sapientiam obumbrat** → ____ _____ _____ (27)

R: **Vīnō sapientia obumbrātur.**
(27)

5. A verb like **adjuvat** or **obumbrat**, which takes an object and which can be transformed to a passive, is called a _____ verb.

A: transitive

6. A verb which does *not* take an object, like the verbs in **Vēritās numquam perit** (7) and **Sub jūdice līs est** (20), is called an _____ verb.

A: intransitive

UNIT TWENTY-NINE

29-1

1. Now for the number 6 form.
Echo. ★ ○ • ○ •

2. Echo the paradigm of the #6 form of **scrībere.**
★ ○ • ○ • scrīpserō   scrīpserimus
scrīpseris   scrīpseritis
scrīpserit   scrīpserint

	Past	Present	Future
Imperfective		pōnēbam[1]	pōnō[2]	pōnam[3]
Perfective		posueram[4]	posuī[5]	posuerō[6]

3. Here is an example of the use of the #6 tense. **Medicus crūdēlis erit. Intemperāns aeger hunc crūdēlem fēcerit.** This says that the doctor will be cruel. But *before* he becomes cruel, some intemperate sick person will h____ m____ him cruel.

A: have made

4. **Fēcerit** ("will have made") shows that the action is ____ (completed/incompleted) in the ____ (past/present/future) time.

A: completed
future

5. The most common use of the #6 tense is in subordinate clauses. **Sī inopī beneficium dederis, omnēs tē laudābimus** means that everybody w____ pr____ you, but they will do this only if *first* you h____ g____ a b____ to a _____.

A: will praise you
have given a benefit to a poor man.

17-2

7-10. Identify the sentence types of these sentences.

7. Nūlla avāritia sine poenā est. (19)
{------}
▪   ▪

A: {-s -t}

8. Ex auribus cognōscitur asinus. (43)
{------}
▪   ▪

A: {-s -tur}

9. Auctor opus laudat. (29) {------}
▪   ▪

A: {-s -m -t}

10. Parva levēs capiunt animōs. (47)
{------}
▪   ▪

A: {-s -m -t}

Two-kernel sentences are common, and they can be made up of any of these three types.

11. Stultī timent Fortūnam, sapientēs ferunt. (42) {------}, {------}
▪   ▪

A: {-s -m -t} {-s -m -t}

12. Missing in **Stultī timent Fortūnam, sapientēs ferunt** is the {_ _} of the ____ (first/second) kernel.
▪   ▪

A: {-m} of the second kernel.

28-70

VOCABULARY INVENTORY

Nouns:
coniūnctiō, coniūnctiōnis, f (266)
febris, febris, f (338-339)
lepus, leporis, m (215)
lūx, lūcis, f (217-221)
vērum -ī, n (233)
vespillō, vespillōnis, m (318)

Proper Names:
Aquilō, Aquilōnis, m (341)
Diaulus -ī, m (321)
Fabulla -ae, f (273)
Gellia -ae, f (222)
Propertius -ī, m (158-159)
Symmachus, -ī, m (353)

Verbs:
comitō (1) (346)
cremō (1) (317)
fugiō, fugere, fūgī (149-150)
gelō (1) (342)
langueō, languēre (334)
nārrō (1) (235)
negō (1) (265)
nōvī (perfective system only) (267-268)
signō (1) (233)
tangō, tangere, tetigī, tāctus (335-336)

Adjectives:
centum (345)   novem (212)
decem (212)   octō (212)
dīves (gen., dīvitis) (260) quattuor (212)
exiguus-a-um (143)   quīnque (212)
formōsus-a-um (216)   sex (212)
nimius-a-um (261)   septem (212)

Miscellaneous:
enim (266)   neque (264)
prōtinus (343)   sē (304-308)
nōn numquam (251)   nūper (320)
sī quandō (225-229)

TEST INFORMATION

From the kinds of tests you have been having and from the Summary you should be able to figure out what you are responsible for. (Oh, no!)

17-3

13. Crūdēlis lacrimīs pāscitur, nōn frangitur. (39) {------}, {------}

A: {-s -tur} {-s -tur}

14. Missing in **Crūdēlis lacrimīs pāscitur, nōn frangitur** is the {--} of the ---- (first/second) kernel.

A: {-s} second

15. The verb **est** in the sentence **Canis est** is an ------------ verb.

A: intransitive

16. Today you will learn another common sentence type. Pronounce this example of it and check. **Vir est jūdex.** √ ★ ○ •

17. Vir est jūdex means, "The --- is a ------."

A: The man is a judge.

18. Simple? Deceptively so, I am afraid. Remember that word order in Latin does *not* carry the same signals as it does in English. The following is an ambiguous sentence. **Vir est jūdex** can *also* mean, "The j---- is a ---."

A: The judge is a man.

19-22. The following four sentences are all the same type as **Vir est jūdex**. Remember that they are *all* ambiguous, and you must give *both* meanings to be correct.

19. Vir amīcus est = The --- is a ------ *or* the ------ is a ---.

A: The man is a friend *or* the friend is a man.

20. Fēmina rēgīna est = _____.

A: The queen is a woman, *or* The woman is a queen.

21. Auctor est fūr = _____.

A: The thief is an author, *or* The author is a thief.

22. Taurī sunt animālia = _____.

A: The animals are bulls, *or* Bulls are animals.

23. Echo a new technical term.
★ ○ • ○ • complement

VCh: "kómm-plu-ment"

24. A transitive verb needs to have an object to complete its meaning. For example, the phrase **Habet blanda ōrātiō** by itself makes no sense; we need the accusative phrase to c_____te the meaning of the verb **habet**.

A: complete

25. Because **venēnum** completes the meaning of **habet**, this direct object of a transitive verb is called the c_____ment of the verb.

A: complement

26. In the same way, in the new type of sentence like **Canis animal est**, one nominative is the subject of **est** and the other is the c_____.

A: complement.

411. "Fōrm___ sep___, Mārce, di___ er___."

R: "Formōsus septem, Mārce, diēbus eris."

412. Sī nōn dērī___, sī vē___, l___ mea, nār___,

R: Sī nōn dērīdēs, sī vērum, lūx mea, nārrās,

413. Ēd___ num___ Gellia, t_____ em.

R: Ēdistī numquam, Gellia, tū leporem.

Here is Reading #2.

[If you had any trouble with this last sequence, turn to your Notebook and review.]

414. Bella __ (nōv___) __ pu___ (v____ est)

R: Bella es (nōvimus) et puella (vērum est)

415. et dī___ (quis en__ po____ negā___?)

R: et dīves (quis enim potest negāre?)

416. Sed c__ t__ nim___, Fabulla, l_____,

R: Sed cum tē nimium, Fabulla, laudās,

417. n__ dīves n__ bel___ n__ puella es.

R: nec dīves neque bella nec puella es.

27. In English, in the sentence "The dog is an animal," the subject of "is" is the word "___," and the complement is the word "_____."

A: dog   animal.

28. Which of the following statements is true about the sentence **Canis est animal?** 1) **Canis** is the subject and **animal** is the complement. 2) **Canis** is the complement and **animal** is the subject. 3) The sentence is ambiguous and you can't tell.

A: The sentence is ambiguous and you can't tell.

29. **Canis est animal** = _____ _____.

A: The animal is a dog, *or* The dog is an animal.

30. Because **est** is by far the most common verb in this type of sentence, we call a sentence like **Auctor est fūr** an {-s -s est} sentence. Copy the following in your Reference Notebook under "Facts About Latin": Because of its ambiguity, the {-s -s est} sentence is one of the most difficult structures in Latin.

31. Whenever you see the verb **est** or **sunt**, be careful! If the sentence doesn't seem to make sense you have probably reversed the subject and the _____.

A: complement.

32. Let us take some new Basic Sentences which illustrate this new {-s -s est} structure. Always keep in mind that the difficulty with this structure lies in the fact that _____. [In your own words]

A: the sentences are ambiguous and you can't tell the subject from the complement.

17-6

33. ★ ○ • ○ • *Vīta vīnum est.* (49) [In doing the next frame, be careful not to look back.]

34. ★ ○ ○ V___ v____ ___.

Cōnf: *Vīta vīnum est.*

35. *Vīta vīnum est* = _____.

A: Life is wine *or* Wine is life.

36. Which of these two meanings makes sense? _____.

A: We would say that they both make sense (if said by someone who approved of drinking wine).

37. The interpretation "Wine is life" means, _____. [In your own words]

A: "Wine is the thing which makes people live happily."

38. The interpretation "Life is wine" means, _____. [In your own words]

A: "The only important thing in life is drinking wine."

---

402. You learned two new Basic Sentences, 137 and 138. Review these now in your Notebook if you are not sure about them.

403. You had four Readings. Go through these in your Notebook for review. If you feel it necessary, do the sequence in the program where these Readings occurred.

404. You learned that the arrangement of phrases, clauses, etc., in sets of three is called a tr_____.

A: tricolon.

405. A common variant of **rīsērunt** is _____.

A: rīsēre.

406. You learned the principal parts of 18 verbs. Turn to your Notebook and memorize any of the following which you do not now know.

trahō, capiō, pōnō, stō, habeō, aperiō, maneō, indicō, serviō, quaerō, fulgeō, neglegō, aspiciō, fugiō, rīdeō, taceō, dēbeō, tangō.

407. Write the Basic Sentence which said that things which used to be considered vices are now just everyday actions. Qu____ f_____ v_____, m____ s____. (137)

R: *Quae fuerant vitia, mōrēs sunt.*

17-7

39. Because it means two things, **Vīta vīnum est** is an _____ statement.

A: ambiguous

40. Copy Basic Sentence 49 and both meanings in your Notebook.

[Are you answering aloud as much as possible?]

41. Authors and poets purposely use ambiguity this way to suggest ___ meanings at the same time.

A: two

42-46. This sentence occurs in a Roman novel which describes the adventures of several most disreputable characters, completely given over to a life of pleasure. Answer the following questions as if you were one of these people, believing that life consisted of nothing but drinking wine.

Question and Answer Drill

42. "In quō est vīta?" "_____ _____."

R: In vīnō.

43. Spelled with a small *f*, the word **fēlīcitās** often means "h____ness."

A: happiness.

44. Remember that your answers in this Question and Answer drill must be in the same ____ and _____ as the question word.

A: case number

SUMMARY

396. In this Unit you learned the number-# - tense of the verb.

A: 4

397. The most common way to translate **Vir fēminam laudāverat** would be, "___ ___ ___ _____."

A: The man had praised the woman.

398. On the other hand, a perfectly good translation of **Quae fuerant vitia, mōrēs sunt** could be, "What ____ v_____, are now customs."

A: were vices

399. The #4 form shows ____ (completed/incomplete) action in ____ (past/present/future) time.

A: completed past

400. The signal for this tense is the three letters {---} added to the active (perfective/imperfective) stem.

A: {-erā-} perfective

401. The active perfective stem may be found from the ____ (1st/2d/3d/4th) principal part.

A: 3d

17-8

45. "Sine quō est nūlla fēlīcitās?" "_____
_____."

R: Sine vīnō.

46. "In quō est omnis fēlīcitās?" "_____
_____."

R: In vīnō. (The people in this novel were a *most* unattractive group!)

47. We proceed to the vocabulary for another Basic Sentence. ★ ○ •

    dux   ducēs
    ducem   ducēs
    duce   ducibus

48. The verb **dūcit** means "_____s."

A: leads.

49. The new noun **dux** means "a l___er."

A: leader.

50. ★ ○ •   ámor   amórēs
           amórem amórēs
           amóre   amóribus

51. Somehow people always seem to know what the word **amor** means: "l___."

A: love.

28-64

391. Decline **tempus** in the plural:

R: tempora
tempora
tempora
temporibus
temporibus
temporum

392. Decline **manus-ūs**, f in the singular:

R: manus
manum
manū
manuī
manūs

393. Decline **manus** in the plural:

R: manūs
manūs
manibus
manibus
manuum

394. Decline **diēs-ēī**, m & f in the singular:

R: diēs
diem
diē
diēī
diēī

395. Decline **diēs** in the plural:

R: diēs
diēs
diēbus
diēbus
diērum

17-9

52. ★ ○ ● ○ ● *Oculī sunt in amōre ducēs.*
(50)

53. ★ ○ ○ Oc___ s___ __ am___ d____.

Cōnf: *Oculī sunt in amōre ducēs.*

54. *Oculī sunt in amōre ducēs* means *either*, "____ are the _____ in ____" *or*, "_____ are ___s in love."

A: Eyes are the leaders in love.   Leaders are eyes in love.

55. The only one of these which makes sense is that _____.

A: eyes are the leaders in love.

56. Copy Basic Sentence 50 in your Notebook.

57. This sentence means that when we fall in love, we are attracted primarily by _____.
[In your own words]

A: _____ the other person's physical appearance.

58. *Oculī sunt in amōre ducēs.* √ ★ ○ ●
[Remember that the check sign means that you are to say the sentence *first* and *then* listen to the tape.]

---

387. Now decline *vitium* in the plural:

℟: vitia
    vitia
    vitiīs
    vitiīs
    vitiōrum

[If you are not satisfied with your performance, study a while in your Notebook.]

388. Decline *lepus, leporis*, m in the singular:

℟: lepus
    leporem
    lepore
    leporī
    leporis

389. Decline *lūx, lūcis*, f in the plural:

℟: lūcēs
    lūcēs
    lūcibus
    lūcibus
    lūcum

390. Decline *tempus, temporis*, n in the singular.

℟: tempus
    tempus
    tempore
    temporī
    temporis

59. Write the paradigm of the Third Declension noun **amor** ("love"). _____ _____
(Auxilium sub hāc līneā)

Aux: Remember that the short **o** of the nominative singular form **amor** is long in all other cases. [If you feel you can't give the correct answer, study nouns in your Notebook before proceeding any further.]

A: amor   amōrēs
    amōrem   amōrēs
    amōre   amōribus

60. Since you know the noun **amor**, you can figure out that the word **amat**, which is the part of speech called a ____, means "_____."

A: verb   loves.

61. amāns = l _ _ ing

A: loving

62. The form **amāns** is the nominative singular of the _____ _____ of **amat**.

A: present participle

Question and Answer Drill

63. In this Question and Answer drill, remember that your answer must be in the same ____ and _____ as the qu_____ w____.

A: case
    number   question word.

---

382. Decline Gellia-ae, f in the singular:

R: Gellia
    Gelliam
    Gelliā
    Gelliae
    Gelliae

---

383. Decline puella-ae, f in the plural:

R: puellae
    puellās
    puellīs
    puellīs
    puellārum

---

384. Decline Marcus-ī, m in the singular:

R: Marcus
    Marcum
    Marcō
    Marcō
    Marcī

---

385. Decline discipulus-ī, m in the plural:

R: discipulī
    discipulōs
    discipulīs
    discipulīs
    discipulōrum

---

386. Decline vitium-ī, n in the singular:

R: vitium
    vitium
    vitiō
    vitiō
    vitiī

17-11

64. Echo the masculine-feminine form of **amāns**, meaning "loving," or, as a noun, "lover."

★ ○ • amāns   amantēs
      amantem   amantēs
      amante   amantibus

65-68. Answer these questions on the Basic Sentence, **Oculī sunt in amōre ducēs.**

65. "In quō oculī animum dūcunt?"
"_____ _____."

R: In amōre.

66. "Quibus membrīs animus dūcitur in amōre?" "_____."

R: Oculīs.

67. "Quibus membrīs virī amantēs dūcuntur?" "_____."

R: Oculīs.

68. "Quālēs virī oculīs dūcuntur?"
"_____."

R: Amantēs.

69. You know, of course, that in Latin it is common to omit parts of the kernel. This is also true of the new {-s -s est} construction in which we often find the two nominatives without any verb at all. Thus **Vir jūdex** (if it is a complete sentence) means: *either* "The ___ is a _____," *or* "The _____ is a ___."

A: The man is a judge, *or*
    The judge is a man.

With all this practice on verbs, you must not forget to keep in practice on the noun forms. We give you a lot of practice on this in the Question and Answer drill on Basic Sentences, but it may help to test yourself by doing a paradigm of each type of noun. We will take nouns which were used in the Readings and Basic Sentences of this Unit. If you wish, review nouns first in your Reference Notebook.

376. "Quōcum vēnēre hī discipulī?"
"_____."

R: Cum Symmachō.

377. "Quālēs manūs habēbant?" "M_____ g_____."

R: Manūs
   gelātās.

378. "Cūrāvitne Symmachus Martiālem?"
"_____."

R: Nōn cūrāvit.

379. "Etiam sī Martiālis languēbat, quid nōn jam habuit?" "_____."

R: Febrem.

380. "Quid Martiālis ex manibus discipulōrum cēpit?" "_____."

R: Febrem.

381. "Quōrum manūs Aquilōne gelātae erant?" "_____."

R: Discipulōrum.

70-72. The sentences in the next three frames are complete sentences. Say them aloud and give the English meanings as complete sentences.

70. **Vir dux** = ________________________.

A: The man is a leader, *or* The leader is a man.

71. **Manus membrum** = _______________.

A: The hand is a part of the body, *or* A part of the body is a hand.

72. **Animal agnus** = ___________________.

A: The animal is a lamb, *or* The lamb is an animal.

73. ★ ○ • ○ • ***Deus jūdex jūstus, fortis, et patiēns.*** (51)

74. Copy in your Answer Pad *without* the three macrons. **Deus judex justus, fortis, et patiens.**

75. Listen and add the missing macrons. ★○○ **Deus judex justus, fortis, et patiens.**

R: Deus jūdex jūstus, fortis, et patiēns.

76. This is an {______} type of sentence with no {___}.

A: {-s -s est} {est}.

369. **Centum mē tetigēre manūs Aquilōne gelātae** = A ______ h___s fr____ by ___ ______ t___ed ___.

A: A hundred hands frozen by the North Wind touched me.

370. Copy.

371. **Nōn habuī fēbrem, Symmache; nunc habeō** = _ ___n't h___ a f____ (before), S_______; (but) _ ____ one n___.

A: I didn't have a fever before, Symmachus; but I have one now.

372. Copy.

Quaestiōnēs et Respōnsa

373. **"Ad quem vēnit Symmachus?"** "__ ________."

R: **Ad Mārtiālem.**

374. **"Quibus membrīs discipulī Symmachī Mārtiālem aegrum tetigēre?"** "M______ s___."

R: Manibus suīs.

375. **"Cujus discipulī Mārtiālem languentem vidēre?"** "________."

R: **Symmachī.**

77. Add the missing element that will make the pattern complete. **Deus ___ jūdex jūstus, fortis, et patiēns.**

A: **Deus est jūdex jūstus, fortis, et patiēns.**

78. Pronounce the original Basic Sentence and check. **Deus jūdex jūstus, fortis, et patiēns.**
√ ★ ○ •

79. One of the most important skills you must master in learning a foreign language is the ability to figure out the meaning of new words. The adjectives **jūstus** and **patiēns** are unknown to you at present. **Jūstus** should be easy to guess. **Patiēns** will be easier to guess if you could see or hear the other cases. The ablative singular of **ēloquēns** is **ēloquentī**. The ablative singular of **patiēns** must therefore be _____.

R: **patientī.**

80. **Deus jūdex jūstus, fortis, et patiēns** = _____.

A: God is a just, brave, and patient judge.

81. Copy in your Notebook.

---

363. "How many students did Symmachus have with him?" "_____."

A: 100

364. "What did these students do?" "_____."

A: They examined Martial.

365. "Why did Martial object to this proceeding?" "_____."

A: Their hands were cold (frozen by the North Wind).

366. "What did Martial say after he had been pawed over by 100 icy hands?" "Although I _____, now _____."

A: Although I didn't have any fever before, now I do have one.

367. **Languēbam; sed tū comitātus prōtinus ad mē vēnistī centum, Symmache, discipulīs.**

"_____ ing in bed s___: b___ y___ c_____ ly to ___, S_____, ac_____ h_____ s_____."

A: I was lying in bed sick; but you came immediately to me, Symmachus, accompanied by a hundred students.

368. Copy. If you like your own translation better, write *that* in your Notebook.

17-14

82. ★ ○ •
    Deus fortis
    Deum fortem
    Deō fortī

83. ★ ○ •
    jūdex jūstus
    jūdicem jūstum
    jūdice jūstō

84. ★ ○ •
    Deus patiēns
    Deum patientem
    Deō patientī

85. Jūdice ____ (is/is not) the same case as fortī.

A: is

86. Virī ____ (is/is not) the same case as fortī.

A: is not

Question and Answer Drill

87. "Quis est jūdex jūstus, fortis, et patiēns?" "_____."

R: Deus.

88. "Quālis jūdex est Deus?" "_____, _____, et _____."

R: Jūstus, fortis, et patiēns.

89. "Quālī sub jūdice stat orbis?" "S____ j____ f___ī, j___ō, et p_____ī."

R: Sub jūdice fortī, jūstō, et patientī.

28-58

Let us check to make sure you understand all the kernels. [If you got the point, skip to #367.]

355. Languēbam = _____.
A: I was sick.

356. Tū vēnistī = _____.
A: You came.

357. Mē tetigēre manūs = _____.
A: Hands touched me.

358. (Nōn) habuī febrem = _____.
A: I (didn't) have a fever.

359. Habeō (febrem) = _____ (a ____).
A: I have (a fever).

360. "What did Symmachus do when he heard that Martial was sick?" "_____." [In your own words]
A: He came to see him.

361. "When did he come?" "_____."
A: Immediately.

362. "Did Symmachus come alone or with someone?" "_____."
A: He came with someone.
[It is still standard practice in medical schools for students to accompany their teachers when they make the rounds of their patients.]

90. "Quālibus oculīs Deus orbem aspicit?"
"O_____ f____bus, j___īs, et p_____bus."

R: Oculīs fortibus, jūstīs, et patientibus.

91. "Quālem Deum colunt sapientēs?"
"_____ _____, _____, et _____."

R: Deum fortem, jūstum, et patientem.

92. "Quālia cōnsilia capit Deus?"
"C_____ f___ia, j____, et p_____."

R: Cōnsilia fortia, jūsta, et patientia.

93. As the English words "quality" and "quantity" remind us, the Latin question word which asks *what kind* of thing (person, etc.) something is is ___lis, while the Latin question word which asks *how big* something is is ____tus.

R: quālis
                              quantus.

94-97. There are not many adjectives of size. See if you can remember the ones which we had in the Basic Sentences.

94. "Quantō ā cane saepe tenētur aper?"
"Ā c____ nōn m_____."

R: Ā cane nōn magnō.

95. "Quanta vīpera taurum spatiōsum morsū necat?" "P_____."

R: Parva.

---

350. In this paradigm you see a common variant for the third person plural. Instead of "tetigērunt," there is a very common variant, which is _____.

A: tetigēre.

Give the new variant for the third person plural (-ēre for -ērunt).

351. dedērunt → d__ēre

R: dedēre

352. dūxērunt → d_____

R: dūxēre

353. ● ○ ★
Languēbam; sed tū comitātus prōtinus
    ad mē
vēnistī centum, Symmache, discipulīs,
Centum mē tetigēre manūs Aquilōne
    gelātae.
Nōn habuī febrem, Symmache; nunc
    habeō.

(Reading #4)

354. Copy in your Notebook.

Do your *best* to get the meaning. The different clauses are all part of the same poem!

17-16

96. "Quanta avāritia sine poenā est?" "N̄_____."

R: Nūlla.

97. "Quantum taurum morsū parva vīpera necat?" "Sp_____."

R: Spatiōsum.

98. Here is a new word, which will occur in a new Basic Sentence. "Quantās aurēs habet asinus, longās an brevēs?" "_____."

R: Longās.

99. "Quantās aurēs habet mūs, longās an brevēs?" "_____."

R: Brevēs.

100. Echo a new Basic Sentence. ★ ○ • •
Ars longa, vīta brevis. (52)

28-56

346.

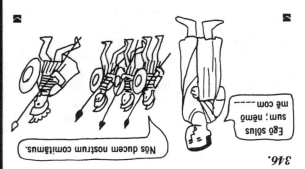

Ego solus sum; nēmō mē com____.

Nōs ducem nostrum comitāmus.

R: comitat

347. "Quid agunt discipulī?" "Mag_____ su_ c_____."

R: Magistrum suum comitant.

348. A brief check on the meaning of these new words: tangō = t_____; comitat = ac_____y; prōtinus = im_____; centum = ___ h_____; Aquilō = the N_____; gelō = fr_____; febris = f_____.

A: touch   accompany
              immediately
   one   the North Wind
   hundred
   freeze   fever.

[If you had trouble with this sequence, go back to frame 334 and run through the frames again.]

349. Echo the paradigm of the #5 tense of tangō. ★ ○ •

tetigī   tetigimus
tetigistī   tetigistis
tetigit   tetigērunt (vel "tetigēre").

17-17

101. Expand with the missing verb. **Ars ___ longa, vīta ___ brevis.**

R: **Ars est longa, vīta est brevis.**

102. ★ ○ ○ [Cover the last frame.] **A__ l____, v___ br____.**

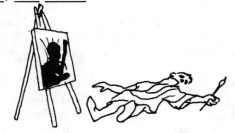

R: **Ars longa, vīta brevis.**

103. **Ars longa, vīta brevis** = _____.

A: Art is long, life is short.

104. Copy in your Notebook.

105. This sentence is usually taken to mean that although the artist himself will soon ___, his work will continue to _____.

A: die live.

106. Interestingly enough, this is not what the sentence meant in its original context. **Ars longa, vīta brevis** is a translation from the works of the Greek physician Hippocrates. He was referring to the science **(ars)** of medicine. He meant that although the lives of both the patient and the physician are short, the science of medicine _____. [In your own words]

A: will live on.

---

342. **Aquilō quoque flūmina gelat. Hic vir trāns flūmen currere potest; hoc flūmen jam ____ (gelātum est/fluit).**

R: **gelātum est.**

343. "**Vīsne mē adjuvāre?**" "**Certē, tē crās adjuvābō.**" "**At crās nimis sērum erit; necesse est tibi mē prōtinus adjuvāre.**" "**Prōtinus**" significat ____ (celeriter/crās/inter decem diēs).

R: **celeriter.**

344. **Prōtinus** = im-_____-ly.

A: immediately

345. **Centum est numerus. In hāc figūrā sunt centum orbēs. Centum est ____ (X/L/C/M).**

|::: |::: |::: |::: |::: |
|::: |::: |::: |::: |::: |

C.

17-18

Question and Answer Drill

107. "Quid manet, vīta an ars?" "____."

R: Ars.

108. "Quid perit?" "____."

R: Vīta.

109. Answer your teacher's questions.
★ ○ ○ ¿ "____."

Cōnf: "Quanta est ars?"

R: Longa.

110. ★ ○ ○ ¿ "____."

Cōnf: "Quanta est vīta?"

R: Brevis.

111. ★ ○ • ○ • *Īra furor brevis est.* (53)

112. ★ ○ ○ Ī__ f____ br____ ___.

R: Īra furor brevis est.

113. The adjective **īrātus, īrāta, īrātum** means "____."

A: angry.

---

336. ★ ○ • **tangō, tangere, tetigī, tāctus**

337. Copy in your Notebook.

338. Hic vir habet *febrem* gravem. Aquam multam bibere vult. Quī febrem habet l____et.

R: languet.

339. Ille aeger quī aquam bibēbat f___m habuit.

R: febrem.

340. *Aquilō* hanc terram niv___ reddit.

R: niveam.

341. Aquilō is the N____ W____.

A: North Wind (or "cold" in general).

17-19

114. Therefore the noun **īra** must mean "_____."

A: anger.

115. The English derivative of **furor** is "___y."

A: fury.

116. In this sentence **furor** means "m___ess."

A: madness.

117. Give just the kernel of **Īra furor brevis est.** _____.

R: Īra furor est.

118. **Īra furor est** means, "_____."

A: "Anger is madness" or "Madness is anger."

119. **Īra furor brevis est.** (53) ✓ ★ ○ •

120. We now have a second ambiguity. **Īra**, being a First Declension noun, belongs to the _____ gender.

A: feminine

121. The adjective **brevis** is _____ or _____ gender.

A: masculine feminine

17-20

122. **Furor** is masculine gender. **Brevis** ____ (could/could not) modify **furor**.

▼

A: could

123. Because there are *two* possible meanings for **Īra furor est**, and because **brevis** could modify either of *two* words (**Īra** or **furor**), there are ____ (1/2/3/4/5/6/7/8) possible interpretations of **Īra furor brevis est**.

▼

A: 4 (But probably only *one* of them will make sense.) [If you are *sure* you know the meaning of this Basic Sentence, write it in your Answer Pad and turn to frame 126 for the answer. But don't do it unless you are sure! If you aren't *positive* of the answer, you need the help of this sequence.]

124. One possibility is that **brevis** modifies **īra**. Give two meanings of **Īra furor brevis est**, first with **īra brevis** as subject, then with it as complement. "_____ _____ is _____." "_____ is a _____ _____."

▼

A: Short anger is madness. Madness is a short anger.

125. Now assume that **brevis** modifies **furor**. Give two meanings of **Īra furor brevis est**, first with **brevis furor** as subject, then with it as complement. "_____ _____ is _____." "_____ is a _____ _____."

▼

A: Short madness is anger. Anger is a short madness.

126. Choose the only meaning of **Īra furor brevis est** which makes sense. _____.

▼

A: Anger is a short madness.

28-52

325. That is, as an undertaker, he helps people on the way to the next world; as a doctor, he had _____.

▲

A: killed off his patients.

326. If you did not understand any point of structure, here is a line-by-line translation. Nūper erat medicus, nunc est vespillo Diaulus = D_____ ly a _____ , ___ he _ __ an _____.

▲

A: Diaulus was recently a doctor, now he is an undertaker.

327. Quod vespillō facit, fēcerat et medicus = What he ____ as an _____, he also ___ ____ as a doctor.

▲

A: What he does as an undertaker, he also had done as a doctor.

328. Copy in your Notebook.

▲

329. "Quālis medicus fuerat Diaulus?" "M_____."

▲

R: Malus.

330. Diaulus medicus aegrōs suōs ne__vit.

▲

R: necāvit.

331. Diaulus, quī nunc est vespillō, mortuōs cr__at.

▲

R: cremat.

17-21

127. Copy in your Notebook.

128. **Īra furor brevis est** means that when a person becomes angry, for a short while he acts like a _____.

A: crazy person.

Question and Answer Drill

129. "**Quantus furor est īra?**" "_____."

R: Brevis.

130. "**Quid virum īnsānum reddit?**" "_____."

R: Īra.

131. "**Quālem virum reddit īra?**" "_____."

R: Īnsānum.

132. The {-s -s est} construction is one of the *most difficult* in Latin because it is always _____.

A: ambiguous.

133. If you happen to guess right the first time, there seems to be no trouble. But if your meaning doesn't make sense, then you must switch the _____ and the _____ around.

A: subject complement

28-51

319. Hoc est, cēpit piscēs ____ (hodiē/inter decem diēs).

[Speech bubble: Suntne hī piscēs bonī?]
[Speech bubble: Sunt bonī; ego ipse hōs piscēs *nūper* cēpī.]

R: hodiē.

320. Nūper = r____ly.

A: recently

321. ● ○ ★
Nūper erat medicus, nunc est vespillō Diaulus.
Quod vespillō facit, fēcerat et medicus. (Reading #3)
[The final "o" on **vespillō** is short here to fit the meter.]

322. Write down what you think the poem means; then go on with the program.

323. Diaulus has held two jobs: he used to be a _____, but he has now become an _____.

A: doctor under">taker.

324. According to Martial, as an undertaker Diaulus ____ (performs a different kind of job from what he did as a doctor/does the same thing he did as a doctor).

A: does the same thing he did as a doctor.

134. In this next Basic Sentence the neuter adjective **bonum** is used as a noun meaning "possession." We used the word "good" in the plural in English in this same meaning, as "Give all your ----s to the poor."

A: goods

135. ★ ○ • ○ • *Forma bonum fragile est.* (54)

136. Forma bonum est = ----------------

A: Beauty is a possession, *or* Possession is beauty.

137. The meaning of the adjective **fragilis, fragile** is easy to guess because of its English derivative. The question is, however, can **fragile** modify either **forma** or **bonum**? ---- (Yes/No)

A: No (If it modified **forma**, the form would be **fragilis**.)

138. ★ ○ ○ F---- b---- fr----- --t.

R: Forma bonum fragile est.

139. Draw an arrow from **fragile** to the noun it modifies. Forma bonum fragile est.

A: Forma bonum fragile est.

17-23

140. Give the one meaning which seems to make sense. **Forma bonum fragile est** = ------------------.

A: Beauty is a fragile possession.

141. Copy in your Notebook.

142. **Forma bonum fragile est** means that ----------------------------------.
[In your own words]

A: youthful good looks don't last very long.

Question and Answer Drill

143. "**Quāle bonum est forma?**" "------."

R: Fragile.

144. "**Quid nōn semper manet?**" "------."

R: Forma.

145. F---- b---- f------ ---. (54)

R: Forma bonum fragile est.

146. ★ ○ • ○ • *Crēdula rēs amor est.* (55)

28-49

307. The dog was washing itself = C------ l---- ab---.

A: Canis sē lavābat.

308. The word **sē** is a little more difficult for you than the pronouns **mē** and **tē** because ----------------------------------.
[In your own words]

A: in English we have four words for it: "him-self," "herself," "itself," and "themselves."

Quaestiōnēs et Respōnsa

309. "**Quantum Fabulla sē laudat?**" "------."

R: Nimium.

310. "**Quem Martiālis dērīdet?**" "------."

R: Fabullam.

311. "**Quid vult Fabulla praeter omnia?**" "------."

R: Laudem.

312. "**Cum Fabulla sē laudat, nōn jam puella pulchra esse vidētur. Cui similis esse vidētur?**" "A------."

R: Anuī.

313. "**Cui Fabulla nōn placet?**" "------."

R: Martiālī.

17-24

147. **Amor** is masculine gender; therefore, the new adjective **crēdula** modifies ____ (amor/rēs).

R: rēs.

148. Write from dictation. ★ ○ ○ Cr_____ r__ am__ ___.

R: Crēdula rēs amor est.

149. Crēdula rēs amor est = _____.

A: Love is a trusting thing. ("A trusting thing is love" would also mean the same thing, but it sounds a little poetical.)

150. Copy in your Notebook.

151. If you were able to get the meaning of this sentence, it was because you knew the English word "credulous." A person who is credulous is one who is much too tr___ing.

A: trusting

Question and Answer Drill

152. "Quālis rēs est amor?" "Cr_____."

R: Crēdula.

---

302. The reason that your teacher doesn't like the young lady is that she _____.

Ego praeter omnēs formōsa sum! Et ego quoque sapiō; mē nimis numquam laudō.

Haec puella mihi nōn placet; sē semper laudat.

A: is always praising herself.

303. Caeciliānus nōn mē, nōn tē, sed semper sē laudat. Caeciliānus doesn't _____ or ____, but he is always _____ing _____.

A: praise me or you praising himself.

304. Sē is used *only* when the verb is *third person* and it refers always to the *subject* of that verb. **Virī semper sē laudant** = ___ s_____ pr____ th____es.

A: Men always praise themselves.

305. **Mulierēs numquam sē laudant** = _____.

A: Women never praise themselves.

306. Thais praised herself too much = Th___ n____ium l___ v___.

A: Thāis sē nimium laudāvit.

28-48

17-25

153. "Quālēs sunt virī amantēs?"
"Cr_____."

R: Crēdulī.

154. "Quālēs sunt fēminae amantēs?"
"_____."

R: Crēdulae.

155. Write the last Basic Sentence. Cr_____ r__ a___ ___. [Two macrons!]

R: Crēdula rēs amor est.

156. Here is the last Basic Sentence of this Unit. ★ ○ • ○ • *Lēgēs sine mōribus vānae.* (56)

157. ★ ○ • mōs   mōrēs   (in the
          mōrem   mōrēs   singular,
          mōre   mōribus "custom";
                           in the
                           plural,
                           "morals")

158. ★ ○ • ○ • English "mores," Latin, **mōrēs.**

159. The plural form **mōrēs** has become an English word, "mores." The mores of a people are the standards of conduct which are considered acceptable. From this word **mōs** we also get another English word: someone who has acceptable standards of conduct is said to possess good m___ls.

A: morals.

Now for Question and Answer drill. But first a new word.

A: three

301. A single sentence could contain a subject which was a tricolon; there would then be _____ different subjects.

A: three

300. A tricolon can be made up of modifiers, but there would have to be _____ of them.

A: three

299. A tricolon can be made up of _____ different sentences.

A: three

298. And a tricolon has _____ different parts.

A: three

297. A tripod has _____ legs.

A: three

296. A TRIangle has _____ angles.

A: Five.

295. How many syllables in nec puella es?

17-26

160. In this sentence **sine mōribus** means "_ _ _ _ _ _ _ m_ _ _ls."

A: without morals.

161. The adjective **vānus** means "useless." Write from dictation. ★ ○ ○ L_ _ _ _ s_ _ _ m_ _ _ _ _ _ v_ _ _ _ _.

R: Lēgēs sine mōribus vānae.

162. Expand to make the structure of the sentence clear. (Remember that **lēgēs** and **vānae** are plural.) Lēgēs sine mōribus vānae _ _ _ _ _.

R: Lēgēs sine mōribus vānae sunt.

163. Say aloud the *original* Basic Sentence, by removing the word which you just added. √ ★ ○ • Lēgēs sine mōribus vānae sunt. _ _ _ _ _ _ _ _ _ _ _ _ _.

R: Lēgēs sine mōribus vānae.

164. Lēgēs sine mōribus vānae = _ _ _s _ _ _ _ _ _ _ _ _ _ _s are _ _ _ _ _ _ _.

A: Laws without morals are useless.

---

288. How many words does the second parenthesis contain?

A: Two.

289. And how many words in the third parenthesis?

A: Four.

290. In these series of threes, the Roman authors often made the last member of the set as long (or even longer) than the first _ _ _ added together.

A: two

291. Echo a new technical term. • ○ • ○ ★ • ○ t r i c o l o n

VCh: "try-cŏle-lon"

292. This arrangement by three is called a tricolon. There is a tricolon in the last line, too. It is emphasized by the three negative connectors _ _ _, _ _ _ _ _ _, and _ _ _.

A: nec neque nec.

293. Observe how each part of the tricolon gets longer. How many syllables are there in **Nec dīves?**

A: Three.

294. How many syllables in **neque bella?**

A: Four.

165. This sentence means that if people do not already have an acceptable code of conduct, there is little use in trying to force them to behave by passing ____s.

A: laws.

Question and Answer Drill

166. "Quālēs sunt lēgēs sine mōribus?" "_____."

R: Vānae.

167. "Sine quibus sunt lēgēs vānae?" "_____ _____."

R: Sine mōribus.

168. "Mōrēs malī sunt; quālēs sunt lēgēs?" "_____."

R: Vānae.

169. Write the paradigm of **mōs**.

R: mōs   mōrēs
    mōrem   mōrēs
    mōre   mōribus

(If you made an error, it shows that you did not properly study frame 157.)

170. ★ ○ ● vírtūs   virtū́tēs
              virtū́tem   virtū́tēs
              virtū́te   virtū́tibus

---

280. Copy in your Notebook.

281. et dīves (quis enim potest negāre?) = and r--- (for --- d--y it?)

A: and rich (for who can deny it?)

282. Copy.

283. Sed cum tē nimium, Fabulla, laudās = But, F------, when ---------------------

A: But, Fabulla, when you praise yourself too much.

284. Copy.

285. nec dīves neque bella nec puella es = --- --------- nor --------- nor a ---- ----.

A: you are (that is, "you appear to be") neither rich nor attractive nor a young girl.

286. Copy.

287. Roman authors frequently reinforced their ideas by arranging them in threes. This device is used here. Look at the poem again. Fabulla is 1) pretty, 2) young, and 3) rich. Each of these qualities is emphasized by a parenthesis which says the same thing in three different ways. But notice: how many words does the first parenthesis contain?

A: One.

17-28

171. Sometimes **virtūs** has the meaning of "manly courage," because **virtūs** is related to the Latin word ____.

R: vir.

172. The common meaning of **virtūs**, however, is "virtue" in the sense of a good quality. For example, **Sapientia virtūs est** means, "_____."

A: Wisdom is a virtue.

173. The antonym of **virtūs** is the Latin word v____m.

R: vitium.

174. ★ ○ • hómō   hóminēs
            hóminem   hóminēs
            hómine   homínibus

175. The scientific name for the species to which we all belong (unless there are some monkeys taking the course) is "h___ sapiens."

A: homo sapiens.

176. There are no macrons in the expression "homo sapiens" because it is not Latin. It is an _____ expression which comes from _____.

A: English   Latin.

177. ★ ○ • áctiō   actiónēs
            actiónem   actiónēs
            actióne   actiónibus

274. Copy in your Notebook.

275. Read it through a few more times. Do you get the point? Don't give up too easily; on the other hand, don't sit staring at it if you don't seem to be making any progress. When you have done what you can, write what you have understood, and proceed. Refer to the poem when necessary.

276. In the first two lines, Martial says Fabulla is a _____, she is _____, and she is _____.

A: attractive   (a) young (girl)   rich.

277. But with all these good qualities Fabulla has one bad fault: she _____. [In your own words]

A: praises herself too much.

278. When she boasts about how pretty, young, and rich she is, says Martial, the listener begins to think that she _____. [In your own words]

A: is not pretty, young, and rich enough to bother with if one has to listen to all that talk.

279. We will go through the poem line by line. We will get you to produce *one* translation out of thousands. If you like your own translation better then copy *that* in your Notebook.

Bella es (nóvimus) et puella (vérum est) = You are _____ (We ____ this) and a y___ g___ (It is ___).

A: You are attractive (We know this) and a young girl (It is true).

17-29

178-185. In this next sequence we are going to have a vocabulary drill, similar to the "Is it animal, vegetable, or mineral?" game. We will ask you, "What is such-and-such?" You are to reply that it is either a person, place, thing, animal, virtue, fault, action, or part of the body. We will practice the meanings of the following Latin words.

āctiō, rēs, virtūs, locus, animal, vitium, membrum, homō

Choose your answer from the list.

178. The Latin word for "place" is _____.

R: locus.

179. The Latin word for "thing" is ____.

R: rēs.

180. fault = _____

R: vitium

181. person = ____

R: homō

182. part of the body = _____

R: membrum

183. virtue = _____

R: virtūs

184. animal = _____

R: animal

28-43

269. "Noster amicus Sabidius qui fuit rāna est jam rēx. Rēgīna Pecūnia enim et genus et formam dōnat. Fuit inops sed nunc est d____."

R: dives.

270. "Sabidium bene hōc tempore nōvī sed nōn amō. Nimium enim mē irrītat!" = _____.

A: I know Sabidius well at this time but I don't like him. For he annoys me too much.

271. "Pecūniam ex Sabidiō quaesīvī, sed neque mihi dōnat neque negat." = _____.

A: I asked Sabidius for money but he neither gave (it) to me nor denied (it.)

272. Just in case you are not sure of these new words, here are the English meanings: Dīves = r____; nimius = t___ m____; neque = n_____ nor; negāre = d___; enim = ___; nōvī = ____ ___ _____; conjūnctiō = c_____tor.

| A: rich | too much | deny | for | I have learned | neither | | | | connector |

[If you missed any of these six, go back to frame 260 and go through the sequence again.]

273. Chorus with your teacher as he reads the poem. ● ○ ★

Bella es (nōvimus) et puella (vērum est) et dīves (quis enim potest negāre?) Sed cum tē nimium, Fabulla, laudās, nec dīves neque bella nec puella es. (Reading #2)

17-30

āctiō, rēs, virtūs, locus, animal,
vitium, membrum, homō

185. action = _____

R: āctiō

Question and Answer Drill [In answering, say the whole sentence.]

186. "Quid est vir?" "____ est vir."

R: Homō est vir.

187. "Quid est porticus?" "_____ est porticus."

R: Locus est porticus.

188. "Quid est agnus?" "_____ est agnus."

R: Animal est agnus.

189. "Quid est saccus?" "___ est saccus."

R: Rēs est saccus.
(*Or,* Locus est saccus.)

190. "Quid est vēritās?" "_____ est vēritās."

R: Virtūs est vēritās.

---

263. Tū tē nimium laudās = _____

A: You praise yourself too much.

264. Mārtiālis puellās quae nōn formōsae sunt nōn amat. Thāis erat neque pulchra neque puella. Haec vōx "neque" signat "__c__."

R: nec.

265. "Tū dentēs ēmptōs habēs, Laecānia." "Ēmptōs dentēs nōn habeō." "Negāre" significat "dī___ n___." Laecānia hoc *negat*:

R: dīcere 'nōn.'

266. "*Enim*" est *conjūnctiō*. "Laecānia habet dentēs niveōs. *Emptōs enim* dentēs habet." = "L___ _____ _____. F__ she __ st___ _____."

A: Laecania has white teeth. For she has store teeth.

267. "*Nōvī*" est verbum simile "*ōdī*," hoc est, nōn habet tempora prīmum, secundum, aut tertium. "Laecānia habet dentēs ēmptōs." "Hoc nōvī; mihi enim ipsa hoc dīxit." = "_____; I kn___ ___ ___." "_____ ___ t__ _____. she t__ ___ _____."

A: Laecania has store teeth; I know this; for she told me herself.

268. "*Nōvī*" means, "I have learned something and therefore I now *know* it." It is related to the familiar Latin verb cog_____re.

A: cognōscere.

17-31

āctiō, rēs, virtūs, locus, animal,
vitium, membrum, homō

191. "Quid est avāritia?" "‑‑‑‑‑‑ est avāritia."

R: Vitium est avāritia.

192. "Quid est oculus?" "‑‑‑‑‑‑‑ est oculus."

R: Membrum est oculus.

193. "Quid est saltus?" "‑‑‑‑‑ est saltus."

R: Āctiō est saltus.

194. Some Latin adjectives can be made into Latin nouns by changing the endings. The Latin ending **-ia** or **-tia** is added to adjectives to show an abstract quality. For example, the word **sapientia**, meaning "‑‑‑dom," is formed by adding **-ia** or **-tia** to part of the word **sapiēns**, which means "‑‑‑‑."

A: wisdom
wise.

195. But **sapiēns**, like many Latin adjectives, can be used as a noun; when used as a noun, **sapiēns** means "‑‑‑‑ ‑‑‑‑‑‑‑."

A: wise person.

196. "Quid est sapientia?" "‑‑‑‑‑‑ est sapientia."

R: Virtūs est sapientia.

28-41

257. "Quid nōn numquam agēbat Gellia?"
"L‑‑‑‑‑m M‑‑‑‑‑‑ dō ā‑‑‑‑."

R: Leporem Mārtiālī dōnābat.

258. "Quid numquam ēderat Gellia?"
"‑‑‑‑‑‑‑."

R: Leporem.

259. "Cui Gellia leporem mittēbat?"
"‑‑‑‑‑‑‑."

R: Mārtiālī.

[The italicized words are new.]

260. Quī *dīves* est magnam pecūniam possidet. Quī exiguam pecūniam habet est "inops." Hoc adjectīvum *dīves* ergō oppōnitur "‑‑‑‑‑‑."

R: inops.

261. **Nimius** est adjectīvum simile "nimis." Avārus *nimiam* pecūniam vult = ‑‑‑‑‑‑‑‑
‑‑‑‑‑‑‑‑‑‑‑‑‑‑‑‑‑‑‑‑‑‑‑‑‑‑‑‑‑‑‑‑.

A: The greedy person wants too much money.

262. The man wants too much praise = V‑‑ n‑‑‑‑‑‑ l‑‑‑‑‑ v‑‑‑.

A: Vir nimiam laudem vult.

17-32

āctiō, rēs, virtūs, locus, animal, vitium, membrum, homō

197. "Quid est sapiēns?" "____ est sapiēns."

R: Homō est sapiēns.

198-208. Here are some new words, whose meanings you can figure out if you remember that the Latin endings **-ia** or **-tia** show a quality (either a vice or a virtue), while the corresponding form to which the **-ia** or **-tia** is added means a person who possesses this quality.

198. For example, if **avāritia** means "greed," the new adjective **avārus, avāra, avārum** must mean "_____."

A: greedy.

199. When used as a noun, **avārus** means a "_____ _____."

A: greedy person.

200. "Quid est avārus?" "____ est avārus."

R: Homō est avārus.

201. "Quid est avāritia?" "_____ est avāritia."

R: Vitium est avāritia.

202. "Quid est stultus?" "____ est stultus."

R: Homō est stultus.

Quaestiōnēs et Respōnsa

251. "Quod dōnum ā Gelliā Martiālī nōn numquam mittitur?" "_____."

R: Lepus. (nōn numquam = sometimes)

252. "Cui Gellia leporem mittit?" "_____."

R: Martiālī.

253. "Sī Gellia vēritātem dīcit, quālem Martiālem lepus reddet?" "_____."

R: Formōsum (vel Bellum vel Pulchrum).

254. "Quid Gellia ipsa edere dēbet?" "_____."

R: Leporem.

255. "Sī hunc leporem edis, septem diēbus bellus eris," dīcit Gellia. Nōn est vēritās sed s_____tiō.

R: superstitiō.

256. "Dērīdetne an laudat Gelliam Martiālis?" "_____."

R: Dērīdet.

In the questions above we have been talking as if Martial and Gellia were doing these actions at the *present* time: "Who *does* Gellia send rabbits to?", "*Is* Martial ridiculing Gellia or praising her?", etc. We will now talk about them in the *past*, "Who *did* Gellia send rabbits to?", etc. When the question is "What *did* she do?", answer with the same tense as the verb *agere*.

17-33

āctiō, rēs, virtūs, locus, animal,
vitium, membrum, homō

203. "Quid est stultitia?" "_____ est stultitia."

▼

R: Vitium est stultitia.

204. Since **stultus** means "stupid person," the new word **stultitia** must mean "_____ity."

▼

A: stupidity.

205. "Quid est malus?" "____ est malus."

▼

R: Homō est malus.

206. "Quid est malitia?" "_____ est malitia."

▼

R: Vitium est malitia.

207. Since **malus** means "___ person," **malitia** must mean "___ness."

▼

A: bad
                                  badness.

208. Latin **-tia** becomes "-ce" in English; the English derivative of **malitia** must therefore be "_____."

▼

A: malice.
(Malice, in case you don't know, is the desire to hurt other people.)

28-39

246. Sī nōn dērīdēs, sī vērum, lūx mea, nārrās = If you are not m__ing ___ of __, if, l__, __ are t__ing the _____

▼

A: If you are not making fun of me, if, my love, you are telling the truth

247. ēdistī numquam, Gellia, tū leporem. = ___ G_____ h___ n_____ _____ a _____.

▼

A: you, Gellia, have never eaten a rabbit.

[If you found it necessary to do this last sequence, it might be desirable to start back at the beginning of the poem, at frame 215, and go through the sequence again which explains the new vocabulary.]

Let us now practice the paradigms of some of the words which you will use in the question-and-answer drill on the poem.

248. ★ ○ •
lepus   leporēs
leporem   leporēs
lepore   leporibus
leporī   leporibus
leporis   leporum

249. ★ ○ •
Martiālis
Martiālem
Martiāle
Martiālī
Martiālis

▼

250. In this sequence of questions on the poem, remember that in asking questions we will shift to the third person. Here is an example in English. The first line says, "Whenever you send me a rabbit, Gellia." An English question is, "Who did Gellia send a rabbit to?" The answer is not "To me," but "To _____."

▼

A: Martial.

17-34

āctiō, rēs, virtūs, locus, animal,
vitium, membrum, homō

209-212. In addition to the Latin words ending in **-tia**, there are also Latin words ending in **-tās** that show qualities, whether good or bad.

209. From the adjective **crūdēlis** (which is a noun when used by itself), comes the new word **crūdēlitās**, which shows the quality of a person who is described as **crūdēlis**. **Crūdēlis** means "_____ person," and **crūdēlitās** must mean "_____ty."

◼   ◼

A: cruel
  cruelty.

210. "Quid est crūdēlitās?" "_____ est crūdēlitās."

◼   ◼

R: Vitium est crūdēlitās.

211. "Quid est crūdēlis?" "____ est crūdēlis."

◼   ◼

R: Homō est crūdēlis.

212. The English ending "-ty" comes from the Latin ending **-tās**. For example, the Latin original of the English word "quality" is a Latin word which you have never seen, but you can figure out that it is _____, [with two macrons.]

◼   ◼

R: quālitās. (How do you like that? You were able to make up a Latin word!)

213-237. Here are more nouns to identify, including some new abstract nouns ending in **-tia** or **-tās**.

28-38

241. Whenever she sends him a rabbit she tells him that if he eats it he ------.

◼

A: will become beautiful (handsome) in seven days.

◼

242. Martial says that if she means this seriously, then it is obvious that she herself has ------.

Gellia sum.

◼

A: never eaten a rabbit.

◼

If you understood the entire poem, skip to the next poem (frame 260). If you have any questions, this next sequence will explain the poem line by line.

243. Sī quandō leporem mittis, mihi, Gellia, dīcis = Wh----- you s---- me a ------, G------ you ---, .

◼

A: Whenever you send me a rabbit, Gellia, you say.

◼

244. Formōsus septem, Mārce, diēbus eris = M---us, you ---- be ---------- in ----------.

◼

A: Marcus, you will be handsome in seven days.

◼

245. That is, he will be handsome in seven days if ------.

◼

A: he eats the rabbit.

17-35

āctiō, rēs, virtūs, locus, animal, vitium, membrum, homō

213. "Quid est vulpēs?" "_____ est vulpēs."

R: Animal est vulpēs.

214. "Quid est plānitiēs?" "_____ est plānitiēs."

R: Locus est plānitiēs.

215. "Quid est morsus?" "_____ est morsus."

R: Actiō est morsus.

216. "Quid est manus?" "_____ est manus."

R: Membrum est manus.

217. "Quid est intemperantia?" "_____ est intemperantia."

R: Vitium est intemperantia.

218. "Quid est intemperāns?" "____ est intemperāns."

R: Homō est intemperāns.

28-37

234. Nōmen nostrī auctōris erat Marcus Valerius Mārtiālis. Puella Gellia leporem amīcō suō Marcō mittit. Ergō lepus dōnātur M_____ ī.

R: Mārtiālī.

235. ★ ○ ●

Sī quandō leporem mittis, mihi, Gellia, dīcis,
  "Formōsus septem, Mārce, diēbus eris."
Sī nōn dērīdēs, sī vērum, lūx mea, *nārrās*,
  ēdistī numquam, Gellia, tū leporem.
(Reading #1)

236. Copy in your Notebook.

237. Read the poem through several times to see if you can understand it without *additional help*. Make a real effort to understand it. When you have done what you can, write down what you think the poem is about. Then continue with the program.

238. The first thing to remember is that the poem is not four separate lines but a whole. The main part of the first half of the poem is a statement by _____. [Refer to the poem where necessary.]

A: Gellia.

239. The main part of the second half is a re--- by _____.

A: by Martial.

240. Martial says that his girl friend, Gellia, often _____.

A: sends him a rabbit as a present.

17-36

āctiō, rēs, virtūs, locus, animal, vitium, membrum, homō

219. "Quid est auris?" "_____ est auris."

R: Membrum est auris.

220. "Quid est lupus?" "_____ est lupus."

R: Animal est lupus.

221. "Quid est lacus?" "_____ est lacus."

R: Locus est lacus.

222. "Quid est levitās?" "_____ est levitās."

R: Vitium est levitās.

223. "Quid est superstitiō?" "_____ est superstitiō."

R: Vitium est superstitiō.

224. "Quid est īgnāvia?" "_____ est īgnāvia."

R: Vitium est īgnāvia.

225. Since īgnāvus means "_____ly _____," the abstract noun īgnāvia must mean "_____ice."

A: _____ cowardly person _____ cowardice.

28-36

229. Sī quandō puella amīcō leporem mittit = _____

A: Whenever the girl sends her boy friend a rabbit.

230. "Hāc in pictūrā quid agit puella? Laudatne an dērīdetne virum?" "P_____ v_____."

R: Puella virum dērīdet.

231. Puella amīcō suō dīcit, "Egō tibi leporem dabō. Sed nōn hodiē mittam nec crās, sed quīnque diēbus." She says that she _____ but she _____ but in _____s.

A: will give him a rabbit but she won't send it today or tomorrow but in five days.

232. "Vērus" est adjectīvum, ut in illā sententiā, "Plōrātur lacrimīs āmissa pecūnia v_____."

R: vērīs.

233. "Vērum" est nōmen secundī dēclīnātiōnis, generis neutrīus, significāns "vēritās." "In omnī rē vincit imitātiōnem vērum" significat "In omnī rē vincit imitātiōnem _____."

R: vēritās.

17-37

āctiō, rēs, virtūs, locus, animal,
vitium, membrum, homō

226. "Quid est pēs?" "_____ est pēs."

R: Membrum est pēs.

227. "Quid est fūr?" "____ est fūr."

R: Homō est fūr.

228. "Quid est musca?" "_____ est musca."

R: Animal est musca.

229. "Quid est dēns?" "_____ est dēns."

R: Membrum est dēns.

230. "Quid est amīcitia?" "_____ est amīcitia."

R: Virtūs est amīcitia.

231. **Amīcus** means "_____." Therefore, **amīcitia** must mean "_____ship."

A: friend
friendship.

232. "Quid est vānitās?" "_____ est vānitās."

R: Vitium est vānitās.

28-35

223. If she had eaten the rabbit she wouldn't now be so _____.

A: homely (ugly, etc.)

224. In sententiā "Certa mittimus dum incerta petimus," haec vōx "mittere" significat "āmittere." Sed si auctor scripsit, "Puella amīcō suō pictūram mittit," significat "Puella amīcō suō pictūram _____." (dat/jūdicat/mūtat/pingit)."

R: dat.

225. Haec vōx "quandō" oppōnitur "_____."

"*Sī quandō mē laudās, mihi placēs.*"
"*Sī numquam mē laudās, mihi nōn placēs.*"

R: numquam.

226. Sī numquam mē laudās = _____ _____

A: If you never praise me.

227. Sī quandō mē laudās = _____ _____

A: If you ever praise me.

228. Often a single word best translates the phrase "Sī quandō": Sī quandō aprō cēnō = Wh____ r____ _____.

A: Whenever I dine on a boar.

17-38

233. vānus = ———

A: useless

234. Therefore the abstract noun **vānitās** must mean "————."

A: uselessness.

235. The English derivative of **vānitās** is "————."

A: vanity.

236. The change from **vānitās** to "vanity" shows the change in endings from Latin ——— to English ———

A: **-tās** ty.

237. The most common meaning of "vanity" today is excessive pride in one's own appearance, ability, etc. The connection with this Latin word **vānitās** is that such pride is ————.

A: useless.

238. At this point you will learn two very common words. In the expression **Auxilium sub hāc līneā est,** the word **hāc** means "————."

A: this.

239. Echo the nominative singular forms of this irregular adjective. ★ ○ • ○ • **hic, haec, hoc** m f n

---

218. Cum caelum serēnum est, lūna nōbis **lūcem** dat. Sī caelum nūbilum erit, nōn dabit lūna l——m.

R: **lūcem.**

219. Something which is "**trans**L**UC**ent" lets l——t through.

A: light

220. From these examples you can see that the Latin word **lūx** has two entirely different meanings. Referring to the sun and moon it means "————."

A: light.

221. A Roman boy would say "**Mea lūx**" to his girl, an American would say, "————."

222. "Haec erat superstitiō Rōmānōrum: sī leporem edis, eris bellus et formōsus inter septem diēs. Utra puella numquam leporem edit?" "————."

A: [This is getting too personal; let's go on.]

Thāis Gellia

R: Gellia

17-39

240. Echo the nominative singular forms of another irregular adjective. ★ ○ • ○ •
   m   f   n
ille, illa, illud

241. Listen to your teacher's description of this picture. ★ ○ ○ **Hic canis est parvus, sed ille canis est magnus.**

242. Write your teacher's description of this picture. ★ ○ ○ H__ an____ s_____ __t, s__ il___ an___ e__ st_____.

Cōnf: **Hoc animal sapiēns est, sed illud animal est stultum.**

243. The word **hic, haec, hoc** shows an object or a person which is *near* the speaker; the word **ille, illa, illud** shows an object or a person which is ___ a___ fr__ the speaker.

A: far away from the speaker.

244. Copy the nominative forms **hic, haec, hoc** and **ille, illa, illud** in your Answer Pad to refer to in doing this next sequence.

[New words in this sequence are italized.]

215. "*Lepus* est animal parvum quod canēs vulpēsque timet. At saepe effugit quod celeriter currere potest. Habet aurēs longās. Cum līber est, in agrīs errat, sed sī *domesticus*, ab hominibus pāscitur. Quotō in orbe vidēs leporem?"

R: Primō in orbe ego videō leporem.

"_____ ego _____"

216. Haec puella est *formōsa*. Hoc adjectīvum "formōsus" sīgnificat "pulcher" vel "b_____."

R: bellus.

217. Hic puer puellam formōsam amat. Puellae blandē dīcit, "_____?"

"mea lūx!"

R: Mea lūx!

245. Echo a word which means "which of the two?" ★ ○ • ○ •
                    m   f   n
uter, utra, utrum

246. Write this in your Notebook under "Question Words."

247. Answer the question about this picture. "Utrum animal est stultum, vulpēs an asinus?" "_____ est an____ st_____."

R: Asinus est animal stultum.

248. "Utrum animal est sapiēns?" "_____ est an____ s_____."

R: Vulpēs est animal sapiēns.

In this sequence you will have new vocabulary explained in Latin. Some of you will find that you will need to go through the sequence several times in order to do the frames correctly. First, let's learn to count to ten. Only the first three numerals change form.

212. Count the fingers. ★ ○ • ○ •

Ūnus digitus | Duo digitī | Trēs digitī | Quattuor digitī | Quīnque digitī | Sex digitī

Septem digitī | Octō digitī | Novem digitī | Decem digitī

213. Count: ★ ○ • Ūnus, duo, trēs, quattuor, quīnque, sex, septem, octō, novem, decem.

214. Hae in pictūrā sunt ___ leōnēs et ___ (duo/trēs/quattuor/quīnque/sex/septem/octō) mūrēs.

R: duo   septem

17-41

249. Haec fēmina est ae____ sed illa fēmina est s____.

R: _____ aegra _____ sāna.

250. "Utra fēmina aegra est, haec an illa?"
"____ _____ ____."

R: Haec fēmina aegra est.

251. Use **hic** and **ille** in the following description. "____ vir est bl_____ sed ____ vir est cr_____."

R: Hic vir est blandus sed ille vir est crūdēlis.

28-31

In this sequence we will give you the principal parts of a verb to echo. Copy them in your Notebook. Then say aloud the #5 tense of the verb.

203. ● ○ ★ • **mittō, mittere, mīsī, missus**

204. Copy these principal parts in your Notebook.

205. Say the #5 tense of **mittere**:
∨ ★ ○ •
____ī   ____imus
____istī   ____istis
____it   ____ērunt

R: mīsī   mīsimus
    mīsistī   mīsistis
    mīsit   mīsērunt

206. ● ○ ★ • **taceō, tacēre, tacuī**

207. Copy in your Notebook.

208. Say the #5 tense of **tacēre**:
∨ ★ ○ •
_____   _____
_____   _____

R: tacuī   tacuimus
    tacuistī   tacuistis
    tacuit   tacuērunt

209. ● ○ ★ • **debeō, debēre, debuī, debitus**

210. Copy in your Notebook.

211. Say the #5 tense of **debēre**:
∨ ★ ○ •
_____   _____
_____   _____

R: debuī   debuimus
    debuistī debuistis
    debuit   debuērunt

17-42

252. These adjectives are frequently used as nouns themselves. For example, **Hic est crūdēlis** means, "____ ___ is _____."

A: This man is cruel.

253. Illud est malum = ____ thing is ___.

A: That thing is bad.

254. Haec est gravis = ____ _____ __ s_____.

A: This woman is serious.

255. Hoc est malum sed illud est bonum = _____.

A: This thing is bad, but that thing is good.

256. In this sequence use this pattern of **Hoc est malum sed illud est bonum** to compare things and people. Study the antonyms which you will use.
crūdēlis/blandus, longus/brevis, certus/incertus, fortis/īgnāvus, sānus/aeger, magnus/parvus

[As you echoed, were you trying to *learn*? Or did you just *say* the words?]

Be sure to use the right gender.

257. Hic est crūdēlis sed ille ___ bl_____.

R: Hic est crūdēlis sed ille est blandus.

28-30

In the perfective system, all verbs are conjugated the same way, regardless of which conjugation they belong to.

196. ★ ○ •
plōrāveram   plōrāvimus
plōrāverās   plōrāvistis
plōrāverat   plōrāverant

However, to form the #4 tense you must know the active perfective stem.

197. ★ ○ • rīdeō, rīdēre, rīsī, rīsus

198. Copy these principal parts in your Notebook.

199. You can find the active perfective stem of rīdēre from the ____ (1st/2d/3d/4th) form in the principal parts given above.

A: 3d

200. Say the #4 form of **rīdēre**: ∧ ★ ○ •

R: rīseram   rīserāmus
   rīserās   rīserātis
   rīserat   rīserant

201. The #5 tense is the *only* tense which has a *special set* of person endings. It is harder to produce but easier to rec____ze.

A: recognize.

202. venīre: vēnī   vēnimus
(#5 tense) vēnistī   vēnistis
★ ○ •   vēnit   vēnērunt

17-43

258. Hoc est longum sed ____d ___ br__e.

R: Hoc est longum sed illud est breve.
[Of course the **hic** does not have to come first; we can have **ille** first.]

259. Illud animal est īgnāvum sed ___ ___ f____.

R: Illud animal est īgnāvum sed hoc est forte.

260. H__ amīcus est cert__ sed ____ est in_____.

R: Hic amīcus est certus sed ille (amīcus) est incertus.

[It is more common to leave out one of the two nouns when they are both the same, like **amīcus**.]

261. Hic juvenis est sān__ sed ____ est ae____.

R: Hic juvenis est sānus sed ille est aeger.

262. Hoc perīc'lum est parvum sed _____ est m_____.

R: Hoc perīc'lum est parvum sed illud est magnum.

263-267. In this sequence you will be asked which of two people or animals is happy, eloquent, large, or cruel. If it is the nearer one, answer with **hic, haec,** or **hoc**; if it is the farther one, answer with **ille, illa,** or **illud**. Answer with a complete sentence.

28-29

191. audīre:
(#3 tense) ∧ ★ ○ •

R: audiam   audiēmus
   audiēs   audiētis
   audiet   audient

192. The verb **esse** is irregular throughout the imperfective system. Echo the synopsis in the second person plural. ★ ○ •

| erātis 1 | estis 2 | eritis 3 |

193. Say the paradigm of the #1 tense of esse: ∧ ★ ○ •

-ra-

R: eram   erāmus
   erās   erātis
   erat   erant

194. Say the paradigm of the #2 tense of esse: ∧ ★ ○ •

s--

R: sum   sumus
   es   estis
   est   sunt

195. Say the paradigm of the #3 tense of esse: ∧ ★ ○ •

R: erō   erimus
   eris   eritis
   erit   erunt

263. "Uter vir est hilaris, hic an ille?"
"____ ___ ___ _____."

R: Ille vir est hilaris.

264. "Uter jūdex est ēloquēns, hic an ille?"
"_____."

R: Ille jūdex est ēloquēns.

265. "Utra rāna est magna, haec an illa?"
"_____."

R: Haec rāna est magna.

---

186. There are two types of regular future verbs: Verbs which have futures ending in -bō, -bis, -bit belong to the ------ and ------ Conjugations; verbs which have futures ending in -am, -ēs, -et belong to the ------ and ------ Conjugations.

A: First   Second
   Third   Fourth

Conjugate the following five verbs in the #3 tense.

187. parāre:
     (#3 tense)
     ∧ ★ ○ •
     -------   -------
     -------   -------
     -------   -------

R: parābō   parābimus
     parābis   parābitis
     parābit   parābunt

188. tenēre:
     (#3 tense)
     ∧ ★ ○ •
     -------   -------
     -------   -------
     -------   -------

R: tenēbō   tenēbimus
     tenēbis   tenēbitis
     tenēbit   tenēbunt

189. pāscere:
     (#3 tense)
     ∧ ★ ○ •
     -------   -------
     -------   -------
     -------   -------

R: pāscam   pāscēmus
     pāscēs   pāscētis
     pāscet   pāscent

190. facere:
     (#3 tense)
     ∧ ★ ○ •
     -------   -------
     -------   -------
     -------   -------

R: faciam   faciēmus
     faciēs   faciētis
     faciet   facient

266. **"Utrum animal est crūdēle, hoc an illud?"** "______________________________."

R: **Illud animal est crūdēle.**

267. Notice that while we say **Illud animal est crūdēle,** if we were to use the word **leō,** we would have to change the gender of the adjective: **Ille leō est cr______.**

R: Ille leō est crūdēlis.

268. Latin nouns have five cases, but before we go on to the other two cases we wish to be sure that you have a good grasp of the nominative, accusative, and ablative. Because you have had less practice on plural forms than on the singular ones, in the following sequence we will stress the _____ (singular/plural) forms.

A: plural

269. Therefore we have frequently transformed a singular noun in a Basic Sentence to the ______.

A: plural.

270. If we ask, "What animals fear pitfalls?" you are to say "C_______ w_____ do."

A: Cautious wolves do.

181. **manēre:** (#2 tense) √ ★ ○ •

_____	_______
_____	_______
_____	______

R:

maneō	**manēmus**
manēs	**manētis**
manet	**manent**

182. **quaerere:** (#2 tense) √ ★ ○ •

______	_________
_______	_________
_______	________

R:

quaerō	**quaerimus**
quaeris	**quaeritis**
quaerit	**quaerunt**

183. **capere:** (#2 tense) √ ★ ○ •

_____	_______
_____	_______
_____	_______

R:

capiō	**capimus**
capis	**capitis**
capit	**capiunt**

184. **servīre:** (#2 tense) √ ★ ○ •

______	________
______	________
______	________

R:

serviō	**servīmus**
servīs	**servītis**
servit	**serviunt**

185. If your performance on this last sequence was unsatisfactory, we suggest that you do one of two things:

1) Review the forms in your Notebook.

2) Go back to Unit 25 and do frames 1 to 286.

Otherwise, proceed with the program.

271-273. First echo the paradigms of nouns which you will use in the next sequence.

271. ★ ○ •

diēs	diēs
diem	diēs
diē	diēbus

272. ★ ○ •

manus	manūs
manum	manūs
manū	manibus

273. ★ ○ •

cautus lupus	cautī lupī
cautum lupum	cautōs lupōs
cautō lupō	cautīs lupīs

[If this single echo is not enough practice for you, practice saying the paradigms several times. Always keep in mind that it is not doing the program which is important, it is *learning* the material which the program presents.]

274. Echo the question word which asks for an adjective, first the masculine-feminine singular, then the neuter singular, etc.

★ ○ •

m&f	n	m&f	n
quālis	quāle	quālēs	quālia
quālem	quāle	quālēs	quālia
quālī	quālī	quālibus	quālibus

Here are the first questions. As in Unit Sixteen, you are to answer with a word that is in the Basic Sentence, but a transformation is necessary. Answer with the same number and case as the question word!

275. Vēritātem diēs aperit. (2) "Quō omnia vitia inveniuntur?" "___."

R: Diē.

---

177. Say the conjugation of this Fourth Conjugation verb.

∧ ★ ○ • --------- audiēbam

R: audiēbam   audiēbāmus
    audiēbās   audiēbātis
    audiēbat   audiēbant

178. Conjugate regere in the #1 form. [Conjugate" means *to give the forms of a verb*.]

∧ ★ ○ • ---ē---   ---------

R: regēbam   regēbāmus
    regēbās   regēbātis
    regēbat   regēbant

179. Conjugate the -iō verb facere in the #1 form.

∧ ★ ○ • ---iē---   ----------

R: faciēbam   faciēbāmus
    faciēbās   faciēbātis
    faciēbat   faciēbant

The #2 tense is the hardest of all, since it is different in all the four conjugations. However, it is the tense which you have practiced the most.

180. cūrāre:
Give the #2 forms of the following five verbs.

∧ ★ ○ • ----   -------
        (#2 tense)
         ----   -------
         ----   -------

R: cūrō   cūrāmus
    cūrās   cūrātis
    cūrat   cūrant

17-47

276. Manus manum lavat. (4) "Quō membrō manus adjuvātur?" "____."

R: Manū.

277. Lupus nōn mordet lupum. (6) "Cum quibus animālibus lupī lītem nōn habent?" "___ _____."

R: Cum lupīs.

278. Cautus metuit foveam lupus. (8) "Quālēs lupī perīc'la cernunt?" "_____ ____."

R: Cautī lupī.

279. ★ ○ •
    intemperāns aeger
    intemperantem aegrum
    intemperantī aegrō

    intemperantēs aegrī
    intemperantēs aegrōs
    intemperantibus aegrīs

280. ★ ○ •
    fūr   fūrēs
    fūrem fūrēs
    fūre   fūribus

281. ★ ○ •
    nox   noctēs
    noctem noctēs
    nocte   noctibus

282. ★ ○ •
    auris facilis   aurēs facilēs
    aurem facilem aurēs facilēs
    aure facilī   auribus facilibus

You now have seen five tenses of the Latin verb.

171. An example of the #1 tense occurred in the sentence about the Roman conqueror who was ruling the whole world: Orbem jam tōtum victor Rōmānus h_____.

A: habēbat.

172. ★ ○ •   habēbam   habēbāmus
                habēbās   habēbātis
                habēbat   habēbant

173. All regular verbs have the same signal for the #1 tense: it is {_____}.

A: {-bā-}.

174. Count yourself right in this last frame if you had {-ba-}, because before final -t, final -m, and any -nt, a ____ vowel becomes a _____ vowel.

A: long   short

175. Habēbam belongs to the ____ (1st/2d/3d/4th) Conjugation.

A: 2d

176. Say the conjugation of this First Conjugation verb.

★ ○ •   errābam
        --------   -------
        --------   -------

R: errābam   errābāmus
     errābās   errābātis
     errābat   errābant

28-25

17-48

283. Nōn semper aurem facilem habet Fēlīcitās. (10) "Quālēs aurēs nōn semper habet Fortūna?" "‑‑‑‑‑‑ ‑‑‑‑‑."

R: Facilēs aurēs.

284. Crūdēlem medicum intemperāns aeger facit. (12) "Ā quālibus aegrīs medicī blandī saepe irrītantur?" "‑‑ ‑‑‑‑‑‑‑‑‑‑‑‑ ‑‑‑‑‑‑."

R: Ab intemperantibus aegrīs.

285. Fūrem fūr cognōscit et lupum lupus. (14) "Ā quibus fūrēs semper cognōscuntur?" "‑ ‑‑‑‑‑‑."

R: Ā fūribus.

286. Diem nox premit, diēs noctem. (16) "Quō diēs premitur?" "‑‑‑‑‑."

R: Nocte.

287. ★ ○ •
    Fortūna   Fortūnae
    Fortūnam   Fortūnās
    Fortūnā   Fortūnīs

288. ★ ○ •
    līs incerta   lītēs incertae
    lītem incertam   lītēs incertās
    līte incertā   lītibus incertīs

289. ★ ○ •
    rēs incerta   rēs incertae
    rem incertam   rēs incertās
    rē incertā   rēbus incertīs

28-24

Quaestiōnēs et Respōnsa

165. "Quantus amor Propertiī fuerat?" "‑‑‑‑‑‑."

R: Magnus.

166. "Quantus amor Propertiī nunc est?" "‑‑‑‑‑‑."

R: Parvus.

167. "Cujus amōrem āmīsit puella?" "Pr‑‑‑‑‑‑."

R: Propertiī.

168. "Quantā viā amor mūtātus est?" "‑‑‑‑‑‑."

R: Longā.

169. "Via Propertiī puellam suam mūtāvit. Quem quoque mūtāvit haec via longa?" "‑‑‑‑‑‑‑‑‑‑ ips‑‑‑."

R: Propertium ipsum.

170. (138)
N‑‑ s‑‑ ‑‑‑ q‑‑ f‑‑‑‑‑: m‑‑‑‑ v‑‑
l‑‑‑‑ p‑‑‑‑‑‑.
Qu‑‑‑‑‑ in ex‑‑‑‑ t‑‑‑‑‑‑ f‑‑‑‑ am‑‑!

R: Nōn sum ego quī fueram: mūtat via longa puellās.
Quantus in exiguō tempore fūgit amor!

17-49

290. ★ ○ •
vēritās
vēritātem
vēritāte

291. Vītam regit Fortūna, nōn Sapientia.
(18) "Sub quō vīta est?" "___ _____."

R: Sub Fortūnā.

292. Sub jūdice līs est. (20) "Haec līs est ____ (certa/incerta)."

R: incerta

293. In omnī rē vincit imitātiōnem vēritās.
(22) "Quō imitātiō semper vincitur?" "_____."

R: Vēritāte.

294. Amīcus certus in rē incertā cernitur.
(24) "Quālibus in rēbus amīcus amīcum cernit?" "_____ __ _____."

R: Incertīs in rēbus.

295. ★ ○ •
vitium   vitia
vitium   vitia
vitiō   vitiīs

296. ★ ○ •
bona mēns   bonae mentēs
bonam mentem   bonās mentēs
bonā mente   bonīs mentibus

28-23

158. Echo the English name of the poet who wrote these two lines. ★ ○ • Propertius

VCh: "pro-pér-shuss"

159. Echo his name in Latin. ★ ○ • Propertius

160. He has been away on a long trip and has returned to discover that the girl no longer seems as attractive as she did when he left. He ascribes this not only to a change in himself, but also to a change in ----

A: her.

161. The two lines of the poem = --------- ----------------

A: I am not the person I was (or "had been"): a long journey changes girls. How great a love has fled in a short time!

162. Copy in your Notebook.

163. Which of these statements is true?
1) You can always translate a Latin tense by the meanings given you in frame 8.
2) There are several different ways to translate each Latin tense into English, and the context tells you which meaning is intended.

A: 2) There are several different ways to translate each Latin tense into English, and the context tells you which meaning is intended.

164. In using the #4 form fueram, Propertius tells us that he was not the person he had been ------------------ before he

A: started out on his trip.

17-50

297. ★ ○ •
sānum córpus   sāna córpora
sānum córpus   sāna córpora
sānō córpore   sānīs corpóribus

298. ★ ○ •
īnsānus   īnsānī
īnsānum   īnsānōs
īnsānō   īnsānīs

299. Nēmō sine vitiō est. (26) "Quās malās rēs omnis homō possidet?" "‗‗‗‗‗."

R: Vitia.

300. Mēns rēgnum bona possidet. (28) "Quālēs mentēs rēgna possident?" "‗‗‗‗‗."

R: Bonae.

301. Mēns sāna in corpore sānō. (30) "Quāle corpus possidet mēns sāna?" "‗‗‗‗‗‗‗‗‗‗."

R: Sānum corpus.

302. Īnsānus mediō flūmine quaerit aquam. (32) "Ā quibus aqua etiam in mediō flūmine nōn invenītur?" "‗‗ ‗‗‗‗‗‗‗."

R: Ab īnsānīs.

303. ★ ○ •
blanda ōrātiō   blandae ōrātiōnēs
blandam ōrātiōnem   blandās ōrātiōnēs
blandā ōrātiōne   blandīs ōrātiōnibus

---

150. ★ ○ ○ • fugiō fugere fūgī

151. Copy in your Notebook.

152-153. Write the two lines of the poem from hearing each one once. There are no clues. If there is a word which you missed, see if you can figure out what it is.

152. ★ ○ ———

153. ★ ○ ———

R: Nōn sum ego quī fueram: mūtat via longa puellās.
Quantus in exiguō tempore fūgit amor!

154. "Fueram" est temporis ‗‗‗‗ (prīmī/secundī/tertiī/quārtī/quīntī/sextī).

R: quārtī.

155. "Mūtat" est temporis ‗‗‗‗‗‗‗.

R: secundī.

156. "Sum" est t‗‗‗‗‗‗‗‗‗‗‗.

R: temporis secundī.

157. "Fūgit" est t‗‗‗‗‗‗‗‗‗‗‗.

R: temporis quīntī.

28-22

17-51

304. ★ ○ •

aquila	aquilae
aquilam	aquilās
aquilā	aquilīs

305. ★ ○ •

malum cōnsilium	mala cōnsilia
malum cōnsilium	mala cōnsilia
malō cōnsiliō	malīs cōnsiliīs

306. Habet suum venēnum blanda ōrātiō. (34) "Quālī in ōrātiōne est magnum peric'lum?" "_____ __ _____."

R: Blandā in ōrātiōne.

307. Aquila nōn capit muscās. (36) "Ā quibus animālibus nōn premuntur muscae?" "__ _____."

R: Ab aquilīs.

308. Malō in cōnsiliō fēminae vincunt virōs. (38) "Quālibus in cōnsiliīs fēminae vincunt virōs?" "_____ __ _____."

R: Malīs in cōnsiliīs.

309. Fortēs Fortūna adjuvat. (40) "Ā quō auxilium dōnātur?" "_ _____."

R: Ā Fortūnā.

Here is the last set in this sequence. If you have not been satisfied with your performance, go back to frame 271 and go through the sequence again before going ahead.

310. ★ ○ •

sapiēns	sapientēs
sapientem	sapientēs
sapiente	sapientibus

28-21

145. Dīcimus "mūs exiguus"; ergō "mūs" est generis ____ (masculīnī/fēminīnī/neutrīus).

R: masculīnī.

146. Dīcimus "animal exiguum"; ergō "animal" est g_____ius.

R: generis neutrīus.

The following explains the difference between the verbs fugere and effugere.

147. Quid accidit aciēī? Aciēs fugit, sed peric'lum ef_____ nōn poterit.

R: effugere

148. Noster amīcus peric'la sua effugere nōn potest. Sīne spē f_____

R: fugit.

149. While the word effugere means "_____," the word fugere means to "f____."

A: escape flee.

17-52

311. ★ ○ •
manus pūra   manūs pūrae
manum pūram   manūs pūrās
manū pūrā   manibus pūrīs

312. ★ ○ •
magna rēs   magnae rēs
magnam rem   magnās rēs
magnā rē   magnīs rēbus

313. ★ ○ •
fātum   Fāta
fātum   Fāta
fātō   Fātīs

314. Stultī timent Fortūnam, sapientēs ferunt. (42) "Ā quibus Fāta feruntur?" "-- ------------."

R: Ā sapientibus.

315. Pūrās Deus, nōn plēnās, aspicit manūs. (44) "Quālēs manūs Deum colunt?" "----- -----."

R: Pūrae manūs.

316. Magna dī cūrant, parva neglegunt. (46) "In quantīs rēbus dī auxilium ferunt?" "-- ------ -----."

R: In magnīs rēbus.

317. Fāta regunt orbem; certā stant omnia lēge. (48) "Sub quibus dīs sunt omnēs hominēs?" "--- -----."

R: Sub Fātīs.

28-20

141. The next Basic Sentence is two lines long. Here is the first line. ★ ○ ○ ○
N___ s___ e___ qui f___ ___ m___ v___ l___ p___.

R: Nōn sum ego quī fueram: mūtat via longa puellās.

142. Now write the second line. ★ ○ ○ ○
Qu___ in ex___ t___ fū___ am___! (138)

R: Quantus in exiguō tempore fūgit amor!

143. "'Exiguus' oppōnitur 'magnus', sig-nificāns 'parvus' vel 'brevis.' Hāc in pictūrā utrum animal est exiguum?" "--------."

144. "Quantum animal est mūs?"
"-------."

R: Exiguum.

R: Mūs est exiguus.

17-53

318. As you know, the forms of **hic** are irregular. We will not ask you to learn them at this time, but we would at least like to introduce you to them. Echo the paradigm. Your teacher will give first the masculine singular, then the feminine singular, and so on. The irregular forms are italicized. ★ ○ •

	singular			plural	
m	f	n	m	f	n
hic	haec	hoc	hī	hae	*haec*
hunc	hanc	hoc	hōs	hās	*haec*
hōc	hāc	hōc	hīs	hīs	hīs

319. Copy this paradigm in your Notebook under "Forms."

320. Observe that only the italicized forms are irregular. We may call **hunc** and **hanc** regular because in Latin **-m-** before **-c** changes to _____.

A: -n-.

321. The forms of **ille,** too, are irregular. We will not ask you to learn them at this time. However, here are its forms to see and hear. ★ ○ •

	singular			plural	
m	f	n	m	f	n
ille	illa	illud	illī	illae	illa
illum	illam	illud	illōs	illās	illa
illō	illā	illō	illīs	illīs	illīs

322. Copy this paradigm in your Notebook under "Forms."

323-330. Echo the paradigms of the nouns you will use in this next sequence.

323. ★ ○ • (1st Decl.)

musca	muscae
muscam	muscās
muscā	muscīs

28-19

136. This saying was written by the Stoic philosopher S-_____.

A: Seneca.

137. Write the paradigm of **quī.** Remember the unusual form of the neuter. Check with your Notebook first if you are uncertain of the forms.

R:
quī	quae	quod
quōs	quās	quae
quibus	quibus	quibus
quibus	quibus	quibus
quōrum	quārum	quōrum

138. Qu— f—— v——, mōr— s—— (137)

Quaestiōnēs et Respōnsa

R: Quae fuerant vitia, mōrēs sunt.

139. "Habentne nostra tempora multa vitia?" "_____."

R: Habent.

140. "Quae nunc videntur quae fuerant tempore praeteritō vitia?" "_____."

R: Mōrēs.

17-54

324. ★ ○ • (5th Decl.)
faciēs
faciem
faciē

325. ★ ○ • (4th Decl.)
gradus   gradūs
gradum   gradūs
gradū   gradibus

326. ★ ○ • (5th Decl.)
aciēs
aciēm
aciē

327. ★ ○ • (4th Decl.)
manus   manūs
manum   manūs
manū   manibus

328. ★ ○ • (3d Decl.)
flūmen   flūmina
flūmen   flūmina
flūmine   flūminibus

329. ★ ○ • (4th Decl.)
anus   anūs
anum   anūs
anū   anibus

330. ★ ○ • (4th Decl.)
morsus   morsūs
morsum   morsūs
morsū   morsibus

28-18

130. Here is the plural paradigm of the relative pronoun. Echo the three forms of the nominative, then the three forms of the accusative, and so on.

★ ○ • quī
quī   quae   quae
quōs   quās   quae
quibus quibus quibus
quōrum quārum quōrum

131. Copy this paradigm in your Notebook.

132. The neuter plural of the pronoun **quī** is unusual because the nominative and accusative _____. [In your own words]

A: both have ae rather than a.

133. **Quae fuerant vitia, mōrēs sunt.** (137) This sentence means, "---- --- ---- v---- s --- c-----s."

A: What had been vices are now customs.

134. Copy in your Notebook.

135. This is a cynical remark, meaning that things that were considered to be terrible in times past are now _____. [In your own words]

A: done by everybody.

331. Write your teacher's description of this picture. ★ ○ ○ H___ ac___ ā f_____ d_____ r_____.

R: Haec aciēs ā fortibus ducibus regitur.

332. "Quō locō sunt hī fortēs ducēs?"
"_____ _____."

R: In aciē.

333. ★ ○ ○ S_____ c__ h__ c_____ l____ h_____.

R: Sīmiae cum hīs canibus lītem habent.

334. "Quibus in locīs sunt hae sīmiae?"
"_____ _____."

R: In gradibus.

---

125. The moon will shine in the clear sky = C___ f___ l___ s_____.

R: Caelō fulgēbit lūna serēnō.

126. The written letter had remained = L_____ sc_____ m_____.

R: Littera scrīpta mānserat.

127. You drank the largest part of your own poison = T__ m_____ p_____ v_____ t___ b_____.

R: Tū maximam partem venēnī tuī bibistī.

128. God was seeing pure hands = P_____ m_____ as_____ D_____.

R: Pūrās manūs aspiciēbat Deus.

129. ★ ○ ○ Qu___ f_____, v_____, m_____ s_____. (137)

R: Quae fuerant vitia, mōrēs sunt.

335. ★ ○ ○ L_____ ab h__ oc____ d_____.

R: Lacrimae ab hīs oculīs dēfluunt.

336. "In quō membrō sunt hī oculī?" "_____ _____."

R: In faciē.

337. ★ ○ ○ H__ a___ r_____ ad_____.

R: Hae anūs rēgīnam adjuvant.

338. "Ā quibus vestis cūrātur?" "_____ _____."

R: Ab anibus.

---

118. Time disclosed the truth = V_____ ____ ap_____.
R: Vēritātem diēs aperuit.

119. The Fates will drag the unwilling = F___ n_____ tr_____.
R: Fāta nōlentem trahent.

120. You are showing an ambush, not grief = V___ in_____, n__ fl_____, in_____.
R: Vōs insidiās, nōn flētum, indicātis.

121. The gods had neglected small things = D__ p___ n_____.
R: Dī parva neglēxerant.

122. Glory will be the shadow of virtue = Gl____ u__ v_____ ____.
R: Glōria umbra virtūtis erit.

123. No free person was a slave to his body = N____ l____ c_____ s____ i____.
R: Nēmō liber corporī serviēbat.

124. We blind people seek a guide = C____ d_____ qu_____.
R: Caecī ducem quaerimus.

17-57

339. ★ ○ ○ H_ el_____ m____ aqu___ ex fl_____ b_____.

R: Hī elephantī magnī aquam ex flūmine bibunt.

340. "Quō locō stant haec animālia spatiōsa?" "_____ _____."

R: In flūmine.

341. ★ ○ ○ H__ m___ ā j_____ t_____.

R: Hic mūs ā juvene tenētur.

342. "Quibus membrīs hic mūs tenētur?" "_____."

R: Manibus.

28-15

Echo and copy these two Fourth Conjugation verbs.

109-10. ★ ○ ● serviō, servīre, servīvī, servītus

111-12. ★ ○ ● aperiō, aperīre, aperuī, apertus

113. In addition to these 13 new verbs, you will be asked to use the verbs bibere and esse. Review these two now in your Reference Notebook if you do not know them.

114. Everything had stood under a fixed law = C---- st------ om--- l----.

R: Certā steterant omnia lēge.

115. We will catch two boars in one jump = N-- ū- in s---- apr-- c------ d----.

R: Nōs ūnō in saltū aprōs capiēmus duōs.

116. You have white teeth = V--- n----- h-----.

R: Vōs niveōs dentēs habētis.

117. You put a happy life in security of mind = Tū b------ v---- in an--- s-------- p-------.

R: Tū beātam vītam in animī sēcūritāte posuistī.

17-58

343. In the next two frames remember that Quibus? asks for a _____ noun while Ā quibus asks for a _____ noun.

A: personal
   non-personal

344. M_____ h___ j_____ m____nt.

R: Muscae hunc juvenem mordent.

345. "Ā quibus hic juvenis irrītātur?"
"_ mus___."

R: Ā muscīs.

346. "Quibus muscae hunc juvenem irrītant?" "Mors____"

R: Morsibus.

SUMMARY

347. In this Unit you learned a new sentence type which uses the verb **est**. We symbolize this new type by { __ __ ___ }.

A: {-s -s est}.

28-14

Echo and copy into your Reference Notebook these two First Conjugation verbs.

87-88. stō, stāre, stetī ★ ○ •

89-90. indicō, indicāre, indicāvī, indicātus ★ ○ •

Echo and copy these three Second Conjugation verbs.

91-92. habeō, habēre, habuī, habitus ★ ○ •

93-94. maneō, manēre, mānsī ★ ○ •

95-96. fulgeō, fulgēre, fulsī ★ ○ •

Echo and copy these four Third Conjugation verbs.

97-98. pōnō, pōnere, posuī, positus ★ ○ •

99-100. quaerō, quaerere, quaesīvī, quaesītus ★ ○ •

101-2. trahō, trahere, trāxī, tractus ★ ○ •

103-4. neglegō, neglegere, neglēxī, neglēctus ★ ○ •

Echo and copy these two Third Conjugatio -io verbs.

105-6. capiō, capere, cēpī, captus ★ ○ •

107-8. aspiciō, aspicere, aspexī, aspectus ★ ○ •

17-59

348. The difficulty which this structure presents is that there is *no* signal by which you can tell which {-s} is the _____ and which {-s} is the _____.

A: _____ subject complement.

349. If the first meaning you think of for an {-s -s est} sentence does not make sense, you should try reversing the _____ and the _____.

A: _____ subject complement.

350-357. You learned eight new Basic Sentences. Say the Latin.

350. Ī__ f____ br____ ____.

R: Īra furor brevis est. (53)

351. ___ l____, v___ br____.

R: Ars longa, vīta brevis. (52)

28-13

79. fulgeō, fulgēre, fulsī ★ ○ •

80. The moon had shone in the clear sky = C____ f____ l____ s____.

R: Caelō fulserat lūna serēnō.

81. sum, esse, fuī ★ ○ •

82. Glory was the shadow of virtue = Gl____ ____ v____ ____ um____.

R: Glōria umbra virtūtis erat.

83. neglegō, neglegere, neglēxī, neglēctus ★ ○ •

84. You gods will neglect small things = V____ d___ p____ n_____.

R: Vōs dī parva neglegētis.

85. aspiciō, aspicere, aspexī, aspectus ★ ○ •

86. God will see pure hands = P___ D___ as____ m____ ____.

R: Pūrās Deus aspiciet manūs.

In this next sequence, we will use the same sentences as in the last but will use the verbs in different tenses. First echo the principal parts of the verbs until you know them well enough to be able to do the next sequence without looking back. Then copy each one into your Reference Notebook so that you may study it for the test on this Unit.

17-60

352. D___ j____ j_____, f_____, __ p_____.

R: Deus jūdex jūstus, fortis, et patiēns. (51)

353. Oc___ s_____ am___ d____.

R: Oculī sunt in amōre ducēs. (50)

354. Cr_____ r__ a_____.

R: Crēdula rēs amor est. (55)

28-12

69. aperiō, aperīre, aperuī, apertus ★ ○ •

70. Time will disclose the truth = V_____ d___ ap_____.

R: Vēritātem diēs aperiet.

71. maneō, manēre, mānsī ★ ○ •

72. The written word will remain = L_____ sc____ m_____.

R: Littera scripta manēbit.

73. indicō, indicāre, indicāvī, indicātus ★ ○ •

74. Prepared tears were indicating an ambush = P_____ l_____ in_____ in_____.

R: Parātae lacrimae īnsidiās indicābant.

75. serviō, servīre, servīvī, servītus ★ ○ •

76. You are being a slave to your body = Tū c_____ s_____.

R: Tū corporī servīs.

77. quaerō, quaerere, quaesīvī, quaesītus ★ ○ •

78. You blind people had sought a leader = V__ c____ d____ qu_____.

R: Vōs caecī ducem quaesīverātis.

17-61

355. ⎯ ⎯ a ⎯ ⎯ m ⎯ ⎯ .

R: Vīta vīnum est.

356. F ⎯ ⎯ b ⎯ ⎯ fr ⎯ ⎯ ⎯ .

R: Forma bonum fragile est.

357. L ⎯ ⎯ s ⎯ ⎯ m ⎯ ⎯ ⎯ v ⎯ ⎯ ⎯ .

R: Lēgēs sine mōribus vānae. (56)

358. The suffixes **-ia** and **-tās** are used to form nouns from adjectives, like **avāritia** from **avārus** and **levitās** from ⎯ ⎯ ⎯ .

A: levis.

28-11

60. Fates had dragged the unwilling = F⎯ ⎯ n⎯ ⎯ ⎯ tr⎯ ⎯ ⎯ .

R: Fāta nōlentem trāxerant.

61. **capiō, capere, cēpī, captus** ★ ○ •

62. You caught two boars in one jump = Tū ⎯ ⎯ s ⎯ ⎯ ap ⎯ ⎯ c ⎯ ⎯ ⎯ d ⎯ ⎯ ⎯ .

R: Tū ūnō in saltū aprōs cēpistī duōs.

63. **pōnō, pōnere, posuī, positus** ★ ○ •

64. You will place a happy life in security of mind = Vōs b⎯ ⎯ ⎯ v⎯ ⎯ ⎯ in an⎯ ⎯ sē⎯ ⎯ ⎯ p⎯ ⎯ ⎯ .

R: Vōs beātam vītam in animī sēcūritāte pōnētis.

65. **stō, stāre, stetī** ★ ○ •

66. Everything stood under a fixed law = C⎯ ⎯ ⎯ st⎯ ⎯ ⎯ ⎯ om⎯ ⎯ l⎯ ⎯ ⎯ .

R: Certā stetērunt omnia lēge.

67. **habeō, habēre, habuī, habitus** ★ ○ •

68. You had black teeth = Tū h⎯ ⎯ ⎯ n⎯ ⎯ ⎯ d⎯ ⎯ ⎯ .

R: Tū habuistī nigrōs dentēs.

359. These suffixes form nouns like **avāritia** and **levitās** which express _____ions.

A: abstractions.

360. **Vānus, vāna, vānum** is the part of speech called an _____, while **vānitās** is a ____.

A: adjective noun

361. You also learned the adjectives **hic** and **ille**. **Hic vir** is the man who is _____ the speaker.

A: near to

362. **Ille vir** is the man who is _____ the speaker.

A: away from

363. Finally you had a review of 24 Basic Sentences by means of a _____ and _____ Drill.

A: Question and Answer Drill.

VOCABULARY INVENTORY

You learned the following nouns:

āctiō, f (177)	**intemperantia**, f (217)
amīcitia, f (231)	**īra**, f (114)
amor, m (59)	**levitās**, f (222)
ars, f (103)	**malitia**, f (207)
bonum, n (134)	**mōs**, m (157)
crūdēlitās, f (209)	**quālitās**, f (212)
dux, m (47-49)	**stultitia**, f (204)
furor, m (116)	**vānitās**, f (234)
homō, m & f (174)	**virtūs**, f (170-172)
īgnāvia, f (225)	***rēs**, f (146-149)

(From now on, an asterisk (*) in this list means a new meaning for a familiar word.)

53. ★ ○ •

quaesīverām	quaesīverāmus
quaesīverās	quaesīverātis
quaesīverat	quaesīverant

54-56. Finally, there are three #5 forms. Like the #4 forms, these are all conjugated alike except that the stems must be learned. Also, this is the only tense in Latin which has a special set of person endings.

54. ★ ○ •

habuī	habuimus
habuistī	habuistis
habuit	habuērunt

55. ★ ○ •

cēpī	cēpimus
cēpistī	cēpistis
cēpit	cēpērunt

56. ★ ○ •

stetī	stetimus
stetistī	stetistis
stetit	stetērunt

57-86. In this sequence, the principal parts of the verb which you will use have been given you; echo them first.

57. **bibō, bibere, bibī** ★ ○ •

58. Malice itself was drinking part of her own poison = M____ i____ p____ v____ s____ b____.

R: **Malitia ipsa partem venēni suī bibēbat.**

59. **trahō, trahere, trāxī, tractus** ★ ○ •

These adjectives:

avārus-a-um (198)	ille, illa, illud (240-255)
brevis-e (99-103)	jūstus-a-um (80-83)
crēdulus-a-um (149)	patiēns (80-84)
fragilis-e (137)	vānus-a-um (161)
hic, haec, hoc (239-255)	uter, utra, utrum (245)

And one verb: **amat** (60)

TEST INFORMATION

In this test you will be given tasks which were *similar* to those you performed in this Unit but not identical. For example, the paradigms you will be asked to produce will not be those which you have practiced in this Unit. However, they will be words with which you are familiar. The questions on Basic Sentences 1-56 will be new questions. There will be questions about new words, asking you to identify in Latin whether they refer to people, qualities, animals, etc. Some of these words will be unknown to you, but you should be able to figure out the meaning, as you were able to understand the meaning of the new word **vānitās**.

46-50. There are five #3 forms, one with the -bō, -bis, -bit endings and four with the -am, -ēs, -et endings.

46. ★ ○ •
neglegam   neglegēmus
neglegēs   neglegētis
negleget   neglegent

47. ★ ○ •
aspiciam   aspiciēmus
aspiciēs   aspiciētis
aspiciet   aspicient

48. ★ ○ •
pōnam   pōnēmus
pōnēs   pōnētis
pōnet   pōnent

49. ★ ○ •
aperiam   aperiēmus
aperiēs   aperiētis
aperiet   aperient

50. ★ ○ •
manēbō   manēbimus
manēbis   manēbitis
manēbit   manēbunt

51-53. There are three #4 forms; except for the fact that you have to know the active perfective stem, they are all conjugated exactly alike.

51. ★ ○ •
trāxeram   trāxerāmus
trāxerās   trāxerātis
trāxerat   trāxerant

52. ★ ○ •
fulseram   fulserāmus
fulserās   fulserātis
fulserat   fulserant

UNIT EIGHTEEN

We will take up here a point of structure which will be of great practical use to you, because it will permit you to recognize English derivatives whose meaning might otherwise escape you.

1. You will remember that in Unit Sixteen you learned that a form like **currēns** is the present participle of the verb _____.

R: currit.

2. Write from dictation. ★ ○ ○ V__ fl____ dē_____ asp____.

R: Vir flūmen dēfluēns aspicit.

3. Although you have never seen it before, you know that the form **dēfluēns** is the _____ _____ of the verb **dēfluit**.

A: present participle.

4. **Dēfluēns**, although a verb, modifies the noun **flūmen**; it is therefore both a v___ and a kind of ad_____.

A: verb adjective.

5. The word "participle" means "sharing," because a participle "shares" features of both a ____ and an _____.

A: verb   adjective.

Fāta regunt orbem; certā stant omnia lēge. (48)
Thāis habet nigrōs, niveōs Lacaenia dentēs. Quae ratiō est? Ēmptōs haec habet, illa suōs. (61)
Vēritātem diēs aperit. (2)
Vōx audīta perit, littera scrīpta manet. (57)
Parītae lacrimae īnsidiās, nōn flētum, indicant. (59)
Nēmō līber est quī corporī servit. (74)
Caecī ducem quaerunt; nōs sine duce errāmus. (107)
Nox erat, et caelō fulgēbat lūna serēnō inter minōra sīdera. (126)
Glōria umbra virtūtis est. (86)
Magna dī cūrant, parva neglegunt. (46)
Pūrās Deus, nōn plēnās, aspicit manūs. (44)

42–44. Here are the paradigms which contain the verb forms which you will use in this next sequence. First there are three #1 forms ("I was blanking.").

42. ★ ○ ●
bibēbam   bibēbāmus
bibēbās   bibēbātis
bibēbat   bibēbant

43. ★ ○ ●
indicābam   indicābāmus
indicābās   indicābātis
indicābat   indicābant

44. ★ ○ ●
eram   erāmus
erās   erātis
erat   erant

There is one #2 form ("I am blanking.").

45. ★ ○ ●
serviō   servīmus
servīs   servītis
servit   serviunt

18-2

6. Write your teacher's description of this picture. ★ ○ ○ **Virī lītigant.**

____ ____ ____ ____

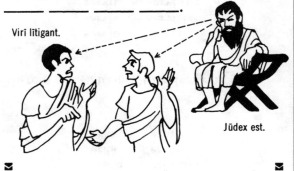

Virī lītigant.

Jūdex est.

R: Jūdex virōs lītigantēs aspicit.

7. Guess at the meaning of the new word. **Jūdex virōs lītigantēs aspicit** means that the ____ ___s the ____ ___.

A: judge sees the quarreling men.

8. Echo these forms of **neglegit**, including a *new* form. ★ ○ •
neglegit, neglegitur, neglegunt, negleguntur, neglegēns, neglēctus

9. The new form is _____.

R: neglēctus.

10. Echo your teacher's description of this picture. ★ ○ • J____ s___ c___ __ c___ n____.

Cōnf: Juvenis sīmiam cūrat sed canem neglegit.
[Be sure to answer aloud for all Latin answers.]

28-7

36. Aquila nōn capiet muscās. "Capiet" est temporis _____.

R: tertiī.

37. Malō in cōnsiliō fēminae vincunt virōs. "Vincunt" est temporis _____.

R: secundī.

38. Fortūna ignāvōs presserat. "Presserat" est temp_____.

R: temporis quārtī.

39. Quī prō innocente dīcet? "Dīcet" est t_____.

R: temporis tertiī.

40. Flōris odōrem nōn pinxerātis. "Pinxerātis" est t_____.

R: temporis quārtī.

As still another way of having you produce these five tenses, we will have you produce a Latin sentence from English. The sentences will be similar to Basic Sentences. Here are the sentences we will use. Read them once to refresh your mind.

41. Malitia ipsa maximam partem venēnī suī bibit. (82)

Dīcunt volentem Fāta, nōlentem trahunt. (45)

Jam egō ūnō in saltū lepidē aprōs capiam duōs. (121)

Nōs beātam vītam in animī sēcūritāte pōnimus. (108)

18-3

11. Ask your teacher what kind of dog this is. [Ask first, *then* check.] "Qu____ hic c_____?"
√ ★ ○ •

Cōnf: Quālis hic canis est?

12. Write his answer. ★ ○ ○ "_____ hic canis est."

R: Neglēctus hic canis est.

13. When you asked what kind of dog this was, he said that this dog was a n_____ dog.

A: neglected

14. Ask your teacher what kind of animal this monkey is. "____e an____ ___ haec s____?"
√ ★ ○ •

Cōnf: Quāle animal est haec sīmia?

15. Write his answer. ★ ○ ○ "_____ animal est."

R: Īrritātum animal est.

(The following items are printed upside-down at the bottom/right of the page:)

29. Cautus metuit foveam lupus. "Metuit" est vel temporis vel _____
R: secundī
quīntī.
(In other words, metuit is an ambiguous form.)

30. Nōn quaesīvistis medicum ēloquentem. "Quaesīvistis" est temporis _____
R: quīntī.

31. Necāveram spatiōsum taurum. "Necāveram" est temporis _____
R: quārtī.

32. Ā fonte pūrō pūra dēfluēbat aqua. "Dēfluēbat" est temporis _____
R: primī.

33. Auctor opus laudāverat. "Laudāverat" est temporis _____
R: quārtī.

34. Et genus et fōrmam dōnāvistī. "Dōnāvistī" est temporis _____
R: quīntī.

35. Mēns rēgnum bona possidēbat. "Possidēbat" est temporis _____
R: primī.

18-4

16. It turns out that the monkey is an _____ animal.

A: irritated

17. Pronounce "participle" and check.
√ ★ ○ •

VCh: "párt-tiss-sip-pull"

18. Latin verbs have another participle, which, like the present participle, also has a similar structure in English. Suppose that you are painting a table. When the job is done, then the table is _____ed.

A: painted.

19. This form "painted" is called the "past participle," while the form "painting" (as in the sentence "He saw the man painting") is called the _____ participle.

A: present

20. In the sentence "The discovered money was returned to the police," the word "discovered" is the _____ of the verb "discover."

A: past participle

21. In the sentence "The man discovering the money turned it over to the police," the word "discovering" is the _____ _____.

A: present participle.

22. Notice that the present participle (like "crying" in "The crying baby was soon comforted") is in the _____ voice.

A: active

28-5

23. Ingrātus ūnus omnibus miseris nocēbat = _____
√ ★ ○ •

A: One ungrateful person was harming all unhappy people.

24-40. We will give you another 15 Basic Sentences (with the tenses of the verb changed). Identify the tense of the verb.

24. Vestis virum reddet. "Reddet" est temporis ____ (prīmī/secundī/tertiī/quārtī/quīntī).

R: tertiī.

25. Vestis virum reddet = _____

A: Clothes will make the man.

26. Elephantus nōn capiet mūrem. "Capiet" est temporis ____ (prīmī/secundī/tertiī/quārtī/quīntī).

R: tertiī.

27. Lupus nōn momordit lupum. "Momordit" est temporis ____.

R: quīntī.

28. Cautī metuērunt foveam lupī. "Metuērunt" est temporis ____.

R: quīntī.

18-5

23. On the other hand, the past participle (like "comforted" in the above sentence) is in the _____ voice.

A: passive

24. The English forms "discovered" and "discovering" are also other forms of the verb "discover." For example, in the sentence "He discovered the money," the word "discovered" is a verb describing ____ (past/present/future) time.

A: past

25. In the sentence "The discovering of the money proved to be an unexpected difficulty," the word "discovering" works like a ____ (noun/verb/adjective).
(Auxilium hāc sub līneā est).

Aux: What slot does "The discovering of the money" fill?

A: noun.

26. In English spelling, the present participle is formed by adding the three letters "____" to the verb.

A: -ing

27. In English spelling, the past participle is formed by adding the two letters "__" to the verb.

A: -ed (The ending "-ed" is often pronounced "t" as in "The dishes are all wiped.")

28-4

16. Quī custōdīverunt ipsōs custōdēs? = ∨ ★ ○ •

A: Who guarded the guardians themselves?

17. Omnia mors poposcit = ∨ ★ ○ •

A: Death demanded everything.

18. Secūrī jūdicāvimus = ∨ ★ ○ •

A: We made our judgment with security.

19. Artēs serviēbant vītae = ∨ ★ ○ •

A: Arts were serving life.

20. Aut inveniēs viam aut faciēs = ∨ ★ ○ •

A: You are either making a way or finding one.

21. Hōrās nōn numerābitis = ∨ ★ ○ •

A: You won't number the hours.

22. Lūna nocturnōs rēxerat equōs = ∨ ★ ○ •

A: The moon had driven her horses of night.

18-6

28. There are, however, some English verbs in which this past participle does not have the signal "-ed." For example, the past participle of "break" is not "breaked" (except in the speech of a few people). Most of us would say, "The dish he dropped is now br_____."

A: broken (some might say "broke").

29. "Brought" is the past _____ of "bring."

A: participle

30. And the past participle of "buy" is "_____."

A: bought.

31. Listen to your teacher's question and then answer it. ★ ○ ○ "Qu__ fr_____ h___ a___?"

Cōnf: Quid frangit haec anus?

32. _____ frangit haec anus.

R: Effigiem

28-3

10. Quiēscent vōcēs hominum = ‒‒‒ ∨ ★ ○ •

A: The voices of men will become quiet.

11. In hōc signō vincēmus = ‒‒‒‒‒‒‒‒‒‒ ∨ ★ ○ •

A: In this sign we had conquered.

12. Fēcistī dē necessitāte virtūtem = ‒‒‒ ∨ ★ ○ •

A: You made a virtue of necessity.

13. Vidētis barbam et pallium = ‒‒‒‒‒‒‒‒ ∨ ★ ○ •

A: You are seeing the beard and the cloak.

14. Tempus abīre tibi erit = ‒‒‒‒‒‒‒‒‒‒ ∨ ★ ○ •

A: It will be time for you to depart.

15. Fidem cōnservāverātis = ‒‒‒‒‒‒‒‒‒‒‒‒ ∨ ★ ○ •

A: You had kept the faith.

18-7

33. Ask him what kind of statue this is. "Qu____ haec ef_____s est?" ✓ ★ ○ •

Cōnf: Quālis haec effigiēs est?

34. Write his answer. ★ ○ ○ "Haec effigiēs _____ est."

R: Haec effigiēs frācta est.

35. What kind of statue is this now? It's a _____ statue.

A: broken

            m   f   n

36. The word **frāctus, frācta, frāctum** is the form of the verb called the ____ _____.

A: past particle.

37. Listen to your teacher's question and then answer. ★ ○ ○ "Qu____ ef_____ v____ d___?"

Cōnf: Quālem effigiem videt dux?

38. **"Fr_____ ef______ v____ d__."**

R: **Frāctam effigiem videt dux.**

39. The past participle in Latin has ____ (1/2/3/4) different genders.

A: 3 (as you can see in the three forms **frāctus** [masculine], **frācta** [feminine], and **frāctum** [neuter])

40. Answer your teacher's question. ★ ○ ○
"Qu__ d__ l_____?"

Cōnf: Quem dux laudat?

41. "__________________________________."

R: **Auctōrem dux laudat.**

42. Ask your teacher what kind of author this is. **"Qu____ ___ hic ______?"** ✓ ★ ○ •

Cōnf: Quālis est hic auctor?

UNIT TWENTY-EIGHT

1. In this Unit we will take up a new tense of the Latin verb. Study the following diagram, which shows the tenses which we have already had.

	Past	Present	Future
Imperfective	**faciēbat** 1	**facit** 2	**faciet** 3
Perfective	? 4	**fēcit** 5	? 6

From the diagram you can see that the #4 tense is going to show completed action in ____ time.

A: past

2. Echo the five tenses. ★ ○ • ○ •

	Past	Present	Future
Imperfective	**faciēbat** 1	**facit** 2	**faciet** 3
Perfective	**fēcerat** 4	**fēcit** 5	? 6

3. Here is an example of the new #4 form. **Medicus erat crūdēlis. Intemperāns aeger hunc medicum crūdēlem fēcerat.** This says that the doctor was cruel because the intemperate sick person ___ ____ him cruel.

A: had made

4. That is, the new form **fēcerat** shows that the act of making the doctor cruel was ____ (completed/not completed) in ____ (past/present/future) time.

A: completed
past

18-9

43. Write his answer. ★ ○ ○ "_____ est hic auctor."

R: Laudātus est hic auctor.

44. He said that this author is a _____ author.

A: praised

45. Ask your teacher what this young man is doing. "Qu__ a___ hic j_____?" √ ★ ○ •

Cōnf: Quid agit hic juvenis?

46. Echo his answer. ★ ○ • ○ • "J_____ p_____ inv_____."

R: Juvenis pecūniam invenit.

47. Ask your teacher what this young man possesses. "Qu__ h__ j_____ poss___et?" √ ★ ○ •

Cōnf: Quid hic juvenis possidet?

TEST INFORMATION

You will be asked to give the #5 paradigm of the verbs which you practiced in this Unit. You will be asked for the principal parts of the 15 verbs which you practiced. You will be asked to recognize #5 forms which you have never seen, such as **Juvenis pecūniam pōposcit**: do you know what verb this must be?

As usual, you are responsible for constructing noun forms, even though you may never have seen or heard them.

ēripiō ēripere ēripuī ēreptus (319) take away
lūdō lūdere lūsī lūsus (248) play
ōdī (329) hate
rīdeō rīdēre (103) laugh/smile
servō (187) save
veniō venīre vēnī (17) come

Prepositions:
ad (2) inter (14) praeter (104) trāns (58) between across

Indeclinables:
nunc (279) sīc (41)

18-10

48. Write his answer. ★ ○ ○ "_____ hic juvenis possidet."

R: Inventam pecūniam hic juvenis possidet.

49. The young man possesses the f____ _____.

A: found money.

50. Since "the found money" sounds awkward in English, we should change it. Perhaps we could say, "The young man possesses the money wh___ he f_____."

A: which he found.

51. Ask your teacher what the young man is doing. "Q___ ____ _____?" ✓ ★ ○ •

Cōnf: Quid agit juvenis?

52. Echo his answer. ★ ○ • ○ • "J_____ s_____ _____."

R: Juvenis saccum aperit.

VOCABULARY INVENTORY

R: Aut amat aut ōdit mulier; nīl est tertium.

390. A. a__ a__ ō__ m____: n__ e__ t_____ (136)

Nouns:
ager, agrī, m (293) field
Caesar, Caesaris, m (268)
certāmen, certāminis, n (181) fight
cursus-ūs, m (184) race
fidēs, fideī, f (190)
Jūlius, Jūliī, m (268)
labor, labōris, m (314)
nīl, n (nom and acc cases only) (310)
Paulus-ī, m (198)
praepositiō, praepositiōnis, f (6)
sīdus, sīderis, n (72) shooting star
*tempus, temporis, n (259)
timor, timōris, m (164)
urbs, urbis, f (296) city

Adjectives:
dīvīnus-a-um (290)
minor, minus (genitive minōris) (76)
sānctus-a-um (198) saint
*serēnus-a-um (76) clear
siccus-a-um (34) dry
sobrius-a-um (39) sober
vester, vestra, vestrum (276) your

Verbs:
abeō abīre abiī (irregular) (240) depart
aedificō (296) build
certō (181) fight
cōnsūmō (181) finish
edō edere ēdī ēsus (245) eat
eō īre iī (7) go

18-11

53. Ask your teacher what kind of sack the thief is finding. "Qu____ s____ in____ ___."
✓ ★ ○ •

Cōnf: Quālem saccum invenit fūr?

54. Echo his answer. ★ ○ • ○ • "Ap____ s____ in____ ___."

R: Apertum saccum invenit fūr.

55. The thief is finding an _____ sack.

A: opened

56. You now know that in the sentence **Vēritātem diēs aperit,** the verb **aperit** meant "_____s," but in the sentence **Juvenis saccum aperit** the verb **aperit** means "_____."

A: discloses   opens.

57. That is, **aperit** means "opens" when used with things like bags. Do you suppose you could use **aperit** in the sense of "He opened the meeting"? ____ (Yes/No/Can't tell).

A: Can't tell.

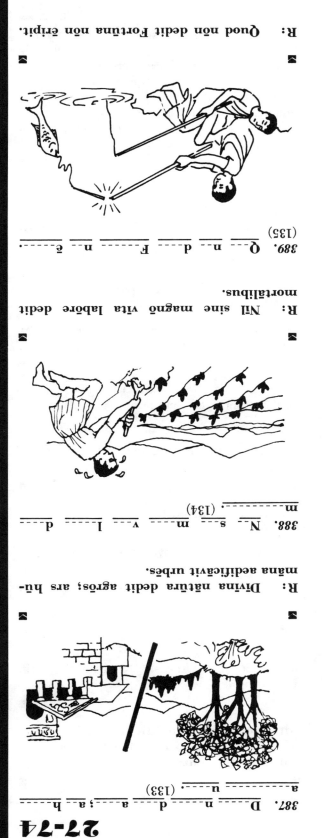

387. D___ n___ d___ a___; a___ h___ m___ a___ u___. (133)

R: Divina nātūra dedit agrōs; ars hūmāna aedificāvit urbēs.

388. N___ s___ m___ v___ l___ d___ m___. (134)

R: Nil sine magnō vita labōre dedit mortālibus.

389. Q___ n___ d___ F___ n___ ē___. (135)

R: Quod nōn dedit Fortūna nōn ēripit.

58. We bring in the past participle at this time because the English derivative which would help you remember the Latin verb is more often formed on the past participle stem than on the stem to which the endings **-t, -tur, -nt, -ntur,** and **-ns** are added. For example, the English word "possess" is formed on the stem of _____ **(possidet/possessus).**

R: possessus.

59. Possessus is the _____ of **possidet.**

A: past participle

60. From **vīsus,** the past participle of **videt,** we have the English word "tele_____."

A: television. (The "tele-" part is from Greek and means "at a distance.")

61. Inventus must be the past participle of the Latin verb _____.

A: invenit.

62. A man who discovers things is an "_____."

A: inventor.

63. Pronounce English "inventor," Latin **inventor.** ★ ○ ● ○ ●

64. The Latin word **inventor** is formed by adding the ending **-or** to the stem of _____. **(inveniēns/inventus).**

R: inventus.

18-13

65. The English words that end in "-ate" are also formed on this past participial stem. For example, the English word "donate" comes from the Latin form ____ (dōnāns/dōnātus).

R: dōnātus.

66. "Irritate" comes from the Latin form _____.

R: irrītātus.

67. On the other hand, the English word "irritant" comes from the Latin form _____.

R: irrītāns.

68. The verb **neglegit** has another spelling, **negligit**. The English word "negligent" comes from the Latin form _____.

R: **neglegēns** (or **negligēns**).

69. The English word "neglect" comes from the Latin form _____.

R: **neglēctus.**

70. This past participle stem is also productive in furnishing Latin nouns. For example, you can now figure out that the unknown Latin word **possessiō** must mean "_____."

A: possession.

71. If you have the misfortune to break your leg we say that you have suffered a fr_____ of the leg.

A: fracture

---

381. I____ t____ mihi p____ a____ r____ (127)

R: Ille terrārum mihi praeter omnēs angulus rīdet.

382. P____ o____ d____ f____ t____ (128)

R: Prīmus in orbe deōs fēcit timor.

383. B____ c____ c____ c____ f____ s____ (129)

R: Bonum certāmen certāvī, cursum cōnsummāvī, fidem servāvī.

18-14

72. "Fracture" does not come directly from **frāctus** but from the Latin word **frāctūra**, which is in turn formed from the _____ **frāctus**.

▼

A: past participle

73. ★ ○ • ○ • English "aperture," Latin **apertūra**.

▼

74. An "aperture" in English is an opening, as in a camera lens. The unknown Latin word **apertūra** is formed on the past participle form of **aperit** and means an "_____ing."

▼

A: opening.

75. The past participle of **aperit** is _____.

▼

R: apertus.

76. Here is another look at how words are formed. You have acquired the ability to identify forms which you have never seen before. For example, you have never seen the form **apertūra**, but you know that it is _____ case and _____ number.

▼

A: ablative
singular

77. You could identify it, although you had never seen it before, because _____.
[In your own words]

▼

A: you have practiced so many other First Declension nouns that you could recognize the form as ablative singular.

378-390. Write the Basic Sentences which the following 13 pictures suggest. Review first in your Notebook if you like.

378. "S_____ Q_____ A_____ m_____?"
S_____ s_____ e_____ l_____ n_____ a_____. (124)

R: "Siccus, sobrius est Aper." Quid ad me?
Servum sic ego laudō, nōn amīcum.

379. C_____ n_____ a_____ m_____ qui tr_____ m_____ c_____. (125)

R: Caelum, nōn animum, mūtant quī trāns mare currunt.

380. N_____ e_____, et c_____ f_____ l_____ i_____ m_____ s_____. (126)

R: Nox erat, et caelō fulgēbat lūna serēnō inter minōra sīdera.

27-12

78. In much the same way, you will not have to learn as separate items all the Latin words you will meet. It will be enough to be able to identify the different "building blocks" out of which the words are built. For example, once you knew that the Latin word **sānus** meant "sound," it was easy to determine that **īnsānus** meant "_____."

A: unsound (or "crazy").

79. The "building block" **in-** means "___."

A: not (or "un-").

80. Because all Latin vowels are long before **-ns**, **in-** plus **sānus** becomes _____.

R: **īnsānus** (with the **ī** long).

81. Sometimes these building blocks (this seems like the best term to describe them) change form, like **in-** becoming **īn-** in **īnsānus**. For example, when **in-** is added to **pūrus**, the form is not *****inpūrus** but _____.

R: **impūrus**.

82. Most of these changes are familiar to you in English because English has borrowed these words from _____.

A: Latin.

83. Something added at the beginning of a word is called a pr___x.

A: prefix.

---

370. **edō** ___ ___ ___
R: **edō edere ēdī ēsus**

371. **lūdō** _____ ____ _____
R: **lūdō lūdere lūsī lūsus**

372. **eō** ___ ___
R: **eō īre iī**

373. **sum** ____ ___
R: **sum esse fuī**

374. **veniō** ____ ____
R: **veniō venīre vēnī**

375. **videō** _____ ____ _____
R: **videō vidēre vīdī vīsus**

376. **vincō** _____ ____ _____
R: **vincō vincere vīcī victus**

377. **ēripiō** _____ _____ _____
R: **ēripiō ēripere ēripuī ēreptus**

18-16

84. Additions are also made at the *ends* of words. Echo a new technical term. ★ ○ • ○ •
suffix

▼

VCh: "súff-fix"

85. In the last unit we practiced making abstract nouns out of adjectives. **Stultus** means "stupid" (or "stupid person" when used as a noun). The abstract noun **stultitia** means "_____ity."

▼

A: stupidity.

86. While the **in-** in **incertus** is a *pre*fix, the **-tia** in **stultitia** is a "_____."

▼

A: suffix.

87. Pronounce "prefix," "suffix." √ ★ ○ •

▼

VCh: "prée-fix," "súff-fix"

88. An element added to the *end* of a word (like the **-tās** of **crūdēlitās**) is called a _____.

▼

A: suffix.

89. An element added to the *beginning* of a word (like the **ob-** in **obumbrat**) is called a _____.

▼

A: prefix.

In this sequence are some new nouns with familiar stems but new suffixes. Try to figure out from the picture what the new words mean.

363-377. Say the principal parts of the 15 verbs that you had. Repeat until you have learned them perfectly. Write them out if necessary.

363. faciō f_ ____ _____
R: faciō facere fēcī factus

▼

364. cōnsumō _____ _____
R: cōnsumō cōnsumāre cōnsumāvī cōnsumātus

▼

365. servō _____ _____ _____
R: servō servāre servāvī servātus

▼

366. laudō _____ _____ _____
R: laudō laudāre laudāvī laudātus

▼

367. dō ____ ____ _____
R: dō dare dedī datus

▼

368. currō _____ _____
R: currō currere cucurrī

▼

369. bibō ____ _____ ____
R: bibō bibere bibī

27-69

SUMMARY

357. This unit covered two different points of structure. The first was a new use of the accusative case. You learned that besides being the object of a verb the accusative case can m___fy a verb.

A: modify

358. When an accusative modifies a verb it is preceded by a pr_____.

A: preposition.

359. The prepositions which pattern with the accusative which you met in this lesson are _____ [Give as many as you can.]

A: ad, trāns, inter, praeter. [Count yourself right if you gave two.]

360. The rest of the unit introduced you to the tense which has a special set of endings, which is number ____.

A: 5.

361. You learned that verbs have ____ (1/2/3/4/5) different stems.

A: three

362. These three stems are shown by four different forms called the pr_____ p__s of the verb.

A: principal parts

---

90. Ask your teacher who that man is. "Qu__ ___ ill_ v__?" ✓ ★ ○ •

Cōnf: Quis est ille vir?

91. Write his answer. ★ ○ ○ "Ille vir est _____."

R: Ille vir est captor.

92. Ille vir est captor = ____ ___ is one who _____ something.

A: That man is one who catches something.

93. Ask your teacher who that young man is. "Qu__ ___ ____ j_____?" ✓ ★ ○ •

Cōnf: Quis est ille juvenis?

94. Write his answer. ★ ○ ○ "Ille juvenis _____ est."

R: Ille juvenis dōnātor est.

18-18

95. Ille juvenis dōnātor est = ____ ____ ___ __ ___ ___ _____ _____.

A: That young man is one who gives something.

96. Ask your teacher who that leader is. "____ ___ ____ ___?" √ ★ ○ •

Cōnf: Quis est ille dux?

97. Write his answer. ★ ○ ○ "Ille dux _____ est."

R: Ille dux laudātor est.

98. Ille dux laudātor est = ____ _____ __ ___ ___ _____ _____.

A: That leader is one who praises something.

99. The Latin suffix **-or** means "_____ _____."

A: "one who does the action."

100. This suffix **-or** is added to the ____ _____ stem of the verb.

A: past participle

---

349. ven- i- e-

Cōnf: veniō venīre vēnī

350. cōnsum-

Cōnf: cōnsumō cōnsumāre cōnsumāvī cōnsummātus

351. sum ee f

Cōnf: sum esse fuī

352. vinc- e i-

Cōnf: vincō vincere vīcī victus

353. fac- e- ē- a

Cōnf: faciō facere fēcī factus

354. ērip- e u e

Cōnf: ēripiō ēripere ēripuī ēreptus

355. vid e i is

Cōnf: video vidēre vīdī vīsus

356. edō e ē ēs

Cōnf: edō edere ēdī ēsus

[If you made any errors, go back over this sequence until you can say the principal parts of these fifteen verbs perfectly.]

18-19

101. **Quaesītus** is the past participle of the verb ‑‑‑‑‑‑‑.

R: quaerit.

102. The unknown word **quaesītor** must mean "‑‑‑ ‑‑‑ ‑‑‑‑‑ ‑‑‑‑‑‑‑‑‑‑."

A: "one who seeks something" (or "a seeker").

103. Here is another suffix. Ask your teacher what action that is. "**Quae āc‑‑‑‑ ill‑ ‑‑‑?**"
✓ ★ ○ •

Cōnf: Quae āctiō illa est?

104. Write his answer. ★ ○ ○ "Illa āctiō ‑‑‑‑‑‑ est."

R: Illa āctiō dōnātiō est.

105. Illa āctiō dōnātiō est = ‑‑‑‑ ‑‑‑‑‑‑ is the act of ‑‑‑ing.

A: That action is the act of giving.

27-66

342-356. You have practiced the principal parts of 15 different verbs; some of them will occur on the test. This next sequence will give you extra practice on them. If you feel you do not need this practice, go directly to the Summary. Otherwise continue for 15 more frames.

Say aloud the principal parts of these verbs and check.

342. lūdō l‑‑e‑‑ l‑s‑ l‑s‑‑

Cōnf: lūdō lūdere lūsī lūsus

343. dō ‑a‑‑ d‑d‑ da‑‑‑

Cōnf: dō dare dedī datus

344. laudō ‑‑‑āre ‑‑‑v‑ ‑‑‑‑t‑

Cōnf: laudō laudāre laudāvī laudātus

345. eō i‑‑ ī

Cōnf: eō īre iī

346. bib‑ ‑‑e‑ ‑‑‑

Cōnf: bibō bibere bibī

347. serv‑ ‑‑‑‑‑‑ ‑‑‑‑‑‑ ‑‑‑‑‑‑‑‑

Cōnf: servō servāre servāvī servātus

348. curr‑ ‑‑‑‑ ‑‑e‑ ‑‑ cuc‑‑‑ ‑‑‑ ‑‑‑ ‑‑cu‑‑‑ ‑‑‑ono

Cōnf: currō currere cucurrī

18-20

106. Ask your teacher what action that is. "Qu__ āc__ ___ ___ ___?" ✓ ★ ○ •

Cōnf: Quae āctiō illa est?

107. Write his answer. ★ ○ ○ "Illa āctiō _____ est."

R: Illa āctiō lavātiō est.

108. Illa āctiō lavātiō est = ____ ___ __ ___ ___ __ _____.

A: That action is the act of washing.

109. Ask your teacher what action that is. "Qu__ ___ ___ ___?" ✓ ★ ○ •

Cōnf: Quae āctiō illa est?

110. Write his answer. ★ ○ ○ "Illa āctiō _____ est."

R: Illa āctiō quaestiō est.

---

337. Echo the paradigm of this new verb, in the #5 form. ★ ○ ○ •

ōdī   ōdimus
ōdistī   ōdistis
ōdit   ōdērunt

338. Ōdī means ____ ("I now hate"/"I hated in the past").

A: I now hate (that is, I have learned to hate).

339. This sentence Aut amat aut ōdit mulier: nil est tertium is by our old friend P_____ S____us.

340. Before you think too harshly of poor Publilius Syrus, remember that these are quotations taken from his plays and that they may not represent his views but the views of _____ [In your own words].

A: people who are talking in the plays.

341. A__ a___ a__ ō___ m_____: n__ e__ t_____. (136)

R: Aut amat aut ōdit mulier: nil est tertium.

18-21

111. Illa āctiō quaestiō est = _____ _____.

A: That action is the act of seeking.

112. In the word **dōnātiō** the suffix **-iō** is added to the _____ stem of the verb **dōnat**.

A: past participle

113. The past participle stem of **dōnat** is _____.

A: **dōnātus**.

114. The suffix which means "act of" is _____.

A: **-iō**.

115. The unknown word **laudātiō** must mean "the ___ of _____."

A: act of praising.

116. The unknown word **obumbrātiō** must mean "_____."

A: the act of overshadowing.

117. The English derivative of **dōnātiō** is "_____."

A: donation.

118. The Latin suffix meaning "act of" is **-iō**; the English suffix is "___."

A: -ion.

---

330. Copy in your Notebook.

331. The reason that you were able to figure out the meaning of **ōdit** was that the context made it clear that **ōdit** was an _____ of **amat**.

A: antonym

332. The opposite of "loves" is "_____."

A: hates.

R: oppōnitur

333. To say the same thing in Latin: "Amat," "ōdit." do _____.

A: hates.

334. There is a curious thing about this verb **ōdit**. It occurs only in the perfective system. The #5 form **ōdit** means, "she has learned to hate," and therefore she now "___s___."

A: hates.

335. In other words, even though it is the #5 form, it has the same meaning as the #___ form.

A: 2

336. This is clear when we recall this last Basic Sentence, where **ōdit** (#5) was connected by **aut** with the #2 verb ____.

A: **amat**.

18-22

119. English words which end in the sound "shun" or "zhun" like "attention," "invention," "occasion," and the like are all derived from a Latin word with the suffix ___.

A: -iō.

120. The English word "litigant" means "someone who is engaged in a ___ s___."

A: law suit.

121. "Litigant" is derived from the participle ____ (lītigāns/lītigātus).

A: lītigāns.

122. The word "litigation" means "the ___ of being in a ___ ___."

A: act of being in a law suit.

123. The word "litigation" is derived from the participle ____ (lītigāns/lītigātus).

A: lītigātus.

124. Is the word "giving" an action or a person? ___.

A: It is an action.

125. Is the word "giver" an action or a person? ___.

A: It is a person.

27-63

326. "Sī ego magnam pecūniam habeō, quantum āmittere possum?" "Tū m___ p___ am___ p___."

R: Tū magnam pecūniam āmittere potes.

327. Qu___ n___ d___ F___ n___ ē___. (135)

R: Quod nōn dedit Fortūna nōn ēripit.

328. ✶ ○ ○ ○ am___ ō___ m___; (136) n___ t t___.

R: Aut amat aut ōdit mulier: nīl est tertium.

329. (Ōdit is a new word; we will ask you to figure out the meaning.) This sentence means, "A w___ either l___ or h___: th___ is ___ c___se."

A: A woman either loves or hates: there is no third course.

18-23

126. We will now do the same thing in Latin: are these Latin words actions (ending in **-iō**) or persons (ending in **-or**)?
"Estne 'laudātiō' āctiō an homō?" " 'Laudātiō' _____ est."

R: "Laudātiō" āctiō est.

127. "Estne 'laudātor' āctiō an homō?"
"_____."

R: "Laudātor" homō est.

128. "Estne 'dōnātor' āctiō an homō?"
"_____."

R: "Dōnātor" homō est.

129. "Estne 'captor' āctiō an homō?"
"_____."

R: "Captor" homō est.

130. "Estne 'quaestiō' āctiō an homō?"
"_____."

R: "Quaestiō" āctiō est.

131. Most Fourth Declension nouns are formed on the past participle stem of verbs and mean "act of." For example, the noun **saltus** comes from the verb **salit** which means "leap." **Saltus** therefore means "the ___ of _____."

A: act leaping.

---

319. Echo the principal parts of a verb that means "take away." ★ ○ ● ○ **ēripiō ēripere ēripuī ēreptus**

320. From these principal parts, it is obvious that this is an ___ verb of the _____ Conjugation.

A: **-iō** Third

321. It has probably become obvious to you that although there are four different conjugations in the imperfective action system, verbs in the _____ system are all conjugated the s___ way.

A: perfective same

322. Quod nōn dedit Fortūna, nōn ēripit = "F___ d___ n___ t___ a___ wh___ she h___ n___ g___."

A: Fortune does not take away what she has not given.

323. Copy in your Notebook.

324. This means that if you don't have very much, you can't _____.

A: lose very much.

Quaestiōnēs et Respōnsa

325. "Sī nil habēs, quantum tū āmittere potes?" "Egō n__ ām_____ p_____."

R: Egō nil āmittere possum.

18-24

132. The great majority of Fourth Declension nouns are formed on the ____ _____ stem of verbs and mean "the ___ of doing something."

A: past participle
 act

133. "Quid agit vīpera?" "V_____ t_____ m_____."

R: Vīpera taurum mordet.

134. "Quae āctiō est?" "Mor___ est."

R: Morsus est.

135. From the noun **morsus** you might guess
that the past participle of **mordet** is ____us, m
 f   n
_____, ____um.

R: m
 morsus,
 f   n
morsa, morsum.

136. This past participle **morsus** means
"_____."

A: bitten.

19-27

Quaestiōnēs et Respōnsa

315. "Quantum Fortūna nōbīs dōnāvit sine magnō labōre?" "_____."

R: Nīl.

316. "Estne nōbīs vīta facilis an difficilis?"
"_____."

R: Difficilis.

317. N___ s___ m___ v___ l___ d___ mo_____. (134)

R: Nīl sine magnō vītā labōre dedit mortālibus.

318. ★ ○ ○ ○ Qu__ n__ d__ F__ n__ ēr____. (135)

R: Quod nōn dedit Fortūna nōn ēripit.

18-25

137. Use the past participle of **mordet** to describe the thief. **"Quālis fūr est?"** **"M_____ f__ ___."**

R: **Morsus fūr est.**

138. When you were asked what kind of thief it was, you answered that it was a _____ thief.

A: bitten

139. ★ ○ •   aspectus   aspectūs
                 aspectum   aspectūs
                 aspectū   aspectibus

140. This is a new word. From the paradigm you know that it belongs to the ____ (1st/2d/3d/4th/5th) Declension.

A: 4th

141. This is a harder task. The unknown word **aspectus** means "_____."

A: the act of seeing (or "sight").

---

309. If **magnō** modifies a noun, draw an arrow on your answer pad from **magnō** to the noun it modifies. If it does not modify any noun, say so.

A: **Nīl sine magnō vītā dedit mortālibus.**

310. **Nīl** is a neuter noun meaning "nothing." When we say that someone's contribution is "nīl," we mean that he has contributed _____

A: nothing.

311. **Nīl sine magnō vītā labōre dedit mortālibus** = _____.

A: Life has given nothing to mortals without great effort (labor, etc.).

312. Copy in your Notebook.

313. In the next frame you will be asked to write the paradigm of **labor**, a word which you have not seen until now. How can you be expected to produce forms which you have never seen or heard? The answer is that _____ [In your own words]

A: You know that it is a Third Declension noun and will be declined like **dolor, dator, amor,** etc.

314. Write the complete paradigm of **labor**. (The o is long in all forms except the nominative singular.)

R: labor   labōrēs
   labōrem   labōrēs
   labōre   labōribus
   labōrī   labōribus
   labōris   labōrum

18-26

142. Write your teacher's description of this picture. ★ ○ ○ "_____."

Cōnf: Īnfāns flet.

143. He said that the ____ is _____.

A: _____ baby is crying.

144. Ask him what the action in that picture is. "Qu__ āc___ illā in pictūrā ___?" √ ★ ●

Cōnf: Quae āctiō illā in pictūrā est?

145. Write his answer. ★ ○ ○ "Āctiō est _____."

R: _____ Āctiō est flētus.

146. Flētus appears to mean "_____."

A: _____ the act of weeping (crying).

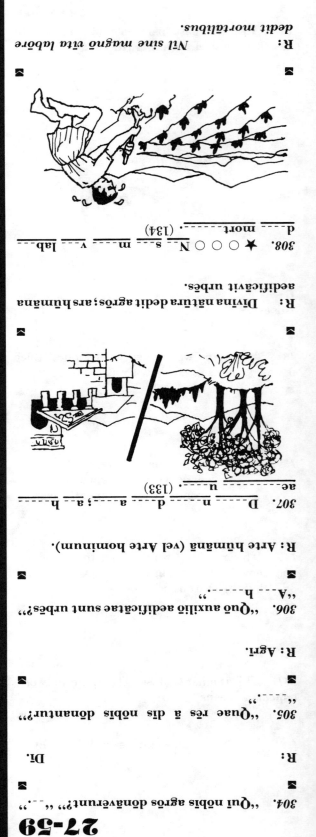

304. "Qui nobis agrōs dōnāvērunt?" "__..."

R: Dī.

305. "Quae rēs ā dīs nōbīs dōnantur?" "_____."

R: Agrī.

306. "Quō auxiliō aedificātae sunt urbēs?" "A____ h____."

R: Arte hūmānā (vel Arte hominum).

307. D____ n____ d____ a____; a____ h____ u____ (133) ae____.

R: Divīna nātūra dedit agrōs; ars hūmāna aedificāvit urbēs.

308. N ○ ○ ○ ★ s____ m____ v____ lab____ d____ mort____. (134)

R: Nīl sine magnō vītā labōre dedit mortālibus.

18-27

147. Of course you can't be sure, but considering what we have been telling you, you would say that the chances are good that **flētus** is the same declension as ____ (taurus/corpus/morsus).

R: morsus.

148. And you would be right. You suspected that it was Fourth Declension because it described an _____ and because it was formed on a stem of the verb ____.

A: action
              flet.

149. The verb **dīcit** means "says." The Latin past participial form which means "said" is ____um. (Hāc sub līneā invenītur auxilium.)

Aux: You have had this word in the neuter form used as a noun in the Basic Sentence **Rem, nōn spem, factum nōn _____, quaerit amīcus.**

R: dictum

150. The past participle of **facit** is _____.

A: factus.

151. Dictus = ____; factus = ____.

A: said   made.

152. We will now take up the numbers which show in what order things are. Echo your teacher as he counts in Latin, "First animal, second animal, third animal, fourth animal." ★ ○ • ○ •
animal prīmum, animal secundum, animal tertium, animal quārtum.

27-58

297. ★ ○ ○ D____ n____ d____ ag____; a____ h____ ae____ ur____. (133)

R: **Divīna nātūra dedit agrōs; ars hūmāna aedificāvit urbēs.**

298. This means that _____.

A: Divine nature gave the fields; human skill built the cities.

299. Copy in your Notebook.

300. Echo the paradigm of **ager**, first in the singular, then in the plural. ★ ● ○ ● ○

Cōnj: ager   agrī
       agrum   agrōs
       agrō   agrīs
       agrō   agrīs
       agrī   agrōrum

Quaestiōnēs et Respōnsa

301. "Cujus dōnātiō sunt agrī?" "D_____."

R: Dīvīnae nātūrae.

302. "Utrī urbēs fēcērunt, hominēs vel dī?" "_____."

R: Hominēs.

303. "Quōrum arte aedificātae sunt urbēs?" "____ ho____."

R: Arte hominum.

18-28

153-156. Echo your teacher as he describes this series of animals.

153. 154. 155. 156.

I	II	III	IV
Agnus est animal prīmum.	Leō est animal secundum.	Sīmia est animal tertium.	Equus est animal quārtum.

157-160. Describe this series of animals in the same way.

I II III IV

157. M____ ___ an____ pr____.

R: Musca est animal prīmum.

158. As____ ___ _____ s_____.

R: Asinus est animal secundum.

159. El_____ ___ _____ t_____.

R: Elephantus est animal tertium.

160. V_____ ___ _____ qu_____.

R: Vīpera est animal quārtum.

---

291. It is an increasingly important part of your job to be able to figure out the meaning of unknown words. This Basic Sentence contains four words which you have not had. However, you ought to be able to make reasonable guesses as to what they mean.

Let us take the first kernel. **Nātūra dedit** means that _____ _____ something.

A: nature gave something.

292. **Divīna nātūra dedit** means that _____ _____ _____.

A: divine nature gave something.

293. The new word **agrōs** is _____ case, _____ and _____ of the verb **dedit**.

A: accusative, object

294. Recalling the word "*agriculture*," you can perhaps figure out that **Divīna nātūra dedit agrōs** = _____ _____ _____ _____.

A: Divine nature gave the fields.

295. In the next clause, we see that divine nature is contrasted with _____ sk____.

A: human skill.

296. The question now arises: if divine nature gave the fields, what was it that human skill did? It _____ the _____ s. [**Auxilium invenītur sub hāc līneā.**]

Aux: A building in English is sometimes called an "edifice." Remembering that **ae** in Latin becomes **e** in English, you should be able to figure out what the verb **aedificāvit** means. Also, "urban" people are people who live in cities.

A: It built the cities.

161-164. Describe this series of people in the same way.

161. M_____ ___ homō ____us.

R: Medicus est homō prīmus.

162. Dux ___ h___ _____.

R: Dux est homō tertius.

163. Īn____ ___ ____ _____.

R: Īnfāns est homō quārtus.

164. F__ ___ ____ _____.

R: Fūr est homō secundus.

165. All four of these new adjectives have English derivatives. The "prime minister" is the _____ minister in the cabinet.

A: first

166. A "quarter" is one _____ of something.

A: fourth

167. Something that is of "secondary" importance takes _____ place to something that is of primary importance.

A: second

18-30

168. You can probably figure out that something which is "tertiary" is something that belongs in the ___ order of things.

A: third

169. Echo a new question word. ★ ○ • ○ •
Quotus?, Quota?, Quotum?

170. The word **Quotus?** is easy to use in Latin but hard to translate into English. It means "Which?" in the sense of "Which in the series?" and gets as an answer such numbers as **prīmus, secundus, tertius,** and **quārtus.** Echo your teacher as he asks, "Which human being is the baby?"

★ ○ • ○ • "**Quotus homō est īnfāns?**"

I   II   III   IV

171. Echo his answer. "___ ___ ___." ★ ○ • ○ •

Cōnf: **Tertius homō est īnfāns.**

172. Ask him which human being is the doctor. "Qu__us h___ m___?" √ ★ ○ •

Cōnf: **Quotus homō est medicus?**

173. Echo his answer. "___ ___." ★ ○ • ○ •

Cōnf: **Prīmus homō est medicus.**

---

281. This means that your friend was formerly very ___ but is now very ___.

A: unimportant (insignificant) important (successful, etc.).

Quaestiōnēs et Respōnsa

282. "**Quantus fuit tempore praeteritō amīcus, parvus an magnus?**" "___."

R: **Parvus.**

283. "**Quantus tempore praesentī est noster amīcus?**" "___."

R: **Magnus.**

284. "**Cui animālī similis fuit tempore praeteritō noster amīcus?**" "___."

R: **Rānae.**

285. "**Cui hominī similis est hōc tempore noster amīcus?**" "___."

R: **Rēgī.**

286. Echo the name of a new part of speech. ★ ○ • ○ • **s u b s t i t u t o r**

287. Because the indeclinable word **nunc** substitutes for the ablative phrase **hōc tempore praesentī, nunc** is a part of speech which we call a ___.

A: substitutor.

18-31

174. The Latin adjective **Quotus?, Quota?, Quotum?** means "Which? (of a numbered set)." It gets as an answer such words as **prīmus** ("first"), **secundus** ("second"), **tertius** ("third"), or _____.

A: quārtus.

175. Your teacher will ask you in which circle one of the animals is. ★ ○ ○

Prīmus orbis   Secundus orbis   Tertius orbis   Quārtus orbis

Cōnf: Quotō in orbe agnus est?

176. Write your answer. "_____ in orbe _____ est."

R: Secundō in orbe agnus est.

177. Ask your teacher which numbered circle the eagle is in. "___tō in or__ aqu___ ___?" √ ★ •

Cōnf: Quotō in orbe aquila est?

178. Write his answer. ★ ○ ○ "_____ aquila est."

R: Quārtō in orbe aquila est.

---

274. "Anus nōn est puella, sed p_____."

R: puella esse vult.

275. "Rāna nōn est rēx, sed _____."

R: rēx esse vult.

276. ★ ○ ○ ○ A____, v____, f____ n___ r___. (132)

R: *Amīcus vester, quī fuit rāna, nunc est rēx.*

277. "Nunc" significat tempor- praesent-.

R: tempore praesenti.

278. "Nostrum" est "quod nōs possidē___."

R: quod nōs possidēmus.

279. *Amīcus vester, quī fuit rāna, nunc est rēx* = _____.

A: Your friend, who was a frog, is now a king.

280. Copy in your Notebook.

18-32

| Prīmus | Secundus | Tertius | Quārtus |
| orbis | orbis | orbis | orbis |

179. Echo the Latin word for "Well done!"
★ ○ • ○ • Bene!

180. You will ask your teacher in which numbered circles different animals are. If he is right, you will compliment him by saying, "-----."

A: Bene!

181. Teachers are not always right, you know. But he will be right this first time, so be ready to praise him. Ask him in which circle the fox is and check. "Qu--- in ---- v------ ---?"
√ ★ ○ •

Cōnf: Quotō in orbe vulpēs est?

182. Listen to his answer and tell him he is right. ★ ○ ○ "B---! ----- in ---- v------ ---."

R: Bene! Prīmō in orbe vulpēs est.

183. This time I am afraid he may make a mistake. If he does, you say sternly, "Minimē!" and then give the correct answer. Ask him in which circle the donkey is and check your question. "-------------------------?"
√ ★ ○ •

Cōnf: Quotō in orbe asinus est?

Quaestiōnēs et Respōnsa

268. "Quid ēgit Jūlius Caesar?" "------, ------, ------."

R: Vēnit, vīdit, vīcit.

269. "Quālis victōria Caesaris fuit, facilis an difficilis?" "------."

R: Facilis.

270. V------, v------, v------.

R: Vēnī, vīdī, vīcī. (131)

271. Echo the principal parts for the irregular verb meaning "to be." ★ ○ ○ • sum esse fuī

272-275. This sequence will say that the person is not such and such but he *wants* to be.

272. "Stultus nōn est philosophus sed philosophus esse ------."

R: vult.

273. "Juvenis nōn est jūdex, sed jūdex es------."

R: vult.

18-33

| Prīmus | Secundus | Tertius | Quārtus |
| orbis | orbis | orbis | orbis |

184. Now listen to his answer. ★ ○ ○

Cōnf: Secundō in orbe asinus est.

185. Tsk, Tsk! Tell him the right answer and don't be gentle about it either. (He should know better.) "M_____; _____ in ____ _____ ___!!!"

R: Minimē; tertiō in orbe asinus est!!!

186. Listen to your teacher's comment. ★ ○

(We couldn't print it.)

187. You seem to have hurt his feelings, so if he's right this time, try to sound encouraging. If he's wrong, be a little more tactful about telling him the right answer. Ask him in which circle the lamb is. "Qu___ in ____ _____ ___?" √ ★ ○ •

Cōnf: Quotō in orbe agnus est?

188. Listen to his answer and see if it is correct. ★ ○ ○

Cōnf: Quārtō in orbe agnus est.

189. Now give the appropriate answer, depending on whether his answer was right or wrong: "B___! _____ in or__ ag___ ___t." or "M____! _____ in or__ ag___ ___t."

R: Minimē! Secundō in orbe agnus est.

27-52

262. Lū___ s___, ēd___ s___ at___ bib___; tem___ ab___ t___ ___t. (130)

R: Lūsistī satis, ēdistī satis atque bibistī; tempus abīre tibi est.

263. ★ ○ ○ ○ V___, v___, v___. [Six macrons] (131)

R: Vēnī, vīdī, vīcī.

264. ★ ○ ○ • veniō venīre vēnī (The past participle is not common.)

265. ★ ○ ○ • videō vidēre vīdī vīsus

266. ★ ○ ○ • vincō vincere vīcī victus

267. Vēnī, vīdī, vīcī was inscribed upon the standards carried in a triumphal celebration by Julius Caesar. He says that the victory was easy for he had only to _____, _____, _____.

A: come, see, and conquer.

18-34

190. "Quotus vir est brevis?" "_____."

| I | II | III | IV |

R: Secundus.

191. "Quota fēmina est hilaris?" "_____."

| I | II | III | IV |

R: Prīma.

192. "Quotus orbis est magnus?" "_____."

| I | II | III | IV |

R: Quārtus.

27-51

255. "Quid hōc tempore necesse facere est?" "Ab____ n_____."

R: Abīre necesse est.

256. "Quid nēmō effugere potest?" "Mor____."

R: Mortem.

257. "Quid nōbīs omnibus accidet?" "M____."

R: Mors.

258. Accidet is tense #____.

A: 3.

259. We can ask this question just as easily in Latin. The word tempus, besides meaning "time," also means "tense." "Quotī temporis est 'accidet?'" "T____ is t____i."

R: Temporis tertiī.

260. "Quotī temporis est 'accidit?'" "T____ qu____."

R: Temporis quīntī.

261. "Quotī temporis est 'accidēbat?'" "_____."

R: Temporis prīmī.

18-35

193. ★ ○ • ○ • *Vōx audīta perit, littera scrīpta manet.* (57)

194. First we will learn the new vocabulary. Listen to your teacher as he talks about these two pictures. Pr___ l_____ m____ __t s__ s_____ l_____ __t p____.

★ ○ ○

I   II

Cōnf: Prīma littera magna est sed secunda littera est parva.

195. "Quotā in pictūrā est littera parva?"
"_____ in _____."

I   II

R: Secundā in pictūrā.

27-50

250. Echo the paradigm of the #5 form of *lūdere*.

★ ○ ○ • lūsī   lūsimus
         lūsistī lūsistis
         lūsit   lūsērunt

251. On the model of *lūsī*, say the #5 paradigm of *edere*.

R: ēdī   ēdimus
    ēdistī ēdistis
    ēdit   ēdērunt

_____

252. Write the #5 paradigm of *bibere*.

R: bibī   bibimus
    bibistī bibistis
    bibit   bibērunt

_____

Quaestiōnēs et Respōnsa

253. Quantum tū ēdistī? Egō s___ s____.

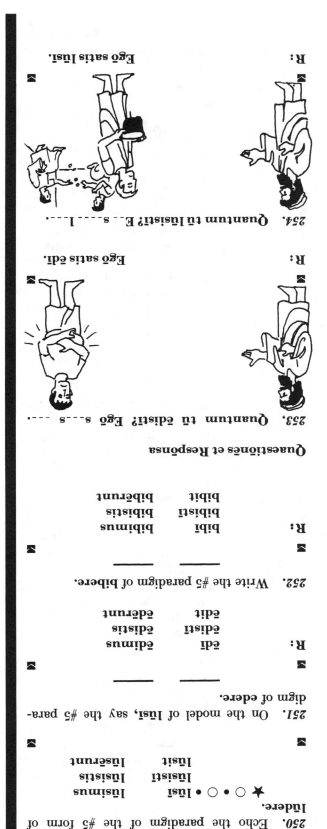

R: Egō satis ēdī.

254. Quantum tū lūsistī? E___ s___ l____.

R: Egō satis lūsī.

18-36

196. Listen to your teacher talk about this picture. ★ ○ ○ J____ ēl_____ __t et m____ d____. J_____ n__ d____ s__ v____ au____.

▼   ▼

Cōnf: Jūdex ēloquens est et multa dīcit. Juvenis nōn dīcit sed vōcem audit.

197. Bearing in mind the English derivative "vocal," you would guess that **Juvenis vōcem audit** means that the _____ ___ _____ the v____.

▼   ▼

A: young man hears the voice.

198. Here is an English equivalent of your teacher's description of the picture. See if you can remember what he said. "The judge is talkative and says many things. The young man does not speak but hears his voice." J____ ē_____ est et m____ d____. J_____ n__ d____ s__ v____ a____.

▼   ▼

R: Jūdex ēloquens est et multa dīcit. Juvenis nōn dīcit sed vōcem audit.

199. Listen to your teacher talk about what is happening in this picture. ★ ○ ○ F_____ l_____ m____ in gr___ scr____, s__ v____ n__ au____.

▼   ▼

Cōnf: Fēmina litterās magnās in gradū scrībit, sed vōcem nōn audit.

27-49

242. Lūsistī satis, ēdistī satis atque bibistī; tempus abīre tibi est = ___ h___ pl____ en____, __ h___ eat___ __ dr___ en____; it __ t___ f___ __ de__ t.

▼

A: You have played enough, you have eaten and drunk enough; it is time for you to depart.

▼

243. Copy in your Notebook.

▼

244-246. Echo the principal parts of the following verbs.

▼

244. ★ ○ ○ • bibō bibere bibī (The past participle of **bibō** is uncommon.)

▼

245. ★ ○ ○ • edō edere ēdī ēsus

▼

246. ★ ○ ○ • lūdō lūdere lūsī lūsus

▼

247. Write the principal parts of **bibere**.

R: bibō bibere bibī

▼

248. Write the principal parts of **edere**.

R: edō edere ēdī ēsus

▼

249. Write the principal parts of **lūdere**.

R: lūdō lūdere lūsī lūsus

200. What did he say that the woman is doing? She _____.

A: She is writing big letters on the step.

201. What did he say that she is not doing? _____.

A: She doesn't hear the voice.

202. The past participle of **scrībit** is **scrīptus**. The original meaning of "manuscript" was "something that was __en by __d."

A: _____ written by hand. (Today a manuscript is usually typed.)

203. Audit = ____s

A: _____ hears

204. Scrībit = ____s

A: _____ writes

205. Say the paradigm of the First Declension noun **littera** ("letter"). _____ _____

R:
littera   litterae
litteram litterās
litterā   litterīs

206. Write the paradigm of the Third Declension noun **vōx** ("voice"). _____

R:
vōx   vōcēs
vōcem vōcēs
vōce   vōcibus

---

236. Sed illī virī quī in angulō sunt ____ (ludunt/lūdunt).

R: lūdunt

237. Echo the principal parts of the irregular verb **īre** ("go"). ✱ ○ • ○ • **eō īre iī**

238. You have had this verb in a compound form with **per**, meaning "go through (one's life)" or more bluntly, "____."

A: _____ die.

239. All mortals die = Om___ m___ p____.

A: **Omnēs mortālēs pereunt.**

240. You should be able to figure out that the new verb **abīre**, a compound of **īre**, means to "go a____."

A: away

241. Unpleasant as it may appear to us, at their feasts Romans often used to display skeletons, either real ones or carved or painted on vases, to remind the guests that they should live a full life because _____ _____ [In your own words]

A: death comes to everybody.

18-38

207. Write. ★ ○ ○ V__ aud___ p____,
l_____ scr____ m____.

R: Vōx audīta perit,
littera scrīpta manet. (57)

208. **Audīta** is the ____ _____ of the
verb **audit**.

A: past participle

209. Therefore **audīta** = _____

A: heard

210. Vōx audīta perit = The _____ _____
___s.

A: The heard voice
dies.

211. This translation has a clumsy sound to it.
In order for someone to "hear" a word, someone
else has to speak it: Therefore, we might better
say "The sp___n word dies."

A: spoken

212. The question arises: Does **audit** mean
"speaks"? ____ (Yes/No)

A: No (Actually, it is a meaningless
question.)

213. In this particular context the phrase **vōx
audīta** corresponds more naturally to the English expression "the _____ word" than to
"the _____ voice."

A: spoken
heard

---

232. Cursum cōnsummāvistī ← ___

R: Vōs
cursum cōnsummāvistis.

233. Medicum crūdēlem fēcistī ← __

R: Tū
medicum crūdēlem fēcistī.

234. ★ ○ ○ ○
L__istī satis, ēd____ s____ at___ b_____;
t____ ab____ t____ t____ (130)
(Tibi is a common variant for tibi.) [Six long vowels]

R: Lūsistī satis, ēdistī satis atque bibistī;
tempus abīre tibī est.

235. Hāc in pictūrā virī nōbīs proximī
aprum edunt vel aprō c_____.

R: _____
cēnant.

214. Vōx audīta perit, littera scrīpta manet
= The spoken word dies; _____.

A: The spoken word dies; the written letter remains.

215. Copy in your Notebook.

216. In **Rem nōn spem, factum nōn dictum, quaerit amīcus** the author was contrasting talk (**dictum**) with _____ (**factum**).

A: actions

217. In **Vōx audīta perit, littera scrīpta manet** the author is contrasting speech with _____.

A: writing.

218. Echo the last Basic Sentence. ★ ○ • ○ •
V__ a_____ p____, l_____ _____ _____.

Cōnf: Vōx audīta perit, littera scrīpta manet. (57)

Quaestiōnēs et Respōnsa

219. "Quid nōn perit?" "_____ _____."

R: _____ _____ Littera scrīpta.

Referring to the paradigm in your Notebook if necessary, expand the following with the subject, using **hic** for the third person singular and **hī** for the third person plural.

224. Haec verba dīxistī → __ h___ v___
 d_____.
R: Tū haec verba dīxistī.

225. Bonum certāmen certāvērunt → __ c_____ c_____.
R: Hī bonum certāmen certāvērunt.

226. Quid ēgistis? → Q___ ___ ēg____?
R: Quid vōs ēgistis?

227. Similēs numquam lāvī → ___ _____.
R: Ego similēs numquam lāvī.

228. Aprō hilariter cēnāvistis → ___ ___ _____.
R: Vōs aprō hilariter cēnāvistis.

229. Fīdem servāvit → ___ ____ _____.
R: Hic fīdem servāvit.

230. Beneficium bis dedimus → ___ _____ ___ _____.
R: Nōs beneficium bis dedimus.

231. Hilariter cucurristī → ___ _____.
R: Tū hilariter cucurristī.

18-40

220. "Quid nōn manet?" "___ _____."

R: Vōx audīta.

221. "Utrum hominēs in mente tenent, vōcem audītam an litteram scrīptam?"
"_____."

R: Litteram scrīptam.

222. "Quid hominēs in mente nōn tenent?" "_____ _____."

R: Vōcem audītam.

223. "Quālēs litterae manent?" "L_____
_____."

R: Litterae scrīptae.

224. V__ aud___ p_____, l_____ _____
_____.

R: Vōx audīta perit, littera scrīpta manet. (57)

225. Quaestiōnēs et Respōnsa = _____
___ _____ (Drill)

A: Question and Answer (Drill)

See if you can predict the four principal parts of **laudāre** (1).
_____.

R: **laudō, laudāre, laudāvī, laudātus**

The #5 form is the only tense in Latin to have special person endings. This makes this tense easier to identify than the others.

219. Echo the following paradigm of **agere** in the #5 tense. Use the pronoun to remind you what person it is. We will use **ille** here for the third person.

★ • ○ • ○ • ego ēgī   nōs ēgimus
              tū ēgistī   vōs ēgistis
              ille ēgit   illī ēgērunt

220. Echo the principal parts of **dare**. (Note that this is an irregular verb since the a is short in **dare** and in almost all the other forms.)

★ • ○ • ○ • **dō dare dedī datus**

221. Echo the paradigm for **dare** in the #5 tense.

★ • ○ • ○ • dedī   dedimus
            dedistī dedistis
            dedit   dedērunt

222. Echo the principal parts of **currere**.
★ • ○ • ○ • **currō currere cucurrī**
(The past participle of **currere** is uncommon.)

223. Using **dedī** as a model, write the paradigm of **currere** in the #5 tense, using **hic** and **hī** for the third person singular and plural.

R: ego cucurrī   nōs cucurrimus
   tū cucurristī   vōs cucurristis
   hic cucurrit   hī cucurrērunt

226. From now on, instead of heading the sequence with "Question and Answer Drill," we will use the Latin equivalent, which is Qu_____ __ _____. [Look back, if necessary.]

R: Quaestiōnēs et Respōnsa.

227. ★ ○ • ○ • *In virtūte posita est vēra fēlīcitās.* (58)

228. The suffix **-tās** is used in Latin to make abstract nouns out of many adjectives. For example, since **crūdēlis** means "cruel," **crūdēlitās** means "_____."

A: cruelty.

229. The English suffix -ty comes from Latin ____.

A: -tās.

230. The word **pūritās** must mean "p_____."

A: purity.

231. Since the word for "heavy" is **gravis**, the Latin word for "heaviness" is ____itās.

A: gravitās.

232. The ending **-tās** is used in Latin to make an abstract ____ out of an adjective.

A: noun

212. **Factus** is the p_____

A: past participle (not all verbs have this form).

213. The form **faciō** is the ____ (1/2/3) person of the ____ (1/2/3/4/5/6) tense.

A: 1   2

214. This form is used in order to show that **faciō** is an ___ verb of the ____ (1/2/3/4) conjugation.

A: -iō   3

215-216. Echo the principal parts of the following verbs.

215. **cōnsummāre** ★ ○ • ○ •

Conf: cōnsummō, cōnsummāre, cōnsummāvī, cōnsummātus

216. **servāre** ★ ○ • ○ •

Conf: servō, servāre, servāvī, servātus

217. Write the principal parts of **servāre**.

A: servō, servāre, servāvī, servātus

218. Most (but not all) First Conjugation verbs form their principal parts in the same way as **servāre** does. We refer to these as *regular* First Conjugation verbs.

233. The noun **vēritās** means "_____."

A: truth.

234. We therefore assume that the unknown adjective **vērus** must mean "_____."

A: true.

235. The verb **pōnit** means "places." The past participle **positus** therefore means "_____."

A: placed.

236. Echo the singular paradigm of **virtūs**. ★ ○ •

Cōnf: virtūs
virtūtem
virtūte

237. Echo the plural. ★ ○ •

Cōnf: virtūtēs
virtūtēs
virtūtibus

238. "Virtue" often means strict conformity to the laws and customs of one's own group. What appeared virtuous to a Roman does not necessarily seem virtuous to us. In addition, the Latin word **virtūs** meant not only "moral excellence" but also "manly excellence" or "manliness" or "courage." In fact, the word **virtūs** is related to the Latin word for "man," which is ____.

A: **vir.**

---

205. The stem on which the forms **fēcī**, **fēcistī**, and **fēcit** are formed is the _____ stem.

A: perfective

206. And then there is the past participle stem from which we get the form **f--tus**.

A: **factus.**

207. The different stems of a verb are called the "principal parts." "Sing, sang, sung" are the _____s of the English verb "sing."

A: principal parts

208. "Run, ran, run" are the _____ of an English verb.

A: principal parts

209. Echo the principal parts of the Third Conjugation **iō** verb **facere**. ★ ○ •

faciō   facere   fēcī   factus

In the same way, Latin verbs have principal parts. These must be learned separately for each verb, but the task is not really as great as it sounds, because there are only a few ways of forming these stems.

210. **Facere** is the in_____ of the verb.

A: infinitive

211. **Fēcī** is the number ____ (1/2/3/4/5/6) form of the verb.

A: 5

18-43

239. ★ ○ ○ __ v_____ p_____ __t

R: In virtūte posita est

240. **In virtūte posita est** tells us that something is _____ in _____.

A: placed in virtue.

241. Needed to complete the pattern of the sentence is the { __ }.

A: {-s}.

242. Because of the words **posita est**, we know that this expected {-s} will be _____ number and _____ gender.

A: singular   feminine

243. ★ ○ ○ **In virtūte posita est** _____.

R: *In virtūte posita est vēra fēlīcitās.* (58)

244. **In virtūte posita est vēra fēlīcitās** = T___ h_____ss __ pl____ in _____.

A: True happiness is placed in virtue.

---

199. "**Prō quō Sānctus Paulus certāvit?**
"___ D___."

R: **Prō Deō.**

200. B___ c_____ c_____, c_____ c___- _____, f_____ s_____ (129).

201. Echo the paradigm of the #5 form of **servāre.**
★ ○ ● ○ ● servāvī   servāvIMUS
servāvISTI   servāvISTIS
servāvIT   servāvĒRUNT

202. Copy this paradigm of a #5 tense in your Notebook under Forms of Latin.
fēcī   fēcimus
fēcistī   fēcistis
fēcit   fēcērunt

203. There are _____ different stems for Latin verbs.

A: three

204. You now know all three. The stem on which the forms **faciēbat, facit,** and **faciet** are formed is the _____ stem.

A: imperfective

18-44

245. Copy in your Notebook.

Quaestiōnēs et Respōnsa

246. "In quō posita est vēra fēlīcitās?"
"-- --------."

R: **In virtūte.**

In this next question we ask **Quid est positum?** and make **positum** agree with the neuter **Quid?** In the answer, however, you must make the participle end in **-a** to agree with the subject which you supply.

247. "Quid in virtūte positum est?" "V___ f_____ in _____ ____ta ___."

R: **Vēra fēlīcitās in virtūte posita est.**

248. Say the paradigm of **virtūs.** _____

R: virtūs   virtūtēs
     virtūtem   virtūtēs
     virtūte   virtūtibus

249. ★ ○ • ○ • *Parātae lacrimae īnsidiās, nōn flētum, indicant.* (59)

250. First, the new vocabulary. Echo your teacher as he describes this picture. ★ ○ • ○ •
H__ v__ f_____ p_____.

Cōnf: Hic vir foveam parat.

27-41

191. Copy in your Notebook.

192. From what St. Paul says here you can see that he expected that he would soon _____ [In your own words]

A: be put to death.

Quaestiōnēs et Respōnsa

193. "Quāle certāmen certāvit Sānctus Paulus?" "_____."

R: **Bonum.**

194. "Quid Sānctus Paulus cōnsummā-vit?" "_____."

R: **Fidem.**

195. "Quid servāvit?" "_____."

R: **Cursum.**

196. ★ ○ • finis   finēs
              fine   finibus
              finī   finibus
              finis   finium

197. Sub quō tempore? = At _____?

A: At what time?

198. (**Dixit** is the #5 form of **dīcit.**) "Sub quō tempore dīxit Sānctus Paulus haec verba?" "Sub fīn-- vīt-- su----."

R: **Sub fīne vītae suae.**

18-45

251. There is an English derivative of **parat**; it is the word "pre___e."

A: prepare.

252. ★ ○ • ○ • H_ _ v_ _ f_ _ _ _ _ in _ _ _ _ _ _.

Cōnf: Hic vir foveam indicat.

253. "Quid agit vir prīmā in pictūrā?" "_ _ _ _ _ _ _ _ _ _ _ _."

R: Foveam parat.

254. "Quid agit vir secundā in pictūrā?" "_ _ _ _ _ _ _ _ _ _ _ _ _."

R: Foveam indicat.

255. The verbs **parat** and **indicat** form their past participle in the same way as **laudat** and **dōnat**. Therefore, the past participle of **parat** is _ _ _ ātus.

A: parātus.

256. The past participle of **indicat** is _____.

A: indicātus.

---

187. Listen to his answer and write it. ★ ○ ○

a_ _ _ ex f_ _ _ _ s_ _ _ _ _ _.

R: Egō agnum ex foveā servāvī.

188. (This new First Conjugation verb **servāre** is *not*, repeat, *not*, the same as the Fourth Conjugation verb **servīre**.) What your teacher says is that he has s_ _ _ _d _ _ _ _ _ _ _ _ _ _ _ _ _ _ _.

A: saved the lamb from the pitfall.

189. ★ ○ ○ ○ B_ _ _ _ _ c_ _ _ _ _ _, c_ _ _ _ _ _ _ _ _ f_ _ _ _ s_ _ _ _ _ _. (129) [Eight long vowels]

R: **Bonum certāmen certāvī, cursum cōnsummāvī, fidem servāvī.**

190. This was written originally (in Greek) by St. Paul to Timothy, bishop of Ephesus, when Paul was brought to Rome for the second time, to appear before Nero. Keeping in mind the English word "fidelity," see if you can guess the meaning of the new noun **fidēs**. **Bonum certāmen certāvī, cursum cōnsummāvī, fidem servāvī** means, "_ _."

A: I have fought the good fight, I have finished the race, I have kept the faith.

18-46

257. The word **īnsidiae** ("ambush") is unusual in that it occurs only in the plural number. Echo the paradigm (plural forms only). ★○●○●

Cōnf: īnsidiae
        īnsidiās
        īnsidiīs

258. Write that the thieves are preparing an ambush. F____ īn_____ p___nt.

R: Fūrēs īnsidiās parant.

Answer the questions following this picture.

259. "Quem locum juvenis indicat?"
"_____."

R: Īnsidiās.

260. "Quō locō sunt fūrēs?" "_____."

R: In īnsidiīs.

261. "Quōs hominēs juvenis indicat?"
"_____."

R: Fūrēs.

27-39

183. It seems that your teacher was equally busy defending himself. Write his description of what he has done. Ego qu____ b_____ c____ i. ○○★○

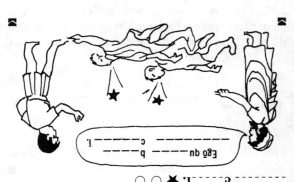

R: Ego quoque bonum certāmen certāvī.

184. Ask your teacher what he has done and write his answer. Quid ēgistī? ∨ ★ ○ ● E____ c____ c____ vī.

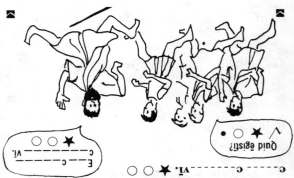

R: Ego cursum cōnsummāvī.

185. Ego cursum cōnsummāvī = I h____ fin____ed the r____.

A: I have finished the race.

186. Ask your teacher what he has done and check your answer. "Quid tū ēg____?" ∨ ★ ○ ●

Cōnf: Quid tū ēgistī?

18-47

262. Write the first part of the new Basic Sentence. ★ ○ ○ _____

R: Parātae lacrimae

263. Parātae lacrimae is the {__} of the sentence.

A: {_s}

264. ★ ○ ○ Parātae lacrimae_____,

R: Parātae lacrimae īnsidiās, nōn flētum,

265. Parātae lacrimae īnsidiās, nōn flētum, means, "_____ ____s blank an am____, not w___ing."

A: Prepared tears blank an ambush, not weeping.

266. ★ ○ ○ Parātae lacrimae īnsidiās, nōn flētum, _____.

R: Parātae lacrimae īnsidiās, nōn flētum, indicant. (59)

267. Parātae lacrimae īnsidiās, nōn flētum, indicant means, "_____ ____ _____ an _____, ___ (real) _____."

A: Prepared tears indicate an ambush, not (real) weeping.

27-38

179. You are doing well and your teacher tells you so. Write down what he says, "B____ c____men c_____." [Two macrons.]

A: Bonum certāmen certās.

180. This means, "___ ___ f___ting a g____ f___t."

A: You are fighting a good fight.

181. Listen to the teacher compliment you on what you *have* done. Write what he says. B____ c____ī_____ c_____. ○ ○ ★

R: Bonum certāmen certāvistī.

182. He tells you, "You h___ f____ a good f____."

A: You have fought a good fight.

268. Copy in your Notebook.

269. This new Basic Sentence means that people who cry deliberately do not feel ____ ____.

A: real grief.

270. Instead, they hope by means of the false tears to _____.

A: get something they want.

271. Echo the paradigm of the Fourth Declension noun **flētus,** first the singular, then the plural. ★ ○ • ○ •

Cōnf: flētus   flētūs
       flētum   flētūs
       flētū   flētibus

272. Write the paradigm of **īnsidiae**; note that there are only three forms.

R: īnsidiae
           īnsidiās
           īnsidiīs

Quaestiōnēs et Respōnsa

273. "Quid parātae lacrimae indicant?" "____."

R: Īnsidiās.

274. "Quid parātae lacrimae nōn indicant?" "____."

R: Flētum.

275. "Quālēs lacrimae īnsidiās indicant?" "____."

R: Parātae.

276. "Quibus indicantur īnsidiae?"
"_ _ _ _ _ īs _ _ _ _ _ _ īs."

R: Parātīs lacrimīs.

277. "Quae rēs lacrimīs parātīs indicantur?" "Īn_ _ _ _ _ _ _."

R: Īnsidiae.

278. "Quid lacrimīs parātīs nōn indicātur?" "Vērus f_ _ _ _ _ _."

R: Vērus flētus.

279. "Quālēs lacrimae flētum vērum indicant?" "V_ _ _ _ _ _ _ _ _ _ _ _ _."

R: Vērae lacrimae.

280. "Quālem flētum indicant lacrimae vērae?" "_ _ _ _ _ _."

R: Vērum.

281. We will have new vocabulary words for the next Basic Sentence. Listen to your teacher describe these two pictures. ★ ○ ○ Pr_ _ _ in p_ _ _ _ _ _ l_ _ _ _ _ _ _ _ ex oc_ _ _ _ d_ _ _ _ _ _ _ _. V_ _ pl_ _ _ _ _. S_ _ _ _ _ _ _ v_ _ n_ _ pl_ _ _ _; h_ _ _ _ _ _ _ _ t.

Prīma pictūra   Secunda pictūra

Cōnf: Prīmā in pictūrā lacrimae ex oculīs dēfluunt. Vir plōrat. Secundus vir nōn plōrat; hilaris est.

---

170. The #5 form of agit is ēgit. "Quid ēgit prīmus timor in orbe?" "_ _ _ _ _ _ _."

R: Deōs fēcit.

171. Quōs prīmus fēcit timor?" "_ _ _ _ _."

R: Deōs.

172. The #5 form of the verb is the only tense in Latin to have a special set of endings. The ending which is added to fēc- to mean "has made" is _ _ _ _ _ _.

A: -it.

173–175. You will now meet the special endings for the First and Second person singular of the #5 tense, meaning "I have done such-and-such" and "You have done such-and-such."

173. Listen to your teacher describe what you are doing now. M_ _ _ _ _ p_ _ _ _ c_ _ _ _. ★ ○ ○

174. Echo your teacher as he compliments you on what you have done. M_ _ _ _ _ p_ _ _ _ istī. ★ ○ ●

Cōnf: Multōs piscēs capis.

Cōnf: Multōs piscēs cēpistī.

282. "Quotā in pictūrā vir hilaris est?"
".."

R: Secundā in pictūrā vir hilaris est.

283. "Quotā in pictūrā vir plōrat?"
".."

R: Prīmā in pictūrā vir plōrat.

284. When we say that a situation is "deplorable," we mean that it is so bad that we are ready to w---- about it.

A: weep

285. "Quid agit vir?" "V-- pl-----."

R: Vir plōrat.

286. Echo your teacher as he describes this same picture. ★ ○ • ○ • Vir plōrat vel flet.

287. Plōrat and flet are both the part of speech called ----s.

A: verbs.

288. The new word vel, since it connects flet and plōrat, must be the part of speech called a ------tor.

A: connector.

---

164. Quid significat hoc nōmen "timor"?
Quī timōrem sentit t--t.

R: timet.

165. Prīmus in orbe deōs fēcit timor means,
"F---- f---- m--- g---- in w-----."

A: Fear first made gods in the world.

166. Copy in your Notebook.

167. This means that according to this Roman author, primitive man conceived the idea of gods because of natural phenomena such as lightning, etc., which awakened the emotion of -----.

A: fear.

168. Does this use of the #5 verb fēcit say that this action happened in the past ("made") or does it say that it is now, at the present time, an accomplished fact which still exists at the present time ("has made")?

A: It happened in the past ("made").

169. Pr--- o--- d--- f--- t------. (128)

R: Prīmus in orbe deōs fēcit timor.

18-51

289. The new connector **vel** is useful for explaining synonyms.

Juvenis pecūniam *habet* **vel** *possidet*.

From these examples you can see that the connector **vel** means "‗‗."

A: or.

Using **vel**, complete the following sentences to indicate synonyms.

290. **Juvenis taurōs videt ‗‗‗‗‗ aspicit.**

R: **Juvenis taurōs videt vel aspicit.**

291. **Lupī cautī foveam timent vel ‗‗‗‗‗‗‗.**

R: **Lupī cautī foveam timent vel metuunt.**

292. Synonyms are tricky, because no two words mean *exactly* the same thing. **Timent** and **metuunt** don't have quite the same "flavor." **Metuunt** means to have a fearful respect for something, while **timent** means to be afr‗‗‗‗ of it.

A: afraid

293. The new verb **āmittit** is an antonym of **invenit. Juvenis pecūniam invenit** = The ‗‗‗‗‗ ‗‗‗ ‗‗‗‗s ‗‗‗‗‗‗.

A: The young man finds money.

294. **Juvenis pecūniam āmittit** = The ‗‗‗‗‗ ‗‗‗ ‗‗‗‗s ‗‗‗‗‗‗.

A: The young man loses money.

295. Since **āmittit** means "loses," **āmissus, āmissa, āmissum** means "‗‗‗‗t."

A: lost.

27-34

160. Here is the same sentence, but the situation is different. The old lady is annoyed because she ‗‗‗‗‗‗‗‗‗‗‗‗ just a few hours ago, but now he is ‗‗‗‗‗‗‗‗‗‗‗.

Anus īnfantem lāvit.

A: The old lady is annoyed because she washed the baby just a few hours ago but now he is dirty again.

161. Copy in your Notebook under Facts About Latin: The #5 tense may describe an act which is now complete at the present time. In the right context, **Mūrēs cēpit** could mean, "He has caught some mice (and still has them in his possession.)"

162. Copy in your Notebook under Facts About Latin: A second common use of the #5 tense is to describe an action which happened in past time, as in telling a story. In the right context, **Mūrēs cēpit** could mean, "He caught some mice." Perhaps he still has them, perhaps he let them go again.

163. Write a new Basic Sentence from dictation. ‗‗‗‗‗‗‗‗ ○ ○ ○ ★ ○ ○ ○ ‗‗‗‗‗‗‗‗ **Pr‗‗‗‗‗ ‗‗ or‗‗‗ d‗‗‗‗ f‗‗‗‗‗ t‗‗‗‗.** (128)

R: **Prīmus in orbe deōs fēcit timor.**

296. There are some verbs in Latin which are sometimes transitive and sometimes intransitive. In the expression **Vir plōrat,** the verb **plōrat** is ____ (transitive/intransitive).

A: intransitive.

297. Ask your teacher what the young man is crying over. "Quid j____ pl____?" √ ★ ○ •

Cōnf: Quid juvenis plōrat?

298. Write his answer. ★ ○ ○ "_____."

R: Āmissam vestem.

299. **Juvenis āmissam vestem plōrat** = The ____ ___ ____s over his ____ _____.

A: The young man weeps over his lost clothes.

300. "Quid fēmina plōrat?" "Pl____ pic_____ ām_____."

R: Plōrat pictūram āmissam.

156. However, this #5 tense (fēcit, lāvit) has another common meaning: it is often used in telling stories to say that an action happened in past time. Notice the following contrast between tenses #1 and #5. **Sabidius hilariter cum convīvīs cēnābat** = S_____ was d_____ ____ ____ _____.

A: Sabidius was dining cheerfully with guests.

157. This action is described as ____ (perfective/going on) in the past.

A: going on

158. We can use the new #5 form, **Sabidius hilariter cum convīvīs cēnāvit**, to merely state that this action happened in the past and we are saying, "_____ d___ p_____ _____."

A: Sabidius dined cheerfully with guests.

Therefore the #5 tense (fēcit, lāvit, cēnāvit) has two meanings:
1) to show that an action is completed in present time;
2) simply to say that an action happened. This tense is therefore ambiguous and the context will tell you which meaning is intended.

159. For example, in the context of the picture, what does the following sentence mean? The old lady _____ (and he is now _____).

Anus īnfantem lāvit.

A: The old lady has washed the baby (and he is now clean).

301. Now let us take a new Basic Sentence, word by word. ★ ○ ○ _____

A: **Plōrātur**

302. From the first word of this sentence (**plōrātur**) you know that you have an {_____} type of sentence.

A: {-s -tur}

303. You expect in the rest of the sentence an {__}.

A: {-s}.

304. Plōrātur = Something is ___t ___r.

A: Something is wept over.

305. ★ ○ ○ Plōrātur _____

A: Plōrātur lacrimīs

306. Lacrimīs ____ (is/is not) the expected {-s}.

A: is not

307. Lacrimīs is _____ case.

A: ablative

308. Lacrimīs is therefore the _____ of the ____.

A: modifier verb.

---

150. The stem of the Latin word for "wash," is lav- in the imperfective system, but lāv- in the _____ system.

A: perfective

151.

I Anus īnfantem lāvat.
II Anus īnfantem lāvit.

152. In the first picture, the old lady _____ the baby.

A: is washing

153. In the second picture, it says that she has c____ed the act of w_____ the b____.

A: completed the act of washing the baby.

154. In other words, in the second picture, the baby is now at the present time all w___ed.

A: washed

155. Lāvit therefore shows _____ action in _____ time.

A: completed present

309. Using the colorless word "something" for the subject, **Plōrātur lacrimīs** means, "_____ _____."

A: Something is wept over by tears.

310. ★ ○ ○ Plōrātur lacrimīs _____

A: Plōrātur lacrimīs āmissa

311. As a participle, **āmissa** must modify something; what it modifies here is the missing {--}.

A: {-s}.

312. Because **plōrātur** is singular, we know that the missing subject will be _____ number.

A: singular

313. The form **āmissa** tells us again that the missing subject is singular number, but it also adds the information that this subject will be _____ gender.

A: feminine

314. Plōrātur lacrimīs āmissa = Something (or somebody) l___ __ ____ ____ by _____.

A: lost is wept over by tears.

315. ★ ○ ○ Plōrātur lacrimīs āmissa _____

R: Plōrātur lacrimīs āmissa pecūnia

316. **Pecūnia** ____ (is/is not) the expected {-s}.

◪

A: is

317. **Plōrātur lacrimīs āmissa pecūnia** = ____ ____ __ ____ ____ __ _____.

◪

A: Lost money is wept over by tears.

318. Write the complete Basic Sentence. ★ ○ ○ **Plōrātur lacrimīs āmissa pecūnia** ____.

◪

R: **Plōrātur lacrimīs āmissa pecūnia vērīs.** (60)

319. In this sentence draw an arrow from **vērīs** to the noun it modifies. If it does not modify a noun but is used as a noun itself, say so.
Plōrātur lacrimīs āmissa pecūnia vērīs (60)

◪

R: Plōrātur lacrimīs āmissa pecūnia vērīs.

320. This Basic Sentence means, "____ ____."

◪

A: Lost money is wept over by true tears.

321. Copy in your Notebook.

◪

---

138. **In factū** we see the p--------p-stem.

◪

A: past participle stem.

◪

139. And finally, in **fēcit** we see the ------ stem.

◪

A: perfective stem.

◪

140-144. Although it is not any easy job to *remember* all the stems of all the Latin verbs, it is not too difficult to *recognize* them. Here are some sample #5 forms which you have never seen. Change them to the #2 form.

140. **Jūdex injūstus innocentem damnā-vit** ←---------- ∨ ★ ○ •

◪

R: **Jūdex injūstus innocentem damnat.**

141. **Equus ad mare cucurrit** ←---------- ∨ ★ ○ •

◪

R: **Equus ad mare currit.**

142. **Laecānia dentēs suōs ēmit** ←---------- ∨ ★ ○ •

◪

R: **Laecānia dentēs suōs emit.**

143. **Īnfāns ad annum vēnit** ←---------- ∨ ★ ○ •

◪

R: **Īnfāns ad annum venit.**

Quaestiōnēs et Respōnsa

322. "Quālibus lacrimīs vir pecūniam āmissam plōrat?" "_____."

R: Vērīs.

323. "Vir pecūniam suam āmittit; quālēs lacrimae dē fāciē dēfluunt?" "_____."

R: Vērae.

324. "Quid vir rē vērā plōrat?" "_____ _____." (Invenītur sub hāc līneā auxilium).

Aux: Rē vērā means "really and truly." To show Latin structure better we might say it means "in a real situation."

R: Āmissam pecūniam.

325. From the position of the words in **Plōrātur lacrimīs āmissa pecūnia vērīs** you know that the word that receives the most emphasis is the Latin word _____.

A: vērīs.

326. Echo this new word. ★ ○ • ○ • cynical

VCh: "sín-nickle"

327. The Cynics were members of a school of philosophy who believed that virtue was the only worthwhile thing in life and that the so-called pleasures of life were actually a _____ to happiness.

A: hindrance (obstacle, etc.)

---

131. The form **fēcit** shows that the action is now c_____ed in pr_____ time.

A: completed present

132. We therefore call **fēcit** the Pr_____ P_____ive tense.

A: Present Perfective tense.

133. Or we can just use the number and call it tense number ____.

A: #5.

134. You will have noticed that the stem of **facere** is **fac**- in the imperfective system, but _____ in the perfective system.

A: fēc-.

135. "I sing," "I sang," "The hymn was sung." From this example, how many different stems does an English verb have?

A: Three.

136. Latin verbs also have three different ____s.

A: stems.

137. In the form **facere** we see the _____ stem.

A: imperfective

328. The Cynics therefore held in contempt many things which other people admired and enjoyed. As a result, a remark that shows contempt for other people or their ideas is sometimes said to be a _____ _____ remark.

A: cynical

329. The word "cynical" comes from a Greek word that means "like a dog." Although we think of dogs as faithful, devoted animals, the Greeks and Romans were more impressed with their less desirable qualities, such as snarling and barking at people. This picture is of the philosopher Diogenes, who is supposed to have lived in an old, abandoned storage jar. There are two ways in which the artist suggested that Diogenes is a cynic. One is the poverty in which he lives; the other is _____.

A: the dog on top of the jar.

330. The Basic Sentence **Plōrātur lacrimīs āmissa pecūnia vērīs** was written by the poet Juvenal. Pronounce his name. √ ★ ○ •

VCh: "Jéw-vuh-null"

331. Juvenal says in effect that when you see a person weeping at his father's funeral, you may not be sure whether he is really sad or not; perhaps he is inwardly rejoicing at the money he will inherit. But, says Juvenal, if a person cries over some money he has lost, you can be sure that his grief is ____.

A: real, true, genuine, etc.

126. Hic medicus, quī blandus erat, jam crūdēlis est. Intemperāns aeger hunc medicum ex blandō crūdēlem fēcit. The reason that the doctor, who used to be kind, is now cruel is that an intemperate sick person has m------ him ------.

A: made   him cruel.

127. That is to say, the action of making the kind doctor cruel ---- (is still going on/is now completed).

A: is now completed.

128. Echo a technical term for action that is completed.

★ ○ ○ • perfective

129. The tenses which you have studied until now (1, 2, and 3) all described actions which were imperfective. The form **faciēbat** is ---- (perfective/imperfective).

A: imperfective.

130. Here is our chart for tenses expanded to include the perfective system. Observe the position of the new form **fēcit**.

	Past	Present	Future
Imperfective	faciēbat 1	facit 2	faciet 3
Perfective		fēcit 5	
	? 4		? 6

18-58

332. This Basic Sentence could be described as c___cal.

A: cynical.

333. Echo a new technical word. ★ ○ • ○ • satire

VCh: "sát-tire"

334. Juvenal was one of the greatest writers of satire that has ever lived. "Satire" is the use of exaggeration, sarcasm, ridicule, humor, etc., to point out the faults of mankind. The name "satire" is given to literary works which show these traits. The sentence **Plōrātur lacrimīs āmissa pecūnia vērīs** is taken from one of the satires of _____.

A: Juvenal.

335. The poems of Juvenal which we possess today are all "_____s."

A: satires.

We will now review the four Basic Sentences of this Unit. Echo each one, then answer the question.

336. ★ ○ • V__ au____ p____, l_____ scr____ m____. (57)

Cōnf: **Vōx audīta perit, littera scrīpta manet.** (57)

27-27

Here we will take a new point of structure.

119. You now know ____ (1/2/3/4/5) different tenses.

A: 3

120. In **Crūdēlem medicum intemperāns aeger facit**, the verb is tense number ____.

A: #2.

121. Notice that we have now made a change in the Basic Sentence. **Crūdēlem medicum intemperāns aeger faciēbat** = _____.

A: An intemperate sick man was making the doctor cruel.

122. **Faciēbat** is tense number ____.

A: #1.

123. **Crūdēlem medicum intemperāns aeger facit** = _____.

A: An intemperate sick man will make a doctor cruel.

124. **Faciet** is tense number ____.

A: #3.

125. Echo a new form of **facere**. ★ ○ • ○ • **Fēcit**

18-59

337. "Utra rēs est vānitās, littera scrīpta an vōx audīta?" "_____."

R: Vōx audīta.

338. ★ ○ • -- v------ p----- --t v---
f--------. (58)

Cōnf: In virtūte posita est vēra fēlīcitās. (58)

339. "Quālem fēlīcitātem possidet vir bonus?" "_____."

R: Vēram.

340. ★ ○ • P------ l------- īn------, ---
fl----, in------. (59)

Cōnf: Parātae lacrimae īnsidiās, nōn flētum, indicant. (59)

341. "Quālibus lacrimīs capitur vir crēdulus?" "_____."

R: Parātīs.

27-26

115. Il--- ter---- m--- pr------- om--- ang----- rī----. (127)

R: Ille terrārum mihi praeter omnēs angulus rīdet.

116-118. You will be asked if someone is of a certain quality and you are to reply enthusiastically that they are beyond all others!

116. "Estne hic conviva hilaris?" "H--- c------ e---- h------ pr----- o------!"

R: Hic conviva est hilaris praeter omnēs!

117. "Estne hic jūdex avārus?" "_____."

R: Hic jūdex est avārus praeter omnēs!

118. "Estne hic magister stultus?" "_____."

R: Hic magister est stultus praeter omnēs!

18-60

342. ★ ○ • Pl_____ l_____ ā_____ p_____ v_____. (60)

Cōnf: Plōrātur lacrimīs āmissa pecūnia vērīs. (60)

343. "Quid homō avārus plōrat?"
"_____ _____."

R: Āmissam pecūniam.

344. We come to an exciting and important point in the program. The main purpose in learning Latin is to read the great _____ which the Romans left to us as a legacy.

A: literature, books, etc.

345-346. Until now you have studied *pieces* of this literature: quotations, famous sayings and the like. Today for the first time you will read a *complete* poem. It isn't long (it's only two lines), and we have chosen it because it contains only the structures that you have studied. However, it is a real poem; it was written by a Roman to entertain his fellow men and not to educate twentieth century students.

Echo the poem, first the first line, then the second. ★ ○ •
Thāis habet nigrōs, niveōs Laecānia dentēs.
    Quae ratiō est? Ēmptōs haec habet, illa suōs. (61)
(Can you read it? Probably not.)

---

108. Write his answer. ★ ○ • "_____ p_____ r_____ o_____."

R: Est pulchra praeter omnēs.

109. He said that the girl was _____

A: pretty beyond all others.

110. Write the Basic Sentence from dictation. ★ ○ • I_____ t_____ m_____ pr_____ o_____ r_____ an_____

R: Ille terrārum mihi praeter omnēs angulus rīdet. [Did you remember to put three macrons in?]

111. This means, "T___ c___ ___ the ___ sm___ s___ upon ___ b_____." (others).

A: That corner of the world smiles upon me beyond all (others).

112. Copy in your Notebook.

Quaestiōnēs et Respōnsa

113. "Cum Horātius hāc in parte orbis terrārum est, estne hilaris an trīstis?"

R: Hilaris.

114. "Cui auctōrī hic angulus placet?"
"H_____."

R: Horātiō.

18-61

347. The author of this poem lived in the first century after the birth of Christ. Echo his name in English, then in Latin. ★ ○ • ○ • Martial, **Mārtiālis**

348. Like Juvenal, he spent his talents and energy in making fun of the human race. Like Juvenal, he wrote _____s.

A: satires.

349. ★ ○ • ○ • satirist

VCh: "sát-tir-rist"

350. Some people, because they feel that the satirical view of life is too negative, do not care for satirists. However, if you realize that he is deliberately exaggerating certain aspects of Roman life, you will learn a great deal about Roman life and customs from reading the works of M_____.

A: Martial.

351. Now for two new adjectives that are antonyms. Listen to your teacher as he describes these pictures and then answer the question. ★ ○ ○ Pr____ t_____ __t n____, s__ s_____ __t n_____.

Prīma pictūra   Secunda pictūra

Cōnf: Prīmus taurus est niger, sed secundus est niveus.

104. A third preposition which takes the accusative is **praeter** which means "beyond" or "in excess of." Ask your teacher what kind of a man Sabidius is. ∧ ★ ○ • "Qu____ v___ ___ S____?"

Cōnf: **Quālis vir est Sabidius?**

105. Write your teacher's answer. ★ ○ ○ "S_____ ___ pr___ om___ ign_____."

R: **Sabidius est praeter omnēs ignāvus.**

106. Your teacher said that Sabidius was _____ be__d ___ others.

A: cowardly beyond all others

107. Ask him what kind of a girl this is. ∧ ★ ○ • "Qu____ p____?"

Cōnf: **Quālis puella est?**

18-62

352. "Utrā in pictūrā est taurus niveus?"
"_ _ _ _ _ _ in _ _ _ _ _ _ _ _."

R: Secundā in pictūrā.

353. "Hic agnus est _ _ _ _ (niger/niveus)."

R: _ _ _ _ _ _ _ _ _ _ _ niger.

354. "Quālis est hic agnus?" "_ _ _ _ _ _ _ _ _ _."

R: _ _ _ _ _ _ _ _ _ _ Niveus est.

355. **Niger** describes things which are _ _ _ _ _ in color.

A: _ _ _ _ _ _ _ _ _ _ _ _ _ _ _ _ _ _ black

356. **Niveus** describes things which are _ _ _ _ _ in color.

A: _ _ _ _ _ _ _ _ _ _ _ _ _ _ _ _ _ _ white

27-23

101. "Quō locō dormiunt īnfantēs?"
"_ _ _ _ _ fl_ _ _ _ _ _."

R: Inter flōrēs.

102. In this next Basic Sentence, the poet (who again is Horace) is talking about a part of Italy which is dear to his heart. ★ ○ ○ I _ _ _ _ t_ _ _ _ _ _ _ _ (127) p_ _ _ _ _ o_ _ _ _ a_ _ _ _ _ r_ _ _ _ _ mihi
(**Mihi** is a common variant in poetry for **mihī**.)
[There are three long vowels.]

R: *Ille terrārum mihi praeter angulus rīdet.*

103. Quī rīdet est hilaris. Quī plōrat est trīstis. Quota in pictūrā vidēmus juvenem rīdentem?

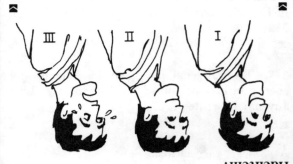

R: Prīma in pictūrā.

357. The adjective **niveus** is a poetic word for "white"; it means "like snow" and comes from a Latin noun that means "snow." When we contrast **niger** and **niveus** we are not only speaking of the contrast between black and white but are emphasizing the difference between black and ‗‗‗w-wh‗‗‗.

A: snow-white.

              m   f   n
358. ★ ○ • ○ • niger, nigra, nigrum

Prīma pictūra   **Secunda pictūra**

359. "Prīmā in pictūrā quālem vestem habet vir?" "‗‗‗‗‗‗."

R: Niveam

360. "Quālis vestis in secundā pictūrā est?" "‗‗‗‗‗‗."

R: Nigra.

361. Complete the description of this picture. Haec sīmia est ‗‗‗‗‗‗ sed illa ‗‗‗‗‗‗.

R: nivea   nigra

362. On the same pattern, describe this picture.
Haec v_____ est n____ sed i___ ____a.
√ ★ ○ •

R: Haec vulpēs est nigra sed illa nivea.

363. The English words "rational" and "reason" come from the word **ratiō**. Although "reason" does not sound very similar to **ratiō**, it comes from _____ through French.

A: Latin

364. If an argument is "rational" it is founded on _____.

A: reason.

365. On the other hand, if a person's argument is irrational, it is _____.

A: not founded on reason.

366. Echo the paradigm of **ratiō** ("reason").
★ ○ • ○ •

Cōnf: rátiō   ratiónēs
       ratiónem   ratiónēs
       ratióne   ratiónibus

18-65

367. The English word "reason" has two very different meanings. One is "the faculty for thinking" (as in "He is a man of reason") and the other is "cause" (as in "What is the reason for this delay?"). The Latin word **ratiō** also has these same two different meanings. Echo your teacher as he gives the Latin for "What's the reason?" ★ ○ • ○ • **Quae ratiō est?**

368. Write the Latin for, "What's the reason?"
_ _ _ _ _ _ _ _ _ _ _ _ _ _ _ _ _ _ .

R: Quae ratiō est?

369. Write your teacher's description of this picture. ★ ○ ○ F_ _ _ _ _ p_ _ _ _ _ em_ _ _.

R: Fēmina piscēs emit.

370. **Fēmina piscēs emit** means that the _ _ _ _ _ is b_ _ _ng _ _ _ _.

A: the woman is buying fish.

371. This is the same woman. Ask your teacher what kind of fish she is holding, and check. "Qu_ _ēs p_ _ _ēs f_ _ _ _ _ t_ _ _ _?" √ ★ ○ •

Cōnf: Quālēs piscēs fēmina tenet?

27-20

91. "Quid agunt sīdera?" "Sīdera quoque
_ _ _ _ _ _ _ _."

R: fulgent.

92. Write the Latin for "It was night, and the moon was shining in the clear sky among the lesser stars."

N_ _ e_ _ _, _ _ c_ _ _ l_ _ f_ _ _ _ _ _ _ l_ _ _ s_ _ _ _ _ _
i_ _ _ _ m_ _ _ _ _ s_ _ _ _ _ _. (126)

R: **Nox erat, et caelō fulgēbat lūna serēnō inter minōra sīdera.**

93. Describe the following pictures, telling where the person is by saying that he is among these various people or animals, using the new preposition "_ _ _ _ _" plus the _ _ _ _ _ive case.

A: inter   accusative

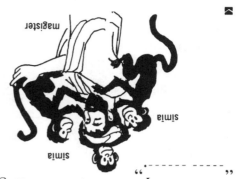

94. "Inter quae animālia est magister?"
"_ _ _ _ _ _ _ _ _ _ _ _ _."

R: Inter sīmiās.

18-66

372. Write his answer. ★ ○ ○ "Piscēs _____ tenet."

R: **Piscēs ēmptōs tenet.**

373. He said that she is holding b____t fish.

A: bought (or "fish that she had bought.")

374. Ēmptus, ēmpta, ēmptum is the _____ of the verb emit.
   m   f   n

A: past participle

375. Emit = ___s; ēmptus = _____.

A: buys ... bought.

376. The word **hic** is used to describe someone who is near the speaker *in space*. It is also used to describe someone who, either *in his thoughts* or *in time*, appears to be near the _____.

A: speaker.

377. Ille vīnum, hic pecūniam dōnat = The former (man) gives wine, the l____ (man) gives money.

A: latter

378. Expand the kernel which has an element missing: **Illa canem, haec agnum quaerit.**

R: Illa canem quaerit, haec agnum quaerit.

27-19

Quaestiōnēs et Respōnsa

84. Copy in your Notebook.

A: It was night, and the moon was shining in the clear sky among the lesser stars.

83. The meaning of this sentence is, "_____."

85. "Quāle est caelum sī lūna fulget?"

R: **Serēnum.**

86. Hoc instrūmentum hōrās nūbilās nōn numerat. Nūbilus-a-um = c_____.

A: cloudy

87. "Fulgetne lūna sī caelum nūbilum est?"

R: **Nōn fulget.**

88. "Inter quanta signa fulget lūna hāc in pictūrā?"

R: **Inter minōra sīdera.**

89. "Quāle tempus est hāc in pictūrā?" "Noct_____."

R: **Nocturnum tempus.**

90. "Quālī tempore fulget lūna hāc in pictūrā?" "_____."

R: **Nocturnō tempore.**

379. Illa canem, haec agnum quaerit = The _____ (woman) looks for a ___; the latter looks for a ____.

A: former   dog   lamb.

380. Illa est jūsta sed haec crūdēlis = The _____ (woman) __ ____, but the _____ (one) is _____.

A: former   is just   latter cruel.

381. Ille hilaris sed hic stultus est = ____ _____.

A: The former (man) is cheerful, but the latter (one) is stupid.

382. Ille verba dīcit, hic audit = _____ _____.

A: The former (man) says words, the latter hears (them.)

383. Ille fraudem, hic laudem vult = ____ _____.

A: The former (man) likes trickery, the latter (likes) praise.

384. "The latter woman (has) a black dress, the former has a snow-white one" = H___ v_____ nig___, i___ niv___ h___t.

A: Haec vestem nigram, illa niveam habet.

79. Hāc in pictūrā caelum serēnum est et lūna ergō fulget. Sī caelum nūbilum erit, lūna nōn ____ēbit.

R: fulgēbit.

80. In the Basic Sentence, Hōrās nōn numerō, nisi serēnās, the word serēnās meant "_____."

A: sunny.

81. However, since this scene takes place at night, the words caelō serēnō cannot mean "in a sunny sky," but must mean "in a _____ sky."

A: clear

82. ★ ○ ○ ─── .

R: Nox erat, et caelō fulgēbat lūna serēnō inter minōra sīdera.

18-68

385. **Ēmptam vestem haec habet, illa suam** = ...

A: The latter (woman) has a bought dress, the former (has) her own (dress).

386. Now for the poem (Basic Sentence 61), which is about two girls named Thais and Laecania. Write the first half of the first line.

★ ○ ○ Th___ h____ nig___,

A: **Thāis habet nigrōs,**

387. The adjective **nigrōs** is a modifier of the {_ _}, but the {_ _} itself is not present.

A: {-m}   {-m}

388. **Thāis habet nigrōs** = _____ ___ some _____ things.

A: Thais has some black things.

389. Write the complete first line of the poem.

★ ○ ○ **Thāis habet nigrōs,** niv___ Lae_____ d_____.

A: **Thāis habet nigrōs, niveōs Laecānia dentēs.**
[Refer to this as you do the following sequence.]

390. Which of these statements is correct?
1) The first kernel is complete but not the second.
2) The second kernel is complete but not the first.
3) Both kernels are complete.
4) Neither kernel is complete.

A: 4) Neither kernel is complete.

Although the word **sīdus** has both the meaning of constellation and single star, we will use it in the sense of single star in this sequence.

75. Echo the paradigm of **sīdus**.

★ ○ ● sīdus   sīdera
        sīdus   sīdera
        sīdere   sīderibus
        sīderī   sīderibus
        sīderis sīderum

In this next Basic Sentence there is another preposition which patterns with the accusative. See if you can identify it and figure out what it means.

76. ★ ○ ○ N___ e____, et c____ f____ l____ s____ m____ s____ (126) i____ s____.

R: *Nox erat, et caelō fulgēbat lūna serēnō inter minōra sīdera.*

77. The new preposition followed by the accusative is the word _____.

A: **inter.**

78. *Intercollegiate* competition in sports is _____ competition _____ different colleges.

A: between

18-69

391. Missing in **Thāis habet nigrōs** is the {--}.

A: {-m}.

392. The modifier of the missing {-m} is the word _____.

A: **nigrōs**.

393. The missing {-m} must therefore be _____ gender and _____ number.

A: masculine   plural

394. Missing in **niveōs Laecānia dentēs** is the {--}.

A: {-t}.

395. Expand the line with the missing two words: **Thāis habet nigrōs _____, niveōs Laecānia dentēs. _____.**

R: **Thāis habet nigrōs dentēs, niveōs Laecānia dentēs habet.**

396. [Cover the previous frame before trying this one.] Pronounce the original line and check with the tape. Th___ h____ n_____, n_____ L_____ d_____. ✓ ★ ○ •

Cōnf: **Thāis habet nigrōs, niveōs Laecānia dentēs.**

397. If we supply the missing element, **Thāis habet nigrōs** means, "_____ ___ _____ _____."

A: Thais has black teeth.

---

71. "**Quō locō stant quercūs?**" "_____."

R: **Trāns lacum.**

72. Your teacher will explain a new word which occurs in the next Basic Sentence. **Signa caelī dīcuntur "sīdera." "Sīdus"** est nōmen generis neutrīus. **Sīdera sunt signa quibus nāvēs errantēs trāns mare dūcuntur. Hāc in imāgine pictum est ____-s.**

73. As you can see from this illustration, **sīdus** is here not a single star, but rather a const. _____ of stars.

A: constellation

74. If you were to hear someone speak about "sidereal time," you would know that this was time that was ascertained by examining the movement of the ____-s.

A: stars.

18-70

398. And similarly, **niveōs Laecānia dentēs** means, "_____ ___ _____ _____."

A: Laecania has white teeth.

399. The meaning of the entire line is that _____.

A: Thais has black teeth and Laecania has white teeth.

400. Write the first half of the second line. ★ ○ ○ **Qu__ r____ e__?**

A: **Quae ratiō est?**

401. **Quae ratiō est?** = ____'s ___ _____?

A: What's the reason?

402. There is only half a line of the poem left. In your own words, what do you think the last half line will say? _____?

A: Of course we don't know what *you* thought, but we expected that you would have looked for an explanation of why one girl has white teeth and the other has black teeth.

403. Write the last line. ★ ○ ○ **Quae ratiō est? Ēm____ h___ h____, i___ s___.**

R: **Quae ratiō est? Ēmptōs haec habet, illa suōs.**

404-405. Pronounce and check, one line at a time.
  Thāis habet nigrōs, niveōs Laecānia dentēs.
  Quae ratiō est? Ēmptōs haec habet, illa suōs. ✓ ★ ○ • (61)

27-15

68-71. In this series, describe where the person is standing by using **trāns** and the accusative to say that he is standing across something. Write your answer.

68. "Quō locō puella stat?" "T____ fl____."
R: **Trāns flūmen.**

69. "Quō locō canēs stant?" "T____ v____."
R: **Trāns viam.**

70. "Quō locō mūrēs stant?" "____ v____."
R: **Trāns vestem.**

406. Only one of these statements is true about **Ēmptōs haec habet, illa suōs.**
1) The first kernel is complete but not the second.
2) The second kernel is complete but not the first.
3) Both kernels are complete.
4) Neither kernel is complete.
The correct statement is ____ (1/2/3/4).

A: 4) Neither kernel is complete.

407. In **Ēmptōs haec habet, illa suōs**, **Ēmptōs** is a modifier of the {__} but the {__} itself is not present.

A: {-m} {-m}

408. **Ēmptōs** is _____ number, _____ case and _____ gender.

A: plural accusative masculine

409. The only masculine plural word in the poem is the word _____.

A: **dentēs.**

410. Expand with the missing masculine accusative plural word: **Ēmptōs** _____ **haec habet.**

R: **Ēmptōs dentēs haec habet.**

411. In **illa suōs** we are missing both the {__} and the {__}.

A: {-m} {-t}.

---

64. "Trāns quid salit lupus?" "_____."

R: flūmen lupus salit.

65. "Trāns quod animal salit juvenis?"

R: Trāns equum juvenis salit.

66. "Trāns" est pars ōrātiōnis quae dicitur "praepositiō." "Ad" et "sub" sunt quoque _____ -tiōnēs.

R: praepositiōnēs.

67. Up to this point the question "Quō locō?" has always gotten as an answer a preposition plus the ablative. From now on, however, the answer may be a preposition like **trāns** which takes the _____ case.

A: accusative

412. Expand: illa suōs _____ _____.

A: illa suōs dentēs habet.

413.
Thāis habet nigrōs, niveōs Laecānia dentēs. Quae ratiō est? Ēmptōs haec habet, illa suōs.

Remember that **haec** refers to the *latter* person mentioned. In this poem, therefore, **haec** refers to ____ (Thais/Laecania).

A: Laecania.

Quaestiōnēs et Respōnsa

414. "Quis habet ēmptōs dentēs?" "_____."

R: Laecānia.

415. "Quis habet suōs dentēs?" "_____."

R: Thāis.

416. Describe the picture and check. Thāis h____ n____ d____ sed h____ s___ d____.
√ ★ ○ •

Cōnf: Thāis habet nigrōs dentēs sed habet suōs dentēs.

---

59. This means that those who _____ sail across the sea change their environment and not their attitude.

A: trāns.

60. The new preposition was the word "_____."

A: trāns.

61. This Basic Sentence was written by Horace. See if you can remember an earlier Basic Sentence in which Seneca imitated Horace. An d____ m____, n____ c____. (104)

R: Animum **dēbēs mūtāre, nōn caelum.** (104)

62. Write the original Horace quotation which Seneca imitated. C____, n____ an____, m____ qui tr____ m____ c____.

R: Caelum, nōn animum, mūtant qui trāns mare currunt.

63-65. The following frames will use such questions as Trāns quās rēs? ("Across what objects?") and Trāns quid? ("Across what?")

63. "Trāns quās rēs suēs saliunt?" "_____ fl____ s____."

R: flōrēs suēs saliunt.

Trans:

18-73

417. Describe this picture and check. L_____
h____ n_____ d_____ sed h____ ēm____
d_____. √ ★ ○ •

Cōnf: Laecānia
habet niveōs dentēs sed habet ēmptōs
dentēs.

418. Thais' teeth were dirty, but at least they
were ___ ____.

A: her own.

419. Laecānia's teeth were nice and white, *but*
____ ____ _____.

A: they were false.

420. See if you can say the poem with part of
it removed.
Thāis h____ nigr___, niv___ Laecānia d_____.
 Quae ratiō est? Ēm____ h___ h____,
  il__ su___.

A:
Thāis habet nigrōs, niveōs Laecānia dentēs.
 Quae ratiō est? Ēmptōs haec habet,
  illa suōs.
[Did you realize that this is the poem which you
were unable to do at the beginning of Unit Nine?]

27-12

54. "Quae pars ōrātiōnis est haec vōx
'siccus'?" _____."

R: Adjectīvum.

55. "Quae pars ōrātiōnis est 'bibit'?"
"_____."

R: Verbum.

56. "Sic____, sob_____. A_____ Q_____?
Ser_____ s___ e___ l_____, n___ am_____.

R: "Siccus, sobrius est Aper." Quid ad mē?"
  Servum sīc ego laudō, nōn amīcum.

57. Copy in your Notebook.

58-62. There are several other prepositions
which pattern with the accusative case, and one
of them occurs in the following sentence. See if
you can not only identify it but discover its
meaning.

58. *Caelum, nōn animum, mūtant quī
trāns mare currunt.* (125) √ ★ ○ •

421. Copy in your Notebook.

422. Now for a translation to put in your Reference Notebook. In a poem like this, there are hundreds of possible translations. Write your own in your Notebook and then compare it with the one given below. Don't be afraid to add extra words to the Latin.

A: Thais has black teeth and Laecania has white ones. What is the reason? Laecania has store teeth, Thais has her own.

423-483. We will now review all 61 sentences of the Basic Text that you have had so far. There is not much help given you; if you wish to go through your Notebook first, do so. If you feel that you know these sentences *thoroughly*, then skip to the Summary at the end of the Unit.

423. El_____ n__ c____ m_____.

R: Elephantus nōn capit mūrem. (5)

424. N__ qu____t aeg__ m_____ ēl_____.

R: Nōn quaerit aeger medicum ēloquentem. (9)

---

48. Servuum sic ego laudo, nōn amīcum
means that Martial ---------------.
[In your own words]

A: praises a slave for being temperate and sober, but wouldn't praise a friend for having these same virtues.

49. Aper has been praised for ------------.
[In your own words]

A: not drinking very much wine.

50. Martial says, "I like my slaves to be -----------, but I prefer that my friends ------------." [In your own words]

A: temperate and sober enjoy drinking with me.

Quaestiōnēs et Respōnsa

51. "Quālēs servōs Martiālis vult?"
"------- et --------."

R: Siccōs et sobriōs.

52. "Quālis amīcus ā Martiāle nōn laudā- tur?" "-------------."

R: Siccus et sobrius.

53. "Quis auctor vult amīcum quī vīnum bibit?" "-------------."

R: Martiālis.

18-75

425. Et___ c_____ ūn__ h____ u____ s____.

R: Etiam capillus ūnus habet umbram suam. (11)

426. F____ f__ c_____ et l____ l____.

R: Fūrem fūr cognōscit et lupum lupus. (14)

427. P_____ n__ s_____ av_____ s__ ir_____.

R: Pecūnia nōn satiat avāritiam sed irrītat. (17)

428. S__ j_____ l__ ___.

R: Sub jūdice līs est. (20)

429. In om__ r_ v_____ im_____ v_____.

R: In omnī rē vincit imitātiōnem vēritās. (22)

430. V____ r____ F_____, n__ S_____.

R: Vītam regit Fortūna, nōn Sapientia. (18)

---

37. In the United States, we refer to a person who takes an active part politically against the use of alcoholic beverages as a "____."

A: Dry.

38. However, the Latin word siccus does not mean quite this but rather someone who is temp____ in his use of wine.

A: temperate

39. Quī "sobrius" est vīnum nōn bibit, et "siccus" significat "sobrius." "Siccus" et "sobrius" oppōnuntur "ēbrius." Quotus vir est siccus sobriusque?

R: Vir secundus.

40. The English derivative of sobrius is the word "_____."

A: sober.

41. Write the Basic Sentence from dictation.
★ ○ ○
"S__, s__ A__ ." "__ m_ ?
S__ s__ l__ , n__ am____."

R: "Siccus, sobrius est Aper." "Quid ad mē? Servum sīc ego laudo, nōn amīcum.

18-77

431. H_____ d_____ d_____ D___.

R: Hilarem datōrem dīligit Deus. (3)

432. A_____ op__ l_____.

R: Auctor opus laudat. (29)

433. N_____ p_____ s___ p_____ v_____.

R: Numquam perīc'lum sine perīc'lō vincitur. (25)

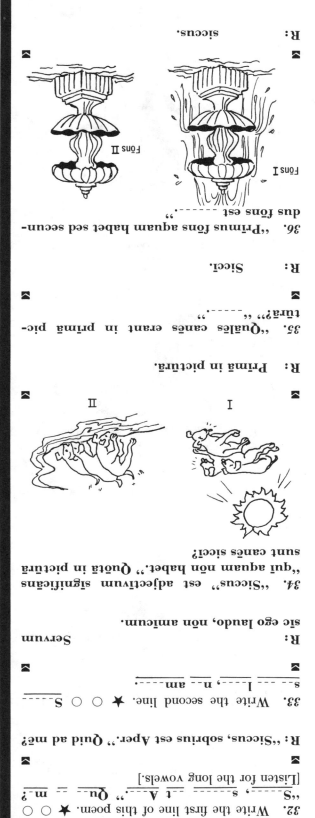

32. Write the first line of this poem. ★ ○ ○
"S_____, s_____ t A_____," Qu__ m__?
[Listen for the long vowels.]

R: "Siccus, sobrius est Aper." Quid ad mē?

33. Write the second line. ★ ○ ○
S_____ l_____, n_____ am_____.

R: Servum sīc ego laudo, non amīcum.

34. "Siccus" est adjectīvum significāns "quī aquam nōn habet." Quota in pictūrā sunt canēs siccī?

35. "Quālēs canēs erant in prīmā pictūrā?" "_____."

R: Prīma in pictūrā.

R: Siccī.

36. "Prīmus fōns aquam habet sed secundus fōns est _____."

R: siccus.

434. M____ m____ l____.

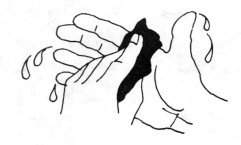

R: Manus manum lavat. (4)

435. H____ s___ v_____ bl____ ōr____.

R: Habet suum venēnum blanda ōrātiō. (34)

436. N__ s_____ aur__ f_____ h____ F_____.

R: Nōn semper aurem facilem habet Fēlīcitās. (10)

26. "Quem ad locum veniunt puellae?" "_____."

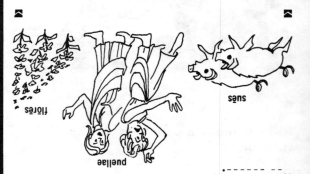

R: Ad flōrēs.

27. "Ā quibus animālibus veniunt puellae?" "_____."

R: Ā suibus.

28-29. Pronounce and check a new Basic Sentence, a poem written by Martial. "Siccus, sobrius est Aper." Quid ad mē? "Servum sīc ego laudō, nōn amīcum. (124)
∨ ✱ ○ •
∨ ✱ ○ •

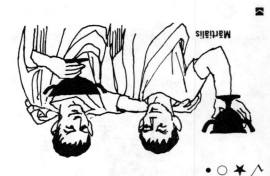

30. Instead of laudō, we find here a variant form, with a _____ vowel.

A: short

31. And instead of egō we find a variant, which is spelled ____.

A: ego (with a short vowel).

437. M____ d_ c____, p___ n_____.

R: Magna dī cūrant, parva neglegunt. (46)

438. D__ n_ pr____, d__ n_____.

R: Diem nox premit, diēs noctem. (16)

439. Cr_____ m_____ in_____ aeg___ f____.

R: Crūdēlem medicum intemperāns aeger facit. (12)

22. "Quō ā locō currit leō?" "_____."

R: Ā foveā.

23. "Quem ad locum currit leō?" "_____."

R: Ad flūmen.

24. "Quō ā locō venit dux?" "_____."

R: Ā nāve.

25. "Quem ad locum venit dux?" "_____."

R: Ad aciem.

440. N___ s___ v____ est.

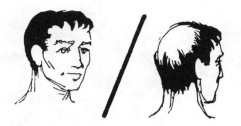

R: Nēmō sine vitiō est. (26)

441. Et g____ et f_____ R_____ P_____ d_____.

R: Et genus et formam Rēgīna Pecūnia dōnat. (31)

442. Aqu___ n__ c____ m_____.

R: Aquila nōn capit muscās. (36)

---

18. "Quibus ab animālibus venit īnfāns?" "_____."

R: Ā canibus.

19. "Quem ad hominem venit īnfāns?" "_____."

R: Ad anum.

20. "Quem ad hominem venit medicus?" "_____."

R: Ad aegrum.

21. "Quibus ab hominibus venit medicus?" "_____."

R: Ā convīvīs.

443. D____ v_____ F___, n_____ tr_____.

R: Dūcunt volentem Fāta, nōlentem trahunt. (45)

444. V_____ v____ red____.

R: Vestis virum reddit. (1)

445. St____ t_____ F_____, s_____ f_____.

R: Stultī timent Fortūnam, sapientēs ferunt. (42)

18-82

446. V_____ d___ ap____.

R: Vēritātem diēs aperit. (2)

447. F_____ F_____ ad_____.

R: Fortēs Fortūna adjuvat. (40)

448. C_____ m_____ f_____ l____.

R: Cautus metuit foveam lupus. (8)

27-3

9–12. In the next four frames you will be asked to what place certain animals or people are going. Answer with **ad** plus the accusative.

9. "Quem ad locum it mūs?" "_____."

R: Ad angulum.

10. "Quem ad hominem it custōs?" "_____."

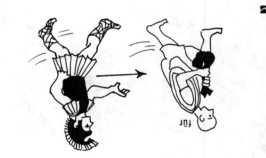

R: Ad fūrem.

11. "Quem ad locum eunt equī?" "_____."

R: Ad mare.

18-83

449. P____ D___, n__ pl____, as____ m____.

R: Pūrās Deus, nōn plēnās, aspicit manūs. (44)

450. Oc___ s___ in am___ d____.

R: Oculī sunt in amōre ducēs. (50)

451. S_____ v___ ob_____.

R: Sapientia vīnō obumbrātur. (27)

---

5. Quis ad fūrem currit, custōs an canis?

R: Custōs ad fūrem currit.

6. Quī ad mare currunt, taurī an equī?

R: Equī ad mare currunt.

7. Echo your teacher as he asks where the lambs are going. ★ ○ ● ○ ● "Qu__ l____ eunt a___?"

Cōnf: Quem ad locum eunt agnī?

8. The expression *quem ad locum* must mean "_____?"

A: to what place?

18-84

452. F____ b____ fr____ ____.

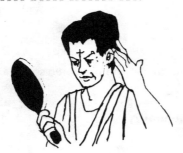

R: Forma bonum fragile est. (54)

453. V____ v___ fr____, l____ ag___, f____ l____.

R: Vulpēs vult fraudem, lupus agnum, fēmina laudem. (15)

454. M___ in c_____ f_____ v_____ v____.

R: Malō in cōnsiliō fēminae vincunt virōs. (38)

UNIT TWENTY-SEVEN

1. So far the only use of the accusative case has been to be the _____ of a verb.

A: object

2. Write your teacher's description of this picture. ★ ○ ○ S____ ab ef____ ad qu____ c____.

R: Simia ab effigiē ad quercum currit.

3. This means that _____.

A: the monkey is running from the statue to the oak tree.

4. While the preposition **ab** patterns with the ablative case, the preposition **ad**, as appears from the expression **ad quercum currit**, patterns with the _____ case.

A: accusative

5–8. In this series you will be asked in which picture are people (or animals) running to certain places (**ad** plus the accusative) or away from certain places (**ā** or **ab** plus the ablative).

455. M___ r____ b___ p_____.

R: Mēns rēgnum bona possidet. (28)

456. L__ v____ īr____, īr____ l___ n__ v____.

R: Lēx videt irātum, irātus lēgem nōn videt. (13)

457. V___ v____ ___.

R: Vīta vīnum est. (49)

TEST INFORMATION

372. As far as verb forms go, you will be asked only to produce the verb forms which you have practiced in this Unit. You should be able to *recognize* any verb which has occurred so far in the program. For example, you should be able to identify the form **dēfluet**, which you have never seen; since you know that there is a #2 form **dēfluit**, then **dēfluet** must be form ----.

A: #3.

Adjectives:

altus-a-um (126)
duo, duae, duo (270)
fēminīnus-a-um (283)
futūrus-a-um (228)
Latīnus-a-um (283)
lepidus-a-um (274)
masculīnus-a-um (283)
neuter, neutra, neutrum (283)
noctūrnus-a-um (123)
Rōmānus-a-um (89)
trēs, tria (270)
trīstis-e (314)

Verbs:

līberō, līberāre (321)
quiēscō, quiēscere (83)
*regō, regere (129)

Connectors:

aut (242)   -que (97)

Indeclinables:

crās (145)   hodiē (4)
herī (10)   jam (83)

18-86

458. Pl_____ l_____ ām____ p_____ v____.

R: Plōrātur lacrimīs āmissa pecūnia vērīs. (60)

459. In v_____ p_____ ___ v___ f_____.

R: In virtūte posita est vēra fēlīcitās. (58)

460. Ex aur____ c_____ as_____.

R: Ex auribus cognōscitur asinus. (43)

26-61

369. S___ qu___ c_____ ip___ c_____? (118)

R: Sed quis custōdiet ipsōs custōdēs?

370. A__ in_____ v___ a__ f_____. (119)

R: Aut inveniam viam aut faciam.

371. Write the Basic Sentence which expresses this thought: Vēritāte vōs līberī eritis.

V_____ v__ l_____. (123)

R: Vēritās vōs līberābit.

VOCABULARY INVENTORY

Nouns:

custōs, custōdis, m (209)
*genus, generis, n (284)
*lingua-ae, f (286)
lūna-ae, f (124)
tempus, temporis, n (225)
via-ae, f (251)
victor, victōris, m (89)

18-87

461. P____ l____ c_____ an____.

R: Parva levēs capiunt animōs. (47)

462. N____ av_____ s___ p____ ___.

R: Nūlla avāritia sine poenā est. (19)

463. R__ n__ sp___, f_____ n__ d_____,
qu_____ am_____.

R: Rem nōn spem, factum nōn dictum,
quaerit amīcus. (33)

26-60

366. J_____ qu_____ v____ h_____
c_____ n____ al__ r_____ eq____. (116)

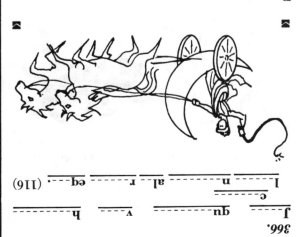

R: Jamque quiēscēbant vōcēs hominumque
canumque
lūnaque nocturnōs alta regēbat equōs.

367. In h___ s___ v_____. (120)

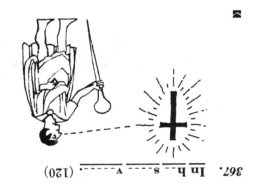

R: In hōc signō vincēs.

368. T_____ er__ s___ s____ er__. (122)

R: Tristis eris sī sōlus eris.

18-88

464. V_____ n_____ p____.

R: Vēritās numquam perit. (7)

465. Cr_____ r__ a___ ___.

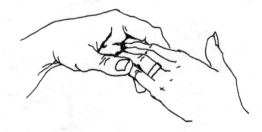

R: Crēdula rēs amor est. (55)

466. Am____ c_____ in r_ inc____ c_____.

R: Amīcus certus in rē incertā cernitur. (24)

---

362. This -ē- becomes short, however, in such positions as before final -t; furthermore, in the First Person it shows up as the variant ---.

A: -a-.

Write the Basic Sentences which these pictures illustrate.

363. Or__ j__ t___ v____ R_____ h_____. (115)

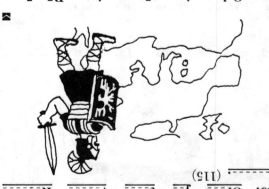

R: Orbem jam tōtum victor Rōmānus habēbat.

364. J___ eg_ ū__ in s____ l____ ap___ c____ d____ (121).

R: Jam ego ūnō in saltū lepidē aprōs capiam duōs.

365. H____ m___, c___ t____. (117)

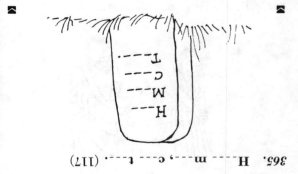

R: Hodiē mihi, crās tibi.

26-59

467. R_____ d___ c____, s_____ v_____.

R: Religiō deōs colit, superstitiō violat. (37)

468. Īn_____ m____ fl_____ qu_____ aqu___.

R: Īnsānus mediō flūmine quaerit aquam. (32)

469. F___ r_____ or___; c____ st___ om___ l____.

R: Fāta regunt orbem; certā stant omnia lēge. (48)

SUMMARY

354. vincere, 1st sg

| egō #1 | egō #2 | egō #3 |

R: vincēbam vincō vincam

355. lavāre, 3d pl

| hī #1 | hī #2 | hī #3 |

R: lavābant lavant lavābunt

356. manēre, 2d sg

| tū #1 | tū #2 | tū #3 |

R: manēbās manēs manēbis

357. effugere (-iō), 2d pl

| vōs #1 | vōs #2 | vōs #3 |

R: effugiēbātis effugitis effugiētis

358. You learned ____ new tenses in this unit.

A: two

359. The signal for the #1 tense for all regular verbs is _____.

A: -bā-.

360. The signal for the #3 tense (future time) for First and Second Conjugation verbs is _____.

A: -bi- (with some variation of -bō and -bu-).

361. The signal for the #3 tense in verbs of the Third and Fourth Conjugations, however, is _____.

A: -ē-.

470. Cr_____ l_____ p_____, n__ fr_____.

R: Crūdēlis lacrimīs pāscitur, nōn frangitur. (39)

471. Ā c___ n__ m____ s____ t_____ a___.

R: Ā cane nōn magnō saepe tenētur aper. (23)

472. Ā f____ p___ p___ dē_____ aqu__.

R: Ā fonte pūrō pūra dēfluit aqua. (35)

473. F_____ f____ m____, īgn____ pr____.

R: Fortūna fortēs metuit, īgnāvōs premit. (41)

474. Thāis h____ n____, n____ Laecānia d____. Quae r____ e__? Em____ h___ h____, i___ s__s.

R: Thāis habet nigrōs, niveōs Laecānia dentēs. Quae ratiō est? Emptōs haec habet, illa suōs. (61)

475. Īr_ f____ br____ est.

R: Īra furor brevis est. (53)

476. M___ s___ in c_____ s____.

R: Mēns sāna in corpore sānō. (30)

477. D___ j____ j_____, f_____, et p_____.

R: Deus jūdex jūstus, fortis, et patiēns. (51)

478. P____ n____ m____ s_____ v_____ t_____.

R: Parva necat morsū spatiōsum vīpera taurum. (21)

Echo the following synopses. [You will later be asked to *write* these same forms.]

331. ★ ○ ● colere (3d conjugation)

#1	#2	#3
colēbāmus	colimus	colēmus

332. ★ ○ ● custōdīre (4th conjugation)

#1	#2	#3
custōdiēbās	custōdīs	custōdiēs

333. ★ ○ ● obumbrāre (1st conjugation)

#1	#2	#3
obumbrābam	obumbrō	obumbrābō

334. ★ ○ ● facere (3d conjugation, -iō)

#1	#2	#3
faciēbat	facit	faciet

335. ★ ○ ● mordēre (2d conjugation)

#1	#2	#3
mordēbātis	mordētis	mordēbitis

336. ★ ○ ● dīcere (3d conjugation)

#1	#2	#3
dīcēbant	dīcunt	dīcent

Rearrange these forms in the proper order, #1 for past time, #2 for present, #3 for future time.

337. ∨ ★ ○ ● dīcunt/dīcent/dīcēbant

#1	#2	#3

R: dīcēbant   dīcunt   dīcent

338. ∨ ★ ○ ● mordēbitis/mordēbātis/mordētis

#1	#2	#3

R: mordēbātis   mordētis   mordēbitis

324. "Quae pars ōrātiōnis est 'vēritās'?"
"_____."

R: Nōmen.

325. "Quae pars ōrātiōnis est 'līberābit'?"
"_____."

R: Verbum.

326. Since the Latin verb is quite regular, we can predict many of the forms. For example, you can predict that the plural of **līberābit** will be _____nt.

A: līberābunt.

327. Echo a new technical term. ★ ● ○ ● ○ •
synōpsis

VCh: "sin-nópp-siss."

328. A brief outline of the plot of a play is called a "synopsis." In language work, a list of just one form of each tense is called a "s_____is" of a verb.

A: synopsis

329. The forms **līberābat, līberat, līberābit** (the Past, Present, and Future Imperfective tenses, 3d person singular) are called a s_____ of **līberāre**.

A: synopsis

330. Echo the synopsis of the verb **stāre** in the third person plural:

Imperfective	Past	Present	Future
	stābant #1	stant #2	stābunt #3

---

479. P_____ l_____ īns_____, n__ fl____, ind_____.

R: Parātae lacrimae īnsidiās, nōn flētum, indicant. (59)

480. L____ n__ m_____ l____.

R: Lupus nōn mordet lupum. (6)

481. L____ s___ m_____ v____.

R: Lēgēs sine mōribus vānae. (56)

482. V__ aud___ p____, l_____ scr____ m_____.

R: Vōx audīta perit, littera scrīpta manet. (57)

483. A__ l____, v___ br_____.

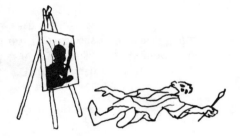

R: Ars longa, vīta brevis. (54)

SUMMARY

484. In this Unit you were reminded of an adjective formed on a verb stem. An example of this is **dōnāns,** which means "_____."

A: giving.

485. The form **dōnāns** is called the "p_____ p_____."

A: present participle.

Quaestiōnēs et Respōnsa

317. "Quālis vir erit qui nūllōs amīcōs habēbit?" "_____."

R: Trīstis.

318. "Sed qui habet multōs amīcōs nōn est trīstis sed h_____."

R: hilaris.

319. Tr____ ____ s____ s___. (122)

R: Trīstis eris sī sōlus eris.

320. V____ ○ ○ V___ l_____. (123)

R: Vēritās vōs līberābit. (123)

321. This means, "The _____."
[See if you can guess the meaning of the new verb **līberābit.**]

A: The truth will set you free.

322. Copy in your Notebook.

Quaestiōnēs et Respōnsa

323. "Cujus cāsūs est 'vōs'?" "_____."

R: Cāsūs accusātīvī.

486. In this Unit you learned another participle, of which an illustration would be **dōnātus**. This form is called the "_____ _____."

A: past participle.

487. While **dōnāns** means "giving," **dōnātus** means "_____."

A: given.

488. The past participle ends (in the nominative masculine singular) in _____ or _____.

A: -tus   -sus.

489. When we say that the English word "position" is derived from Latin **pōnit**, the relationship is not very clear until you understand that the past participle of **pōnit** is _____**tus**.

A: **positus**.

490. You learned more about word formation; you discovered that the suffix **-or**, as in **dōnātor**, means _____

A: a person who does something; a **dōnātor** is a person who gives.

491. In words like **laudātiō**, the **-iō** part is called a _____.

A: suffix.

492. You also learned the numbers for "first," "second," "third," and "fourth." The question word that asks for these numbers is _____.

A: Quotus?

---

311. Hodiē tū stultus ____ (eris/es/erās).
   ∨ ★ ○ ●

R: Hodiē tū stultus es.

312. Crās victor ____ (erit/est/erat) fēlix.
   ∨ ★ ○ ●

R: Crās victor erit fēlix.

313. ★ ○ ○ ○ Tr____ er____ s____ ____ ____
(122)

314. Haec vōx tristis oppōnitur vōcī hilaris. Quī tristis est dolōrem sentit. Ex oculīs hominis tristis dēfluunt lacrimae. Quota in pictūrā cernis canem tristem?

R: Prīma in pictūrā ego cernō canem tristem.

315. Tristis eris sī sōlus eris = _____.

A: You will be sad if you are alone.

316. Copy in your Notebook.

493. You also learned four new Basic Sentences. Pl_____ l_____ ā_____ p_____ v_____.

R: Plōrātur lacrimīs āmissa pecūnia vērīs. (60)

494. V__ au____ p____, l_____ scr____ m_____.

R: Vōx audīta perit, littera scrīpta manet. (57)

495. P_____ l_____ īn_____, ___ fl____, in_____.

R: Parātae lacrimae īnsidiās, nōn flētum, indicant. (59)

Choose the verb form which the words **herī** ("yesterday"), **hodiē** ("today"), and **crās** ("tomorrow") suggest.

303. Hodiē vōs hilarēs ____ (erītis/erātis/estis). ∨ ★ ○ •

R: Hodiē vōs hilarēs estis.

304. Hodiē nāvēs parvulae ____ (erant/erunt/sunt). ∨ ★ ○ •

R: Hodiē nāvēs parvulae sunt.

305. Herī tempora difficilia ____ (erant/erunt/sunt). ∨ ★ ○ •

R: Herī tempora difficilia erant.

306. Herī tū bella ____ (es/eris/erās). ∨ ★ ○ •

R: Herī tū bella erās.

307. Crās ego mortuus ____ (sum/erō/eram). ∨ ★ ○ •

R: Crās ego mortuus erō.

308. Hodiē ego ____ (sum/eram/erō) miser. ∨ ★ ○ •

R: Hodiē ego sum miser.

309. Crās dolōrēs ____ (erant/sunt/erunt). ∨ ★ ○ •

R: Crās dolōrēs erunt.

310. Crās vōs vīvī ____ (estis/erātis/erītis). ∨ ★ ○ •

R: Crās vōs vīvī erītis.

496. -- v------ p----- --- v--- f--------.

R: In virtūte posita est vēra fēlīcitās.
(58)

497. In this Unit you read your first complete Latin poem, which was written by the satirist M-------.

A: Martial.

498.
Thāis h---- n----, n----- Laecānia d------.
Qu--- r---- e---? Ēm---- h--- h----,
i--- s----.

R: Thāis habet nigrōs, niveōs Laecānia dentēs.
Quae ratiō est? Ēmptōs haec habet,
illa suōs. (61)

VOCABULARY INVENTORY

The vocabulary is large because many words were combinations of familiar parts.

294. Verba ōrātōris blanda erunt ⟶ --------------.
R: Crās verba ōrātōris blanda erunt.

295. Tū lepida erās ⟶ --------------
R: Herī tū lepida erās.

296. Dux erit sēcūrus ⟶ --------------
R: Crās dux erit sēcūrus.

297. Fūrēs erant ignāvī ⟶ --------------
R: Herī fūrēs erant ignāvī.

298. Custōdēs erunt honestī ⟶ --------------
R: Crās custōdēs erunt honestī.

299. Lūna erat alta ⟶ --------------
R: Herī lūna erat alta.

300. Vīta erit beāta ⟶ --------------
R: Crās vīta erit beāta.

301. Egō erō jūcundus ⟶ --------------
R: Crās egō erō jūcundus.

302. Vōs estis acerbī ⟶ --------------.
R: Hodiē vōs estis acerbī.

In this Unit you learned the following nouns:

apertūra (73)	laudātor (98)
aspectus (139)	lavātiō (108)
captor (92)	littera (225)
dōnātiō (105)	obumbrātiō (116)
dōnātor (95)	pictūra (195)
flētus (146)	possessiō (70)
frāctūra (71-72)	pūritās (230)
gravitās (231)	quaestiō (111)
īnsidiae (257)	quaesītor (102)
inventor (63-64)	ratiō (366)
laudātiō (115)	vōx (206-207)

You also learned these past participles:

āmissus (295)	laudātus (43-44)
apertus (54-55)	morsus (135-136)
audītus (208-209)	neglēctus (12-13)
dictus (149-151)	parātus (255)
dōnātus (65)	positus (235)
ēmptus (374-375)	possessus (58-59)
factus (150-151)	quaesītus (101)
frāctus (35-36)	scrīptus (202)
indicātus (256)	vīsus (60)
irrītātus (15-16)	inventus (48-49)

You learned these new verbs:

āmittit (293)	flet (142-143)	pōnit (235)
*aperit (56)	indicat (252-254)	salit (131)
audit (203)	lītigat (6-7)	scrībit (204)
dīcit (149)	parat (251-253)	
emit (375)	plōrat (284-285)	

You learned two new question words:

Quotus? Quota? Quotum? (170)   **Quae ratiō?** (368)

Three adjectives:

vērus-a-um (234)   **niger, nigra, nigrum** (355)
niveus-a-um (356)

---

285. "Estne hoc nōmen 'saltus,' generis fēminīnī an masculīnī?" "———."

R: Generis masculīnī.

286. "Estne nōmen 'animal,' generis masculīnī an neutrīus?" "———."

R: Generis neutrīus.

287. A few special adjectives have the genitive singular in -ius. The only one you know is neuter, whose genitive singular form is ———.

A: neutrīus.

288-289. The verb est is irregular in the #1, #2, and #3 tenses. Echo the paradigms of est, singular, then plural.

288. ✱ ○ • ○ •   289. ✱ ○ • ○ •

#1 eram	erāmus	#2 sum	sumus
erās	erātis	es	estis
erat	erant	est	sunt

290. ✱ ○ • ○ •

#3 erō	erimus
eris	eritis
erit	erunt

291-292. Copy the #1 and #3 tenses in your Notebook.

293-302. Expand these sentences with the word which the tense of the verb suggests, **heri** ("yesterday") for #1, **hodiē** ("today") for #2, and **crās** ("tomorrow") for #3. Remember that erat is #1 and erit is #3.

293. Vir erat caecus. ⟶ ———.

R: Herī vir erat caecus.

18-99

Two names:

Thāis (386)   **Laecānia** (386)

Four numbers:

prīmus-a-um (153-174)   **secundus-a-um** (154-174)   **tertius-a-um** (155-174)   **quārtus-a-um** (156-174)

One exclamation:

bene (180)

And finally, one connector:

vel (288)

[For your convenience, the frame number is given in parentheses. Review if necessary. The asterisk before **aperit** shows that there is a new meaning for this word.]

TEST INFORMATION

In this test you will be tested more on the skills which you have learned than on the answers to specific frames. For example, you will be asked to decline nouns which you have not practiced; by now you have declined so many First Declension nouns that you ought to be able to decline a First Declension noun without having ever seen or heard its paradigm. You will be told what declension the noun belongs to, and you will be asked only words which are known to you.

You will be asked to write Basic Sentences, as in the last sequence in the Unit, and you will be asked new questions on other Basic Sentences.

You will be asked to figure out the meaning of new words which contain familiar stems and prefixes or suffixes.

26-48

279. "Quālis vir est sī hoc facere potest?"
 "------."

R: Lepidus.

▲

280. "Quae animālia hoc lepidō saltū capientur?" "------."

R: Aprī.

▲

281. "Quid hic homō lepidē aget?" "D--- ap--- c------."

R: Duōs aprōs capiet.

▲

282. J--- e--- ū--- in s---(121) lep--- ap--- c------ d---.

R: *Jam egō ūnō in saltū lepidē aprōs capiam duōs.*

▲

283. In linguā Latīnā sunt tria genera. "Via" est generis fēminīnī, "oculus" est generis masculīnī, et "corpus" est generis neutrīus.

From the above sentences, you can see that the word **lingua**, besides meaning "tongue," can also mean "------."

A: language.

▲

284. The word **genus**, besides meaning "family," can also mean "------."

A: gender.

▲

UNIT NINETEEN

1. Echo after each number as your teacher counts ("First, second, etc."); ★ ○ • ○ •

   I   II   III   IV   V
prīmus secundus tertius quārtus quīntus

  VI   VII   VIII   IX   X
sextus septimus octāvus nōnus decimus

[Repeat until you have learned them all.]

2. **Animal octāvum est** _____. [Dashes do not indicate the number of missing letters.]

R: leō.

3. **Animal sextum est** _____.

R: aper.

4. **Animal quīntum est** _____.

R: sīmia.

5. **Animal decimum est** _____.

R: musca.

6. **Animal septimum est** _____.

R: elephantus.

274. Lepidus significat "*bellus.*" **Fēmina quae est lepida est mulier quae mente formāque omnibus placet. Quota in pictūrā cernis puellam lepidam?**

R: **ego c----- p------- I------.**

R: **Prīma in pictūrā ego cernō puellam lepidam.**

275. This ambitious young man says, "_____."

Jam ego ūnō in saltū lepidē aprōs capiam duōs.

A: I will cleverly capture two boars in one jump.

276. Copy in your Notebook.

277. Our expression for the same idea is to kill two -----s with one -----.

A: birds   stone.

Quaestiōnēs et Respōnsa

278. "**Quāliter hic homō duōs aprōs capiet?**" "_____."

R: **Lepidē.**

19-2

7. Animal nōnum est _____.

R: taurus.

8. Animal prīmum est _____.

R: rāna.

9. "Quotum animal est sīmia?"
   "Sīmia est animal _____."

R: quīntum.

10. Leō est animal _____.

R: octāvum.

11. Aper est animal _____.

R: sextum.

12. Elephantus est animal _____.

R: septimum.

13. Musca est animal _____.

R: decimum.

14. Taurus est animal _____.

R: nōnum.

15. "Quotum animal est mūs?" "Mūs est animal _____."

R: quārtum.

16. Equus est animal _____.

R: secundum.

---

270. The forms of the Latin numeral for "two" are slightly irregular. Echo your teacher as he counts these flowers. ★ ○ ○ ●

Ūnus flōs.   Duo flōrēs.   Trēs flōrēs.

271. Finally he will count the animals. ★ ○ ○ ●

Ūnum animal.   Duo animālia.   Tria animālia.

272. ★ ○ ●

	m	f	n
	duo	duae	duo
	duo	duās	duo
	duōs	duābus	duōbus
	duōbus		

[You need not learn these forms yet.]

273. ★ ○ ○ ○ ○ ● Ū__ e__ ū__ in__ s____ l____ apr____ c____ d____. [There are seven long vowels.] (121)

R: Jam ego ūnō in saltū lepidē aprōs capiam duōs.

I II III IV
V VI
VII VIII IX X

17. "Quotō in orbe est quercus?"
    "S_____ō in orbe est quercus."

R: Secundō in orbe est quercus.

18. "Quotō in orbe est auris?"
    "_____ in orbe est auris."

R: Octāvō in orbe est auris.

19. "Quotō in orbe est fōns?"
    "_____ in or___ est fōns."

R: Quīntō in orbe est fōns.

20. "Quotō in orbe est manus?"
    "_____ in ____ est m_____."

R: Sextō in orbe est manus.

21. "Quotō in orbe est oculus?"
    "_____ __ ____ est _____."

R: Septimō in orbe est oculus.

22. "Quotō in orbe est pēs?"
    "_____ __ ____ est ____."

R: Decimō in orbe est pēs.

23. "Quotō in orbe est pecūnia?"
    "_____ __ ____ est _____."

R: Tertiō in orbe est pecūnia.

---

265. h____ s____ v____. (120)

R: In hōc signō vincēs.

266. Echo your teacher as he counts these ships. ★ ○ ○ ●

Here are the first three Latin numerals.

Ūna nāvis.
Duae nāvēs.
Trēs nāvēs.

267. A UNIcorn has only ___ horn.
A: one

268. A car with DUal controls has ___ sets of controls.
A: two

269. And a TRIangle has ___ angles.
A: three

24. "Quotō in orbe est effigiēs?"
"_ _ _ _ _ _ _ _ _ _ est _ _ _ _ _ _ _ _ _."

R: Prīmō in orbe est effigiēs.

25. "Quotō in orbe est flūmen?"
"_ _ _ _ _ _ _ _ _ est _ _ _ _ _ _."

R: Nōnō in orbe est flūmen.

26. Because the word **orbe** is masculine gender, the adjectives in the sequence you just did are all _ _ _ _ _ _ _ _ gender to agree with **orbe**.

A: masculine

27. Because **orbe** is _ _ _ _ _ _ _ _ case and _ _ _ _ _ _ _ number, the adjectives in the sequence are all _ _ _ _ _ _ _ _ case and _ _ _ _ _ _ _ _ number to agree with **orbe**.

A: ablative singular ablative singular

28. Let us review the four different sentence types which we have had. The first one is the kind containing a verb which patterns with an accusative as its object. This kind of sentence we call the { _ _ _ _ _ _ } type.

A: {-s -m -t}

29. The second type of sentence which we have had is the kind containing a verb which does *not* have an accusative as its object. An example is the sentence **Vēritās numquam perit**. We call this kind the { _ _ _ _ } type.

A: {-s -t}

30. The third type of sentence can be made by transforming an {-s -m -t} sentence to the passive voice. Sentences with passive verbs are called the { _ _ _ _ _ _ } type.

A: {-s -tur}

---

259. _ _ _ _ in _ _ _ v _ _ t f _ _ _ _ _ _ (119)

R: **Aut inveniam viam aut faciam.**

260. ★ ○ ○ ○ h _ _ s _ _ v _ _ _ _ _ _ [Four long vowels]. (120)

R: **In hōc signō vincēs.** [Did you include four macrons?]

261. Constantine the Great, Emperor of Rome from A.D. 324 to 337, is said to have been converted to Christianity by seeing a cross in the heavens and hearing the words, "**In hōc sign-** _ _ _ _ _."

R: **In hōc signō vincēs.**

262. This means, "_ ."

A: In this sign (or "under this sign,") you will conquer.

263. Copy in your Notebook.

264. The sign by which he was to conquer was the _ _ _ _ _ .

A: cross.

31. The last type we have had is the one that states that two things are the same. Both nouns are in the nominative case. We call this kind of sentence the {_ _ _ _ _ _} type.

A: {-s -s est}

32. From here on we will try to rely almost entirely on symbols rather than English directions. If you are ever in doubt about their meaning, refer to your Notebook. In particular, remember that the check sign [√ ★ ○] means "_ _."

A: Say your answer aloud and *then* check with the tape or with the Visual Check.

33. The sentence below is of one of the four types reviewed in frames 28-31. Identify its pattern and then say the complete sentence. Choose the *only* verb which will fit into the pattern.

$$\text{Agnus lupus nōn} \begin{cases} \text{est.} \\ \text{stat.} \\ \text{videt.} \\ \text{capitur.} \end{cases}$$

Say the complete sentence and check. _ _ _ _ _ _ _ _.
√ ★ ○ •

R: Agnus lupus nōn est.

34. This is an {_ _ _ _ _} sentence.

A: {-s -s est}

35.
$$\text{Virōs vestis} \begin{cases} \text{manet.} \\ \text{est.} \\ \text{facit.} \\ \text{redditur.} \end{cases}$$

Say the complete sentence and check. _ _ _ _ _ _ _ _.
√ ★ ○ •

R: Virōs vestis facit.

36. This is an {_ _ _ _ _} sentence.

A: {-s -m -t-}

---

253. Read and check. Vir viam quaerit.
√ ★ ○ •

254. Here we see that the word *via* has three different meanings. The dog is lying in the _ _ _ _ _ _; the pigs are lying in the r_ _ _ _; whereas the man is trying to find his _ _ _ through the woods.

A: street
   road
   way

255. If you send something *via* Chicago, it means it goes by _ _ _ of Chicago.

A: way

256. Expand with the missing elements. _ _ _ aut inveniam viam aut _ _ _ faciam.

R: Egō aut inveniam viam aut egō faciam viam.

257. This motto, Aut inveniam viam aut faciam, means, "_ _ _ _ _ _ _ _ _ _ _ _ _ _ _ _ _."

A: I'll either find a way or make one.

258. Copy in your Notebook.

37. Piscis ā virō { est. / capitur. / quaerit. / stat.

Say the complete sentence. ----------------
√ ★ ○ •

R: Piscis ā virō capitur.

38. This is an {_____} sentence.

A: {-s -tur}

39. Dux vir { est. / timet. / cernitur. / perit.

---------------------- √ ★ ○ •

R: Dux vir est.

40. This is an {_____} sentence.

A: {-s -s est}

41. Taurōs fēminae { sunt. / regunt. / stant. / dūcuntur.

---------------------- √ ★ ○ •

R: Taurōs fēminae regunt.

42. This is an {_____} sentence.

A: {-s -m -t}

43. Vulpēs ā leōne nōn { reddit. / manet. / premitur. / est.

---------------------- √ ★ ○ •

R: Vulpēs ā leōne nōn premitur.

44. This is an {_____} sentence.

A: {-s -tur}

---

249. "Metuisne vīperamque taurumque?" "--------; --------."

R: Minimē; metuō aut vīperam aut taurum.

250. ★ ○ ○ ○ (119) A. ____ in ____ v ____ f ____.

R: Aut inveniam viam aut faciam.

251. The word via has several meanings. Read the description of this picture and check with the tape. Canis in viā currit. √ ★ ○ •

252. Read and check. Suēs in viā quiēscunt. √ ★ ○ •

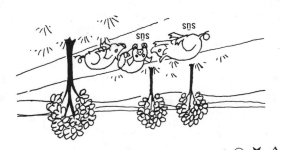

45.
Īnfāns homō { est.
videt.
irrītātur.
currit.

---------------------- √ ★ ○ •

R: Īnfāns homō est.

46. This is an {_____} sentence.

A: {-s -s est}

47.
Sīmiae taurī nōn { dīligunt.
mordentur.
currunt.
sunt.

---------------------- √ ★ ○ •

R: Sīmiae taurī nōn sunt.

48. This is an {_____} sentence.

A: {-s -s -est}

49.
Īnsidiās fūr { parātur.
indicat.
est.
perit.

---------------------- √ ★ ○ •

R: Īnsidiās fūr indicat.

50. This is an {_____} sentence.

A: {-s -m -t}

51.
Manūs saccum { est.
tenent.
tenētur.
stant.

---------------------- √ ★ ○ •

R: Manūs saccum tenent.

52. This is an {_____} sentence.

A: {-t -m -s-}

Sometimes, however, the situation is not so clear: the existence of ambiguous forms in Latin means that you cannot always tell from the form alone whether a word is subject or object. In some of the following frames there is more than one possible interpretation; you must give both possibilities to consider yourself right. For example, **Jūdex auxilium** could fit into two sentences: **Jūdex auxilium dōnat**, and **Jūdex auxilium est**.

53. In **Jūdex auxilium dōnat**, the word **auxilium** is _____ case, while in **Jūdex auxilium est**, the word **auxilium** is _____ case.

A: accusative
   nominative

54. **Jūdex auxilium est** = The _____ is a _____.

A: The judge is a help.

55. **Jūdex auxilium dōnat** = The _____ _____s help.

A: The judge gives help.

Remember that in this sequence some of the sentences will have *two* possible choices, and others will have only *one*. Say the whole sentence (or sentences).

56.
Fēminae hominēs { pereunt.
                  laudantur.
                  sunt.
                  dīligunt. } √ ★ ○ •

R: Fēminae hominēs sunt, Fēminae hominēs dīligunt.

57. Fēminae hominēs sunt = _____.

A: Women are human beings.

---

234. Tempore praesentī muscās _____ (capitis/capiētis/capiēbātis). √ ★ ○ •

R: Tempore praesentī muscās capitis.

235. Tempore futūrō lupōs _____ (metuam/metuō/metuēbam). √ ★ ○ •

R: Tempore futūrō lupōs metuam.

236. Tempore praesentī rēgnum _____ (possidēbō/possidēbam/possideō). √ ★ ○ •

R: Tempore praesentī rēgnum possideō.

237. Tempore praeteritō ducī _____ (serviō/serviēbam/serviam). √ ★ ○ •

R: Tempore praeteritō ducī serviēbam.

238. Tempore futūrō manūs datōris _____ (aspiciet/aspicit/aspiciēbat). √ ★ ○ •

R: Tempore futūrō manūs datōris aspiciet.

239. Tempore praeteritō Titō _____ (nūbis/nūbēs/nūbēbās). √ ★ ○ •

R: Tempore praeteritō Titō nūbēbās.

240. Tempore futūrō pecūniam āmissam _____ (plōrāmus/plōrābimus/plōrābimus).

R: Tempore futūrō pecūniam āmissam plōrābimus.

241. Under Facts About Latin copy the following: The #3 tense shows incomplete action in future time. **Plōrābimus** may be translated in English by "We are going to cry," "We will cry," and in several other ways.

242. Echo a new connector. ★ ○ • aut

58. Fēminae hominēs dīligunt = _____.

A: Women love human beings.

59. Saccum mūrēs { nōn sunt. / aperiuntur. / stant. / inveniunt. } ✓ ★ ○ •

R: Saccum mūrēs inveniunt.

60. Saccum mūrēs inveniunt = The ____ ____ing the ____.

A: The mice are finding the sack.

61. Mūrēs elephantī nōn { capiunt. / irrītantur. / sunt. / sapiunt. } ✓ ★ ○ •

R: Mūrēs elephantī nōn sunt, Mūrēs elephantī nōn capiunt.

62. Mūrēs elephantī nōn capiunt = _____ don't _____ ____.

A: Elephants don't catch mice.

63. Mūrēs elephantī nōn sunt = _____ aren't ____, or ____ aren't _____.

A: Elephants aren't mice. Mice aren't elephants.

64. Agnī ab aquilīs { capiuntur. / sunt. / aspiciunt. / currunt. } ✓ ★ ○ •

R: Agnī ab aquilīs capiuntur, Agnī ab aquilīs currunt.

---

226. Tempore praeteritō = In p--- t-------

A: In past time

227. Tempore praesentī = In t------- -----

A: In present time

228. Tempore futūrō = ----------------

A: In future time

In this sequence, choose the tense of the verb that makes the best sense with the time expression. Use #1 with tempore praeteritō, #2 with tempore praesentī, and #3 with tempore futūrō. Check with the tape.

229. Tempore praeteritō auctōrēs opus ---- (laudant/laudābunt/laudābant). ✓ ★ ○ •

R: Tempore praeteritō auctōrēs opus laudābant.

230. This means that ---------------------. [In your own words]

A: in the past authors used to praise (were praising, etc.) their works. [Without the context, you can't tell which meaning is intended.]

231. Tempore futūrō imāginem flōris ---- (pingō/pingēbam/pingam). ✓ ★ ○ •

R: Tempore futūrō imāginem flōris pingam.

232. Tempore praesentī pecūniam ---- (tenēs/tenēbās/tenēbis). ✓ ★ ○ •

R: Tempore praesentī pecūniam tenēs.

233. Tempore futūrō inopī beneficium ---- (damus/dabimus/dabāmus). ✓ ★ ○ •

R: Tempore futūrō inopī beneficium dabimus. (The verb *dare* is *irregular*; the -a- is short in *almost* all the forms.)

65. Agnī ab aquilīs capiuntur = _____ are _____ by _____.

A: Lambs are caught by eagles.

66. Agnī ab aquilīs currunt = _____ ___ f___ _____.

A: Lambs run from eagles.

67. Opus ab auctōre ⎰neglegitur.
⎨est.
⎨manet.
⎩scrībit. ✓ ★ ○ •

R: Opus ab auctōre neglegitur.

68. Opus ab auctōre neglegitur = The _____ is _____ by ___ _____.

A: The work is neglected by the author.

69. Vīpera animal ⎰obumbrātur.
⎨perit.
⎨mordet.
⎩est. ✓ ★ ○ •

R: Vīpera animal est, Vīpera animal mordet.

70. Vīpera animal est = A _____ __ an _____, *or* An _____ __ a _____.

A: A snake is an animal. An animal is a snake.

71. Vīpera animal mordet = The _____ _____ the _____.

A: The snake bites the animal.

Copy the following paradigms in your Notebook and label them #3 tense. Indicate also the conjugation.

218. **facere (-iō)** ★ ○ •

faciam faciēmus
faciēs faciētis
faciet facient

219. **servīre** ★ ○ •

serviam serviēmus
serviēs serviētis
serviet servient

220. 1st Conjugation

adjuvābō adjuvābimus
adjuvābis adjuvābitis
adjuvābit adjuvābunt

221. 2nd Conjugation

mordēbō mordēbimus
mordēbis mordēbitis
mordēbit mordēbunt

222. 3d Conjugation

reddam reddēmus
reddēs reddētis
reddet reddent

223. 3d Conjugation (-iō)

aspiciam aspiciēmus
aspiciēs aspiciētis
aspiciet aspicient

224. 4th Conjugation

saliam saliēmus
saliēs saliētis
saliet salient

225. ★ ○ • ("time")

tempus tempora
tempus tempora
tempore temporibus
temporī temporibus
temporis temporum

19-11

You will now learn a new part of speech.

72. Describe this picture, in which the happy old lady is giving money. **Haec hil____ an____ pec_____ dōn___.**

R: **Haec hilaris anus pecūniam dōnat.**

73. In this sentence the word **hilaris** is the part of speech called an _____, and it modifies the word _____.

A: adjective
                    anus.

74. Now echo your teacher as he describes this same picture. However, he will transform **hilaris** to a new part of speech. ★ ○ ● ○ ● **H___ an___ p_____ h_____ter d____.**

Cōnf: **Haec anus pecūniam hilariter dōnat.**

75. The new signal on **hilariter** is the three letters _____.

A: **-ter.**

The new word **hilariter** now modifies **dōnat**; it is the giving which is cheerful.

76. Haec anus pecūniam hilariter dōnat =
The ___ ___ is ___ing _____ ch_____ly.

A: The old lady is giving money cheerfully.

77. Echo a new technical term. ★ ○ • ○ •
a d v e r b

VCh: "ádd-verb"

78. Hilariter is an adverb. Adverbs, as the last part of the name suggests, modify ____ (nouns/adjectives/verbs).

A: verbs.

Adverbs tell *IN WHAT WAY* the action of the verb happens.

79. Anus hilariter dōnat means that the old lady gives _____ly.

A: cheerfully.

80. Echo as your teacher asks *IN WHAT WAY* the old lady gives money. ★ ○ • ○ • "**Quāliter** an__ pec_____ dō___?"

Cōnf: Quāliter anus pecūniam dōnat?

81. Echo the answer. ★ ○ • ○ • "Hilari____."

Cōnf: Hilariter.

82. The question word which asks "in what way" is qu_____.

A: quāliter.

Many adverbs are formed on adjectives by using the signal **-ter**.

83. ★ ○ • ○ • **intemperanter, ēloquenter, crūdēliter, patienter, hilariter**

---

205. Echo the paradigm of the #3 tense of a Fourth Conjugation verb: ★ ○ •

R: custōdiam   custōdiēmus
    custōdiēs   custōdiētis
    custōdiet   custōdient

206. Say the paradigm of the #3 tense of **servīre**:

R: serviam   serviēmus
    serviēs   serviētis
    serviet   servient   ★ ○ •

207. Write the #3 tense of **audīre**:

R: audiam   audiēmus
    audiēs   audiētis
    audiet   audient

208. ★ ○ ○ ○ S____ qu____ c_____ ip c_____? [There are four long vowels.] (118)

R: *Sed quis custōdiet ipsos custōdēs?* (118)

209. *Custōs est vir qui c____dit.*

R: custōdit

210. We need custodians to watch our property, but the question is, _____?

A: but who will watch the custodians themselves?

19-13

84-88. In this sequence, echo your teacher's answers.

84. "Hī juvenēs hilarēs sunt. Quāliter sub jūdice manent?" ★ ○ • ○ • "H_____ter."

📧

Cōnf: Hilariter.

85. "Hī auctōrēs ēloquentēs sunt. Quāliter opus suum laudant?" ★ ○ • ○ • "Ēl_____."

📧

Cōnf: Ēloquenter.

86. "Hī hominēs intemperantēs sunt. Quāliter vīnum bibunt?" ★ ○ • ○ • "_____."

📧

Cōnf: Intemperanter.

87. "Hī lupī crūdēlēs sunt. Quāliter animālia blanda necant?" ★ ○ • ○ • "_____."

📧

Cōnf: Crūdēliter.

88. "Deus est patiēns. Quāliter orbem jūdicat?" ★ ○ • ○ • "_____."

📧

Cōnf: Patienter.

89. ★ ○ • hilariter, ēloquenter, crūdēliter, patienter, intemperanter

📧

90. These adverbs in **-ter** are formed from the adjectives **hilaris, patiēns, quālis, ēloquēns, intemperāns,** and **crūdēlis,** all of which belong to the ____ (1/2/3/4/5) Declension.

📧

A: 3d

Adjectives of the First-and-Second Declension (like **jūstus-a-um**) have a variant signal. Echo these adverbs formed on familiar adjectives of the First-and-Second Declension.

91. ★ ○ • ○ • cautē, jūstē, vērē, īnsānē

📧

---

199. Echo the paradigm of the #3 form of a Third Conjugation verb: ★ ○ •

R: premam premēmus
premēs premētis
premet prement

📧

200. On the model of **premam,** say the paradigm of **colere** in the #3 tense:

\-\-\-am \-\-\-ēmus
\-\-\-ēs \-\-\-ētis ∨ ★ ○ •
\-\-\-et \-\-\-ent

📧

R: colam colēmus
colēs colētis
colet colent

📧

201. Write the #3 tense of **pāscere.**

_____ _____

R: pāscam pāscēmus
pāscēs pāscētis
pāscet pāscent

📧

202. Echo the paradigm of the #3 form of a Third Conjugation **-iō** verb: ★ ○ •

effugiam effugiēmus
effugiēs effugiētis
effugiet effugient

📧

203. Say the paradigm of the #3 tense of **sapere** (an **-iō** verb):

\-\-\-iam \-\-\-iēmus
\-\-\-iēs \-\-\-iētis ∨ ★ ○ •
\-\-\-iet \-\-\-ient

📧

R: sapiam sapiēmus
sapiēs sapiētis
sapiet sapient

📧

204. Write the #3 tense of **capere.**

_____ _____

R: capiam capiēmus
capiēs capiētis
capiet capiet

📧

19-14

92-106. Echo your teacher as he answers in what way these actions take place.

92. "Quāliter lupī foveam metuunt?"
★ ○ • ○ • "C___ē."

Cōnf: Cautē.

93. "Quāliter aqua mediō flūmine quaeritur?" ★ ○ • ○ • "Īns___."

Cōnf: Īnsānē.

94. "Quāliter āmissa pecūnia plōrātur?"
★ ○ • ○ • "V___."

Cōnf: Vērē.

95. "Quāliter Deus orbem jūdicat?"
★ ○ • ○ • "J___."

Cōnf: Jūstē.

96. "Quāliter Deus orbem jūdicat?" "Pat___."

R: Patienter.

97. "Quāliter hī auctōrēs opus laudant?" "Ēl___."

R: Ēloquenter.

98. "Quāliter hī lupī animālia blanda quaerunt?" "Cr___."

R: Crūdēliter.

99. "Quāliter hī hominēs vīnum bibunt?" "Int___."

R: Intemperanter.

100. "Quāliter juvenēs sub jūdice manent?" "Hil___."

R: Hilariter.

---

193. Echo the paradigm of the #3 form of a first conjugation verb: ★ ○ •

R: parābō   parābimus
   parābis   parābitis
   parābit   parābunt

194. On the model of parābō, say the paradigm of irritābō and check with the tape.

___bō   ___bimus
___bis   ___bitis √ ★ ○ •
___bit   ___bunt

R: irritābō   irritābimus
   irritābis   irritābitis
   irritābit   irritābunt

195. On the model of these last two verbs, write the #3 form of lavāre. [Or say it.]

R: lavābō   lavābimus
   lavābis   lavābitis
   lavābit   lavābunt

196. Echo the paradigm of the #3 form of a Second Conjugation verb: ★ ○ •

   tenēbō   tenēbimus
   tenēbis   tenēbitis
   tenēbit   tenēbunt

197. On the model of tenēbō, say the paradigm of nocēbō.

___bō   ___bimus
___bis   ___bitis √ ★ ○ •
___bit   ___bunt

R: nocēbō   nocēbimus
   nocēbis   nocēbitis
   nocēbit   nocēbunt

198. Write the #3 form of tacēre.

R: tacēbō   tacēbimus
   tacēbis   tacēbitis
   tacēbit   tacēbunt

19-15

101. ★ ○ • **cautē, īnsānē, vērē, jūstē**

102. "Quāliter plōrātur āmissa pecūnia?" "V__ē."

R: **Vērē.**

103. "In what way is lost money wept for?" "___ly."

A: **Truly.**

104. "Quāliter foveam metuunt lupī?" "C____."

R: **Cautē.**

105. "Quāliter aqua quaeritur mediō flūmine?" "Īns___."

R: **Īnsānē.**

106. "Quāliter Deus orbem jūdicat?" "J____."

R: **Jūstē.**

107. The new word **jūdicat** is the part of speech called a ____ and must mean "____s."

A: verb   judges

108. The variant signal of **-ter** which changes many First and Second Declension adjectives (like **cautus**) is _____.

A: **-ē.**

In this sequence the **-ter** type and the **-ē** type will be mixed.

109. Echo first three new **-ē** adverbs. ★ ○ •
īgnāvē, blandē, avārē

Echo the infinitives of the verbs which we will use in the next four frames.

187. ★ ○ • Second Conjugation
dēbēre
movēre
nocēre
placēre
tacēre
tenēre
vidēre

188. ★ ○ • Third Conjugation
crēdere
currere
dūcere
fluere
oppōnere
metuere
premere
regere

189. Write the forms which are #3 tense (future time): **metuēs, crēdēs, dēbēs, placēs, dūcēs, tenēs, tacēs, oppōnēs, movēbis.**

A: **metuēs, crēdēs, dūcēs, oppōnēs, movēbis.**

190. Write the forms which show present time (#2 tense): **nocēmus, cernimus, vidēmus, premēmus, placēbimus, regēmus, movēmus.**

A: **nocēmus, cernimus, vidēmus, movēmus**

191. Write the verbs which are #3 tense. **dūcēs, movēmus, tenētis, metuēmus, crēdēs, flēbit, tacēs.**

A: **dūcēs, metuēmus, crēdēs, flēbit**

192. Write the verbs which are #2 tense. **nocēmus, vidēs, oppōnēmus, premētis, regēmus, dēbēs.**

A: **nocēmus, vidēs, dēbēs**

110. Copy these three adverbs in your Notebook under "Forms" and label them "Adverbs." **īgnāvē, blandē, avārē**

111. Echo three new **-ter** adverbs. ★ ○ •
fortiter, leviter, sapienter

112. Copy these three adverbs in your Notebook under "Forms." **fortiter, leviter, sapienter**

Read the questions aloud, and write your teacher's answer.

113. "**Quāliter fūrēs canem timent?**" ★ ○ • ○ • "_____."

R: Īgnāvē.

114. "**Quāliter medicī aegrōs cūrant?**" ★ ○ • ○ • "_____."

R: Blandē.

115. "**Quāliter mūs elephantum premit?**" ★ ○ • ○ • "_____."

R: Fortiter.

116. "**Quāliter juvenēs perīc'la cernunt?**" ★ ○ • ○ • "_____."

R: Leviter.

117. "**Quāliter stultī pecūniam quaerunt?**" ★ ○ • ○ • "_____."

R: Avārē.

118. "**Quāliter līs jūdicātur?**" ★ ○ • ○ • "_____."

R: Sapienter.

---

181. **Timēbit** is tense number ____ (1/2/3).

A: 3.

182. In learning anything, we must be careful to distinguish between things which resemble one another but are actually different. For example, **tenēbimus** looks a great deal like **tenēbāmus.** They differ only in the fact that _____ [In your own words]

A: **tenēbimus** has **-i-** where **tenēbāmus** has **-ā-**.

183. From the following list, write those verbs which are #1 tense and show *past time*. **possidēbit, satiābās, tenēbō, irritābunt, nocēbam, manēbunt, serviēbam, stābant**

A: **satiābās, nocēbam, serviēbam, stābant**

184. Write the verbs which are #3 tense and show *future time*. **dēlūebat, nūbēbam, timēbit, necābō, premēbant, aspiciēbās, parābis, habēbunt**

A: **timēbit, necābō, parābis, habēbunt**

185. A harder distinction to make is the one between the forms of the #2 tense (present) for verbs of the Second Conjugation and the forms of the #3 tense (future) for verbs of the Third Conjugation. Although **habet** and **premet** both end in **-et**, you know the **-e-** in **habet** signals _____ time.

A: present.

186. The **-e-** in **premet**, however, signals _____.

A: future time.

119. ★ ○ • blandē, avārē, īgnāvē, fortiter, leviter, sapienter

Give these same answers yourself.

120. "Quāliter stultī pecūniam quaerunt?" "Av___."

R: Avārē.

121. "Quāliter medicī aegrōs cūrant?" "Bl___."

R: Blandē.

122. "Quāliter līs jūdicātur?" "S___."

R: Sapienter.

123. "Quāliter mūs elephantum premit?" "F___."

R: Fortiter.

124. "Quāliter fūrēs canem timent?" "Īg___."

R: Īgnāvē.

125. "Quāliter juvenēs perīc'la cernunt?" "L___."

R: Leviter.

126. Next we will read another poem, written about 2,000 years ago. Like the first poem in this course, this one is by the satirist M___.

A: Martial.

---

174. In lītigābō the -i- on the signal -bi-d___s.

A: disappears.

175. Also notice that in emam the signal for future time is the variant ___-a-.

176. The contrast between timēbat/timet/timēbit is called the "tense" of the verb. Timēbat is therefore the Past T___.

A: Tense.

177. Echo a new technical term. ★ ○ • ○ •

i m p e r f e c t i v e

178. You may notice that we have stressed the fact that such forms as capiēbam and capit show action that is not complete, but either was going on in the past or is going on in the present time. The technical term for this kind of action is *imperfective*. Therefore the complete name for the form such as timēbāmus would be p___ imp___ t___.

A: past imperfective tense.

Imperfective	Past	Present	Future
	timēbat	timet	timēbit
	1	2	3

179. However, it is easier to use the numbers in the boxes. Timēbat is tense number ___ (1/2/3).

A: 1.

180. Timet is tense number ___ (1/2/3).

A: 2.

127. The experience of going back into the past through reading is particularly valuable for Americans, because America is such a new country. America is composed of peoples who came from all parts of the world to start a new life. Many people have little idea of where their grandparents were born, except that it was "somewhere in the old country." This "New World" has been a wonderful thing, but it means that America does not have the traditions of hundreds and thousands of years which exist in many other parts of the world. A literary critic named Kazin wrote recently, "Our culture is stupefyingly without support from tradition." This is perhaps an extreme statement, but what he meant was that our nation suffers severely from the fact that it is so new that it lacks ----------.

A: traditions.

128. The study of Latin helps fill this gap. When you read Latin, you are undergoing an experience which almost every educated man in Europe has had for the last two thousand years. The poems which you will read in this program have been read by ---- (hundreds/thousands/millions) of people.

A: millions

Now to our poem. There is one new point of structure, used in calling people.

129. Most men's names in Latin end in **-us**. Echo the name of the man who appears in this poem. ★ ○ • ○ • **Caeciliānus**

130. Echo the name of Martial's friend to whom he addresses this poem. ★ ○ • ○ • **Titus**

For men's names that end in **-us** there is a special calling form. Echo your teacher as he calls these people.

167-169.

★ ○ ○   ★ ○ ○   ★ ○ ○
Past   Present Future

H. l----- ag--- noc-----, h--- aqu---, c--- leō t---bit.

R: Herī lupus agnō nocēbat, hodiē aquam quaerit, crās leōnem timēbit.

Echo verbs which show *two ways* of forming the form which shows future time. First the singular, then the plural.

170. ★ ○ • ○ •
litigābō   litigābunt
litigābis   litigābitis
litigābit   litigābimus

171. ★ ○ • ○ •
emam   emēmus
emēs   emētis
emet   ement

172. In **emēs** the signal for future time is the sound ----, while in **litigābis** it is the sound ----.

A: -ē-   -bi-.

173. Note that in **litigābunt** the -i- of the signal -bi- changes to ----.

A: -u-

19-19

131.

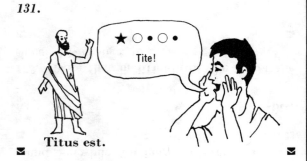

Titus est.

132.

Caeciliānus est.

133.

Mārcus est.

Now call these people yourself, changing the nominative **-us** to **-e**.

134.

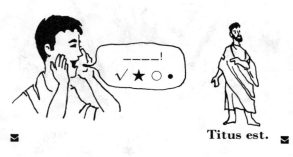

Titus est.

R: Tite!

R: Herī fēmina vestem lavābat, hodiē cōnsilium capit, crās piscēs emet.

H___ f___ ves___ la___, h___ cōnsi___ c___, c___ p___ em___.

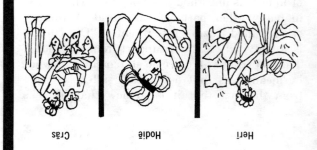

Herī   Hodiē   Crās

★ ○ ○   ★ ○ ○   ★ ○ ○
Past   Present   Future

164-166.

R: Herī agnus currēbat, hodiē sub quercū stat, crās celeriter saliet.

H___ ag___ curr___, h___ sub qu___ s___, c___ cel___ter sal___.

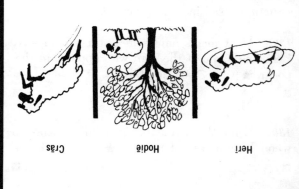

Herī   Hodiē   Crās

★ ○ ○   ★ ○ ○   ★ ○ ○
Past   Present   Future

161-163.

19-20

135.

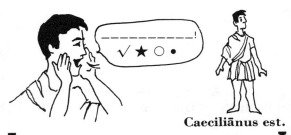

Caeciliānus est.

R: Caeciliāne!

136.

Mārcus est.

R: Mārce!

137-138. Here's the poem. ★ ○ •
Nōn cēnat sine aprō noster, Tite,
    Caeciliānus.
★ ○ •
    Bellum convīvam Caeciliānus habet. (62)

139. You are not expected to understand the poem yet; there are too many new words, for one thing. But we do expect you to see the structure of the poem at once. In the first place, the new calling form tells us that Martial is addressing a person named _____.

A: Titus.

140. **Nōn cēnat sine aprō Caeciliānus** is an {_____} type of sentence.

A: {-s -t}

26-28

154-156.

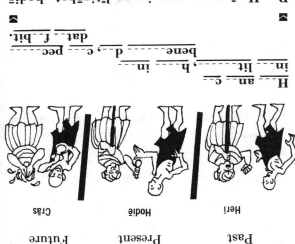

Past ○ ○ ★
Present ○ ○ ★
Future ○ ○ ★

R: Herī anus cum inope litigābat, hodiē inopī beneficium dat, crās pecūniam datam flēbit.

H__ an__ c_____ in_____ lit_____, h____ in____ bene_____ d___, c____ pec_____ dat___ f__bit.

157. The contrast between the future **premet** with the signal **-e-** and **flēbit** with the signal **-bi-** shows that there are ___ variant signals to show future time in Latin.

A: two

158-160.

Past ○ ○ ★
Present ○ ○ ★
Future ○ ○ ★

R: Herī jūdex injūstē agēbat, hodiē mentem mūtat, crās nocentem damnābit.

H__ j____ inj_____ ag____, h____ men___ m____, c____ noc_____ dam_____.

19-21

141. The new verb **cēnat** is modified by the prepositional phrase s___ ap__ and the negator ___.

A: sine aprō nōn.

142. Bellum convīvam Caeciliānus habet is an {_____} sentence.

A: {-s -m -t}

143. The subject of both lines is _____.

A: Caeciliānus.

Now for the new vocabulary.

144. Ask your teacher what this man is doing. √ ★ ○ • Qu__ ___ h__ v__?

Cōnf: Quid agit hic vir?

145. Echo and write his answer. ★ ○ • ○ • "_____."

R: Cēnat.

146. Cēnat = He is d__ing.

A: He is dining.

151–153. Write, if you have a tape recorder, your teacher's description of what the young man was doing *yesterday*, what he is doing *now*, and what he is going to be doing *tomorrow*. If you do not have a tape recorder, then of course you can't have the practice in writing from dictation. Instead, copy the **Respōnsum** in your Answer Pad and study it and the pictures.

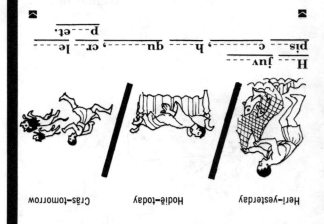

151.	152.	153.
★ ○ ○	★ ○ ○	★ ○ ○
Herī-yesterday	Hodiē-today	Crās-tomorrow

R: Herī juvenis piscēs capiēbat, hodiē quiēscit, crās leōnēs premet.

H___ c___ cr__ le___
juv___ qu___ p___et.
pis___

R: Hodiē mihi, crās tibi.

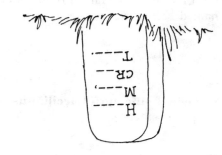

150.

26-27

19-22

147. Answer the question below and check. "**Quid agit haec fēmina?**" "**H__c f_____ c_____.**" √ ★ ○ •

R: Haec fēmina cēnat.

148. Ask your teacher this question, and write his answer. "**Cum quibus vir cēnat?**" ★ ○ ○ "_____."

A: Cum convīvīs.

149. The word **convīva** means "guest." Ask your teacher in Latin in what way the guests are dining. "**Qu_____ con___ae c__ant?**" √ ★ ○ •

Cōnf: Quāliter convīvae cēnant?

150. Write his answer. ★ ○ ○ "_____."

R: Hilariter.

26-29

144. Copy these pronouns in your Notebook.

145. ✱ ○ ○ ○ **H**_____ **m**___, **c**___ **t**____. [Four macrons] (117)

R: Hodiē mihi, crās tibī.

146. The star and circles and the number 117 told you that you were to write from dictation a new _____.

A: Basic Sentence.

147. When we say that a person proCRAStinates, we mean that he doesn't do his job today, but keeps putting it off until t_____ w_____.

A: tomorrow.

148. Here is where this Basic Sentence is found. The person inside the tomb is supposed to be saying to the passerby, "Death happens _____ but will happen _____ _____ _____."

HODIE MIHI, CRAS TIBI.

A: Death happens to me today but will happen to you tomorrow.

149. Copy in your Notebook as "Today to me, tomorrow to you."

19-23

151. Ask your teacher in Latin what the guests are dining on. "**Quō convīvae cēnant?**"
✓ ★ ○ •

152. Write his answer. ★ ○ ○ "_____."

R: Aprō.

153. This means that the guests are dining on a _____.

A: boar.
[The Romans considered wild boar a great delicacy to eat; it was very expensive.]

154. Quō convīvae cēnant? = What are _____ s _____ on?

A: What are the guests dining on?

155. Write the paradigm of the First Declension noun **convīva**. [You have never seen or heard the paradigm, but it is like **fēmina** or **sīmia**.]

R: convīva   convīvae
        convīvam   convīvās
        convīvā   convīvīs

---

137. "**Cujus equī caelō nocturnō currebant?**" "_____."

R: Lūnae.

Echo and learn the paradigm of the pronoun of the first person.

138. singular "I," **139.** plural "we," "us," "me." ★ ○ • ○   ★ ○ • ○

R: nom ego   nom nōs
      acc mē   acc nōs
      abl mē   abl nōbīs
      dat mihī   dat nōbīs
      gen meī   gen nostrum

140. Write this paradigm of the first person pronoun. [Or, of course, say it if you prefer.]

R: ego   nōs
      mē   nōs
      mē   nōbīs
      mihī   nōbīs
      meī   nostrum

Echo the paradigm of the pronoun of the second person.

141. singular "you," **142.** plural "you." ★ ○ • ○   ★ ○ • ○

      nom tū   nom vōs
      acc tē   acc vōs
      abl tē   abl vōbīs
      dat tibī   dat vōbīs
      gen tuī   gen vestrum

143. Write the paradigm of the second person pronoun.

R: tū   vōs
      tē   vōs
      tē   vōbīs
      tibī   vōbīs
      tuī   vestrum

19-24

156. ★ ○ ○ "Quō convīvae cēnant?"
"_____."

R: Pisce.

157. ★ ○ ● ("attractive guest")

singular	plural
bellus convīva	bellī convīvae
bellum convīvam	bellōs convīvās
bellō convīvā	bellīs convīvīs

158. **Convīva** is a First Declension noun, but because it refers here to a male guest it is here _____ gender.

A: masculine

159. "Quō bellus convīva cēnat?" "____."

R: Aprō.

160. "Quōcum convīva cēnat?" (**Quōcum?** is more common than **Cum quō?**) "___ ____."

R: Cum aprō.

26-24

131. Copy the poem and the *first* line of the English (but not the second).

132. Once again we have an illustration of how we must use a different structure in English to translate the Latin. It would sound much better if we were to use something like this for the second line. **lūnaque nocturnōs alta regēbat equōs** = A__ the m___ on h___ was _____ her h_____ of n_____.

A: And the moon on high was driving her horses of night.

133. Copy in your Notebook.

134. Write the two lines. ★ ○ ○ J_____ qu_____/qu_____que h_____que c_____que/ l_____que n_____ al___ r_____ equ___. [There should be eight macrons.]

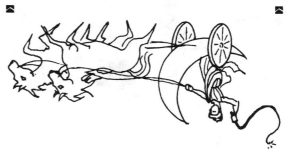

R: Jamque quiēscēbant vōcēs hominumque canumque/ lūnaque nocturnōs alta regēbat equōs.

Quaestiōnēs et Respōnsa

135. "Quae animālia tacēbant?" "_____."

R: Canēs.

136. "Cui serviēbant equī nocturnī?" "_____."

R: Lūnae.

19-25

161. "Quōcum fēmina cēnat?" "_____."

R: Cum mūre.

162. The attractive guest is dining *with* a boar = B_____ c_____ c__ a___ cē____.

R: Bellus convīva cum aprō cēnat.

163. The attractive guest is dining *on* a boar = B_____ c_____ ___ō c_____.

R: Bellus convīva aprō cēnat.

164. ★ ○ • ○ • m____ f____ n____
                  noster nostra nostrum

165. Noster means "our." In the expression noster Caeciliānus, it means "___ fr___d Caeciliānus."

A: our friend

26-23

125. A lunar flight is one that is made towards the _____.

A: moon.

126. When we determine the *altitude* of a mountain, we find out how _____ it is.

A: high

127. Write your teacher's description of this picture. ★ ○ ○ H____ qu____ b_____ e_____, sed i_____ e_____ a_____.

R: Haec quercus brevis est, sed illa est alta.

128. In Vītam regit Fortūna, nōn Sapientia, the word regere meant "r_____."

A: rule.

129. Lūna regēbat equōs, however, means that the moon was dr__-ing her horses.

A: driving

130. Jamque quiēscēbant vōcēs hominum-que canumque lūnaque nocturnōs alta regēbat equōs.

If we give a translation that corresponds to the structure of the Latin, we would get something like this: ---- and ---- of ---- ---- ---- b_____ qu_____ a____ the h____ m____ was dr_____ her n_____ h_____.

A: And now the voices of men and dogs became quiet/and the high moon was driving her night horses.

19-26

166. Pronounce the first line of the poem: **Nōn cēnat sine aprō noster, Tite, Caeciliānus.** √ ★ ○ •

167. Martial says, "Titus, ___ _____ Caecilianus d___ not d___ w_____ a b___."

A: Titus, our friend Caecilianus does not dine without a boar.

168. Cēnat sine aprō could mean either **Nōn cēnat aprō** or **Nōn cēnat cum aprō**. **Nōn cēnat aprō** = He doesn't ____ on a ____ (as f___).

A: He doesn't dine on a boar (as food).

169. Nōn cēnat cum aprō = He doesn't ____ w___ a ____ (as his g___t).

A: He doesn't dine with a boar (as his guest).

170. The phrase **Nōn cēnat sine aprō** ("He does not dine without a boar") is therefore ambiguous, meaning either:
"He dines __ a boar (as ____)."
or "He dines ____ a boar (as his _____)."

A: He dines on a boar (as food).
He dines with a boar (as his guest).

171. Pronounce the second line: **Nōn cēnat sine aprō noster, Tite, Caeciliānus/Bellum convīvam Caeciliānus habet.** √ ★ ○ •

172. This second line means, "_____ ___ an _____ _____."

A: Caecilianus has an attractive guest.

---

119. Vōcēs hominum quiēscunt = T__ v_____ of m__ a__ qu____.

A: The voices of men are quiet.

120. However, the new form in **-bā-** shows that this action was "incomplete," and in this context we might say that **quiēscēbant vōcēs hominum** = __ v_____ of ___ became _____.

A: The voices of men became quiet.

121. Jamque quiēscēbant vōcēs hominumque canumque = _____ ___ _____ __ ___ _____.

A: And now the voices of dogs and men became quiet.

122. *Nocturnal* animals are animals, like owls, that sleep by day but are active by _____.

A: night.

123. The new adjective **nocturnus, nocturna, nocturnum** means "belonging to the _____."

A: night.

124. Write your teacher's description of this scene. ★ ○ ○ N_____ e_____. In c_____ l_____.

R: Nox est. In caelō nocturnō est lūna.

19-27

173. Remembering the first line, we realize that the attractive guest can only be the ____.

▼

A: boar.

174. In other words, the wild boar is an attractive guest for Caecilianus, because Caecilianus is just like a ____ ____ himself.

▼

A: wild boar

Nōn cēnat sine aprō noster, Tite, Caeciliānus/Bellum convīvam Caeciliānus habet. (62)

175. This poem means, "____, our ____ ____ d___ not ____ ____ a ____. ____ ____ an ____ ____."

▼

A: Titus, our friend Caecilianus does not dine without a boar. Caecilianus has an attractive guest.

176. Copy in your Notebook.

▼

177. As you learned in Unit 16, "phrase" is a general term for any group of words which is tied together in some way. For example, in the sentence **Ex auribus cognōscitur asinus**, the preposition **ex** patterns with the ablative form ____.

▼

A: **auribus.**

178. The group of words **ex auribus** is a pr_____ _____.

▼

A: prepositional phrase.

---

115. Write the second line from dictation.

★ ◯ ◯ ◯ ◯ l_____ n_____ al_____ r_____ eq____. [There are four long vowels.] (116)

R: **lūnaque nocturnōs alta regēbat equōs.** (116)

This Basic Sentence is taken from a poem of Ovid. For reasons that are not entirely clear to us today, he had been exiled by the emperor Augustus to one of the border towns of the Roman Empire on the Black Sea, in what is now Russia. In this poem he tells us of the torment which he went through on this, his last night in Rome before being separated from his home and his friends.

116. The first thing to notice is that in the context of the whole poem, the **-que** on the first word **jamque** must have connected this sentence with _____. [In your own words]

A: the sentence which came before.

117. The **-que** ... **-que** in the first line connects two words in the same case, _____ and _____.

A: **hominum** ... **canum.**

118. The **-que** of **lūnaque** connects _____.

A: the first kernel (clause) and the second kernel (clause).

19-28

179. In **Hilarem datōrem dīligit Deus**, the object is a phrase consisting of the two Latin words _____ _____ .

A: **hilarem datōrem**.

180. Echo another technical term. ★ ○ • ○ •
c l a u s e

VCh: "claws"

181. A group of words which contains a subject, verb, and complement (if there is one) is a "clause." Thus in **Sub jūdice līs est**, **Sub jūdice** is a _____ al _____ while **līs est** is a _____ .

A: prepositional phrase
 clause.

182. The sentence "I went to the movies" contains only one clause. But in the sentence "After I ate my dinner I went to the movies" there are ___ clauses.

A: two

183. Echo a technical term. ★ ○ • ○ •
s u b o r d i n a t e

184. There are two kinds of clauses. Those introduced by such words as "since," "when," and "if" are called "subordinate" clauses. In the sentence "After I ate my dinner I went to the movies," the clause "I went to the movies" is the "main" clause, and "After I ate my dinner" is the _____ clause.

A: subordinate

185. A person who holds a "subordinate" position is not so important as someone above him. In the same way, a subordinate clause is ____ (not so important as/more important than) the main clause.

A: not
 so important as

19-29

Identify the italicized clauses as main or subordinate. (Remember that the presence of the words "after," "when," "since," "if," etc. signal a subordinate clause.)

186. "Dinner was ready *when I sat down to eat*." The italicized clause is ____ (main/subordinate).

A: subordinate.

187. "*When dinner was ready* I sat down to eat." The italicized clause is ____ (main/subordinate).

A: subordinate.

188. In "He went home after the play was over," the *subordinate* clause is "_____ _____."

A: after the play was over.

189. Echo another technical term. ★ ○ • ●
subórdinating conjúnction

190. In English subordinate clauses are introduced by subordinating conjunctions, such as "si___," "af___," "wh__," etc.

A: since after when

191. In the sentence "If you are ready to leave, I'll start the car," the *main* clause is "_____."

A: I'll start the car.

192. In the same sentence, the *subordinate* clause is "_____."

A: If you are ready to leave.

---

101. Jūstitia est domina et rēgīna virtū-tum ★ ○ ○ • ∫ _____.

Conf: Jūstitia est domina rēgīnaque virtūtum.

Make these same changes (from et or atque to -que).

102. Jūstitia est domina et rēgīna virtū-tum → ∨ ★ ○ • _____.

R: Jūstitia est domina rēgīnaque virtūtum.

103. Multae rēgum aurēs atque oculī → ∨ ★ ○ • _____

R: Multae rēgum aurēs oculīque.

104. Genus et formam Rēgīna Pecūnia dōnat → ∨ ★ ○ • _____.

R: Genus formamque Rēgīna Pecūnia dōnat.

Change the et to -que in these new sentences.

105. Deō et Rēgī → D____ R____que. ∨ ★ ○ •

R: Deō Rēgique.

106. Rēgī et Patriae → R____ P____. ∨ ★ ○ •

R: Rēgī Patriaeque.

107. Magna dī cūrant et neglegunt parva → ← M____ n____ c____ nt p____. ∨ ★ ○ •

R: Magna dī cūrant neglegunt que parva.

193. The word "if" is a _____ _____.

▼

A: subordinating conjunction.

194. When there is no subordinating conjunction starting a clause, then the clause is a ____ clause.

▼

A: main

195. Latin, too, has both main clauses and subordinate clauses. We have not had any Latin subordinating conjunctions yet; all of the Latin Basic Sentences so far have consisted of ____ _____.

▼

A: main clauses.

196. The sentence **Plōrātur lacrimīs āmissa pecūnia vērīs** (60) contains only one k_____, **plōrātur pecūnia**; it consequently has just one m___ c_____.

▼

A: kernel main clause.

197. **Thāis habet nigrōs, niveōs Laecānia dentēs** has two _____; it has ___ m____ _____s.

▼

A: kernels two main clauses.

198. You are familiar with the fact that in English there are some words which sound alike and are spelled alike but have different meanings. For example, one meaning of "bear" is the verb "carry." But when we say, "The bear came near our tent," we are referring to a _____ _____. [In your own words]

▼

A: plantigrade quadruped of the genus Ursus belonging to the Carnivora.

96. You have learned several connectors, words whose function is to connect equal things. We will now introduce you to a connector which is the most common word in the Latin language. Echo your teacher as he describes this picture.

★ ● ○ ● V___ v___ b____ p_____.

Conf. **Vir videt barbam et pallium.**

▲

97. Here is another description of the same picture, using a new connector in place of et.

★ ● ○ ● **Vir videt barbam palliumque.**

▲

98. The position of this new connector is that it is added to the _____. [In your own words]

▲

A: second of the two words (or phrases) that it connects.

▲

Echo your teacher as he substitutes this new connector -que for et or atque in these sentences.

99. Genus et formam Rēgīna Pecūnia dōnat. → ★ ● ○ ● G____ ____que R____ P____ d____.

Conf. **Genus formamque Rēgīna Pecūnia dōnat.**

▲

100. Multae rēgum aurēs atque oculī → ★ ● ○ ● M____ r____ au____ oc____.

Conf. **Multae rēgum aurēs oculīque.**

19-31

199. In the same way, there is a Latin word **cum** which you have already learned as a preposition meaning "_ _ _ _."

A: with.

You will now meet a Latin subordinating conjunction **cum,** which means "when" or "because" or "since" or "although." For a while we will use it in the sense of "when."

Your teacher will now use the Latin subordinating conjunction **cum** to subordinate one of these two main clauses: **Caeciliānus cēnat; bellum convīvam habet.** (62)

200. Echo as he makes one of these clauses a subordinate clause. ★ ○ • ○ • C_ _ _ _ _ _ _ _ _ _, _ _ _ c_ _ _ _, b_ _ _ _ _ c_ _ _ _ _ _ _ h_ _ _ _.

Cōnf: **Caeciliānus, cum cēnat, bellum convīvam habet.**

201. He said that when _ _ _ _ _ _ _ _, Caecilianus _.

A: he dines, Caecilianus has an attractive guest.

202. Echo as he makes the other clause subordinate instead. ★ ○ • ○ • C_ _ _ _ _ _ _ _ _ _, _ _ _ b_ _ _ _ _ c_ _ _ _ _ _ _ h_ _ _ _, c_ _ _ _.

Cōnf: **Caeciliānus, cum bellum convīvam habet, cēnat.**

203. He said that when _, he _ _ _ _ _.

A: Caecilianus has an attractive guest, he dines.

204. Make the first clause (italicized) a subordinate clause by introducing it with *cum*: *Vōx audīta perit,* littera scrīpta manet. (57) C_ _ v_ _ _ _ _ _ p_ _ _ _, l_ _ _ _ _ scr_ _ _ _ m_ _ _ _ _.

A: **Cum vōx audīta perit, littera scrīpta manet.**

19-32

205. This sentence means that _____ _____, the _____.

A: _____ when the spoken word dies, the written letter remains.

206. Now make the second clause (italicized) the subordinate clause and place it first in the sentence. [Say the whole sentence aloud.] **Vōx audīta perit,** *littera scrīpta manet.* C___ _____ _____ m____, v__ _____ p____.

A: _____ **Cum littera scrīpta manet, vōx audīta perit.**

207. This sentence means that _____ _____, the_____.

A: _____ when the written letter remains, the spoken word dies.

208. Subordinate the italicized clause. **Fāta regunt orbem,** *certā stant omnia lēge.* (48)
_____.

R: **Cum Fāta regunt orbem, certā stant omnia lēge.**

209. This sentence means that _____

A: _____ when the Fates rule the world, all things stand under a sure law.

210. When the same word is subject of both clauses, Latin usually expresses it only with the main verb. Subordinate the italicized clause, and put the subject first. **Magna dī cūrant,** *parva neglegunt.* (46)
Dī, cum m____ c_____, p____ n_____.

R: **Dī, cum magna cūrant, parva neglegunt.**

211. **Dī, cum magna cūrant, parva neglegunt** = When the ____ ____ ____ of _____ _____, they _____ _____ _____.

A: _____ When the gods take care of large things, they neglect small things.

26-16

85. **Orbem jam tōtum victor Rōmānus habēbat** = Now the _____ h_____ the _____ _____.

A: Now the Roman victor held the whole world.

86. Copy in your Notebook.

87. Was he *still* holding it victoriously or had he *finished* holding it and let someone else take over? _____.

A: He was still holding it.

88. You will remember that we explained that the signal {-bā-} in a Latin verb showed that the action was going on in past time. From this Basic Sentence you can see that **habēbat,** showing an act of holding going on in the past, can be translated either by "The Roman victor h___-ing" or "The Roman victor h___-held.

A: was holding

89. Echo the paradigm of this phrase, first the singular, then the plural. ★ ○ ●
victor Rōmānus
victōrem Rōmānum
victōre Rōmānō
victōrī Rōmānō
victōris Rōmānī
victōrēs Rōmānī
victōrēs Rōmānōs
victōribus Rōmānīs
victōribus Rōmānīs
victōrum Rōmānōrum

19-33

212. When the gods neglect small things, they take care of large things = D_, cum _____ _____, _____ _____.

R: **Dī, cum parva neglegunt, magna cūrant.**

213. Subordinate the italicized clause. **Fortūna fortēs metuit,** *ignāvōs premit.* (41)
F_____, ___ _____ _____, _____ _____.

R: **Fortūna, cum ignāvōs premit, fortēs metuit.**

214. ★ ○ • ○ • **Jūdex damnātur, cum nocēns absolvitur.** (63)

215. ★ ○ ○ **J____ d_____, c_ n____ ab_____.**

R: **Jūdex damnātur, cum nocēns absolvitur.**

216. At a glance you see that **Jūdex damnātur** is the ____ clause, while **cum nocēns absolvitur** is the _____ clause.

A: main
   subordinate

217. Both **damnātur** and **absolvitur** are _____ voice.

A: passive

218. Show that you understand the structure of the sentence by using the colorless verb "blanks" and by using the Latin word **nocēns** as if it were an English word. **Jūdex damnātur, cum nocēns absolvitur** = _____.

A: _____ The judge is blanked when the **nocēns** is blanked.

---

81. Whether the action actually in fact does eventually get completed is not the point; both the #1 and #2 tenses say that at the time described the action was ____ (complete/incomplete).

A: incomplete.

82. Write a new Basic Sentence as your teacher says it. ○ ○ ○ ○ ★ O____ j____ t____ h_____. [There are four long vowels.] (115)

R: v_____ (115)

R: **Orbem jam tōtum victor Rōmānus habēbat.** (115)

83. Jam is a common word in Latin; its general sense is to indicate that the situation has now changed from what it was before. **Jam** may often be translated by the English word "now," but only when English "now" means that there is a change.

Heri   Jam

Heri leō taurōs premēbat sed jam quiēscit. = _____. [Guess the new verb **quiēscit**.]

A: Yesterday the lion was pursuing bulls but now he is quiet.

84. Because of the word **jam** you know that the situation _____. [In your own words]

A: was different from what it had been.

19-34

219. The English derivative of **damnat** is a word which we are accustomed to think of as a profane word; it is "d____."

A: damn.

220. The Latin **condemnat** is a compound form of **damnat**. You can now guess that **Jūdex damnātur** means, "The _____ __ con____ed."

A: The judge is condemned.

221. The Latin adjective **innocēns** has a common English derivative, which is the word "_____nt."

A: innocent.

222. The prefix **in-** means "not." A person who is innocent is *not* guilty. Therefore the Latin adjective **nocēns** must mean "_____."

A: guilty.

223. What noun, if any, does **nocēns** modify in **Jūdex damnātur, cum nocēns absolvitur**?
_____.

A: It doesn't modify any noun.

224. Since it doesn't modify any noun, it is used as _____ and must mean "_____."

A: a noun itself   guilty person.

225. Use the colorless verb "blanks" for the unknown word **absolvitur**. **Jūdex damnātur, cum nocēns absolvitur** = _____.

A: The judge is condemned, when the guilty person is blanked.

Now comes the big jump. Use your common sense. Under what conditions would we condemn a judge? What happened to the guilty person so that people condemned the judge? Find a reasonable verb for **absolvitur**.

26-14

75. **Necessitātēs nōn effugiō** ← ___ ___ __ iē_____.

R: Herī neces- sitātēs nōn effugiēbam.

76. **Corporī nōn serviō** ← ___ ____ ___ iē____.

R: Herī corporī nōn serviēbāmus.

77. Latin has three kinds of time, past, present, and future. Since we are used to reading from left to right, we arrange the verbs in a box like this:

Past	Present	Future
cēnābam #1	cēnō #2	? #3

We call **cēnābam** "Form Number ___."

A: One.

78. And **cēnō** is Form N___ ____.

A: Form Number Two.

79. Copy this in your Notebook under Facts About Latin:

The #1 form of the verb describes an action which was not completed in the past. Possible English translations of **cēnābat** are "He began to dine," "He dined (frequently)," "He used to dine," "He tried to dine," "He was in the act of dining," etc.

80. Copy this in your Notebook under Facts About Latin:

The #2 form of the verb describes an action which is not completed in present time. Possible English translations of **cēnat** are "He is dining (right now)," and "He dines (regularly)."

226. Jūdex damnātur, cum nocēns absolvitur = _____.

A: The judge is condemned when the guilty person (or "man") is acquitted.

227. Copy this sentence (63) and meaning in your Notebook. Refer to it if you need to answer these questions.

228. "Quem omnēs damnant cum nocēns absolvitur?" "_____."

R: Jūdicem.

229. "Absolviturne nocēns ā jūdice bonō an malō?" "_ _____ ____."

R: Ā jūdice malō.

230. "Damnāturne an laudātur jūdex cum innocēns absolvitur?" "_____."

R: Laudātur.

231. "Quālī ā jūdice nocēns absolvitur?" "____ _ _____."

R: Malō ā jūdice.

232. "Quālī ā jūdice innocēns absolvitur?" "____ _ _____."

R: Bonō ā jūdice.

Now back to adverbs.

233. In the sentence "The quick horse is running," the idea of speed is shown by the adjective "quick," which modifies the word "_____."

A: horse.

234. It would be equally possible, however, to assign the idea of speed to the verb phrase and say, "The horse is running qu___ly."

A: quickly

67. Sapientēs hōrās nōn numerant → H____ s____ h____ n____ n____ ā____.

R: Sapientēs hōrās nōn numerābant.

68. Vidētis barbam et pallium → H____ v____ b____ et p____.

R: Vidēbātis barbam et pallium.

69. Omnia poscimus → ____ ____ p____ ē____.

R: Heri omnia poscē-bāmus.

70. Fortis necessitātēs nōn effugit → ____ _____ ef____ iē____.

R: Heri fortis necessitātēs nōn effugiēbat.

71. Corporī nōn serviō → ____ ____ ____ iē____.

R: Heri corporī nōn serviēbam.

72. Hōrās nōn numerāmus → ____ ____ ā____.

R: Heri hōrās nōn numerābāmus.

73. Vidēmus barbam et pallium → ____ _____ ē____.

R: Heri vidēmus barbam et pallium.

74. Omnia poscitis → ____ ____ ____ ē____.

R: Heri omnia poscē-bātis.

19-36

235. In this last sentence, the word "quickly" modifies the verb phrase "__ _____."

A: _____ is running.

236. "What kind of horse is that?"
"It's a quick horse."
"In what way is he running?"
"He is running _____."

A: _____ quickly.

237. A word like "quickly" is called an "_____."

A: adverb.

238. As the last part of this technical term suggests, adverbs modify the part of speech called ____s.

A: verbs.

239. In English to make an adverb out of an adjective like "rapid" we add the suffix "__."

A: _____ ly.

240. Some common adjectives have "irregular" adverbs. For example, if we use the adverb of "good," we would not say that the girl sang *goodly; we would say that she sang w____.

A: _____ well.

241. Echo two irregular Latin adverbs.
★ ○ • ○ • **bene, male**

242. Hic medicus aegrōs male cūrat =
____ _____ c___s for his ____ _____ ___ly.

A: This doctor cares for his sick people (or patients) badly.

243. **Ille medicus aegrōs bene cūrat =** ________________________________.

A: That doctor cares for his patients well.

244. In Unit 18 you used **"Bene!"** as an expression meaning "___ ____!"

A: Well done

245. You know now that **bene** is the part of speech called an ______.

A: adverb.

246. ★ ○ • ○ • ***Mulier, cum sōla cōgitat, male cōgitat.*** (64)

247. Echo a new adjective. ★ ○ • ○ • **sōlus, sōla, sōlum**

The English derivatives of this word are "solo," "solitude," and "solitaire." With this hint, read the following description of this picture and check.

248. **Haec fēmina nōn sōla est sed cum virīs stat.** √ ★ ○ •

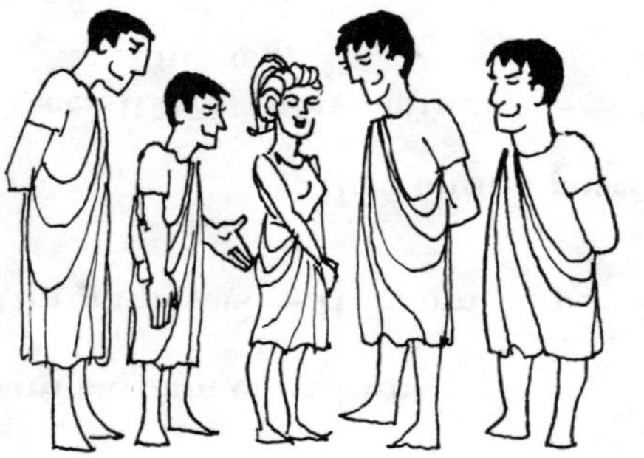

53. ★ ○ • **poscere** (Third Conjugation)

____**ēba**_	____**ēbā**___
____**ēbā**_	____**ēbā**___
____**ēba**_	____**ēba**__

Cōnf:

poscēbam	**poscēbāmus**
poscēbās	**poscēbātis**
poscēbat	**poscēbant**

54. ★ ○ • **effugere** (Third Conjugation, **-iō**)

_____**iēba**_	_____**iēbā**___
_____**iēbā**_	_____**iēbā**___
_____**iēba**_	_____**iēba**__

Cōnf:

effugiēbam	**effugiēbāmus**
effugiēbās	**effugiēbātis**
effugiēbat	**effugiēbant**

55. ★ ○ • **servīre** (Fourth Conjugation)

____**iēba**_	____**iēbā**___
____**iēbā**_	____**iēbā**___
____**iēba**_	____**iēba**__

Cōnf:

serviēbam	**sērviēbāmus**
serviēbās	**serviēbātis**
serviēbat	**serviēbant**

56. One thing which will help you to remember the pronunciation of this tense is that in *every* conjugation the vowel before the **-bā-** is *always* ___ (short/long).

A: long.

The following sentences are in the form which shows present time. Transform each verb into the new form which shows action going on in past time ("I was doing such-and-such") and expand with the word which means "yesterday" **(herī)**. You will use the verbs which you just practiced.

57. **Hōrās nōn numerās → Herī h____ nōn n____ābā__.**

R: **Herī hōrās nōn numerābās.**

19-38

Here is a contrasting picture.

249. Haec fēmina est sōla et sine virīs plōrat. √ ★ ○ •

250. Haec fēmina, cum sōla est, plōrat = ____ ____ __ _____ when ___ __ _____.

A: This woman is crying when she is alone.

251. The new word **mulier** is a synonym of **fēmina.** Say that this woman is standing alone and check. H___ m_____ s___ st___. √ ★ ○ •

R: Haec mulier sōla stat.

252. This picture represents a statue known as "The Thinker." Echo your teacher's description. ★ ○ • ○ • H__ v__ s____ c_____.

Cōnf: Hic vir sōlus cōgitat.

253. Mulier, cum sōla cōgitat, male cōgitat. (64) √ ★ ○ •

254. This sentence is another of those attacks on women by Publilius Syrus. He says that when a _____ _____ al___, she _____ _____.

A: woman thinks alone, she thinks badly.

255. Copy in your Notebook.

256. Pronounce the author's name in English and check. Publilius Syrus √ ★ ○ •

VCh: "pooh-blíll-lee-yuss sír-russ"

257. Publilius Syrus (or rather, one of the characters in his plays) says that a woman has no business to try to think for herself. She should leave this to _____.
[In your own words]

A: her husband, her father, or whatever male relative she was **in manū** to.

258. The phrase **in manū** means "_____ the p___r" of someone.

A: under the power

259. ★ ○ ○ M_____, ___ s___ c_____, m___ c_____. [Three long vowels]

R: Mulier, cum sōla cōgitat, male cōgitat.

260. ★ ○ •
   sōla mulier   sōlae mulierēs
   sōlam mulierem sōlās mulierēs
   sōlā muliere   sōlīs mulieribus
[Remember to repeat the paradigm as many times as needed to remember it.]

Answer the following questions, pretending that you live in the first century before Christ and are much upset at the fact that women are allowed more freedom than in the good old days.

Ask him the same question for the next four frames. [If you have no tape recorder, study the **Respōnsum**.]

43. "Quid herī tū ag___ ?" √ ★ ○ •

Cōn: **Quid herī tū agēbās?**

44.

45. "Qu__ h__ tū ag__ ?" √ ★ ○ •

Cōn: **Quid herī tū agēbās?**

R: **Ego magnum opus scrībēbam.**

"E__ m__ op__ scr_____."

46.

R: **Ego hilaribus convīvīs placēbam.**

"___ h_____ c_____ plac_____."

47. "_____?" √ ★ ○ •

Cōn: **Quid herī tū agēbās?**

261. "Quāliter cōgitat mulier sōla?"
"_____."

R: Male.

262. "Quāle cōnsilium capiunt mulierēs sōlae, bonum an malum?" "_____."

R: Malum.

263. "Quālī in cōnsiliō mulierēs virōs vincunt?" "_____."

R: Malō.

264. "Ā quō malum cōnsilium capitur?"
"Ā m_____ s_____."

R: Ā muliere sōlā.

265. "Quālēs mulierēs malum cōnsilium capiunt?" "_____ _____."

R: Mulierēs sōlae.

266. The kernel of the main clause of **Mulier, cum sōla cōgitat, male cōgitat** is _____ _____.

A: Mulier cōgitat.

267. The verb **cōgitat** is modified by the adverb _____.

A: male.

268. The verb **cōgitat** in the main clause is also modified by the _____ cl_____ **cum sōla cōgitat**.

A: subordinate clause

---

37. Label the **cēnābam** paradigm as 1st conjugation; then copy just the first person of the other conjugations, like this:

2d	3d
nocēbam	scrībēbam
etc.	etc.
3d-iō	4th
capiēbam	audiēbam
etc.	etc.

38. The signal {-bā-} on a verb shows an action which _____.
[In your own words]

A: _____ was going on in the past.

39. Looking at the paradigm you notice that **-bā-** changes to **-ba-** (with a short vowel) before _____.

40. The person endings are the same as in **cēnō, cēnās, cēnat,** except that this tense has the variant _____ in the _____ (1st/2nd/3d) person.

A: -m, -t, and -nt

A: -m 1st

In the next sequence, ask your teacher, "What were you doing yesterday?", check your question and write down his answer. The balloon shows he is recalling what he did.

41. "Quid herī tū agēbā_____?" ∨ ★ ○ •

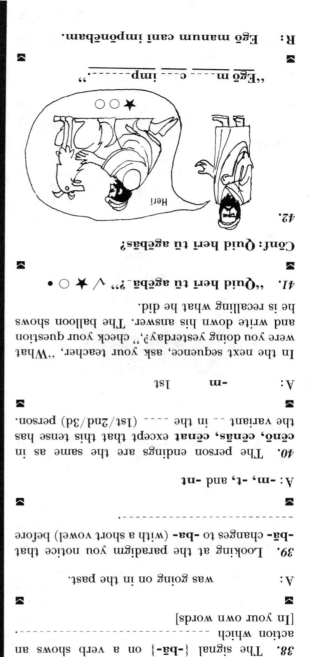

Cōnf: Quid herī tū agēbās?

42.

"Egō m___ c___ imp___."

R: Egō manum cānī impōnēbam.

19-41

269. In the sentence **Jūdex damnātur cum nocēns absolvitur,** the verb **damnātur** is modified by the subordinate clause _____ _____.

A: cum nocēns absolvitur.

270. We will take up another way of making a main clause a subordinate one. Read the description of this picture. There are two main verbs. **Vir crūdēlis est; vir canem tenet.** ✓ ★ ○ •

271. We could perhaps rewrite the sentence by placing one clause in parentheses, like this: **Vir (vir crūdēlis est) canem tenet.** ✓ ★ ○ •
This means, "The ___ (___ ___ is ____) is ____ing the ___."

A: The man (the man is cruel) is holding the dog.

272. A far more common way in English to express this thought would be to use the word "who." The man, ___ is cruel, is ____ing the ___.

A: The man, who is cruel, is holding the dog.

273. In this sentence the clause "who is cruel" describes the ____ (man/dog).

A: man.

274. Echo a new technical term. ★ ○ • ○ •
rélative prónoun

---

30. ★ ○ •   II
nocēre
nocēBAm   nocēBAmus
nocēBAs   nocēBAtis
nocēBAt   nocēBAnt

31. ★ ○ •   III
scrībere
scrībēbam   scrībēbāmus
scrībēbās   scrībēbātis
scrībēbat   scrībēbant

32. ★ ○ •   III (-iō)
capere
capiēbam   capiēbāmus
capiēbās   capiēbātis
capiēbat   capiēbant

33. ★ ○ •   IV
audīre
audiēbam   audiēbāmus
audiēbās   audiēbātis
audiēbat   audiēbant

34. All four conjugations ____ (have the same/ have a variant) signal for this new tense.

A: have the same

35. The signal for this new tense is { ____ }.

A: -bā- (with the vowel becoming short in the usual places).

36. Copy in your Notebook the paradigm of **cēnābam** as a model.
cēnābam   cēnābāmus
cēnābās   cēnābātis
cēnābat   cēnābant

Since all the other conjugations have the same signal {-bā-} it is not necessary to copy their complete paradigm.

275. Because the clause "who is cruel" refers to or is related to the word "man," it is called a "re____ve cl____," and the word "who" is called a "re_____ pr_____."

A: relative clause
   relative pronoun.

276. Echo the nominative forms of the Latin relative pronoun. ★ ○ • ○ •
   m   f   n
   quī, quae, quod

277. Here is our same sentence, this time written with the relative pronoun. Read and check. **Vir, quī crūdēlis est, canem tenet.** √ ★ ○ •

278. This sentence means, "The ___, who _____, is _____ the ___."

A: The man, who is cruel, is holding the dog.

279. The main idea of this sentence, as now expressed, is that the man _____.

A: is holding the dog.

280. We can easily change the importance and make the holding of the dog the subordinate idea. Read and check. **Vir, quī canem tenet, crūdēlis est.** √ ★ ○ •

281. This means that _____.

A: the man, who is holding the dog, is cruel.

282. You know that Latin does not use word order to signal such structures as subject, object, and modification. However, word order *does* show in which clause a word belongs. In the sentence **Vir, quī crūdēlis est, canem tenet, quī** is the subject of ____ (est/tenet).

A: est.

---

22. Omnia mors poscēbat → ········ √ ★ ○ •

R: Herī omnia mors poscēbat.

23. Tū vidēs barbam et pallium → ····· √ ★ ○ •

R: Hodiē tū vidēs barbam et pallium.

24. Nōs necessitātēs nōn effugimus → ········ √ ★ ○ •

R: Hodiē nōs necessitātēs nōn effugimus.

25. Vōs corporī nōn serviēbātis → ········ √ ★ ○ •

R: Herī vōs corporī nōn serviēbātis.

26. Ego horās nōn numerābam → ········ √ ★ ○ •

R: Herī ego horās nōn numerābam.

27. From this last example you can see that in this tense the signal for First Person Singular is not **-ō** but the variant ___ .

A: -m-.

28. Variant signals are ____ (common/rare) in the Latin verb system.

A: rare (Aren't you glad?)

29. ★ ○ • ○ I
cēnāre
cēnāBAm   cēnāBAmus
cēnāBAs   cēnāBAtis
cēnāBAt   cēnāBAnt

Echo the paradigms of representative verbs of the four conjugations in this new form that shows that something was happening in the past. Repeat as many times as necessary to learn.

19-43

283. In the sentence **Vir, quī canem tenet,** **quī** is the subject of ____ (est/tenet).

A: tenet.

284. Make the clause in parentheses a relative clause by substituting **quī** for the italicized word. **Deus (Deus hominēs regit) jūdex jūstus est** → D___, quī h_____ r____, j____ j_____.

R: **Deus, quī hominēs regit, jūdex jūstus est.**

285. This means, "_____."

A: God, who rules men, is a just judge.

286. Make the second clause a relative clause. Substitute **quī** for **auctor**. **Auctor opus laudat; auctor est ēloquēns** → A_____, ___ ___ ē_____, o___ l_____.

R: **Auctor, quī est ēloquēns, opus laudat.**

287. This sentence means that _____.

A: the author, who is eloquent, praises his own work.

288. Make the second clause a relative clause. Substitute the feminine form **quae** for **mulier**. **Mulier bella est; mulier laudem vult** → M_____, quae l____ v___, b____ ____.

R: **Mulier, quae laudem vult, bella est.**

289. This sentence means that _____.

A: the woman, who likes praise, is pretty.

---

16. **Vir vestem lavat** = ___ ___ ___ ___ing _____, while **Vir vestem lavābat** = ___ ___ ___ ___ing _____.

A: The man is washing clothes (at the present time); The man was washing clothes (in the past).

Expand these sentences with **hodiē** ("today"), if you hear the familiar verb form (which means that the action is going on now), or with **herī** ("yesterday") if you hear the new form in {-bā-} (which means that the action was going on in the past).

17. **Hōrās nōn numerō** → H___ ē hō___ n___ ∨ ★ ○ •
R: **Hodiē hōrās nōn numerō.**

18. (Hodiē = today; herī = yesterday) **Vidēbant stultī barbam et pallium** ← ____ ∨ ★ ○ •
R: **Herī vidēbant stultī barbam et pallium.**

19. (Hodiē = today; herī = yesterday) **Omnia mors poscit** ← _____ ∨ ★ ○ •
R: **Hodiē omnia mors poscit.**

20. (Hodiē = today; herī = yesterday) **Nōs necessitātēs nōn effugiēbāmus** ← _____ ∨ ★ ○ •
R: **Herī nōs necessitātēs nōn effugiēbāmus.**

21. (Hodiē = today; herī = yesterday) **Vōs corporī nōn servītis** ← _____ ∨ ★ ○ •
R: **Hodiē vōs corporī nōn servītis.**

26-5

290. Make a relative clause out of the second clause. Use the feminine relative pronoun **quae**. Vīpera parva est; *vīpera* taurum necat → ------, ---- ------ ----, ----- ---.

R: Vīpera, quae taurum necat, parva est.

291. Again, make a relative clause out of the second clause by using **quae**. Lēx jūsta est; *lēx* omnēs cūrat → L--, qu-- ----- -----, j----- ---.

R: Lēx, quae omnēs cūrat, jūsta est.

In this sequence, make a relative clause out of the second clause by substituting **quod** for the subject.

292. Auctor opus laudat; *opus* bonum est → A----- o---, quod b---- ---, l-----.

R: Auctor opus, quod bonum est, laudat.

293. This sentence means that _____.

A: the author praises his work, which is good.

294. Echo new forms of the relative pronoun.
          m   f   n
★ ○ • ○ • quem, quam, quod

295. These three forms are in the _____ case.

A: accusative

296. Read aloud and check. **Vir, quem aper premit, ignāvus est.** √ ★ ○ •

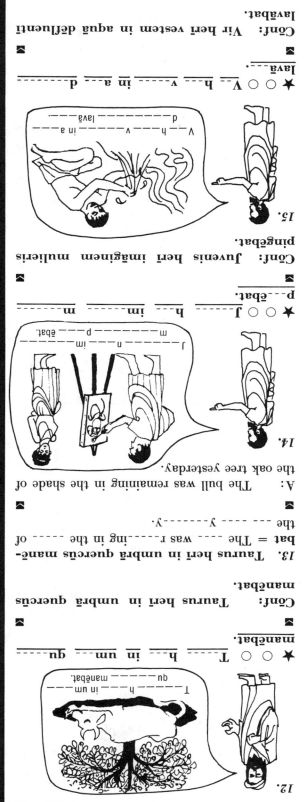

297. Relative pronouns are the same number and gender as the word to which they refer. In the sentence above, **quem** refers to the masculine singular word ___.

A: **vir.**

298. Rewrite **quem aper premit** by replacing the relative with the accusative form of the word to which it refers. _____ **aper premit.**

R: **Virum aper premit.**

299. Virum aper premit = The ___ is _____ing the ___.

A: The boar is pursuing the man.

300. Vir ignāvus est = ___ ___ ___ ___.

A: The man is cowardly.

301. Vir, quem aper premit, ignāvus est = ___ ___, ___ ___ ___ is _____, is _____.

A: The man, whom the boar is pursuing, is cowardly. [Although some people might say "*who* the boar is pursuing," the form "whom" would be preferred by most people. This is a different situation from the question "Who did the boar pursue?", in which almost everyone would use "Who."]

302. Read this description and check. **Vir, quī aprum premit, nōn ignāvus est.** √ ★ ○ •

---

8. Does the sentence **Vestis virum reddit** describe an action about one particular man which is going on at the present time or does it make a statement which is true about men in general?

A: It is true about men in general.

9. In making this statement, is your teacher talking about what this one man is doing at this time, or is he making a general statement about what men generally do?

A: He is talking about what this one man is doing at this time.

10. We will now learn how to make statements about things that were happening in the past. Echo the Latin word for "yesterday." ★ • ○ •

Herī

Your teacher will now describe the last four pictures which you just saw. However, he will say that these things were happening *yesterday*, using a new form of the verbs which means "was happening in the past." The balloon shows that he is *thinking* about these things which happened.

11. Copy what he says.

★ ○ ○ ●
R____ h____ v____ f____ fl____ audiēbat.

Cōnf: **Rēx herī vōcem fēminae flentis audiēbat.**

19-46

303. This means, "_____, _____ _____, _____."

✉ ✉

A: The man, who is pursuing the boar, is not cowardly.

304. Give the English for these sentences, all of which include relative clauses. If the relative form is accusative (**quem, quam,** or **quod**) the relative pronoun is ____ (subject/object) of the verb.

✉ ✉

A: object

305. **Agnus, quem lupus capit, niveus est** = _____.

✉ ✉

A: The lamb, which the wolf catches, is snow-white.

306. **Vir, quī lupum capit, fortis est** = ____ _____.

✉ ✉

A: The man, who catches the wolf, is brave.

307. **Perīc'lum, quod magnum est, ā duce cernitur** = _____.

✉ ✉

A: The danger, which is great, is discovered by the leader.

308. **Mulierem, quam aeger laudat, omnēs dīligunt** = _____.

✉ ✉

A: Everyone loves the woman, whom the sick person praises.

309. **Medicus, quī aegrum laudat, nōn ēloquēns est** = _____.

✉ ✉

A: The doctor, who praises the sick person, is not talkative.

The forms of the verb which you have learned so far have been used for two purposes: 1) to describe something which is *actually happening at the present time.* 2) to describe something which is *generally true.*

Echo your teacher's descriptions of these actions that are all happening today.

5. ★ ○ ● ○ ●

Cōnf: **Rēx hodiē vōcem fēminae flentis audit.**

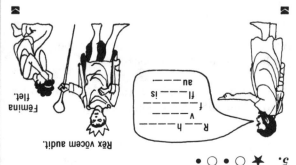

6. ★ ○ ● ○ ●

Cōnf: **Taurus hodiē in umbrā quercūs manet.**

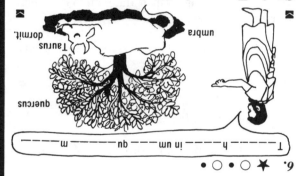

7. ★ ○ ● ○ ●

Cōnf: **Juvenis hodiē imāginem mulieris pingit.**

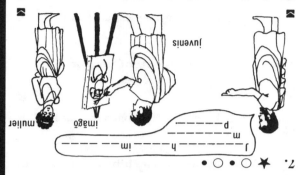

19-47

310. Umbra, quam capillus habet, nigra est = _____.

A: The shadow, which the hair casts, is black.

311. Jūdex, sub quō līs est, irrītātus est = _____.

A: The judge, before whom the lawsuit is (being tried) is irritated.

312. Canis, ā quō aper tenētur, fortis est = _____.

A: The dog, by whom the boar is being held, is brave.

313. Vīnum, quod vir bibit, sapientiam obumbrat = _____.

A: Wine, which the man is drinking, overshadows wisdom.

314. Lēx, quam īrātus nōn videt, jūstē vītam regit = _____.

A: Law, which the angry person doesn't see, rules life justly.

Note that **lēgem** is now the object of the main clause.

315. Lēgem, quae vītam jūstē regit, īrātus nōn videt = The _____ _____ n't _____ _____, _____ _____ _____ _____.

A: The angry person doesn't see the law, which rules life justly.

316. Jūdex respōnsum quod fūr nōn audit dīcit. The *subordinate* clause is qu__ ___ ___ _____.

A: quod fūr nōn audit.

UNIT TWENTY-SIX

1. Echo the Latin word for "today."

✱ ○ • ○ Hodiē

A: Hodiē.

2. Write down your teacher's description of what the wolf is doing *today*. ✱ ○ ○ [If you have no tape recorder, then study the Response.]

H____ l____ a____ s____ pl____.
[Four macrons!]

R: Hodiē lupus agnōs salientēs plōrat.

3. This new word **hodiē** is a combination of two familiar words in the ablative case meaning "on this day." The first part of the word is **hōc** and the second part is _____.

A: diē.

4. But when these two words **hōc diē** were combined into one word, the first long vowel became short, and the expression **hōc diē** became _____.

A: hodiē.

317. **Jūdex respōnsum quod fūr nōn audit dīcit.** The main clause is _____.

A: **Jūdex respōnsum dīcit.**

318. **Jūdex respōnsum quod fūr nōn audit dīcit** = _____.

A: The judge says an answer which the thief doesn't hear.

319. **Fortūnam, quae fortēs adjuvat, stultī timent** = _____.

A: Stupid people fear Fortune, who helps the brave.

320. **Vitium, quod stultus habet, sapiēns nōn possidet** = _____.

A: The wise man doesn't possess the fault which the stupid person has.

321. Some of the forms of the relative pronoun are like the interrogative pronoun. Echo first the singular paradigm of the *interrogative* pronoun. ★ ○ •

m&f	n
quis?	quid?
quem?	quid?
quō?	quō?

322. Now echo the singular paradigm of the *relative* pronoun. ★ ○ •

m	f	n
quī	quae	quod
quem	quam	quod
quō	quā	quō

323. Copy the singular paradigm of the relative pronoun in your Notebook under "Forms."

TEST INFORMATION

You are expected to be able to produce any verb form which we have practiced, either in Question-and-Answer drill, in paradigms, in completions, etc., but you will not be asked to produce verb forms which you have never seen. You are still not responsible for producing the forms of the irregular word **hic, haec, hoc.**

However, you are now responsible for producing *any form of any* noun we have had, whether you have practiced that particular form in the program or not. For example, you have not been shown the complete paradigm of **barba.** You should be able to do this now, since you have practiced so many other First Declension nouns. In this Unit you were given practice in doing this; for example, in frame 303 you were asked to write the paradigm of a new word, **dolor, amor.** You could do this because you had practiced

324. We will take up four Basic Sentences, all of which use some form of this new _____ pronoun **quī**.

A: relative

325. ★ ○ • ○ • **Nāvis quae in flūmine magna est in marī parvula est.** (65)

326. The subordinate clause is _____ _____.

A: **quae in flūmine magna est.**

327. And the main clause is _____ _____ _____.

A: **Nāvis in marī parvula est.**

As before, show that you understand the structure of the sentence by treating the unknown words **nāvis**, **marī**, and **parvula** as if they were English words and placing them in the correct English slots to show their structure.

328. **Nāvis quae in flūmine magna est in marī parvula est** = The **nāvis** _____ _____ _____ _____ is **parvula** _____ _____ **marī**.

A: The **nāvis** which is big in the river is **parvula** in the **marī**.

329. Because it follows the preposition **in**, the new word **marī** must be the _____ case.

A: ablative

R: **Certa mittimus dum incerta petimus.**

466. C―― m―― d―― in―― p――. (109)

VOCABULARY INVENTORY

Nouns:
adjectīvum-ī, n 64   nōmen, nōminis, n 62
dolor, dolōris, m 302   persōna-ae, f 49
*dux, ducis, m 172   Sabīdius-ī, m 412
Mamōna-ae, m 446   sēcūritās,
necessitās,   sēcūritātis, f 216
necessitātis, f 73   verbum-ī, n 63

Adjectives:
beātus-a-um 212   serēnus-a-um 29-30
caecus-a-um 171   tantus-a-um 378
falsus-a-um 451

Verbs:
effugiō, effugere 317
errō, errāre 174
mittō, mittere 238
numerō, numerāre 45
petō, petere 239
possum, posse (irregular) 290

Be sure that you know the six forms of the 23 regular verbs you learned in this Unit, as well as the two irregular verbs, **est** and **potest**.

Phrases:
dē 95   *quā rē 374
dum 224   *pars ōrātiōnis 70
ergō 342
nec 389
nisi 22

Indeclinables:

330. "Naval" architects design sh_ _ _s.

A: ships.

331. "Marine" animals live in the o_ _ _n.

A: ocean.

332. Prīma nāvis est magna; secunda est parva; sed tertia est parvula. The first ship is _ _ _; the second is _ _ _ _ _; but the third is t_ _ _ _.

A: big   small   tiny.

333. ★ ○ ○ N_ _ _ _ qu_ _ _ _ fl_ _ _ _ _ m_ _ _ _ _ _ _ m_ _ī p_ _ _ _ _ _ _ _ _. [Listen for and mark the three long vowels.]

R: Nāvis quae in flūmine magna est in marī parvula est.

334. This means that _.

A: the ship which is big in the river is tiny in the ocean.

335. Copy in Notebook.

336. The "poetical meaning" of this is that a person who seems _ _ _ _ _ _ _ _ _ will seem _ _ _ _ _ _ _ _.

A: important in a small town will seem unimportant in a big city.

337. From the phrase **parvula nāvis** you know that the new word **nāvis** is _ _ _ _ _ _ _ _ gender.

A: feminine

19-51

338. ★ ○ •

nāvis parvula	nāvēs parvulae
nāvem parvulam	nāvēs parvulās
nāve parvulā	nāvibus parvulīs

339. ★ ○ • ○ •

mare	maria
mare	maria
marī	maribus

[Practice this 3d Declension neuter *thoroughly*. Notice that it is declined like **facile, omne,** etc.]

340. From the paradigm it appears that **mare** is like **animal** in two ways; they are both _____ gender and they both have the ablative singular in ___.

A: neuter
  -ī.

341. "Quanta est haec nāvis in marī?"
"_____."

R: Parvula.

342. "Quanta est haec nāvis in flūmine?"
"_____."

R: Magna.

---

458. Animus sēcūrus hominem fēlīcem reddit. Nōs b____ v____ in an____ s____ p____. (108)

R: Nōs beātam vītam in animī sēcūritāte pōnimus.

459. Difficile est vērum dolōrem adjuvāre. L____ t d____ q____ c____ c____ p____. (110)

R: Levis est dolor quī capere cōnsilium potest.

460. Mārtiālis Sabīdium nōn amat. Quā rē? Causa obumbrātur. N____ am t____, S____ p____, nec p____ d____ q____ r____. H____ t____ p____ d____ : nōn a____ t____. (113)

R: Nōn amō tē, Sabidī, nec possum dīcere quā rē. Hoc tantum possum dīcere: nōn amō tē.

461. Necesse est Deum vērum, nōn falsum, colere. N____ p____ D____ s____ et M____. (114)

R: Nōn potestis Deō servīre et Mamōnae.

462-466. Now write the five Basic Sentences which the following pictures suggest.

462. C____ d____ qu____ ; n____ s____ d____ er____. (107)

R: Caecī dūcem quaerunt; nōs sine duce errāmus.

```
           m   f   n
```
The pronoun **hic, haec, hoc** is irregular. We will introduce its use gradually.

343. ★ ○ • ○ • haec nāvis   hae nāvēs
               hanc nāvem   hās nāvēs
               hāc nāve   his nāvibus

344. The suffix **-c** occurs on about half of the forms of this word. Note that the expected form *hamc becomes _____.

A: hanc.

345. Before the final **-c** Latin **-m** becomes _____.

A: **-n**.

346. "Quō locō est haec nāvis magna?" "_____."

R: In flūmine.

347. "Quō locō est haec nāvis parvula?" "_____."

R: In marī.

348. "Uter locus reddit hanc nāvem parvulam, flūmen an mare?" "____."

R: Mare.

349. "Uter locus reddit hanc nāvem magnam?" "_____."

R: Flūmen.

Here is a new use of the relative pronoun. You will find that clauses can be substituted for subject and object in both Latin and English.

SUMMARY

452. In this Unit, you learned that the plural of **Egō aprum teneō** is **___ aprum _____**.

R: **Nōs aprum tenēmus**.

453. And the plural of **Tū opus laudās** is **___ opus _____**.

R: **Vōs opus laudātis**.

454. You learned about two kinds of order in sentences, the _____ order and the _____ order.

A: criss-cross parallel

455. There are ____ (1/2/3/4/5) different Conjugations, but there is a special sub-class of the 3d Conjugation called "____ verbs of the 3d Conjugation."

A: 4   **-iō**

456. You learned two irregular verbs, **est** and its compound _____.

A: **potest**.

457-461. You learned ten Basic Sentences which used the new person endings. Write the Basic Sentence which the Latin sentence suggests. Review first in your Notebook if you do not know these Basic Sentences thoroughly.

457. Necessitās, nōn virtūs, tē bonum reddit. F___ dē n_____ v_____. (106)

R: **Facis dē necessitāte virtūtem.**

350. In Shakespeare's sentence "Who steals my purse steals trash," the subject of "steals trash" is not a noun phrase (like "A stupid thief steals my purse"). The subject of "Who steals my purse steals trash" is "_____."

A: Who steals my purse.

351. The use of a relative clause as subject is particularly common in sayings like our Basic Sentences. Echo this new Basic Sentence, in which the {-s} has been replaced by a relative clause. ***Crūdēlis est, nōn fortis, quī īnfantem necat.*** (66)

352. The kernel is an {-s -s est} sentence, ***Crūdēlis est quī īnfantem necat.*** The subject of **est** is the relative clause ___ _____ _____; the complement of **est** is the adjective _____.

A: quī īnfantem necat crūdēlis.

353. The kernel **nōn fortis** must be expanded to be another {-s -s est} kernel; add the missing subject and verb. ___ _____ _____ **nōn fortis** ___.

R: **Quī īnfantem necat nōn fortis est.**

354. ★ ○ ○ Cr_____ ___, n__ f_____, __ īn_____ n____. [Listen for the five long vowels.]

A: **Crūdēlis est, nōn fortis, quī īnfantem necat.**

355. This means, "Who ____ s a _____ __ ____, ___ _____."

A: Who kills a child is cruel, not brave.

---

445. ★ ○ ○ N__ p_____ D__ s_____ et M_____. (114)

R: **Nōn potestis Deō servīre et Mamōnae.**

446. This Basic Sentence comes from a Latin translation of the New Testament. Mammon was a god who represented money and worldly power. This Basic Sentence means that _____.

A: you can't serve God and Mammon. (Note that the spelling of the last name is different in English.)

447. Copy in your Notebook.

Quaestiōnēs et Respōnsa

448. "Cujus cāsus est 'Deō'?" "_____."

R: Cāsūs datīvī.

449. "Uter est deus falsus?" "_____."

R: Mamōna.

450. "Utrum colere dēbēmus, Deum vērum an Mamōnam?" "_____."

R: Deum vērum.

451. "Quālis deus est Mamōna?" "_____."

R: deus Falsus.

356. Copy in your Notebook. You may wish to know that this saying, like many of our others, is by Publilius Syrus.

All of these questions require the transformation of a word in the original to another case. So be sure that you answer with the form which the question word requires.

357. "Quālēs sunt hominēs quī īnfantēs necant, fortēs an crūdēlēs?" "_____."

R: Crūdēlēs.

358. "Ā quālī homine necātur īnfāns?" "_____ ab _____."

R: Crūdēlī ab homine.

359. The verb **agit** and **agunt** may be used without an object and means to "act." **Quāliter agunt hominēs** means, "In ____ ____ do people ____?"

A: _____ In what way do people act?"

360. The expected answer for **Quāliter** is a word like ____ (crūdēlis/agit/jūstē/fortem).

A: jūstē. [The adverb question word is answered with an adverb.]

361. "Quāliter agit quī īnfantem necat?" "_____."

R: Crūdēliter.

362. "Quāliter nōn agit quī īnfantem necat?" "_____ nōn agit."

R: Fortiter nōn agit.

363. "Quālēs hominēs īnfantem necant?" "_____."

R: Crūdēlēs.

---

438. Let us see how a poet can use this criss-cross order in the structure of an entire poem.

Nōn amō tē, Sabidī, nec possum dīcere
quā rē.
Hoc tantum possum dīcere: "Nōn amō tē."

There are two phrases that are repeated: ____ and _____.

A: Nōn amō tē
possum dīcere.

▼

439. The two clauses Nōn amō tē are in the _____ order.

A: criss-cross

▼

440. The two phrases possum dīcere are in the _____ order.

A: criss-cross

▼

441. Even a person who did not know the language would notice at once that the first three words of the poem are also the _____ words of the poem.

A: last three

▼

442. The poem gets much of its humor from the fact that through these devices the blunt and impolite statement, "Nōn amō tē," has received unusual _____.

A: emphasis.

▼

443. *Nōn potestis Deō servīre et Mamōnae.* (114) ∨ ★ ○ •

▼

444. Expand with the predictable pronoun subject. ____ nōn potestis Deō servīre et Mamō-nae. ∨ ★ ○ •

▼

Conf: Vōs nōn potestis Deō servīre et Mamōnae.

364. ★ ○ • ○ • *Quī prō innocente dīcit satis est ēloquēns.* (67)

365. The word **quī** tells us that this sentence contains a r_____ clause.

A: relative

366. The first verb to follow **quī** is ____ (dīcit/est).

A: dīcit.

367. Therefore **dīcit** is the ____ (main/subordinate) verb of the sentence.

A: subordinate

368. This means that the main verb is ____.

A: est.

369. *Satis* is a word which does not change form. It means "enough" and modifies **ēloquēns.** *Quī prō innocente dīcit satis est ēloquēns* is an {-s -s est} sentence. One of the {-s} elements is the adjective _____.

A: ēloquēns.

370. The other {-s} is not a noun at all but the relative clause ___ ___ _____.

A: *Quī prō innocente dīcit.*

Prō is a new preposition which means "for" in the sense "in favor of" or "in behalf of." Note that when **dīcit** is used without an object (as here) we translate it in English by a different word than "say."

371. *Quī prō innocente dīcit* = He ___ sp___s ___ the _____.

A: He who speaks for the innocent.

---

430. If we were to draw a line connecting the subjects of these two kernels and another line connecting the verbs, these two lines would ____

Religiō deōs colit, superstitiō violat.

A: be parallel to each other.

431. These kernels, therefore, are written in a _____ order.

A: parallel

432. *Fūrem fūr cognōscit et lupum lupus* is in the _____ order.

A: parallel

433. *Videō barbam et pallium; philosophum nōndum videō* is in the _____ order.

A: parallel

434. *Dīcunt volentem Fāta, nōlentem trahunt* is written in the _____ order.

A: criss-cross

435. *Vōx audīta perit, littera scrīpta manet* is written in the _____ order.

A: criss-cross

436. *Ars longa, vīta brevis* is written in the _____ order.

A: parallel

437. Change this last Basic Sentence to the criss-cross order: *Ars longa,* _____.

R: *Ars longa, brevis vīta.*

19-56

372. ★ ○ ○   ___ p__ in_____ d____ s____
___ ē_____.

R: Quī prō innocente dīcit satis est ēloquēns.

373. This means, "_____."

A: He who speaks for the innocent is "talkative" enough. [Don't write this meaning in your Notebook.]

We placed quotes around "talkative" to suggest that this meaning doesn't sound right here. There is an English derivative of **ēloquēns** which sounds much better.

374. He who speaks for the innocent is _____ enough.

A: He who speaks for the innocent is eloquent enough.

375. Perhaps the word "eloquent" is new to you; if so, you can probably figure out from the way we have just used it that it means someone who sp___s very w____.

A: speaks very well.

376. The meaning of this Basic Sentence is that if the accused person is _____, his lawyer doesn't need to be very _____ to get him acquitted.

A: innocent
             eloquent (good, etc.)

377. Is this good advice? ____ (Yes/No)

A: Innocent or not, you had better hire a good lawyer!

378. The new word **satis** has an English derivative. When someone has had enough, we say that he is "_____fied."

A: satisfied.

25-68

425. This arrangement of clauses is therefore called the "criss-cr..." order.

A: criss-cross

426. Two clauses which are arranged
{-s – m –}
{-s – m – t}
are said to be in the ____ (criss-cross/parallel) order.

A: parallel

Here is a two kernel sentence with the second kernel directly underneath the first kernel:
**Effugere nōn potes necessitātēs;
potes vincere.**

427. The infinitive **effugere** comes ____ (before/after) the verb **potes** in the first kernel; the infinitive **vincere** comes ____ (before/after) the verb **potes** in the second kernel.

A: before
     after

428. If we draw a line from one **potes** to the other **potes** and from one infinitive to the other, the lines ____ (cross each other/are parallel to each other).

**Effugere nōn potes necessitātēs;
potes vincere.**

A: cross each other.

**Effugere nōn potes necessitātēs;
potes vincere.**

429. The kernels in this Basic Sentence are therefore written in the ____ (parallel order/criss-cross order).

A: criss-cross order.

19-57

Expand these {-s -s est} sentences to say that these people and animals are good (bad, etc.) enough.

379. Hī medicī sunt bonī → Hī medicī sunt s____ bonī. ★ ○ •

Cōnf: Hī medicī sunt satis bonī.

380. Haec animālia sunt fortia → H___ an_____ sunt s____ f_____. ★ ○ •

Cōnf: Haec animālia sunt satis fortia.

381. Haec verba sunt blanda → H___ v____ s___ s____ bl____. ★ ○ •

Cōnf: Haec verba sunt satis blanda.

So far we have had six Latin prepositions which pattern with the ablative. Write the missing prepositions in these five Basic Sentences:

382. Nāvis quae _____ flūmine magna est _____ marī parvula est. (65)

R: Nāvis quae in flūmine magna est in marī parvula est.

383. _____ auribus cognōscitur asinus. (43)

R: Ex auribus cognōscitur asinus.

384. Lēgēs _____ mōribus vānae. (56)

R: Lēgēs sine mōribus vānae.

385. _____ jūdice līs est. (20)

R: Sub jūdice līs est.

386. _____ cane nōn magnō saepe tenētur aper. (23)

R: Ā cane nōn magnō saepe tenētur aper.

25-67

R: Mārtiālis.

420. "Cujus verba sunt, 'Nōn amo tē?' "

We will now discuss Latin word order.

421. As you well know, Latin word order is *almost* (but not quite) completely free, and instead of being used as a structural signal, is used to show _____.

A: emphasis.

422. For example, in the sentence Cautus metuit foveam lupus, the word lupus is emphasized two ways. For one thing, lupus comes in the ____ part of the sentence; for another thing, lupus is separated from its _____.

A: last modifier (adjective).

Let us look at the symbols for a two kernel {-s -m -t} sentence, with the second kernel written under the first:

{-s -m -t}
{-s -m -t}

423. If we draw a line connecting these symbols for subjects and a line connecting these symbols for objects, the lines will ____ (cross each other/be parallel to each other).

{-s -m -t}
↕   ↕
{-s -m -t}

A: be parallel to each other.

424. If we draw lines connecting the two subjects and the two objects, these lines will ____ (cross each other/be parallel to each other).

{-s -m -t}
{-s -m -t}

A: cross each other.

{-s -m -t}
✕
{-s -m -t}

19-58

387. In addition we have had the antonym of **sine**, which is ____.

A: cum.

388. The prepositions **in, ex, sine, sub, ā, (and ab) cum,** and **prō** pattern with the ablative. Copy this in your Notebook under "Facts about Latin."

389. The new preposition **prō,** like the others you have learned so far, patterns with the _____ case.

A: ablative

390. ★ ○ • innocēns   innocentēs
           innocentem   innocentēs
           innocente   innocentibus

391. In the Basic Sentence **Quī prō innocente dīcit satis est ēloquēns,** the word **innocēns** means "the innocent" and is used as a n____.

A: noun.

392. The ablative case of this word in the singular is **innocentE**. But when the same word is used as an adjective, the ablative case of **innocēns** in the singular would more likely be the form _____.

A: innocentī.

393. "Ā quō vēritās dīcitur?" "Ā fēminā inn_____."

R: innocentī.

394. ★ ○ • līs   lītēs
            lītem   lītēs
            līte   lītibus

Quaestiōnēs et Respōnsa

412. Sabidius ★ ○ •

413. Martialis ★ ○ •

Cōnf: Martialis
        Martialem
        Martiāle
        Martiālī
        Martialis

Cōnf: Sabidius
        Sabidium
        Sabidiō
        Sabidiō
        Sabidiī

414. "Quem Martialis nōn amat?"

R: Sabidium.

415. "Quis Sabidium nōn amat?"

R: Martialis.

416. "Ā quō Sabidius nōn dīligitur?"

R: Martiāle.

417. "Cui Sabidius nōn placet?"

R: Martiālī.

418. "Quis dīcit, 'Nōn amō tē?'"

R: Martialis.

419. "Cui Martialis dīcit, 'Nōn amō tē?'"

R: Sabidiō.

These question-and-answers refer to the general idea that an innocent man has nothing to fear and doesn't need a lawyer. In some questions you will have to use words which are not in the Basic Sentence at all. Remember to answer with the form which the question word expects.

395. "Quālis vir in līte perīc'la nōn timet?" "In_____."

R: **Innocēns.**

396. "Quō locō vir innocēns perīc'lum nōn metuit?" "__ l____."

R: In līte.

397. "Quālis jūdex innocentem semper absolvit?" "J_____."

R: Jūstus.

398. "Quālem virum jūdex jūstus numquam damnat?" "In_____."

R: Innocentem.

399. "Quālī ab homine līs nōn timētur?" "In_____ī __ h_____."

R: **Innocentī ab homine.**

400. "Ā quō līs nōn timētur?" "__ _____e."

R: Ab innocente.

401. That is, **innocente** is used for the n____ and **innocentī** for the ad_____.

A: noun adjective.

402. ★ ○ • ○ • *Absentem laedit, cum ēbriō quī lītigat.* (68)

407. Nōn amō tē, Sabidī, nec possum dīcere quā rē = _____

A: I do not love you, Sabidius, and I cannot say why.

408. Hoc tantum possum dīcere: "Nōn amō tē." = _____

A: I can say at least this much; "I do not love you."

409. Copy the poem in your Notebook.

410. N__ __ o t__, S_____; n__ p____d__ qu__ r__. H__ t____ p____ d____; "N__ __ o t__."

R: Nōn amō tē, Sabidī, nec possum dīcere quā rē. Hoc tantum possum dīcere: "Nōn amō tē."

411. This poem has been translated into English in the following way. Remembering the original Martial poem, see if you can predict the last line:

I do not like thee, Doctor Fell;
The reason why, I cannot tell.
But this alone I know full well:
"_____."

A: "I do not like thee, Doctor Fell."

412-420. Answer the questions, remembering that when Martial used the First Person in the poem, he was referring to himself, and when he used the Second Person he was referring to Sabidius. Therefore, in our answers we cannot use the pronouns **ego** and **tū**, but must use the names **Martiālis** and **Sabidius**. Echo the singular paradigm of these two names.

403. The subject of the subordinate clause **cum ēbriō quī lītigat** is the relative pronoun ____.

A: quī.

404. By looking at the clause **cum ēbriō quī lītigat,** you can see that occasionally parts of the clause may occur _____ the relative pronoun.

A: before

405. In order to achieve extra emphasis the Romans could place an item like a prepositional phrase before the _____ _____.

A: relative pronoun (or the subordinating conjunction).

406. The unknown word **absentem** is _____ case.

A: accusative

407. Since **absentem** is the object, the sentence must be an {_____} type.

A: {-s -m -t}

408. In **Absentem laedit cum ēbriō quī lītigat,** it is plain that the {-m} is the word _____ and that the {-t} is the word _____. The {-s}, however, is not a noun but is a _____ cl____.

A: absentem   laedit.
      relative
clause.

409. The relative clause which is the subject of **laedit** is ___ _____ ___ _____.

A: cum ēbriō quī lītigat.

405-406. (In this poem the verb **amō** has a poetical variant **amo,** with a short vowel.)
Nōn amō tē, Sabidī, nec possum dīcere
quā rē.
Hoc tantum possum dīcere: "Nōn amō tē." (113) ∨ ★ ○ •

R: Sabidī!

404.

R: Segī!

403.

R: Tuccī!

402.

402-404. Call these people as they identify themselves.

19-61

410. The word **absentem** is an adjective. If there is a noun for it to modify, draw an arrow from **absentem** to the noun it modifies; if there is no noun for it to modify, say so.

A: There is no noun for it to modify.

411. You can guess from the English derivative that **absēns** means "_ _ _ _ _ _ p_ _ _ _ _."

A: absent person.

412. Use the colorless word "blanks" for the verb, and use **ēbriō** as an English word to show you understand the structure of the sentence, even if you do not know all the words. **Absentem laedit, cum ēbriō quī lītigat** = _ _ _ _ _ _ _ _ _ s _ _ _ _ an _ _ _ _ _ _ _ _ _ _ s an _ _ _ _ _ _ _ _ _ _ _ _.

A: Who quarrels with an **ēbriō** blanks an absent person.

413. Multum vīnum virum ēbrium reddit. √ ★ ○ •

414. Vir ēbrius est vir īnsānus. √ ★ ○ •

415. Quī vīnum intemperanter bibit est ēb_ _ _ _ _.

R: **ēbrius.**

416. The adjective **ēbrius, ēbria, ēbrium** means "dr_ _ _ _."

A: drunk (as a noun, "drunken person").

417. Cum ēbriō quī lītigat = _ _ _ _ _ _ _ _ _ s _ _ _ _ a _ _ _nken p_ _ _ _ _

A: Who quarrels with a drunken person

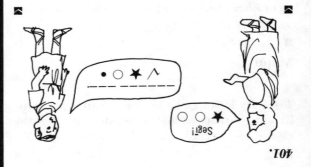

401. Cōn: Segius sum.

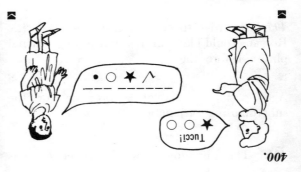

400. Cōn: Tuccius sum.

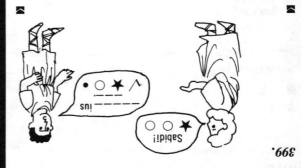

399. Cōn: Sabidius sum.

name is.

399-401. However, if the last three letters are **-ius**, the calling form ends in **-ī.** In this sequence, your teacher will call you by name. And you, pretending that you are this person, will answer in Latin, "I am Sabidius," or whatever the

A: ē.

398. When the last two sounds of the nominative of a man's name are **-us**, the calling form ends in _ _.

25-63

418. ★ ○ ○ Ab_____ l_____, ___ ē___
___ l_____.

R: Absentem laedit, cum ēbriō quī lītigat.

419. Now put "blanks" in place of the unknown verb **laedit**. Absentem laedit, cum ēbriō quī lītigat = Who _____ ____ _____ _____s an _____ _____.

A: Who quarrels with a drunken person blanks an absent person.

The next step is hard. What does the unknown verb **laedit** mean?

420. Absentem laedit, cum ēbriō quī lītigat = ___ _____ ____ a _____ _____ h___s an _____ _____. (Auxilium invenītur sub hāc līneā.)

Aux: **Laedit** is an antonym of **adjuvat**.

A: Who quarrels with a drunken person harms an absent person.

421. Copy this sentence and its meaning in your Notebook.

422. It would be unfair to attack someone who wasn't present and couldn't defend himself. This Basic Sentence says that it is equally unfair to quarrel with a drunken person because _____ _____. [In your own words]

A: although he may actually be present in body, on account of the wine his intelligence has disappeared and he might as well be absent, as far as defending himself goes.

423. In this sentence the word **ēbrius**, although it is the part of speech called an _____ ____, is used here as a ____.

A: adjective noun.

19-63

These questions require the use of a word in the last Basic Sentence. Sometimes the word has to be transformed, sometimes it does not. Observe closely the question word; the answer must be in the same case and number as the question word.

424. "Quālis vir est quī ēbrius est?" "Ab____ vir est."

R: Absēns vir est.

425. "Quōcum lītigat quī cum ēbriō lītigat?" "C__ a_____."

R: Cum absente.

426. "Quis absentem laedit?" "___ ___ _____ _____."

R: Quī cum ēbriō lītigat.

These questions are on the general sense that wine steals away one's wits.

427. "Quid āmittit vir ēbrius?" "Men___ su___."

R: Mentem suam.

428. "Quāliter nōn agit quī cum ēbriō lītigat?" "Jūs__ n__ ag___."

R: Jūstē nōn agit.

429. The in- part of the word **incertus** is called a "_____."

A: prefix.

430. While **certus** means "sure," **incertus** means "un__e" or "___ sure."

A: unsure   not

25-61

388. I can see this much = H. t_____ v_____ p_____.

R: Hoc tantum vidēre possum.

If we wish to connect two equal things in Latin, we use et.

389. Pecūniam quaerō et inveniō = _____ _____ and I ____ it.

A: I seek money and I find it.

If we wish to connect two equal things in a *negative* way, (I do one thing and not another) we use the connector nec.

390. Pecūniam quaerō nec inveniō = _____ _____ and I do ___ f___ it.

A: I seek money and I do not find it.

391. Īnfāns canem magnum metuit nec amat = _____ _____ _____ _____ _____.

A: The child fears the big dog and does not love him.

392. Aprum nōn cernō nec timeō = I __ ___ see and do ___ ___ the ____.

A: I do not see and do not fear the boar.

393. Hunc nōn dīligō nec possum laudāre = _____ _____ _____ _____ _____.

A: I do not love him and I cannot praise him.

394-397. In Unit 19 you learned that to call people whose names ended in **-us** (like **Marcus**, **Quīntus**, and **Titus**) you used the special calling form ending in **-e**. In this sequence, your teacher will call you by name. Pretending that you are this person, answer in Latin, "I am **Marcus**," or whatever the name is.

431. The prefix **in-** makes an adjective negative; for example, the antonym of **sānus** is formed by adding the prefix **in-** to **sānus**, resulting in the word _____. [Don't forget to make the vowel long before **-ns-**.]

A: **īnsānus.**

432. There is another Latin prefix **in-**, which means "into." When someone is "inducted" into the army he is ____ (*not* brought into the army/brought *into* the army).

A: brought *into* the army.

433. The prefix in the English word "inflammable" is the one that means "into." Therefore material which is "inflammable" is ready to burst ___o fl___s.

A: into flames.

434. However, there were many people who mistakenly thought that the prefix in "inflammable" was the one which made the idea negative. These people therefore *wrongly* thought that material which is "inflammable" ____ (would/would not) burn.

A: would not

435. Therefore many gasoline trucks changed their danger signs from "INFLAMMABLE" (which people misunderstood) to a new word "FL_____."

A: FLAMMABLE.

436. A person who is "inebriated" ____ (is/is not) drunk.

A: is [Of course, if you didn't know the word "inebriated," you could not have answered the question.]

382.

Quanta est littera?

T___ a ___
___ ___

R: **Tanta est littera.**

383. Ask your teacher, "How much are you doing?" Qu____ m f____? ✓ ★ ○ •

Cōnf: **Quantum facis?**

384. Write down his answer. ("I am doing this much.") _____ ★ ○ ○

R: **Tantum faciō.**

385. How much can you say? = Qu_____ dīc___ po___?

R: **Quantum dīcere potes?**

386. I can say this much = T_____ dīc_____ pos___.

R: **Tantum dīcere possum.**

387. I can say this much = **Hoc tantum dīcere possum.**

If the word that corresponds to the English "this" is expressed, it is **hoc.**

I can do this much = H___ t___ f_____ p_____.

R: **Hoc tantum facere possum.**

SUMMARY

437. This Unit started off with the numerals that tell "in what order," from one through ten. Echo as your teacher numbers in Latin from "first animal" to "tenth animal"; echo after each numeral. ★ ○ • animal **prīmum**, animal **secundum**, animal **tertium**, animal **quārtum**, animal **quīntum**, animal **sextum**, animal **septimum**, animal **octāvum**, animal **nōnum**, animal **decimum**.

438. You learned a new part of speech that tells HOW something is done. This part of speech is formed by putting the ending _____ or _____ on the stem of the adjective.

A: -ē   -ter

439. You learned that the more common expression for **Cum quō** was _____, written as one word.

A: **Quōcum**

440. Write the Martial poem.
N__ c____ sine ap__ n_____, T___,
  C_____.
  B_____ c_____ C_____ h____.

A: **Nōn cēnat sine aprō noster, Tite,
   Caeciliānus.
   Bellum convīvam Caeciliānus habet.**

441. You learned that in a two-kernel sentence one kernel may be more important than the other. The important kernel (with its modifiers) is called the "____ clause."

A: main clause.

---

375. Write the Latin for, "Why do you (plural) seek dangers?" Qu__ r__ vōs p_____ pet____?
R: **Quā rē vōs perīc'la petītis?**

376. Why are you (sg) counting the hours? = ___ hōr__ num____? ∨ ★ ○ •
Cōnf: **Quā rē hōrās numerās?**

377. Why are you (pl) changing your mind? = ___ an___ m_____? ∨ ★ ○ •
Cōnf: **Quā rē animum mūtātis?**

378. The answer to **Quantus** is often **tantus** ("this big").

A: this big.

379. When the teacher asked, "How big is the fish?", the pupil held up his hands and said, "The fish is ___ ___."
R: **Tantus est piscis.**

380. Your teacher will ask you how big the bull is. ★ ○ ○
Cōnf: **Quantus est taurus?**

381. Tell him, "It's this big." ___ s___ ∨ ★ ○ •
Cōnf: **Tantus est taurus.**

442. The less important kernel (with its modifiers) we call the _____ cl___e.

A: subordinate clause.

443. The signal for a subordinate clause is a sub_____ting con_____n.

A: subordinating conjunction.

444. The one Latin subordinating conjunction you know is the word which means "when": ____

A: **cum.**

445. You then learned that a relative clause may modify a noun or even replace a noun. Such clauses are introduced by a form of the word **quī, quae, quod,** which is called a "_____ _____."

A: relative pronoun.

Besides the Martial poem, you learned six sentences, all of which contained subordinate clauses.

446. The judge is condemned when the guilty man is acquitted = J____ d_____ c__ n_____ abs_____. (63)

A: **Jūdex damnātur cum nocēns absolvitur.**

447. When a woman thinks alone she thinks badly = M_____, c__ s___ c_____, m___ c_____. (64)

A: **Mulier, cum sōla cōgitat, male cōgitat.**

448. Who kills a child is cruel, not brave = Cr_____ ___, n__ f_____, qu_ īn_____ _____. (66)

A: **Crūdēlis est, nōn fortis, quī īnfantem necat.**

---

368. Quem lupī metuunt? _____.

R: **Tē lupī metuunt.**

369. The question "Why?" may be asked in Latin by **Quā rē?**. The **quā** is the interrogative word and **rē** is the ablative of the Latin word whose nominative form is ____.

A: **rēs.**

370. We told you before that **rēs** was a word of wide meaning. **In omnī rē** = In every s_____.

A: situation.

371. Rem, nōn spem, quaerit amīcus = A friend seeks _____, not a promise.

A: support

372. Crēdula rēs amor est = Love is a trusting _____.

A: thing.

373. Rēs also means "reason"; **quā rē** therefore means "bec____ of w_____?" or "for w_____?"

A: because of what reason? for what reason?

374. The most common English equivalent of **quā rē** is "Why?" Echo your teacher as he says in Latin, "Why are you (singular) holding the boar?" ★ ○ • ○ ○ Q__ r. ap__ t____?

Cōnf: **Quā rē tū aprum tenēs?**

449. Who speaks for the innocent is eloquent enough = Qu_ pr_ in_____ d____ s____ ___ ēl_____. (67)

A: **Quī prō innocente dīcit satis est ēloquēns.**

450. Who quarrels with a drunken person harms an absent person = Ab_____ l_____, c__ ē____ qu_ l_____. (68)

A: **Absentem laedit, cum ēbriō quī lītigat.**

451. N____ qu__ fl_____ m____ __ in ____ p_____ ___.

A: **Nāvis quae in flūmine magna est in marī parvula est.** (65)

452. By now you know paradigms well enough to construct paradigms even of words you have never seen. For example, you have done so many First Declension nouns that you should have no trouble writing the paradigm of **puella**, a First Declension noun which you have never seen. Try it:

puella _____
puellam _____
_____ _____

R: puella   puellae
    puellam   puellās
    puellā   puellīs

365. Here is some new vocabulary for another poem by Martial. The accusative of the Latin word **tū** is **tē**. Tell your teacher that the dog loves him.

T_ c___ d_____ p_____

Quem canis dīligit?

R: **Tē canis dīligit.**

366-368. Your teacher will ask a similar question in each of these pictures. But answer truthfully; if he asks you, "Who is the bull chasing?", don't say that he is chasing your teacher, if the bull is actually chasing someone else.

366.

Quem taurus premit?

R: **Suem taurus premit.**

367.

Quem fēmina cognōscit?

R: **Tē fēmina cognōscit.**

453. Try a new Second Declension Noun:

    servus   servī
    _____   _____
    _____   _____

R: servus   servī
    servum servōs
    servō   servīs

We clue you in two ways: we tell you what declension the noun belongs to and we give you two of the six forms.

454. Decline a Second Declension neuter noun:

    _____   sīgna
    _____   _____
    sīgnō   _____

R: sīgnum sīgna
    sīgnum sīgna
    sīgnō   sīgnīs

455. Decline a Third Declension noun:

    mors   _____
    mortem _____
    _____   _____

R: mors   mortēs
    mortem mortēs
    morte   mortibus

456. Decline a Third Declension neuter:

    nōmen   _____
    _____   nōmina
    _____   _____

R: nōmen   nōmina
    nōmen   nōmina
    nōmine nōminibus

457. Decline a Fourth Declension noun:

    _____   _____
    cāsum   cāsūs
    _____   _____

R: cāsus   cāsūs
    cāsum   cāsūs
    cāsū   cāsibus

360-363. Read aloud your teacher's question; then answer for you-and-your-friends who share your discouraged feeling about your ability to do all these things.

360. Magister: "Numerātisne horās serēnās?"

Discipulus: "H——s——n——non p——mus."

R: Horās serēnās numerāre non possumus.

361. Magister: "Errātisne sine duce?"

Discipulus: "S——d——e——non p——."

R: Sine duce errāre non possumus.

362. Magister: "Vincitisne necessitātēs?"

Discipulus: "N——v——n——."

R: Necessitātēs vincere non possumus.

363. Magister: "Depōnitisne longum amōrem?"

Discipulus: "L——a——d——n——."

R: Longum amōrem depōnere non possumus.

364. Write the compound paradigm of est that means "can," remembering about the change pot- to pos- before -s-.

_____ _____

R: possum possumus
    potes   potestis
    potest   possunt

458. Finally, a Fifth Declension noun (singular only):

        _____
        speciem
        _____

R: speciēs
        speciem
        speciē

VOCABULARY INVENTORY

In this Unit you learned the following nouns:

        convīva (158)   mulier (251)
        mare (327-31)   nāvis (325-30)

You learned these adjectives:

absēns (405)   noster, nostra,
bellus-a-um (157)   nostrum (164)
ēbrius-a-um (415)   parvulus-a-um (332)
innocēns (221)   sōlus-a-um (247)
nocēns (222)

You learned six more numerals:

quīntus-a-um, sextus-a-um,
septimus-a-um, octāvus-a-um,
nōnus-a-um, decimus-a-um (1)

You learned the following verbs:

absolvit (223)   cēnat (146)   cōgitat (252)
damnat (214)   laedit (419)   lītigat (417)
*agit (359)   jūdicat (107)

You learned a new part of speech formed on adjectives called an adverb. The question word is quāliter (82).

You learned these adverbs which end in -ē:

        avārē (109)   īnsānē (91)
        blandē (109)   jūstē (91)
        cautē (91)   vērē (91)
        īgnāvē (109)

---

355. Magister: "Egō taurum necō."
Discipulus: "Tū t---- n---- nōn p----."
◄

R: Tū taurum necāre nōn potes.
◄

356. Magister: "Egō perīc'la vincō."
Discipulus: "Tū p------- v------ nōn
------."
◄

R: Tū perīc'la vincere nōn potes.
◄

357. Magister: "Egō flūmen aspiciō."
Discipulus: "Tū f------ as------ nōn
------."
◄

R: Tū flūmen aspicere nōn potes.
◄

358. Magister: "Egō cum bellō convīvā cēnō."
Discipulus: "-- cum b------ c------ c------ ------."
◄

R: Tū cum bellō convīvā cēnāre nōn potes.
◄

359. Now your teacher will ask you and your friends whether you can do certain things, using the form potestisne. You, speaking for you-and-your friends, are most pessimistic and say, "We can't do such-and-such," using the new form p------s.
◄

A: possumus.

19-70

These adverbs end in **-ter**:

crūdēliter (83)	**intemperanter** (83)
ēloquenter (83)	**leviter** (111)
fortiter (111)	**patienter** (83)
hilariter (78)	**sapienter** (111)

This adverb is irregular: **male** (241)

Then there were three indeclinable words:

cum (250)   **prō** (370)   **satis** (369)

Finally, there was the relative pronoun

quī, quae, quod (322)

TEST INFORMATION

You will be asked questions on Basic Sentences 1-68, both new and old. You will be tested on new sentences which contain relative pronouns.

---

349. C-----, er--- s---. (112)

R: Cōgitō, ergō sum.

350. Echo the paradigm of the verb meaning "can." (Its infinitive form is **posse**, but you will not now be held responsible for it.)
★ ○ •

possum	possumus
potes	potestis
potest	possunt

351. Copy this paradigm in your Notebook.

352. You can see that before **sum** the prefix **pot-** becomes ———.

A: pos-.

353. In this sequence your teacher will make a number of statements. You are to contradict him, saying, "You cannot do this." For example:

Magister: "Ego fūrem cognōscō."
Discipulus: "Tū fūrem cognōscere nōn p--es."

R: Tū fūrem cognōscere nōn potes.

354. Magister: "Ego manūs lavō."
Discipulus: "Tū manūs lav--- nōn ---es."

R: Tū manūs lavāre nōn potes.

UNIT TWENTY

We will begin with a review of the various question words.

1. The interrogative adjective has the forms of the relative pronoun; in other words, we say **Quī vir est?** for "What man is it?" To ask "What woman is it?" we would ask ___ae **mulier est?**

A: **Quae mulier est?**

2. "Sub quō stat leō?" "___ _____."

quercus   leō

R: **Sub quercū.**

3. "Quō locō est nāvis?" "__ ____."

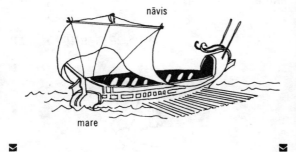

nāvis   mare

R: **In marī.**

---

343. **Cōgitō, ergō sum.** (112) √ ★ ○ •

344. ★ ○ ○ C_____, e____ ____

R: **Cōgitō, ergō sum.**

345. Expand as indicated: ___ **cōgitō, ergō** ___ **sum.**

R: **Ego cōgitō, ergō ego sum.**

346. **Cōgitō, ergō sum** = ------------------

A: I think, therefore I am.

347. Copy in your Notebook.

348. This statement is by the famous French philosopher, Descartes. He was discussing a fundamental problem, namely, how do we know that we actually exist. His answer means, "I know that I exist because I can perceive that I ------."

A: think.

4. "Quō locō stat elephantus?" "_____."

R: In nāve.

[Remember that the word **uter, utra, utrum** means "which of the two."]

5. "Utrum animal habet aurēs longās?" "_____."

R: Asinus.

6. "Quotō in orbe est mulier?" "_____."

R: Secundō in orbe.

7. "Quāliter hic vir cantat?" "_____."

R: Male.

339.

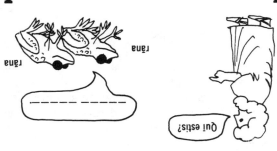

R: Rānae sumus.

340.

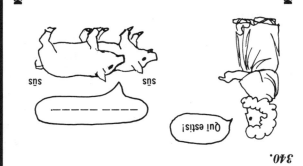

R: Suēs sumus.

341. Write the paradigm of the irregular verb **est**.

R: sum   sumus
   es   estis
   est   sunt

342. In the next Basic Sentence there is a new indeclinable word, **ergō**, which means "therefore." This word is occasionally used in English with the same meaning it has in Latin. It is used in summing up an argument to show the logical conclusion. "This and this is true; ergo, we should behave thus and so." This English word "ergo" (written in English without a macron) means "_____."

A: therefore.

20-3

8. **Male vir cantat** = The _ _ _ is s_ _ _ing _ _ _ly.

A: The man is singing badly.

9. We have had three cases, the _____, the _____, and the _____.

A: nominative accusative ablative.

10. The nominative serves not only as the subject of verbs but also as the c_____t of certain verbs, such as **est**.

A: complement

11. There are two nominatives in such a pattern, which we call the { _ _ _ _ _ _ _ } construction.

A: {-s -s est}

12. The only use of the *accusative* which we have had so far has been as the _____ of a transitive verb.

A: object (or complement)

13. The pattern in which the accusative enters is the { _ _ _ _ _ _ } construction.

A: {-s -m -t}

14. The only use of the *ablative* we have had so far has been to _____ verbs.

A: modify

In this Unit we will take up a new case. We will start with examples. We have had a Basic Sentence which meant, "The author praises his own work." We could expand this to say, "The author praises his own work *to the leader*." The new case which we are going to learn now expresses the idea of "to the leader."

337-340. Your teacher will now ask you who you are, except that you are now one of a group. Tell him who you are.

336. ★ ○ ● **sum**   sum   est
es   estis
sumus   sunt

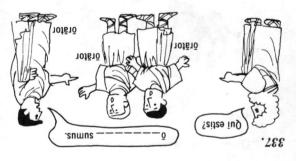

335.

20-4

15. In the Third, Fourth, and Fifth Declensions, the signal for this new case is -ī. Listen to your teacher describe this picture by saying that the author is praising his work TO THE LEADER. ★ ○ ○ D_ _ _ _ _ _ _ o_ _ _ l_ _ _ _ _ _.

Cōnf: **Ducī auctor opus laudat.**

16. Write this same description.
_____ **auctor opus laudat.** ★ ○ ○

A: **Ducī auctor opus laudat.**

17. Echo a new technical term. d á t i v e case ★ ○ • ○ •

VCh: "dáy-tive"

18. This new case is called the "dative case." The **dative** case of **dux** is _____.

A: **ducī.**

19. Ducī auctor opus laudat = _____ _____.

A: The author is praising his work to the leader. [If you need this reminder, you're hopeless: say your answers aloud.]

332-335. In the following sequence, your teacher will ask you who you are. You are to take the part of the person in the picture and reply, for example, **Fēmina sum.** ("I am a woman.")

332. Your teacher will ask you, "Who are you?" (**Quis es?**). You are to answer for the figure pictured on the right, "I am so-and-so."

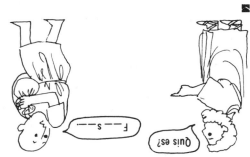

R: **Fūr sum.**

333.

R: **Anus sum.**

334.

R: **Medicus sum.**

20-5

20. ★ ○ • ○ • A_____ ī d___ n___ pr_____.

Cōnf: Auctōrī diem nox premit.
[*You* will not need this reminder, but your friends may have forgotten that they should keep on repeating the sentence until they feel that they have learned it.]

21. ★ ○ • ○ • ___ ī v_____ d___ ap_____.

Cōnf: Anuī vēritātem diēs aperit.

22. Write what you have just echoed. _____ vēritātem diēs aperit.

R: Anuī vēritātem diēs aperit.

23. Anuī vēritātem diēs aperit = ____ _____ ___ for ___ ___.

A: Time discloses the truth for the old lady.

---

325. We will now practice the irregular verb **est.** You are a human being = ★ ○ • ○ •
H___ ___.

Cōnf: Homō es.

326. I am a human being. = ___ ___
★ ○ • ○ •

Cōnf: Homō sum.

327. Who am I? = _____ ★ ○ • ○ •

Cōnf: Quis sum?

328. Tell him that he is a human being.
T___ h___ es. √ ★ ○ •

Cōnf: Tū homō es.

329. Echo the paradigm of the verb **est.** (The infinitive of **est** is **esse,** but you will not be held responsible for it at this time.) ★ ○ • ○ •

sum sumus
es estis
est sunt

330. Copy this paradigm in your Notebook.

331. Notice that the signal for the First Person is **-m** instead of the signal you have been practicing, which has been - - .

A: -ō.

24. ★ ○ • ○ • In_____ ī s__ j_____ l__ e___.

Cōnf: Innocentī sub jūdice līs est.

25. Write what you just echoed. _____ sub jūdice līs est.

R: Innocentī sub jūdice līs est.

26. ★ ○ • ○ • S_____ ī v___ n_____ p____.

Cōnf: Sapientī vēritās numquam perit.

27. Write what you just echoed. _____ vēritās numquam perit.

R: Sapientī vēritās numquam perit.

28. ★ ○ • ○ • H____ ī v___ v___ ___.

Cōnf: Hominī vīta vīnum est.

20-6

25-48

318. In this Basic Sentence, the word necessitās has the meaning of "necessary evil." Effugere nōn potes necessitātēs; potes vincere = _____.

A: You cannot escape necessary evils; (but) you can conquer them.

319. Copy in your Notebook.

Quaestiōnēs et Respōnsa

320. "Pereuntne an manent necessitātēs?"
"Nec_____."

R: Manent.

321. "Quibus sapiēns nōn servit?"
"Nec_____."

R: Necessitātibus.

322. "Quōrum sub rēgnō nōn manet sapiēns?" "Nec_____ ___ s_____ m_____."

R: Necessitātum sub rēgnō nōn manet sapiēns.

323. "Quibus sapiēns imperāre potest?"
"N_____."

R: Necessitātibus.

324. We have said that potest is a compound of the irregular verb _____.

A: est.

20-7

29. Write what you just echoed. _____ vīta vīnum est.

R: Hominī vīta vīnum est. [Did you remember to put the macron in?]

30. Echo the six datives you have just used. ★ ○ • ○ • innocentī, anuī, auctōrī, homīnī, sapientī, ducī

31-36. Do these same six sentences again, expanding with the new case ("dative") to show that this Basic Sentence is true as far as the person mentioned is concerned.

31. In_____ s__ j____ l__ e__. ✓ ★ ○ •

innocēns

R: Innocentī sub jūdice līs est.

32. A_____ d___ n__ p_____. ✓ ★ ○ •

auctor

R: Auctōrī diem nox premit.

---

314. Potes is another form of the irregular verb **potest**; note that it ends in **-s**. Expand the sentence with the two subjects which this signal -s suggests. __ effugere nōn potes necessitā- tēs; __ potes vincere.

R: Tū effugere nōn potes necessitā- tēs; tū potes vincere.

315. As the sentence is now expanded in the answer to the frame above, which of these state- ments is true?
1) Both kernels are complete.
2) Neither kernel is complete.
3) The first kernel is complete but not the second.
4) The second kernel is complete but not the first.

A: 3) The first kernel is complete but not the second.

316. Expand the second kernel: Tū potes vincere _____.

R: necessitātēs.

317. Listen to your teacher's description of this picture. ★ ○ • [The italicized word is new.] Hāc in pictūrā leō ā virō captus est. Leō mortem in foveā *effugere* nōn potest. Dolōrem sentiō prō leōne īnfēlīcī quī in foveā tenētur et perīclum effugere nōn potest.

The verb *effugere* (-iō) means "es_____."

A: escape.

20-8

33. S_____ v_____ n_____ p____. √ ★ ○ •

sapiēns

Cōnf: Sapientī vēritās numquam perit.

34. A___ v_____ d___ a_____. √ ★ ○ •

anus

R: Anuī vēritātem diēs aperit.

35. D___ a_____ o___ l_____. √ ★ ○ •

dux

R: Ducī auctor opus laudat.

25-46

308. "Quāliter plōrat quī capere cōnsilium potest, graviter an leviter?" "_____."

R: Leviter.

309. "Quantus dolor cōnsilium capere nōn potest?" "_____."

R: Gravis (vel māgnus).

310. "Quid agere nōn potest quī gravī dolōre movētur?" "_____ _____ _____."

R: Cōnsilium capere nōn potest.

311. "Quantō dolōre movētur vir quī cōnsilium capere potest?" "_____ _____."

R: Levī dolōre.

312. Effugere nōn potes necessitātēs; potes vincere. (III) √ ★ ○ •

313. Ef_____ n_____ pot___ n_____-___; p____ v_____. ★ ○ ○ √

Cōnf: Effugere nōn potes necessitā- tēs, potes vincere.

36. H_____ v___ v____ e___. ✓ ★ ○ •

R: Hominī vīta vīnum est.

37. Pronounce the technical term "dative case."
✓ ★ ○ •

VCh: "dáy-tive case."

38. In the first declension, the combination of the characteristic vowel **-a** and the signal for the dative results in the combination **-ae**. The dative of **fēmina** is **fēminae**. This form is identical with the _____ case of the _____ number.

A: nominative   plural

39. Fēminae is then another one of the amb_____ forms that are found in Latin.

A: ambiguous

40. From now on, whenever you meet the form **fēminae**, you must determine whether it is _____ _____ or _____ _____.

A: dative singular   nominative plural.

41. There are certain words which *almost always require* a dative. The Latin adjective that means "like" or "similar" is an example of this. It makes very little sense to say, "The fly is similar"; one would immediately ask, "The fly is similar __ _____?"

A: to what?

---

302. The new word **dolor** means "gr____."

A: grief.

303. Write the paradigm of the new Third Declension noun **dolor, dolōris, m.**

R:
dólor   dolōrēs
dolōrem   dolōrēs
dolōre   dolōribus
dolōrī   dolōribus
dolōris   dolōrum

304. Levis est dolor qui capere cōnsilium potest = The ___ ___ ___ ____ ____ ___ _ ____ is _____.

A: The grief which can make a plan is light.

305. Copy in your Notebook.

306. This means that a person's grief cannot be very deep if the person involved can look beyond that grief to something else and can _____.

A: make a plan.

Quaestiōnēs et Respōnsa

307. "Quantum dolōrem sentit qui cōnsilium capere potest?", "———— dolōrem."

R: Levem dolōrem.

20-10

42-47. In this sequence of pictures your teacher will comment that one of these persons or objects is similar to the other. After echoing, repeat the sentence until you have learned it.

42. ★ ○ • ○ • Musca muscae similis est.

43. This sentence means that one ___ is l___ ano___r ___.

A: one fly is like another fly.

44. ★ ○ • Aquila a___l__ similis est.

Cōnf: Aquila aquilae similis est.

45. This means that one eagle _____.

A: _____ is like another eagle.

46. ★ ○ • Sīmia s_____ similis est.

Cōnf: Sīmia sīmiae similis est.

296. Ingrātus miseris nocet ← ★ ○ • ○ •
In_____ m_____.

Cōnf: Ingrātus miseris nocere potest.

297-300. Make these same changes yourself, to say that these things can happen.

297. Absentem laedit → Ab_____ l_____re potest.

R: Absentem laedere potest.

298. Impōnit fīnem sapiēns → _____.

R: Impōnere fīnem sapiēns potest.

299. Sapientia vītae imperat → _____.

R: Sapientia vītae imperāre potest.

300. Ingrātus miseris nocet → _____.

R: Ingrātus miseris nocēre potest.

301. Listen to your teacher's description of this picture. ★ ○ [The italicized word is new.] Fūr pecūniam hujus juvenis capit. Juvenis pecūniam āmissam plōrat et, *dolōrem* sentit. Lacrimae dēfluunt ex oculīs juvenis qui dolōrem sentit. Hae lacrimae sunt signa dolōris.

47. ★ ○ • Fēmina _____ similis est.

Cōnf: Fēmina fēminae similis est.

48. Enter this as "Facts About Latin." The dative case is used with adjectives like **similis**.

49-56. We will practice the First Declension nouns along with those of the Third, Fourth, and Fifth Declensions.

49. ★ ○ • ○ • L__ l____ similis __t.

Cōnf: Leō leōnī similis est.

50. ★ ○ • ○ • Ef_____ ef_____ s_____ __t.

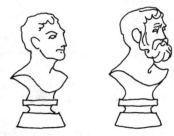

Cōnf: Effigiēs effigiēī similis est.

---

288. ★ ○ ○ _____

R: Levis est dolor qui capere cōnsilium potest.

289. This new verb **potest** is a combination of the irregular verb **est** preceded by the prefix **pot-**.

A: pot--.

290. In this program the only use which you will meet of this new verb **potest** is to pattern with an infinitive. Echo your teacher as he says that clothes *can* make the man. ★ ○ • ○ •

Cōnf: Vestis virum reddere potest.

291. Now write what he just said, that clothes can make the man. Vestis virum _____

R: Vestis virum reddere potest.

292. The word that means "can" in this sentence is _____.

A: potest.

293-296. Echo your teacher as he says that the action in the kernel *can* happen, using the new verb **potest** and transforming the original verb of the Basic Sentence to the infinitive.

293. Absentem laedit → ★ ○ • ○ •
Ab_____ l_____ ere potest.

Cōnf: Absentem laedere potest.

294. Sapientia vitae imperat → ★ ○ • ○ •
S_____ v_____ im_____ āre p_____

Cōnf: Sapientia vitae imperāre potest.

295. Impōnit fīnem sapiēns → ★ ○ • ○ •
Im_____ ere f_____ s_____ p_____

Cōnf: Impōnere fīnem sapiēns potest.

20-12

51. ★ ○ • ○ • Ar___ ar___ s_____ ___t.

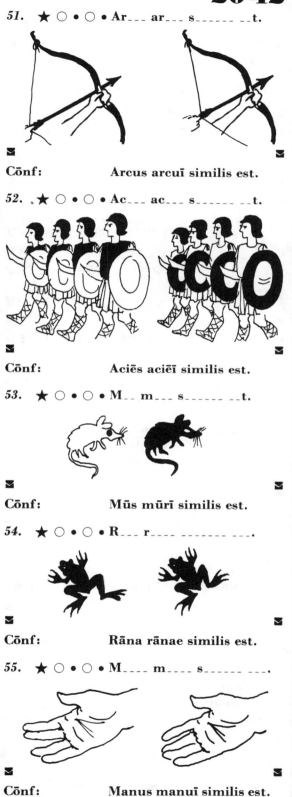

Cōnf: Arcus arcuī similis est.

52. ★ ○ • ○ • Ac___ ac___ s_____ ___t.

Cōnf: Aciēs aciēī similis est.

53. ★ ○ • ○ • M__ m___ s_____ ___t.

Cōnf: Mūs mūrī similis est.

54. ★ ○ • ○ • R___ r_____ _____.

Cōnf: Rāna rānae similis est.

55. ★ ○ • ○ • M____ m____ s____ ____.

Cōnf: Manus manuī similis est.

---

279. **Egō corpor. serv___** ⟵‧‧‧‧‧‧‧‧ ∧‧‧‧‧‧‧‧ ★ ○ •

R: **Egō corporī serviō.**

280. **Vōs corp___** s___ ⟵‧‧‧‧‧‧‧ ∧‧‧‧‧‧‧‧ ★ ○ •

R: **Vōs corporī servītis.**

281. **Tū cor___** s___ ⟵‧‧‧‧‧‧‧ ∧‧‧‧‧‧‧‧ ★ ○ •

R: **Tū corporī servīs.**

282-286. Copy in your Notebook these sample verbs of the four different conjugations. Be sure you copy them correctly!

282. First Conjugation

satiō	satiāmus
satiās	satiātis
satiat	satiant

283. Second Conjugation

placeō	placēmus
placēs	placētis
placet	placent

284. Third Conjugation
(regular)

neglegō	neglegimus
neglegis	neglegitis
neglegit	neglegunt

285. Third Conjugation
(iō)

sapiō	sapimus
sapis	sapitis
sapit	sapiunt

286. Fourth Conjugation

custōdiō	custōdīmus
custōdīs	custōdītis
custōdit	custōdiunt

287. **Levis est dolor quī capere cōnsilium potest.** (110) ∧ ★ ○ •

56. ★ ○ • ○ • V_____ v_____ _____ ___.

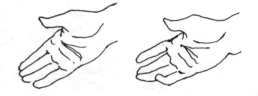

Cōnf: Vīpera vīperae similis est.

57-65. You will now be asked to describe some of these same pictures. Say and check.

57. M____ m___ī sim___s ____. √ ★ ○ •

R: Manus manuī similis est.

58. M__ca m___ae sim_____ ____. √ ★ ○ •

R: Musca muscae similis est.

59. R___ r__ae s_____ est. √ ★ ○ •

R: Rāna rānae similis est.

60. Ef___iēs ef____ēī s_____ ____. √ ★ ○ •

R: Effigiēs effigiēī similis est.

20-14

61. L_ _ l_ _ ī _ _ _ _ _ _ _ _ _ _ √ ★ ○ •

R: Leō leōnī similis est.

62. _ _ _ _ _ _ _ _ _ _ _ _ _ _ _ _ √ ★ ○ •

R: Aciēs aciēī similis est.

63. _ _ _ _ _ _ _ _ _ _ _ _ _ _ _ _ √ ★ ○ •

R: Arcus arcuī similis est.

64. _ _ _ _ _ _ _ _ _ _ _ _ _ _ _ _ √ ★ ○ •

R: Vīpera vīperae similis est.

25-40

264. petere _____ _____

R: petō petimus
    petis petitis
    petit petunt

265. cūrāre _____ _____

R: cūrō cūrāmus
    cūrās cūrātis
    cūrat cūrant

266. facere _____ _____

R: faciō facimus
    facis facitis
    facit faciunt

267. dīligere _____ _____

R: dīligō dīligimus
    dīligis dīligitis
    dīligit dīligunt

268. quaerere _____ _____

R: quaerō quaerimus
    quaeris quaeritis
    quaerit quaerunt

269. manēre _____ _____

R: maneō manēmus
    manēs manētis
    manet manent

270-272. Echo the paradigms of these Fourth Conjugation verbs.

270. custōdīre ★ ○ •
    custōdiō custōdīmus
    custōdīs custōdītis
    custōdit custōdiunt

65. .... ✓ ★ ○ •

R: Mūs mūrī similis est.

66. The dative singular of the Second Declension is always like the ablative singular. Thus the form **lupō** from now on is an _____ form.

A: ambiguous

67. From now on, **lupō** can be either _____ or _____.

A: ablative singular   dative singular.

68. Now we will continue in this sequence with commenting on the likeness of the following persons and animals, using just Second Declension nouns in the dative, which ends in __.

A: -ō.

69. ★ ○ • ○ • T_____ t____ s_____ __t.

Cōnf: Taurus taurō similis est.

70. ★ ○ • ○ • Ap___ ap__ _____ ___.

Cōnf: Aper aprō similis est.

---

260. The type like **capiō** we call "-iō verbs" (because they have the vowel -i- in the first person). The first person singular of the great majority of Third Conjugation verbs, however, (the "regular" ones) have a form like **quaerō**, that is, without any -i-.

Write down all the "-iō" verbs which occur in the following list, all of which are Third Conjugation verbs: **dīligō, reddō, capiō, currō, metuō, quaerō, faciō, premō, regō, cognōscō, cernō, vincō, bibō, neglegō, trahō, sapiō, aspiciō, dīcō, āmittō, emō, pōnō, absolvō, laedō, agō, colō, impōnō, pingō, oppōnō, accidō, dēpōnō.** _____.

A: **capiō   faciō   sapiō   aspiciō**

261. In this sequence, remember that you can tell to what conjugation a verb belongs by the ch_____ v_____ of the infinitive.

A: characteristic vowel

262. However, you must remember that **aspicere, capere, facere,** and **sapere** are not regular Third Conjugation verbs but are __ verbs of the Third Conjugation.

A: -iō

263-269. [You may say these instead of writing if you feel you can learn them that way just as well.]

263. aspicere _____ _____

R: **aspiciō   aspicimus**
aspicis   aspicitis
aspicit   aspiciunt

71. ★ ○ • ○ • Equ___ ___ ___ .

Cōnf: Equus equō similis est.

72. ★ ○ • ○ • As___ ___ ___ .

Cōnf: Asinus asinō similis est.

73. Expand the following sentence to say that this (that is, what the kernel says) is true as far as a *doctor* is concerned. M___ō ars l___a est.
√ ★ ○ •

Cōnf: Medicō ars longa est.

252-259. Complete the sentences with the verb form which the person pronoun requires. Remember: there will be a short -i in every form.

252. Vōs nōn capi___ mūrem ← _____ .
∨ ★ ○ •

R: Vōs nōn capitis mūrem.

253. Tū nōn cap___ mūr___ ← _____ .
∨ ★ ○ •

R: Tū nōn capis mūrem.

254. Egō nōn ca___ m___ ← _____ .
∨ ★ ○ •

R: Egō nōn capiō mūrem.

255. Nōs nōn c___ m_____ ← _____ .
∨ ★ ○ •

R: Nōs nōn capimus mūrem.

256. Egō crūdēlem medicum fac___ ← _____ .
∨ ★ ○ •

R: Egō crūdēlem medicum faciō.

257. Nōs crūdēl___ medicum fac___ ← _____ .
∨ ★ ○ •

R: Nōs crūdēlem medicum facimus.

258. Vōs crūd___ med___ f___ ← _____ .
∨ ★ ○ •

R: Vōs crūdēlem medicum facitis.

259. Tū cr___ m___ f___ ← _____ .
∨ ★ ○ •

R: Tū crūdēlem medicum facis.

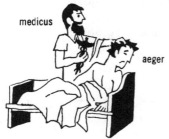

74. Expand the following sentence to say what is true as far as the *patient* is concerned. Aeg___ v___ br____ ____. ✓ ★ ○ •

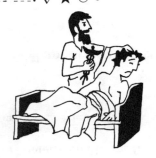

Cōnf: Aegrō
vīta brevis est.

75. Echo the dative forms which you will use in the next sequence: ★ ○ • ○ • Agnō, vīperae, piscī, quercuī, muscae, elephantō, mūrī, canī

76-83. Now use the same pattern to describe the following pictures, all of which anticipate a speedy end for someone.

76. ___ō v___ br____ ____.

R: Agnō vīta brevis est.

77. V____ae ___ br____ ___.

R: Vīperae vīta brevis est.

246-248. There is a special sub-class of Third Conjugation verbs, slightly different from mittere and pōnere. Echo sample paradigms of this class.

246. sapere • ○ ★ •
sapiō   sapimus
sapis   sapitis
sapit   sapiunt

247. aspicere • ○ ★ •
_____iō   _____imus
_____is   _____itis
_____it   _____iunt

Cōnf:
aspiciō   aspicimus
aspicis   aspicitis
aspicit   aspiciunt

248. facere • ○ ★ •
fac___   fac___
fac___   fac___
fac___   fac___

Cōnf:
faciō   facimus
facis   facitis
facit   faciunt

249. Note that in this paradigm there is a short *i* in ___ of the forms.

A: all

250. Using these verbs as models, write the paradigm of the -*iō* verb capere.

R:
capiō   capimus
capis   capitis
capit   capiunt

251. These special Third Conjugation verbs are called "-*iō* verbs" because they _____ _____ instead of _____ in the _____.

A: have -*iō*   just -*ō*   First Person Singular.

78. P__ī ____ _____ ___.

R: Piscī vīta brevis est.

79. _____ ____ _____ ___.

R: Quercuī vīta brevis est.

80. _____ ____ _____ ___.

R: Muscae vīta brevis est.

81. _____ ____ _____ ___.

R: Elephantō vīta brevis est.

---

238. Echo the paradigm of the Third Conjugation verb mittere. ★ ○ •

Cōnj: mittō   mittimus
       mittis   mittitis
       mittit   mittunt

239. On the model of mittere, write the paradigm of petere.

R: petō   petimus
    petis   petitis
    petit   petunt

240. Change the sentence by transforming the verb to the person which the new subject requires.

Egō certa mitt_ dum incerta pet_.

R: Egō certa mittō dum incerta petō.

241. Tū c____ m____ d___ inc____ p_____.

R: Tū certa mittis dum incerta petis.

242. Vōs c____ m____ ____ p_____.

R: Vōs certa mittitis dum incerta petitis.

243. Stultus _____ dum _____ _____.

R: Stultus certa mittit dum incerta petit.

Quaestiōnēs et Respōnsa

244. "Quotae persōnae sunt 'mittimus' et 'petimus'?" "Sunt p_____."

R: Sunt prīmae persōnae.

245. "Cujus cāsūs et numerī est haec vōx 'certa'?" "_____" est c_____ et n_____ _____."

R: "Certa" est cāsūs accūsātīvī et numerī plūrālis.

82. _____ .

R: Mūrī vīta brevis est.

83. _____ .

R: Canī vīta brevis est.

84. **Vir pecūniam dōnat** means that the ___ is _____ _____.

A: man is giving money.

85. However, something is missing in this sentence to make it sensible. Besides knowing *who* does the giving and *what* he gives, we should also like to know _____. [In your own words]

A: to whom he gives it.

---

231. If **certa** modifies a noun, draw an arrow to the noun it modifies; if it does not modify a noun say so.

A: It does not modify any noun.

232. Therefore the adjective **certa** in this sentence is used _____.

A: as a noun itself.

233. **Certa mittimus** = We l___ s___ th___s.

A: We lose sure things.

234. Write the sentence. _____

R: Certa mittimus dum incerta petimus.

235. Using "blank" for the unknown verb **petimus**, this means, "_____."

A: We lose sure things while we blank unsure things.

236. An English derivative of **petere**, formed from the past participle form **petītus**, is the word "petition." We draw up a petition when we are seeking something. **Certa mittimus dum incerta petimus** (109) = We s___ s___ wh___ we s___ ___ ___ ones.

A: We lose sure things while we seek unsure ones.

237. Copy in your Notebook.

20-20

86. In order to give something, we generally have to have three parties: a person who does the giving, an object to give, and a person to whom we give it. Let's put a woman into the picture. ★ ○ • ○ • **Vir pecūniam fēminae dōnat.**

87. This means that the man gives the money -- --- -----.

A: to the woman.

88. Or we can say in English that he is giving the ----- the -----.

A: woman   money.

89. Say a Latin sentence that describes this picture. -----ae v-- v----- dōnat.

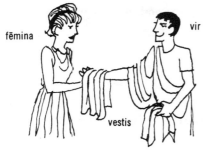

fēmina   vir   vestis

R: **Fēminae vir vestem dōnat.**

---

225. *Certa mittimus dum incerta petimus.* (109) ∨ ★ ○ • (The subordinating conjunction **dum** means "while.")

226. C----- m----- d-- in--- p-----.

R: *Certa mittimus dum incerta petimus.*

227. The verb **āmittere**, which you met in the Basic Sentence *Plōrātur lacrimis āmissa pecūnia vēris*, means "to l-----."

A: lose.

228. **Āmittere** is a compound of the prefix -**ā** and the verb **mittere**. In this Basic Sentence, the simple verb **mittere** is used with the same meaning as the compound verb ---------.

A: **āmittere.**

Expand with the only possible subjects.

229. --- *certa mittimus dum --- incerta petimus.* ∨ ★ ○ •

Conf: *Nōs certa mittimus dum nōs incerta petimus.*

230. Since the predictable subject of **mittimus** is **nōs**, **certa** cannot be the subject but must be --------- case, --------- gender, and --------- number.

A: accusative   neuter   plural

20-21

90. Write a Latin sentence that describes this picture. F_____ j_____s as_____ d_____.

fēmina — juvenis — asinus

R: Fēminae juvenis asinum dōnat.

91. Fēminae juvenis asinum dōnat = The ____ ___ is ___ing the _____ a _____.

A: The young man is giving the woman a donkey.

92. Echo a synonym for **dōnat**: ★ ○ • ○ •
dat

93. The verb **dat** ("gives") so commonly patterns with the dative case (because you can't give anything without giving it TO someone) that the name "dative" comes from an adjective **datīvus,** which consists of the adjective ending **-īvus** (in English, "-ive") added to the stem of **datus,** which is the p___ p_____ of **dat**.

A: past participle

94. Echo the dative of the question word **quis? quid?** ★ ○ • ○ • **cui?**

95. Ask your teacher to whom the young man is giving water. "Cui j_____ aq___ dat?" √ ★ ○ •

Cōnf: Cui juvenis aquam dat?

25-33

Quaestiōnēs et Respōnsa

217. "Quid Cicerō vult?" "Sē_____."

R: Sēcūritātem animī.

218. "In quō posita est vīta fēlix?" "_____ s_____."

R: In animī sēcūritāte.

219. "Quālem animum possidet vir beātus?" "An___ s_____."

R: Animum sēcūrum.

220. "Quī auctor pōnit vītam beātam in animī sēcūritāte?" "C_____."

R: Cicerō.

221. "Cujus cāsūs est 'sēcūritāte'?" "_____, _____ est c_____ ivī."

R: "Sēcūritāte" est cāsūs ablātīvī.

222. "Quotae persōnae est 'pōnimus'?" "_____, _____ est per_____."

R: "Pōnimus" est prīmae persōnae.

223. "Cujus numerī est hoc verbum 'pōnimus'?" "Est n_____."

R: Est numerī plūrālis.

224. "Cujus cāsūs et cujus numerī est hoc nōmen 'animī'?" "Est c_____ et n_____."

R: Est cāsūs genitīvī et numerī singulāris.

20-22

96. Write the one important word of his answer [that is, the one that answers **cui?**].
★ ○ ○ "_____."

Cōnf: Canī juvenis aquam dat.

R: Canī.

97-115. You will now be asked questions about a series of pictures in which you will use nouns in four different cases. You will be asked *who* is doing the giving, *what* he is giving, *to whom* it is given, or *by whom* it is given.

97. "Quod animal dux rēgīnae dat?"
"_____."

R: Aprum. [If you would like extra help, use the previous picture and answer for the next three questions.]

98. "Quis aprum rēgīnae dat?" "_____."

R: Dux.

99. "Cui dux aprum dat?" "_____."

R: Rēgīnae.

100. "Quid rēgīnae ā duce datur?"
"_____."

R: Aper.

25-32

211. In the New Testament there is a section where each sentence begins with the expression "Blessed are they who . . . ." This section is called "The Beatitudes," because the Latin version begins, "Beātī sunt quī . . . ." Beātam vītam pōnimus = We place a h---y life.

A: happy

212. The verb **pōnere** occurred in the Basic Sentence **In virtūte posita est vēra fēlicitās**. In this new Basic Sentence the verb **pōnimus** has a slightly different meaning. However, the way to proceed is to use the meaning it had before and then try to figure out the new meaning from the context. So as a try, we would say that **Nōs vītam beātam in animī sēcūritāte pōnimus** means, "-- pl--- a ---- l---- in ------ m---------."

A: We place a happy life in security of mind. [Do not put this meaning in your Reference Notebook.]

213. We might better say, "We believe that a ------- l---- lies in -------- m------."

A: happy life lies in security of mind.

214. Copy in your Notebook.

215. ★ ○ ○ N--- b----- v----- an----
s------------ p----------.

R: Nōs beātam vītam in animī sēcūritāte pōnimus.

216. Write the singular paradigm of **sēcūritās, sēcūritātis**, f. _____.

R: sēcūritās
sēcūritātem
sēcūritāte
sēcūritātī
sēcūritātis

20-23

101. How do we know in the sentence **Dux rēgīnae aprum dat** that the ambiguous form **rēgīnae** is dative singular and not nominative plural? There are *two* ways of telling. For one thing, **rēgīnae** could not *possibly* be the subject of **dat** because _____ . [In your own words]

A: **dat** is singular number and therefore requires a singular subject.

102. For another thing, with the verb **dat** you expect a noun (usually a personal noun) in the _____ case.

A: dative

Now back to our question-and-answer practice on the pictures.

103. "Quis piscī aquam dat?" "_____."

R: _____ Juvenis.
[Use the picture and question from the previous frame if you wish to.]

104. "Quid piscī juvenis dat?" "_____."

R: _____ Aquam.

105. "Cui juvenis aquam dat?" "_____."

R: _____ Piscī.

106. "Quid ā juvene piscī datur?" "_____."

R: _____ Aqua.

25-31

204. N ○ ○ ✱ b _____ v _____ in an_____ s _____ p _____

R: **Nōs beātam vītam in animī sēcūritāte pōnimus.**

205. From sentences like **Oculī sunt in amōre ducēs** you know that the preposition in patterns with the _____ case.

A: ablative

206. In the sentence **Nōs beātam vītam in animī sēcūritāte pōnimus** which word is in the ablative case and patterns with the in? _____

A: **sēcūritāte.**

207. **Animī** is _____ case and its use in the sentence is _____ [In your own words]

A: genitive to modify **sēcūritāte.**

208. Guess the new word: **in animī sēcūritāte** = _____

A: in security of mind.

209. You know that **vītam** is the part of speech called a _____

A: noun.

210. The unknown word **beātam** must therefore be the part of speech called an _____ and its use in the sentence is to _____ [In your own words]

A: adjective modify **vītam**.

20-24

107. "Quid fēmina anuī dat?" "_____."

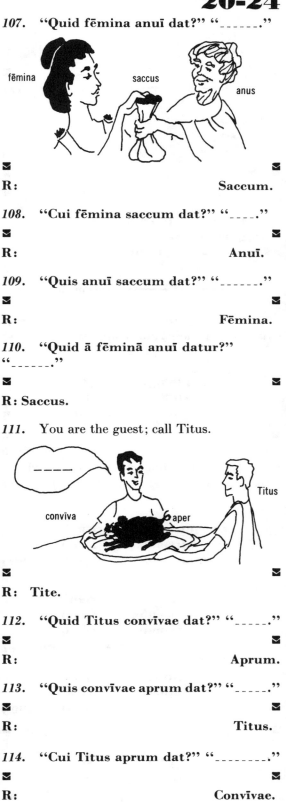

R: Saccum.

108. "Cui fēmina saccum dat?" "_____."

R: Anuī.

109. "Quis anuī saccum dat?" "_____."

R: Fēmina.

110. "Quid ā fēminā anuī datur?" "_____."

R: Saccus.

111. You are the guest; call Titus.

R: Tite.

112. "Quid Titus convīvae dat?" "_____."

R: Aprum.

113. "Quis convīvae aprum dat?" "_____."

R: Titus.

114. "Cui Titus aprum dat?" "_____."

R: Convīvae.

25-30

195-202. In this sequence complete the sentence with the verb form which the person-noun requires.

195. Nōs parva neglegī---- ← ----------

R: Nōs parva neglegimus.

196. Ego parv- negleg- ← ----------

R: Ego parva neglegō.

197. Vōs parv- negl- ← ----------

R: Vōs parva neglegitis.

198. Tū p---- negl- ← ----------

R: Tū parva neglegis.

199. Vōs mediō flūmine quaerī---- aquam ←

R: Vōs mediō flūmine quaeritis aquam.

200. Tū medi- flūmin- quaer- aqu- ←

R: Tū mediō flūmine quaeris aquam.

201. Ego med- flūm- qu- aqu- ←

R: Ego mediō flūmine quaerō aquam.

202. Nōs med- fl- qu- aq- ←

R: Nōs mediō flūmine quaerimus aquam.

203. Pronounce and check a new Basic Sentence, this one written by Cicero. *Nōs beātam vītam in animī sēcūritāte pōnimus.* (108)

20-25

115. "Quid datur?" "____."

R: Aper.

116. Echo your teacher. ★ ○ • ○ •
Ph_____ c_____ r_____ d___.

Cōnf: Philosophus cōnsilium rēgīnae dat.

117. Philosophus cōnsilium rēgīnae dat =
The _____ is ___ing ad____ __ ___ _____.

A: The philosopher is giving advice to the queen.
[Although **philosophus** was a new word, we hope you were able to guess it.]

118. Echo these six dative forms, which you will use in the next sequence. ★ ○ • ○ •
ducī aegrō convīvae effigiēī anuī īnfantī

119-124. Describe these pictures by using the appropriate dative to show TO WHOM the object or advice is given. Put the new dative form first for emphasis.

119. C_____ f_____ aq___ dat. √ ★ ○ •

R: Convīvae fēmina aquam dat.

---

189. regere ★ ○ •

Cōnf:	regō	regimus
	regis	regitis
	regit	regunt

___ō
___is   ___itis
___it   ___unt

190. quaerere ★ ○ •

Cōnf:	quaerō	quaerimus
	quaeris	quaeritis
	quaerit	quaerunt

quaer__   quaer____
quaer__   quaer____
quaer__   quaer____

191. On the model of these verbs, write the paradigm of the Third Conjugation verb **dīligere**.

R: dīligō   dīligimus
dīligis   dīligitis
dīligit   dīligunt

192-194. Write the conjugation of these verbs of the first three conjugations.

192. 3d quaerere

R: quaerō   quaerimus
quaeris   quaeritis
quaerit   quaerunt

193. 1st stāre

R: stō   stāmus
stās   stātis
stat   stant

194. 2d vidēre

R: videō   vidēmus
vidēs   vidētis
videt   vident

20-26

120. D--- h--- v---- d--- . √ ★ ○ •

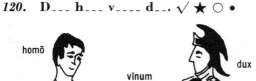

R: Ducī homō vīnum dat.

121. Ef------ ē----- cōnsilium ----. √ ★ ○ •

R: Effigiēī ēbrius cōnsilium dat.

122. M----- ae--- p----- -----. √ ★ ○ •

R: Medicō aeger pecūniam dat.

123. An-- q----s ------ ----. √ ★ ○ •

R: Anuī quercus umbram dat.

25-28

180. "Quem nōs stultī nōn quaerimus?"
"D-----."

R: Ducem.

181. "Cui servīre dēbēmus?" "Nāt------."

R: Nātūrae.

182. "Quae pars ōrātiōnis est 'errāmus'?"
"------."

183. "Quae pars ōrātiōnis est 'duce'?"
"------."

R: Verbum.

184. "Cujus cāsūs est hoc nōmen 'duce'?"
"--- c--- ------."

R: Nōmen.

R: "Duce" est cāsūs ablātīvī.

185. "Quotae persōnae est hoc verbum 'quaerunt'?"
"--------- , ------ est p------ae."

R: "Quaerunt" est tertiae persōnae.

186. "Quotae persōnae est hoc verbum 'errāmus'?" "------, ------, ------."

R: "Errāmus" est prīmae persōnae.

187. "Cujus numerī est 'errāmus'?"
"Est n----- ----- is."

R: Est numerī plūrālis.

188-190. Echo the paradigms of the following Third Conjugation verbs.

188. neglegere ★ ○ •

neglegō   neglegimus
neglegis   neglegitis
neglegit   neglegunt

20-27

124. Ī_ . ✓ ★ ○ •

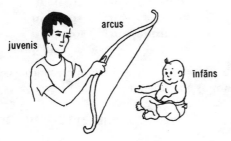

R: Īnfantī juvenis arcum dat.

125-130. In the following pictures, different people will be offering objects or advice to other people.

125. "Cui nocēns pecūniam dat?" "J_ ."

R: Jūdicī nocēns pecūniam dat.

126. "Cui opus auctor dat?" "_ _ _ _ _ _ _ _ _ _ _ _ _ _ _ _ _ ."

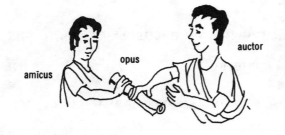

R: Amīcō opus auctor dat.

---

174. Now if blind people seek a guide, what is it that we ordinary people do without a guide? What must **Nōs sine duce errāmus** mean? [In your own words] _

A: We wander without a guide.

175. Copy in your Notebook.

176. This means that although blind people recognize their limitations and ask for guidance, the rest of us _ . [In your own words]

A: are so sure of ourselves that we foolishly blunder through life without trying to get any assistance.

177. C_ _ _ d_ _ _ _ qu_ _ _ _; s_ _ _ d_ _ _ _ er_ _ _ _ _ .

R: Caecī dūcem quaerunt; nōs sine duce errāmus.

178. **Errāre** can also mean to wander from the truth; the English derivative which has this same meaning is the word "_ _ _ _ _ ."

A: err.

Quaestiōnēs et Respōnsa

179. "Ā quō caecī adjuvantur?" "_ _ _ _ _ _ _ _ _ ."

R: Ā _ _ _ _ dūce.

127. "Cui rāna cōnsilium dat?"
"_____ ____ _____ ___."

R: Philosophō rāna cōnsilium dat.

128. "Cui fōns aquam dat?" "_____
____ _____ ___."

R: Sapientī fōns aquam dat.

129. "Cui cōnsilium anus dat?" "____
_____ ____ ___."

R: Fūrī cōnsilium anus dat.

---

169. **Vir caecus** est quī oculōs nōn sānōs habet et hāc dē causā nōn videt. Vir caecus pingitur in orbe ____ (prīmō/secundō/tertiō/quārtō).

R: In orbe secundō.

170. In **Caecī ducem quaerunt** the adjective **caecī** ____ (does/doesn't) modify any noun.

A: doesn't

171. In this Basic Sentence, therefore, the word **caecus** means a "_____."

A: blind person.

172. Notice that **dux** has a slightly different meaning here from what it has meant before. **Caecī ducem quaerunt** = Bl--- p---le s--- a g---e.

A: Blind people seek a guide.

173. There is a new word in this sentence. Use the colorless word "blank" for it. **Caecī ducem quaerunt; nōs sine duce errāmus** = _____; _____.

A: Blind people seek a guide; we blank without a guide.

20-29

130. "Cui rānās juvenis dat?" "———— ——— ———."

R: Puellae rānās juvenis dat.

131-135. Echo the singular paradigms of sample nouns of the five declensions.

	First *131.* ★ ○ •	Second *132.* ★ ○ •	Third *133.* ★ ○ •
nom	musca	ēbrius	mulier
acc	muscam	ēbrium	mulierem
abl	muscā	ēbriō	muliere
dat	muscae	ēbriō	mulierī

	134. Fourth ★ ○ •	*135.* Fifth ★ ○ •
nom	manus	faciēs
acc	manum	faciem
abl	manū	faciē
dat	manuī	faciēī

[REPEAT UNTIL LEARNED!]

136. Now for the vocabulary of a new Basic Sentence. Qu—— in sac—— est?

Cōnf: Quid in saccō est?

---

162. Nōs m—— c———— ← ∧ ★ ○ •

R: Nōs magna cūrāmus.

163. Nōs necā—— spatiōsum taurum ← ∧ ★ ○ •

R: Nōs necāmus spatiōsum taurum.

164. Tū nec— spatiōs— taur— ← ∧ ★ ○ •

R: Tū necās spatiōsum taurum.

165. Egō n—— sp———— t———— ← ∧ ★ ○ •

R: Egō necō spatiōsum taurum.

166. Vōs n—— ds———— t———— ← ∧ ★ ○ •

R: Vōs necātis spatiōsum taurum.

167. Caecī dūcem quaerunt; nōs sine duce errāmus. (107) ∧ ★ ○ •

168. ★ ○ ○ C———— d———— qu———— ; n———— nb———— s———— d———— er————.

Cōnf: Caecī dūcem quaerunt; nōs sine duce errāmus.

20-30

137. Chorus the answer. ★ ◉ [The italicized words are new to you.]

Quid est hoc animal quod in saccō est? Hoc animal quod in saccō est dīcitur "sūs." Sūs similis aprō est, sed aper est animal *ferōx*, quod saepe hominēs laedit et etiam necat. Sūs est animal *domesticum*. Multī hominēs *sue* necātō cēnant.

138. The passage compares two animals, similar in appearance, but one is wild and the other is domesticated. With this in mind, read the passage again if you did not understand it. The animal in the sack is a ___.

A: _____ pig. [Now that you know the answer, you can read the passage again if you like.]

139. Echo these forms of a new Latin word:
              m   f   n
★ ○ • ○ • pulcher, pulchra, pulchrum

140. Listen to your teacher as he describes this girl. ★ ○ H___ p_____ p_____ est.

Cōnf: Haec puella pulchra est.

25-24

155-156. In the next two frames you will be asked to conjugate one verb from each of the two conjugations which you have practiced, the First and the Second.

155. cūrāre _____
R: cūrō   cūrāmus
    cūrās   cūrātis
    cūrat   cūrant

156. manēre _____
R: maneō   manēmus
    manēs   manētis
    manet   manent

157. The characteristic vowel becomes short before a v___.
A: vowel.

158. It also becomes short before -t (when -t is final) and before the two consonants __ (in any position in the word).
A: -nt.

159-166. Complete the sentence by using the person ending which the person pronoun requires.

159. Egō magna cūr___ ← ∧ ★ ○ • _____.
R: Egō magna cūrō.

160. Tū magna cūr___ ← ∧ ★ ○ • _____.
R: Tū magna cūrās.

161. Vōs mag___ cūr___ ← ∧ ★ ○ • _____.
R: Vōs magna cūrātis.

141. He says that this young girl is pr___y (or h_____e).

⊠

A: .... pretty handsome.

142. The passive of the verb **videt** is often used in a sense of "seem." ★ ○ • ○ • **Vir pulcher vidētur.**

⊠

143. **Vir pulcher vidētur** means, "The ___ ___s _____."

⊠

A: .... The man seems handsome.

144-149. Change the following sentences from saying that the persons (or animals, etc.) *are* such, to saying that the persons (or animals, etc.) *seem to be* such.

144. **Medicus crūdēlis est** → Me_____ cr_____ v_____.

⊠

R: .... **Medicus crūdēlis vidētur.**

145. **Rāna pulchra est** → R___ _____ v_____.

⊠

R: .... **Rāna pulchra vidētur.**

146. **Dicta vāna sunt** → _____ _____ ___entur.

⊠

R: .... **Dicta vāna videntur.**

147. **Datōrēs hilarēs sunt** → _____ _____.

⊠

R: .... **Datōrēs hilarēs videntur.**

148. **Vīta brevis est** → ____ _____ _____.

⊠

R: .... **Vīta brevis vidētur.**

149. Nōs m____ nōn pl____ ← _____.
∨ ★ ○ •

⊠

R: **Nōs multīs nōn placēmus.**

150. Tū m____ nōn pl____ ← _____.
∨ ★ ○ •

⊠

R: **Tū multīs nōn placēs.**

151-153. Echo the paradigm of the following *First Conjugation verbs,* first the singular, then the plural.

151. **satiāre** ★ ○ • satiō   satiāmus
                       satiās   satiātis
                       satiat   satiant

⊠

152. **stāre** ★ ○ • __ō   __āmus
                       __ās   __ātis
                       __at   __ant

Conj: stō   stāmus
      stās   stātis
      stat   stant

⊠

153. **cūrāre** ★ ○ • cūr___   cūr___
                        cūr___   cūr___
                        cūr___   cūr___

Conj: cūrō   cūrāmus
      cūrās   cūrātis
      cūrat   cūrant

⊠

154. On the model of these verbs, write the paradigm of the First Conjugation verb **lītigāre,** remembering that in the *first person singular* the characteristic vowel has disappeared.

_____   _____

⊠

R: lītigō   lītigāmus
   lītigās   lītigātis
   lītigat   lītigant

[You will be tested on the verbs which you practice in this Unit, so be sure to learn them well.]

20-32

149. Vīta brevis vidētur = _____.

A: Life seems to be short.

150. You now know that in a {-s -s est} construction, you may also use the verb _____.

A: vidētur.

151. ★ ○ • ○ • *Asinus asinō, sūs suī pulcher.* (69)

152. This is a two kernel {-s -s est} sentence, but the {___} is missing.

A: est

153. In this sentence it would seem that the verb which makes the most sense is **vidētur**. Write your teacher's description of this picture.
★ ○ ○ _____.

R: Sūs suī pulcher vidētur.

154. The word **asinus** is _____ case; **asinō** is _____ case.

A: nominative dative

155. In the same way, the **sūs** is _____ case; **suī** is _____ case.

A: nominative dative

25-22

140. Metuitis foveam ← ─────── .
∨ ★ ○ •

R: Vōs metuitis foveam.

141. Crūdēlem medicum facimus ← ──── .
∨ • ★ ○ •

R: Nōs crūdēlem medicum facimus.

142. ∨ ★ ○ • ○ • Egō, tū, nōs, vōs

143-150. In this sequence, transform the verb to the person required by the person pronoun. Egō ("I"), tū ("you"), nōs ("we"), vōs ("you plural").

143. Vōs omnibus miseris nocē─── ← ─────── .
Vōs om─── m────tis. ∨ ★ ○ •

R: Vōs omnibus miseris nocētis.

144. Egō omni─── miseris nocē─── ← ──────── .
∨ ★ ○ •

R: Egō omnibus miseris noceō.

145. Nōs omni─── miser─── noc─── ← ──────── .
∨ ★ ○ •

R: Nōs omnibus miseris nocēmus.

146. Tū om─── mis─── n─── ← ─────── .
∨ ★ ○ •

R: Tū omnibus miseris nocēs.

147. Egō multīs nōn plac─── ← ─────── .
∨ ★ ○ •

R: Egō multīs nōn placeō.

148. Vōs mult─── nōn plac─── ← ─────── .
∨ ★ ○ •

R: Vōs multīs nōn placētis.

156. Write a description of this picture.
As____ as___ p_____ v_____r.

R: Asinus asinō pulcher vidētur.

157. This sentence means that _____
_____.

A: _____ one donkey seems handsome to another.

158. Sūs suī pulcher vidētur = One ___
___s _____ __ a_____ ___.

A: _____ One pig seems handsome to another pig.

159. When we expand **Asinus asinō**, we must add both the missing {est} and the missing {-s}. Expand as indicated.

A: **Asinus asinō pulcher vidētur.** [The verb used for {est} is here **vidētur**.]

160. ★ ○ ○ As___s as___, s__ s__ p_____.

R: Asinus asinō, sūs suī pulcher.

20-34

161. This sentence means, "A d_____ s____ h_____ to _____ d_____; a p__ s____ h_____ to _____ p___."

✉   ✉

A: A donkey seems handsome to another donkey; a pig seems handsome to another pig.

162. Copy in your Notebook.

✉   ✉

163. This Basic Sentence means that no matter how ugly you are, somewhere in the world you can find someone who will think that you are _____.

✉   ✉

A: handsome.

Quaestiōnēs et Respōnsa

164. "Quis asinum laudat?" "_____."

✉   ✉

R: Asinus.

165. "Quis suem laudat?" "____."

✉   ✉

R: Sūs.

166. "Quem asinus laudat?" "_____."

✉   ✉

R: Asinum.

167. "Quem sūs laudat?" "____."

✉   ✉

R: Suem.

168. "Cui asinus pulcher vidētur?" "_____."

✉   ✉

R: Asinō.

169. "Cui sūs pulcher vidētur?" "____."

✉   ✉

R: Suī.

170. "Quālis vidētur asinus asinō?" "_____."

✉   ✉

R: Pulcher.

---

124. Opus laudātis ← ---- l_____ ∨ ★ ○ •

✉

R: Vōs opus laudātis.

✉

125. Flōrem pingimus ← --- ------ ∨ ★ ○ •

✉

R: Nōs flōrem pingimus.

✉

126. Prō innocente dīcimus ← -------- ∨ ★ ○ •

✉

R: Nōs prō innocente dīcimus.

✉

127. Absentem laedimus ← -------- ∨ ★ ○ •

✉

R: Nōs absentem laedimus.

✉

128. Corporī servītis ← -------- ∨ ★ ○ •

✉

R: Vōs corporī servītis.

✉

129. Vēritātem aperītis ← -------- ∨ ★ ○ •

✉

R: Vōs vēritātem aperītis.

✉

130. Crūdēlem medicum facitis ← -------- ∨ ★ ○ •

✉

R: Vōs crūdēlem medicum facitis.

✉

131. Nōlentem trahitis ← -------- ∨ ★ ○ •

✉

R: Vōs nōlentem trahitis.

20-35

171. Write the Basic Sentence. As____ as___, s__ s__ p_____.

R: Asinus asinō, sūs suī pulcher.

172-175. On the model of **Asinus asinō pulcher vidētur**, describe these pictures.

172. L____ l__ō p_____r v___tur.

R: Lupus lupō pulcher vidētur.

173. S____ ___ae p_____a v_____.

R: Sīmia sīmiae pulchra vidētur.

174. A_____ _____ _____um v_____.

R: Animal animālī pulchrum vidētur.

175. P_____ _____ _____r v_____.

R: Piscis piscī pulcher vidētur.

25-19

116. Note that before **-t** in final position (that is, at the end of a word) and before **-nt-** in any position, the long vowel becomes a _____ vowel.

A: short

117. Placēre belongs to the ____ (1st/2d/3d/4th) conjugation.

A: 2d

118. Using the verbs above as models, write the paradigm of **vidēre**.

R: vídeō   vidēmus
    vidēs   vidētis
    videt   vident

119. ★ ○ ○ **Egō** ("I"), **tū** ("You-one-person"), **nōs** ("we"), **vōs** ("You-one-than-one").

120-142. Here are Basic Sentences with the verb transformed to the First or Second Person Plural. Add the pronoun which fits the person endings.

120. Metuimus foveam ← N__ m_____ f_____ ∧ ★ ○ •

R: Nōs metuimus foveam.

121. Metuimus foveam = _____.

A: We fear the pitfall.

122. Ignāvōs premitis ← V__ ig_____ pr_____ ∧ ★ ○ •

R: Vōs ignāvōs premitis.

123. Ignāvōs premitis = _____.

A: You (plural) crush the cowards.

20-36

176. A verb like **dat** almost always has a nominative which is the _____ of the verb.

A: subject

177. It also has an accusative which is the _____ of the verb.

A: object

178. From now on we will call the accusative the "direct ob____."

A: direct object.

179. A verb like **dat** also patterns with the dative, which shows the person TO WHOM the subject gives the object. The common name for this dative is the "ind___ct ob____."

A: indirect object.

180. Copy under "Facts about Latin": "The indirect object in Latin is expressed by the dative case."

181. In **Vir fēminae pecūniam dat**, the word **pecūniam** is the d_____ o_____; the word **vir** is the _____ and the word **fēminae** is the _____ o_____.

A: direct object
    subject
  indirect object.

182. The person in the dative case is the one who is the least concerned with the activity. The man is doing the action directly to the money; the action affects the woman to whom the money is given only in_____ly.

A: indirectly.

---

111. Quālibus canibus placētis?

R: **Blandīs canibus nōs placēmus.**

112. Cujus pallium vidētis?

R: **Philosophī pallium nōs vidēmus.**

113–115. Echo the paradigm of these Second Conjugation verbs, first the singular, then the plural.

113. **placēre** ★ ○ • placeō placēmus
                               placēs placētis
                               placet placent

114. **nocēre** ★ ○ • ___eō ___ēmus
                              ___ēs ___ētis
                              ___et ___ent

R: noceō nocēmus
   noces nocētis
   nocet nocent

115. **manēre** ★ ○ • ___ō ___mus
                            ___s ___tis
                            ___t ___nt

R: maneō manēmus
   manēs manētis
   manet manent

183. Many times the woman would be the one who would be the most interested in this transaction; after all, she is the one who is receiving the money. But the use of the dative case shows that *in the mind of the speaker or writer* she is less important than either the ___ or the _____.

A: man   money.

184. If we wanted to focus the primary attention on the *woman*, we could make her the _____ of the sentence.

A: subject

185. **Fēmina pecūniam ā virō capit** = ____
_____.

A: The woman takes money from the man.

186. If we wished to focus the primary attention on the *money*, we could make *it* the _____ of the sentence.

A: subject

187. **Pecūnia fēminae ā virō datur** = ____
_____.

A: The money is given to the woman by the man.

188. To indicate the woman as the person *to whom* or *for whom* this action was performed the Romans used the _____ case.

A: dative

189. In the sentence **Vir aquam canī dōnat**, **aquam** is the direct object and **canī** is the _____ _____.

A: indirect object.

---

107. Listen to your teacher as he says, "In what kind of situation are you (more than one person) weeping?" ★ ○ ● ○ ●

Conf: **Quālī in rē vōs flētis?**

108-112. Your teacher will ask you questions about what you and your friends are doing, using the new signal **-tis** that means "You-more-than-one," and the pronoun **vōs** ("You-more-than-one"). You reply, giving the right answer and transforming the verb from **-tis** to **-mus** and the **vōs** ("you") to **nōs** ("we").

108. Quālī in rē vōs flētis?

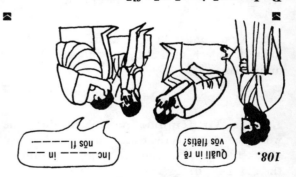

R: **Incerta in rē nōs flēmus.**

109. Cujus in umbrā vōs manētis?

R: **Quercūs in umbrā nōs manēmus.**

110. Cujus effigiem frāctam movētis?

R: **Ducis effigiem frāctam nōs movēmus.**

190. In the sentence **Philosophus cōnsilium ducī dat,** the direct object is _____ and the indirect object is ____.

A: **cōnsilium ducī.**

191. **Dux aprum convīvae dōnat.** The direct object is _____; the indirect object is _____.

A: **aprum**   **convīvae.**

192-198. Describe the following pictures using both direct and indirect objects.

192. V__ l__ō f_____ in__cat.

R: Vir lupō foveam indicat.

193. **Vir foveam lupō indicat** means that the man is showing the pitfall __ ___ ____.

A: to the wolf.

194. J_____ l____ j_____ ind___t.

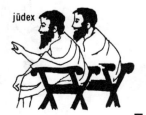

R: Jūdex lītem juvenī indicat.

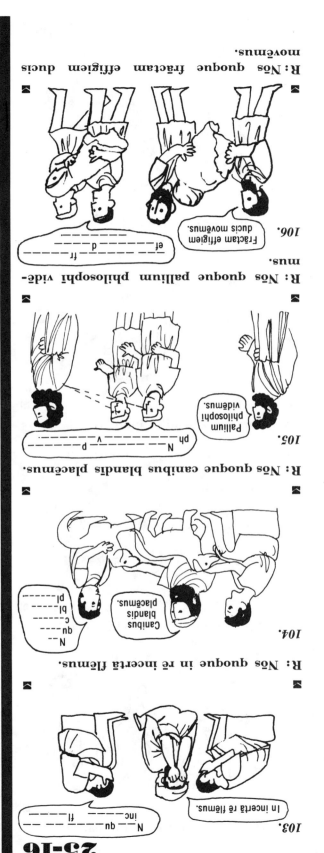

20-39

195. M_____s an__ equ__ ind__ant.

R: Mulierēs anuī equōs indicant.

196. D__ ac___ īns_____ ind___t.

R: Dux aciēī īnsidiās indicat.

197. F____ pe_____ j_____ ind___nt.

R: Fūrēs pecūniam jūdicī indicant.

198. Au____ rē_____ o___ ind___t.

R: Auctor rēgīnae opus indicat.

---

99. Latin has a First Person plural. Listen to your teachers describe what they are doing. "Nōs in __ nb_____ m_____nus."

Cōnf: **Nōs in umbrā quercūs manēmus.**

100. As you know, Latin uses pronouns to show em_____.

A: emphasis.

101. **Nōs in umbrā quercūs manēmus** = _____.

A: We are remaining in the shade of the oak.

102-107. This sequence is a familiar one. Your two teachers will say, "We are remaining in the shade of the oak tree," using the new signal **-mus**. You are to answer by saying "We too are remaining in the shade of the oak tree." You do this by repeating your teacher's statement about himself and the other teacher and adding "**Nōs quoque**." ("We too."). Remember, you and your friends are speaking.

102.

R: **Nōs quoque in umbrā quercūs manēmus.**

199. It would be a little difficult to *give* things if you were on a desert island with no one to give them *to*. Therefore such verbs as **dat** almost always have a _____ to make a sensible sentence.

A: dative (indirect object)

200. Some Latin verbs can sometimes be transitive and sometimes be intransitive. For example, the sentence **Mulier plōrat** means, "The _____ is w___ing."

A: The woman is weeping.

201. However, the sentence **Mulier pecūniam āmissam plōrat** means that the _____ is _____ ___r the ____ _____.

A: the woman is weeping over the lost money.

202. In **Mulier plōrat** the verb is _____ive, but in **Mulier pecūniam āmissam plōrat** the verb is _____.

A: intransitive transitive.

203. You know the verb **timet** only as transitive verb. **Stultī Fortūnam timent** = _____ p___le ____ _____.

A: Stupid people fear Fortune.

204. But when used *without* any object **Stultī timent** would mean that stupid people are afr____.

A: afraid.

94. "**Cujus cāsūs et cujus numerī est hoc nōmen 'virtūtem'?**" "**Est c_____, n_____ n_____.**"

R: **Est cāsūs accūsātīvī, numerī singulāris.**

95. You have met the prefix **dē-** in the Basic Sentences **A fonte pūrō dēfluit aqua** and **Difficile est longum subitō dēpōnere amōrem.** The meaning of the prefix was "d____" or "a___e."

A: down aside.

96. In the sentence **Facis dē necessitāte virtūtem**, the preposition **dē** means "___ ___."

A: out of.

97. When a person wishes to say in English that he is doing something alone, as the subject he uses the pronoun "__."

A: I

98. If, however, he wishes to include a friend in this statement, he uses the pronoun "__."

A: we

20-41

205. ★ ○ • Vir canem timet.

206. In this picture the man fears ___ ___.

A: _____ the dog.

207. ★ ○ • Vir canī timet.

208. But in this picture the man is afraid ___
___ ___.

A: _____ for the dog.

209-216. In this sequence your teacher will describe one of the two pictures. He will say either the person *fears* the animal or the person is *afraid for* the animal. Write on the righthand side of your Notebook if the answer describes the righthand picture; write on the lefthand side if it describes the lefthand picture.

(The following items are printed upside down on the right side of the page, belonging to page 25-13.)

86. "Cujus causā agit hic homo honestē?"

R: Necessitātis causā.

87. Suppose that you have just done something nice; your friends have complimented you. But you have the honesty to admit that you act this way only because you have to. You say manfully (or womanfully), "Egō fac— dē neces— virt—."

R: Egō faciō dē necessitāte virtūtem.

88. One of your friends comes to your defense. This is true of everyone, he says, everybody acts this way. He says: "Om— f—iunt n— v——."

R: Omnēs faciunt dē necessitāte virtūtem.

89. Quae pars ōrātiōnis est 'facis'?"

R: Verbum.

90. "Quotae persōnae est 'facis'?"

R: Secundae.

91. "Et cujus numerī est 'facis'?"

R: Singulāris.

92. "Quae pars ōrātiōnis est 'necessitāte'?"

R: Nōmen.

93. "Cujus cāsūs et numerī est hoc nōmen 'necessitāte'?" "Est c—— —— n——."

R: Est cāsūs ablātīvī, numerī singulāris.

78. This means that you are doing right only because _____ [In your own words].

A: you have to.

79. ★ ○ • ○ • ("this man")

hic homo	hī hominēs
hunc hominem	hōs hominēs
hōc homine	hīs hominibus
huic homini	hīs hominibus
hujus hominis	hōrum hominum

[You do not have to learn this yet.]

80. Notice that some of the forms of hic are irregular. They resemble somewhat the forms of quis; for example, the genitive singular of quis is _____.

A: cujus.

81. And the genitive singular form of hic is _____.

A: hujus.

82. However, many of the forms of hic end in the one letter suffix _____.

A: -c.

83. Note that before the suffix -c, the accusative signal -m changes to _____.

A: -n.

Quaestiōnēs et Respōnsa

84. "Utrum reddit hunc hominem honestum, virtūs an necessitās?" "_____."

R: Necessitās.

85. "Quālis redditur hic homo dē necessitāte?" "_____."

R: Honestus.

---

209. ★ ○ • ○ •

Fēmina _____ timet.

Cōnf: Fēmina mūrī timet.

R: mūrī

210. ★ ○ • ○ •

Juvenis _____ timet.

Cōnf: Juvenis taurō timet.

R: taurō

211. ★ ○ • ○ •

Anus _____ timet.

Cōnf: Anus equō timet.

R: equō

212. ★ ○ • ○ •

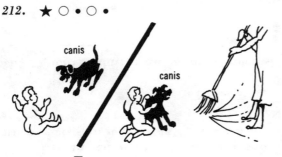

Infāns _____ timet.

Cōnf: Infāns canem timet.

R: canem

213. (puella = girl) ★ ○ • ○ •

Puella _____ timet.

Cōnf: Puella rānae timet.

R: rānae

214. ★ ○ • ○ •

Juvenis _____ timet.

Cōnf: Juvenis sīmiae timet.

R: sīmiae

---

70. Secondly, you had been asked in Latin, "What part of speech is **numerō**?" "What part of speech is **hōra**?" and then "**Quae pars ōrātiōnis est 'serēnās'?**" You could therefore figure out the meaning of **adjectīvum** from the c....t.

A: context.

71. **Facis dē necessitāte virtūtem.** (106)
V ★ ○ •

72. F_____ n_____ v_____
★ ○ ○ •

R: Facis dē necessitāte virtūtem.

73. Echo the paradigm of a new word, first the singular, then the plural.
• ○ ★ **necessitās** (Third Declension)

Cōnf: necessitās   necessitātēs
necessitātem   necessitātēs
necessitāte   necessitātibus
necessitātī   necessitātibus
necessitātis   necessitātum

74. Remembering that the Latin suffix -tās becomes "-ty" in English, the word **necessitās** has an English derivative, "n_____-ty."

A: necessity.

75. **Facis dē necessitāte virtūtem.** (106)
Expand with the missing element: _____

R: Tū facis
dē necessitāte virtūtem.

76. This means, "___ are ___ a ___ out of _____."

A: You are making a virtue out of necessity.

77. Copy in your Notebook.

215. ★ ○ • ○ •

Anus _____ timet.

Cōnf: Anus equum timet.

R: equum

216. ★ ○ • ○ •

Īnfāns _____ timet.

Cōnf: Īnfāns canī timet.

R: canī

217-220. Now describe these pictures. Use the accusative when the person fears the animal and the dative when he is afraid *for* him.

217. Juvenis _____ timet.

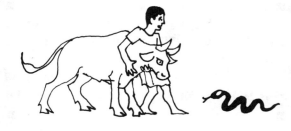

R: taurō

---

61. Write his answer. ★ ○ ○ _____

R: **Adjectīvum.**

62. The Latin word **nōmen** means "_____."

A: noun.

63. The Latin word **verbum** means "_____."

A: verb.

64. The Latin word **adjectīvum** means "_____."

A: adjective.

65. "Quae pars ōrātiōnis est 'hōrās'?"

R: Nōmen.

66. "Quae pars ōrātiōnis est 'numerō'?"

R: Verbum.

67. "Quae pars ōrātiōnis est 'serēnās'?"

R: Adjectīvum.

68. You will notice that you were using new words (**verbum, nōmen, adjectīvum**) before you were told what they meant. It will be part of your task to learn to _____ the meaning of new Latin words.

A: guess

69. There are two ways by which you can guess the meaning of new words. You could associate the Latin word **adjectīvum** with its English derivative "_____."

A: adjective.

218. Fēmina _____ timet.

R: mūrem

219. Puella _____ timet.

R: rānam

220. Juvenis _____ timet.

R: sīmiae

221-227. The following sentences are called "echelon" sentences; you are asked to expand the sentence one item at a time.

20-46

221. The queen gives advice = Rēg___ cōn_____ d___. ✓ ★ ○ •

R: Rēgīna cōnsilium dat.

[Add the new item to the *beginning* of the Latin sentence each time.]

222. The queen gives advice *to the leader* = D___ r_____ c_____ d___. ✓ ★ ○ •

R: Ducī rēgīna cōnsilium dat.

223. The queen gives advice to the leader *in all circumstances* = In om_____ r____ d___ r_____ c_____ d___. ✓ ★ ○ •

R: In omnibus rēbus ducī rēgīna cōnsilium dat.

224-227. In **Vestis virum reddit**, the verb **reddit** means "make." A common use, however, is "give something back," and we will use it in that sense in the following sentences.

224. The thief gives back the money = F__ p_____ r_____. ✓ ★ ○ •

R: Fūr pecūniam reddit.

225. The thief gives back the money *to the guest* = Conv____ f__ p_____ r_____. ✓★○•

R: Convīvae fūr pecūniam reddit.

226. The thief gives back the money to the guest *without a lawsuit* = S___ l___ c_____ f__ p_____ r_____. ✓ ★ ○ •

R: Sine līte convīvae fūr pecūniam reddit.

227. The thief *never* gives back the money to the guest without a lawsuit = N_____ s___ l___ c_____ f__ p_____ r_____. ✓ ★ ○ •

R: **Numquam sine līte convīvae fūr pecūniam reddit.**

228. ★ ○ • ○ • *Inopī beneficium bis dat quī dat celeriter.* (70)

229. With the verb **dat** we expect to find a s_____t, a d_____ object, and an in_____ object.

A: subject direct object indirect object.

230. The subject of **dat** in this sentence is the clause ___ ___ _____.

A: **quī dat celeriter.**

231. The direct object is _____.

A: **beneficium.**

232. And the dative that shows the indirect object, the person *to whom* the benefit is given, must be the new Latin word _____.

A: **inopī.**

233. ★ ○ • nom inops
acc inopem
abl inope
dat inopī

---

42. Copy this in your Notebook.

43. Like many of our sayings, this has two levels of meanings. The obvious one is that a sundial can only _____ [In your own words]

A: tell time when the sun is shining.

44. The "poetical" meaning is that the owner wished to express his own attitude toward life, which was that he _____ [In your own words]

A: remembered just the happy days of his life and chose to forget the ones that had brought him trouble.

45. H___ n___ n___ s_____.

R: **Hōrās nōn numerō, nisī serēnās.**

45-48. Pretend that you are the person who owns the sundial and had placed this inscription on it. Answer these questions, using a full sentence that contains a verb.

46. "Quālēs diēs in memoriā tenēs, jūcundās an acerbās?" "Egō _____ _____ _____."

R: **Egō jūcundās diēs in memoriā teneō.**

47. "Quālēs diēs in memoriā nōn tenēs?" "_____."

R: (Egō) Acerbās diēs in memoriā nōn teneō.

234. Describe this picture. V__ bl_____ in___ p_____ dat.

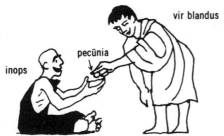

R: Vir blandus inopī pecūniam dat.

235. The man who was giving the money was a ____ man; the one who received it was a p___ man.

A: kind   poor

236. If a sentence were to begin with **Inops,** you would interpret it to mean that _____.

A: a (the) poor man blanks.

237. If the sentence were to begin with **Inopem,** you would interpret it to mean that _____ _____s a ____ ___.

A: somebody blanks a (the) poor man.

238. Because the sentence begins with **Inopī,** you know that somebody blanks _____. [In your own words]

A: to (or for) the poor man.

239. Since the verb in this Basic Sentence is **dat,** you know that somebody _____.

A: gives something to the poor man.

---

36. The only word in the kernel is the word **serēnās,** which is neither the {-s}, the {-m}, nor the {-t}, but is a _____ of the missing {--}.

A: modifier {-m}.

37. The adjective **serēnās** is _____ gender and _____ number.

A: feminine plural

38. Supply all the missing parts of the two {-s -m -t} kernels. ___ **hōrās nōn numerō, nisi** ___ **as serēnās** ___ **o**____.

A: **Egō hōrās nōn numerō, nisi ego hōrās serēnās numerō.**

39. Let us translate our Basic Sentence into a version which shows the Latin structure. It will not be good English. **Hōrās nōn numerō, nisi serēnās** = I don't _____ the _____ unless I _____ the _____s.

A: I don't count the hours unless I count the sunny hours. [Don't copy this into your Notebook.]

40. This means that the sundial doesn't count the hours unless the ____s are _____.

A: hours are sunny.

41. We have been emphasizing the fact that it is becoming more and more difficult to give English translations which reflect a corresponding Latin structure. It will sound much better in English if we translate the Latin subordinate clause **nisi serēnās** by an English prepositional phrase, using the preposition "except." **Hōrās nōn numerō, nisi serēnās** = I don't _____ the _____, except the _____ ones.

A: I don't count the hours, except the sunny ones.

20-49

240. ★ ○ • nom   **beneficium**
            acc   **beneficium**
            abl   **beneficiō**
            dat   **beneficiō**

241. Beneficium is a _____ Declension noun belonging to the _____ gender.

A: Second
                     neuter

242. There is an English derivative of **beneficium.** If we do someone a favor, we say that we have given him a b_____t.

A: benefit.

243. Write the sentence from dictation. ★ ○ ○
In___ b_____ b__ ___ q____ c_____.

R: **Inopī beneficium bis dat quī dat celeriter.**

244. Because of the **-ter** signal, you know that **celeriter** is the part of speech called an _____.

A: adverb.

245. There are several English derivatives of
               m   f   n
the Latin adjective **celer, celeris, celere,** from which the adverb **celeriter** is formed. When you step on the ac*celera*tor of your car, it makes the car go more qu___ly.

A: quickly.

246. The adverb **celeriter** means "_____."

A: quickly.

247. One last point: the word **bis** [which does not change form] means "twice."

Inopī beneficium bis dat quī dat celeriter.
   √ ★ ○ •

20-50

248. This sentence means, "Who ____s ____ly ____s a _____ to the ____ ___ ____."

A: Who gives quickly gives a benefit to the poor man twice.

249. Copy in your Notebook.

250. This translation means that if a needy person asks you for something he will be twice as grateful if you ____ it _____.

A: give it quickly.

Quaestiōnēs et Respōnsa

251. "Quāliter dat quī beneficium bis inopī dat?" "_____."

R: Celeriter.

252. "Quis celerem datōrem dīligit?" "_____."

R: Inops.

253. "Quālem datōrem dīligit inops?" "_____."

R: Celerem.

254. Echo a new adjective. ★ ○ • ○ •
grātus, grāta, grātum

255. The English derivative of this word is "____ful."

A: grateful. (**Grātus** means "grateful.")

256. Then **ingrātus** means "_____ful."

A: ungrateful.

---

22. Nisi is a subordinating conjunction and is the antonym of **si. Sī nocēns absolvitur, jūdex damnātur** = _____.

A: If the guilty man is acquitted, the judge is condemned.

**23. Nisi innocēns absolvitur, jūdex damnātur = Unl___ an ____ ____ is ac_____, the ____ is _____ed.

A: Unless an innocent person is acquitted, the judge is condemned.

**24. Lacrimae, nisi vērae sunt, insidiās indicant = Unless ____s are ____, they _____ an _____.

A: Unless tears are real, they indicate an ambush.

25. Hōrās nōn numerō, nisi serēnās. ∧ ★ ○ •

26. This sentence illustrates one of the chief difficulties you meet in reading Latin. You know the noun **numerus** ("number"). But in this sentence the word **numerō** is not the dative-ablative form of **numerus** but is a new word. First decide what part of speech it must be; then check by listening to your teacher expand the sentence. ★ ○ • ○ •

Conf: **Egō hōrās nōn numerō nisi serēnās.**

27. This **numerō** must be a ____ verb.

A:

28. Hōrās nōn numerō = _____.

A: I don't count the hours.

20-51

257. "Estne inops grātus an ingrātus sī amīcus pecūniam celeriter dat?" "_____."

R: Grātus est.

258. "Quālis est inops sī dator nōn celer dator est?" "_____."

R: Ingrātus est.

259. "Quem adjuvat quī beneficium celeriter dat?" "_____."

R: Inopem.

260. "Quis inopem bis adjuvat?" "Quī ___ _____."

R: Quī dat celeriter.

261. The English prefix "bi-" is a derivative of **bis**. An animal described as a "biped" has ___ feet.

A: two

262. I____ be_____ b__ ___ qu_ ___ c_____.

R: Inopī beneficium bis dat quī dat celeriter. [Did you remember to put two macrons in?]

263. √ ★ ○ • *Mors īnfantī fēlīx, juvenī acerba, nimis sēra senī.* (71)

---

18. Most of you are familiar with this instrument; it is used to tell time by the shadow of the sun and is called a s_____.

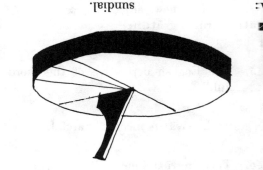

A: sundial.

19. Naturally, a sundial works only _____ [In your words]

A: when the sun is shining.

20. Our next Basic Sentence is one that is occasionally inscribed on sundials. Pronounce and check the inscription written on this Roman sundial. √ ★ ○ • [Do not look at this frame when doing the next one.]

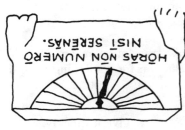

21. H ○ ○ ★ n___ n___ s___. [Seven macrons]

R: *Hōrās nōn numerō, nisī serēnās.* (105)

264. **Mors fēlīx** is an {_ _ _ _ _ _ _} kernel with the {_ _ _} missing.

A: {-s -s est}
  {est}

265. Expand: **Mors īnfantī fēlīx _ _ t.**

R: est.

266. **Acerba** is an adjective. To expand this kernel, you must add both the {-s} and the verb. ____ **juvenī acerba** ____.

R: Mors juvenī acerba est.

267. Expand the last kernel. ____ **nimis sēra senī** ____.

R: Mors nimis sēra senī est.

268. Here is the completely expanded sentence. **Mors īnfantī fēlīx est, mors juvenī acerba est, mors senī nimis sēra est.** Say the original Basic Sentence, check, and write it. M___ in____ f____, j____ a____, n____ sēr_ sen_.
√ ★ ○ •

R: Mors īnfantī fēlīx, juvenī acerba, nimis sēra senī.

269. This says that Death is different for _____ (a number) groups of people.

A: three

---

10. Metuis foveam → _____
∨ ★ ○ •

R: Tū metuis foveam.

11. Crūdēlem medicum faciō → _____
∨ ★ ○ •

R: Ego crūdēlem medicum faciō.

12. Fortēs adjuvō → _____
∨ ★ ○ •

R: Ego fortēs adjuvō.

13. Corporī servīs → _____
∨ ★ ○ •

R: Tū corporī servīs.

14. Fortēs adjuvās → _____
∨ ★ ○ •

R: Tū fortēs adjuvās.

15. Metuō foveam → _____
∨ ★ ○ •

R: Ego metuō foveam.

16. Corporī serviō → _____
∨ ★ ○ •

R: Ego corporī serviō.

17. Crūdēlem medicum facis → _____
∨ ★ ○ •

R: Tū crūdēlem medicum facis.

20-53

270. This Basic Sentence contains new vocabulary, which we will now explain. Echo your teacher as he describes this picture. ★ ○ • ○ •
S____ j____ c_____ d___.

Cōnf: **Senex juvenī cōnsilium dat.**

271. ★ ○ •   nom   **senex**
              acc   **senem**
              abl   **sene**
              dat   **senī**

272. While a **juvenis** is a _____ ___, a **senex** is an ___ ___.

A: young man old man.

273. **Senex juvenī cōnsilium dat** = ____
_____.

A: The old man is giving advice to the young man.

274. "**Quis vīnum bibit?**" "S___x v____ b_____." ✓ ★ ○ •

R: **Senex vīnum bibit.**

UNIT TWENTY-FIVE

25-1

In this Unit you will learn the forms of the other conjugations. Here are examples of the singular.

	1. First	2. Second	3. Third	4. Third -iō	5. Fourth
	★ ○	★ ○	★ ○	★ ○	★ ○
	adjuvō	**mordeō**	**metuō**	**faciō**	**serviō**
	adjuvās	**mordēs**	**metuis**	**facis**	**servīs**
	adjuvat	**mordet**	**metuit**	**facit**	**servit**

[You need not learn these paradigms yet; just observe them.]

6. In all these verbs, regardless of conjugation, the signal for First Person is _____, for Second Person is _____, and the Third Person is _____.

A: -ō   -s   -t.

7. The different conjugations, however, have different _____ s_____ before these person endings.

A: characteristic vowels

8-18. This sequence will contain sentences (parts of Basic Sentences) with verbs in the First Person or Second Person. Expand with **Egō** ("I") if the verb is First Person Singular (ends in **-ō**); expand with **Tū** ("You") if the verb is Second Person Singular (ends in **-s**). Check after your answer. [If you make an error, repeat the correct answer until you have learned it.]

8. **Non mordeō lupum** ← ___ **nōn mordeō lup---.** ✓ ★ ○ •

R: **Egō nōn mordeō lupum.**

9. **Non mordēs lupum** ← **n-- m------ l-----.** ✓ ★ ○ •

R: **Tū nōn mordēs lupum.**

20-54

275. Ask your teacher what kind of wine the old man is drinking. "____e v____ b____ s___x?" √ ★ ○ •

Cōnf: Quāle vīnum bibit senex?

276. Write his answer. ★ ○ ○ "_____ vīnum bibit senex."

R: Acerbum vīnum bibit senex.

277. Your teacher said that the old man was drinking b___er wine.

A: bitter

278. In a recent Basic Sentence we had the phrase **satis ēloquēns**, which meant "_____ _____."

A: eloquent enough.

279. In this new sentence there is a word which, like **satis**, does not change form. It means "too much" or "too." ★ ○ • ○ • **nimis**

280. Nimis ēloquēns medicus est = The _____ is ___ _____.

A: The doctor is too eloquent.

281. The sick person is too intemperate = _____.

A: Aeger nimis intemperāns est.

TEST INFORMATION

24-62

Verbs: (Notice that we now give both the First Person and the infinitive).
debeō, dēbēre (347-348)
dēpōnō, dēpōnere (81-84)
mūtō, mūtāre (124-125)
poscō, poscere (149)
recitō, recitāre (64-65)
significō, significāre (320)
taceō, tacēre (49)

Indeclinables: **Personal Pronouns:**
nōndum (318-319)   egō (217)
quidem (113-116)   tū (217)
quoque (222)

You will be expected to produce the First, Second, or Third person singular of any Second Conjugation verb, in the types of drills which you have practiced in this Unit. You will also be expected to *identify* the person of a verb of any conjugation and place the correct pronoun with it. We will use familiar Basic Sentences for this. You are now expected to be able to produce the form of any noun which you have practiced in any Unit.

20-55

282. Echo your teacher as he explains why Titus missed his boat. ★ ○ • ○ • T____ n____ sērus ____.

◼ ◼

Cōnf: Titus nimis sērus est.

283. It turns out that Titus arrived too l____.
◼ ◼
A: late.

284. Since the sick man is dying, the doctor is too late = C__ ae___ p___t, m_____ n__s s____ ____. ✓ ★ ○ •
◼ ◼
R: Cum aeger perit, medicus nimis sērus est.

285. Working back from the abstract noun **fēlicitās**, which means "happiness," you can figure out that the adjective **fēlīx** means "_____."
◼ ◼
A: happy.

286. ★ ○ • nom **mors**
acc **mortem**
abl **morte**
dat **mortī**
◼ ◼

287. Something is "im*mort*al" if it never suffers d_____.
◼ ◼
A: death.

288. On the other hand, all *mort*als have one thing in common. They will eventually find _____.
◼ ◼
A: death.

24-61

403. "Quid est 'porticus' in cāsū genitīvō et numerō singulārī?" ("Porticus" est quārtae declīnātiōnis.) "_____."
◼ ◼
R: Porticūs.

404. "Quid est 'servus' in cāsū accūsātīvō et numerō plūrālī?" "_____."
◼ ◼
R: Servōs.

405. "Quid est 'regnum' in cāsū nōminātīvō et numerō plūrālī?" "_____."
◼ ◼
R: Regna.

VOCABULARY INVENTORY

(Remember that the asterisk shows a new meaning for a familiar word.)

Nouns:
*amor, amōris, m (90)
*animus -ī, m (365-366)
barba -ae, f (325)
caelum -ī, n (369-373)
difficultās, difficultātis, f (178)
discipulus -ī, m (180)
magister, magistrī, m (180)
Marōn, Marōnis, m (53)
nātūra, -ae, f (123)
pallium -ī, n (331)
*rēs magna, reī magnae, f (49-54)
signum -ī, n (328-329)
subitum -ī, n (88)

Adjectives:
difficilis, difficile (67-69)
Graecus-a-um (332)
immortālis, immortāle (170-171)
injūstus-a-um (174-175)
singulāris, singulāre (399)
subitus-a-um (87)

289. Before you proceed any further, we should explain that this Basic Sentence is extremely cynical, and you will not (we hope) agree with it at all. **Mors īnfantī fēlīx** = _____ is _____ for a _____.

A: Death is happy for a baby. [What is meant by that?]

290. juvenī acerba = _____ is _____ ___ a _____ ___.

A: Death is bitter for a young man.

291. nimis sēra senī = _____ is ___ ___ an ___ ___.

A: Death is too late for an old man.

292. Mors īnfantī fēlīx, juvenī acerba, nimis sēra senī. √ ★ ○ •

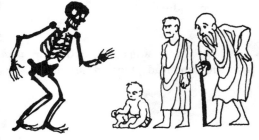

293. If a person dies when he is a baby, it is a happy thing for him because life would have turned out to be _____. [In your own words]

A: nothing but trouble.

294. However, young people are foolishly optimistic (this author thinks) and do not realize how difficult life will be. Therefore, if a young man dies, it seems to him that death is a _____ thing.

A: bitter

295. Yet, if this young man does not die and lives to suffer all the misfortunes of this wretched world, then at the end, after he has lost his teeth, his hair, his hearing, and perhaps his money, it seems that death has come ___ ___.

A: too late.

296. This view of life is called c_____.

A: cynical.

Quaestiōnēs et Respōnsa

297. "Quālis mors īnfantī est?" "_____."

R: Fēlīx.

298. "Quālis mors juvenī est?" "_____."

R: Acerba.

299. "Quālis mors senī est?" "_____ _____."

R: Nimis sēra.

300. "Cui est mors nimis sēra?" "_____."

R: Senī.

301. "Cui est mors fēlīx?" "_____."

R: Īnfantī.

302. "Cui est mors acerba?" "_____."

R: Juvenī.

303. Echo two new adverbs. ★ ○ • ○ •
fēlīciter   acerbē

304. Now answer these questions. "Quāliter perit īnfāns?" "_____."

R: Fēlīciter.

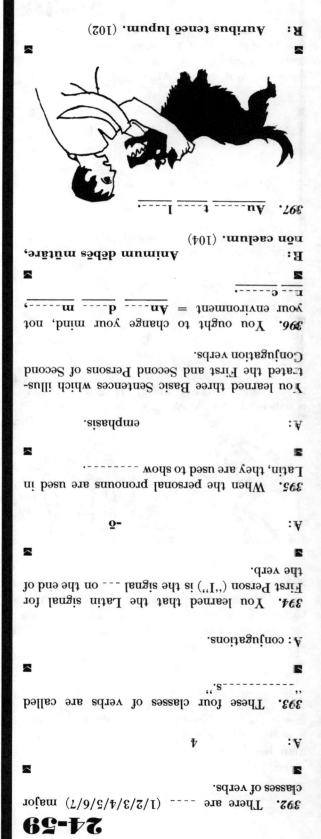

392. There are ____ (1/2/3/4/5/6/7) major classes of verbs.

A: 4.

393. These four classes of verbs are called "_____s."

A: conjugations.

394. You learned that the Latin signal for First Person ("I") is the signal ___ on the end of the verb.

A: -ō

395. When the personal pronouns are used in Latin, they are used to show _____.

A: emphasis.

396. You ought to change your mind, not your environment = An___ d___ m___, n___ c___.

R: Animum dēbēs mūtāre, non caelum. (104)

397. Au____ t____ l____.

R: Auribus teneō lupum. (102)

20-58

305. "Quāliter perit juvenis?" "_____."

R: Acerbē.

306. Write the Basic Sentence you have just been studying. M___ īn_____, f____, j_____ ac____, n____ s____ s____.

R: Mors īnfantī fēlīx, juvenī acerba, nimis sēra senī.

307. This sentence means, "_____."

A: Death is happy for a baby, bitter for a young man, too late for an old man.

308. Copy in your Notebook.

309. For the next Basic Sentence you have to know the word **rēx**. You have met the **reg/rēg** stem in three different words. **Rēgīna** = _____

A: queen

310. **rēgnum** = _____

A: kingdom

311. **regit** = ____s

A: rules

312. If we tell you that **rēx** is a noun which refers to a masculine person, you could guess that **rēx** = _____.

A: king.

313. ★ ○ •   rēx
                rēgem
                rēge
                rēgī

---

385. The signal for the Latin infinitive is _____

A: -re.

386. The infinitive is the n____ of the verb.

A: noun

387. However, the Latin infinitive cannot be substituted for *any* noun in *any* slot. So far the only constructions where you have seen the Latin infinitive is in the {-s -- ___-} construction and as object of the verb d___re.

A: {-s - s est}
      dēbēre.

388-391. Four Basic Sentences illustrated the {-s - s est} construction for the infinitive. Write the Basic Sentences which the Latin thought suggests.

388. Sapiēns, sī aeger est, tacet, nōn recitat. R____ m____ t____.

R: Rēs est magna tacēre. (98)

389. Amor nōn celeriter perit. D_____ l____ s____ d____ a____.

R: Difficile est longum subitō dēpōnere amōrem. (99)

390. Nātūra magnā difficultāte mūtātur. N____ qu____ m____ p____.

R: Nātūram quidem mūtāre difficile est. (100)

391. Mors omnibus imperat; sed nōn est dominus crūdēlis. O____ m____ p____ l____: n____ p____ p____.

R: Omnia mors poscit: lēx est, nōn poena, perīre. (101)

24-58

314. When someone acts in a kingly fashion, we say that he acts in a _ _ _al fashion.

A: regal

315. We will now study a Basic Sentence that is a motto. It is composed entirely of datives. In such a situation, the person whose motto it is says that he acts for the persons or institutions named.

★ ○ • ○ • *Deō, Rēgī, Patriae.* (72)

316. From the unknown word **Patria** comes the English word "patriotic." A person who is patriotic loves his _ _ _ _ _ _ _.

A: country.

317. The holder of the motto *Deō, Rēgī, Patriae* says that he acts for his _ _ _, his _ _ _ _, and his _ _ _ _ _ _ _.

A: God   King   Country.

318. ★ ○ •   patria
                patriam
                patriā
                patriae

319. ★ ○ ○ D_ _, R_ _ _, P_ _ _ _ _ _.

R: *Deō, Rēgī, Patriae.*

Quaestiōnēs et Respōnsa

320. "Quōs cūrat hic homō?" "D_ _ _ et Rē_ _ _ _."

R: *Deum et Rēgem.*

321. "Quem locum cūrat hic homō?" "_ _ _ _ _ _ _."

R: *Patriam.*

377. Expand the last part of the sentence as indicated: **Tū animum dēbēs mūtāre;** _ _ _ nōn caelum.

A: **Tū animum dēbēs mūtāre; tū nōn dēbēs mūtāre caelum.**

378. The author of this Basic Sentence (Seneca) says here that you ought to _ _ _ _ _ _ one thing and not another.

A: change

379. Seneca says that you ought to change your _ _ _ _ _ _ _ but not your _ _ _ _ _ _ _ _ _ _ _.

A: attitude   environment.

380. This means that if you are unhappy in East Podunk you _ _ _ _ (will/will not) be happier in New York.

A: will not

381. The secret of being happy, according to Seneca, isn't to go to New York but to stay in East Podunk and ch_ _ _ your at_ _ _ _ _ _.

A: change your attitude.

382. You ought to change your attitude (and) not your environment = A_ _ _ _ _ m_ _ _ _, n_ _ c_ _ _ _ _.

R: **Animum dēbēs mūtāre, nōn caelum.**

383. Copy in your Notebook.

SUMMARY

384. In this Unit you learned a new form of the verb called the in_ _ _ _ _ _ _ _ _.

A: infinitive.

322. "Quōs hic homō custōdit?" "____ et _____." (Auxilium sub līneā)

Aux: A "custodian" is one who guards something. Remember that **quōs** asks for *personal* nouns.

R: Deum et Rēgem.

323. "Quem locum hic homō custōdit?" "_____."

R: Patriam.

324. "Prō quibus fortiter agit hic homō?" "Prō D__ et R____." (Auxilium est sub līneā.)

Aux: As an intransitive verb, **agit** means "acts."

R: Prō Deō et Rēge.

325. "Prō quō locō fortiter agit hic homō?" "___ _____."

R: Prō Patriā.

SUMMARY

326. This lesson dealt with a new case called the _____ case.

A: dative

327. The subject shows the person who does the action (if the verb is one that is an action); the person (or thing) that receives this action is shown by the d____t ob____.

A: direct object.

371. English "celestial" comes directly from the Latin adjective caelestis, caeleste, meaning "h____ly."

A: heavenly.

372. "Quō locō di mortālēs jūdicant?"

R: In caelō.

373. **In caelō** = __ h_____.

A: In heaven.

374. Besides meaning "heaven," the word **caelum** often means "location," or "environment." The woman is changing her environment = F_____ c_____ m_____ m_____.

R: Fēmina caelum mūtat.

375. The woman ought to change her environment = F_____ c_____ m____re d____t.

R: Fēmina caelum mūtāre dēbet.

376. You remember that when the verb ends in **-ō** or **-s**, the subject pronoun is usually not expressed. When it *is* expressed it shows emphasis. Add this emphasis to the sentence by adding the subject. __ animum dēbēs mūtāre.

A: Tū animum dēbēs mūtāre.

328. The dative, on the other hand, shows someone who is considered to be less involved in this action; in English we often show this relationship by the prepositions "▁▁" and "▁▁▁."

A: to for.

329. The dative form of a noun shows the ▁▁▁▁t▁▁▁▁.

A: indirect object.

330. The sign of the dative case in the Third, Fourth, and Fifth Declensions is ▁▁▁▁.

A: -ī.

331. However, the dative of **fēmina** is ▁▁▁▁.

A: fēminae.

332. And the dative of **equus** is ▁▁▁▁.

A: equō.

333. You practiced the dative with the Latin word for "like" or "similar," saying that one animal was like the other. For example, seeing two flies, you said: M▁▁▁ m▁▁▁ s▁▁▁ est. √ ★ ○ •

Cōnf: Musca muscae similis est.

334. You also used the dative with certain verbs that also require an accusative to complete their meaning. Give at least two verbs you know which pattern with the dative.

A: **dat dōnat reddit indicat**

365. But **animus**, like most words, has ▁▁▁▁ (one area/many areas) of meaning.

A: many areas of meaning.

366. It is hard for us to understand the meaning of **animus** because it involves the Romans' views on psychology. It means "mind" or "soul" and sometimes "personality." In the sentence that you are about to meet, it means "attitude." The philosopher is changing his attitude = Ph▁▁▁ an▁▁▁ m▁▁▁.

A: **Philosophus animum mūtat.**

367. Echo the singular paradigm of a new word. ★ ○ ○ • **caelum**

Cōnf: caelum
caelum
caelō
caelō
caelī

368. You can tell from these forms that **caelum** is a ▁▁▁▁ noun of the ▁▁▁▁ Declension.

A: neuter Second

369. Write the singular paradigm of **caelum**:

R: caelum
caelum
caelō
caelō
caelī

370. Latin **ae** becomes "e" in English. "Celestial," as in "celestial beings live in the sky," comes indirectly from the Latin word ▁▁▁▁.

A: caelum.

20-62

335-338. You had four Basic Sentences. Write them.

335. In___ b_____ b__ ___ quī ___ c_____.

R: Inopī beneficium bis dat quī dat celeriter.

336. A_____ a____, s__ s__ p_____.

R: Asinus asinō, sūs suī pulcher.

337. M___ īn_____ f____, j_____ a_____, n____ s___ s____.

R: Mors īnfantī fēlīx, juvenī acerba, nimis sēra senī.

338. Finally, the motto of one who fights for God, King, and Country. D__, R___, P_____.

R: Deō, Rēgī, Patriae.

24-54

357. Lupus foveam metuit. ← L____ f_____ere dēbet. ★ ○ • ○ •

Cōnf: Lupus foveam metuere dēbet.

358. Īrātus lēgem videt. ← I___ē__ d____. ★ ○ • ○ •

Cōnf: Īrātus lēgem vidēre dēbet.

359. Pecūnia avāritiam satiat. ← P_____ā_____. ★ ○ • ○ •

Cōnf: Pecūnia avāritiam satiāre dēbet.

360. Vestis virum reddit. ← _____e_____. ★ ○ • ○ •

Cōnf: Vestis virum reddere dēbet.

361. Animum dēbēs mūtāre, nōn caelum. ∨ ★ ○ • (104)

362. ★ ○ ○ ____.

R: Animum dēbēs mūtāre, nōn caelum.

363. The last time we met the word animus, -ī, m, it was in the Basic Sentence Par__ lev__ cap___ ani____.

A: Parva levēs capiunt animōs.

364. Parva levēs capiunt animōs = Small things capture light ____.

A: minds.

VOCABULARY INVENTORY

In this Unit you learned eight new nouns:
  beneficium (240)   puella (213) (130)
  mors (286)   rēx (312-313)
  patria (318)   senex (271)
  philosophus (117)   sūs (137)

You also learned these new adjectives:
acerbus (276)
celer, celeris,
  celere (245)
domesticus-a-um (137)
fēlīx (289)
ferōx (137)
grātus-a-um (254)
ingrātus-a-um (256)
inops (233)
pulcher, pulchra,
  pulchrum (139)
sērus-a-um (282)
similis,
  simile (42)

You learned the following verbs:
*agit (324)   cantat (7)   custōdit (322)
dat (92)   *reddit (223)   *timet (203)
vidētur (142)

[Remember that the asterisk indicates a familiar word with a new meaning.]

You learned these adverbs:
acerbē (303)   celeriter (246)   fēlīciter (303)

You learned two indeclinable words:
bis (247)   nimis (279)

You learned the dative case of the question word **quis?**, which is **cui?** (94).

TEST INFORMATION

You will not be asked to produce any dative forms except those used in this Unit. However, you will be shown pictures similar to those used in this Unit.

350. The judge ought to condemn the guilty person = J----- n------- d------ dē-----.
■
A: Jūdex nocentem damnāre dēbet.
■
351. The judge owes money = Jū---- p------- dē-----.
■
A: Jūdex pecūniam dēbet.
■
352. Echo your teacher as he says in Latin, "Religion ought to cherish the gods." ★ ○ • ○ •
R----- d---- c----- d-----.
■
Conf: Religiō deōs colere dēbet.
■
353-360. Echo your teacher as he says that these things ought to happen.
353. Vēritātem diēs aperit. ← V--------- d----īre dēbet. ★ ○ • ○ •
■
Conf: Vēritātem diēs aperīre dēbet.
■
354. Manus manum lavat. ← M----- m----- lavāre dēbet. ★ ○ • ○ •
■
Conf: Manus manum lavāre dēbet.
■
355. Fēlicitās aurem facilem habet. ← F----- a---- f----ēre d----. ★ ○ • ○ •
■
Conf: Fēlicitās aurem facilem habēre dēbet.
■
356. Jūdex lītem audit. ← J----- l----īre ★ ○ • ○ •
■
Conf: Jūdex lītem audīre dēbet.

21-1

UNIT TWENTY-ONE

1-4. Echo your teacher as he changes the following datives from singular to *plural*.

1. ★ ○ • ○ • *Anuī* vēritātem diēs aperit →
   ---ibus v-------- d--- ap----.

Cōnf: Anibus vēritātem diēs aperit.

2. ★ ○ • ○ • *Ducī* auctor opus laudat →
   ---ibus au---- op-- l------.

Cōnf: Ducibus auctor opus laudat.

3. ★ ○ • ○ • *Muscae* musca similis est →
   M---īs m---- s-------.

Cōnf: Muscīs musca similis est.

4. ★ ○ • ○ • *Agnō* vīta brevis est → ---īs
   v--- br---- ----.

Cōnf: Agnīs
vīta brevis est.

5. You will observe that the dative forms **anibus**, **ducibus**, **muscīs** and **agnīs** are ambiguous forms. They are identical with the -------- plural.

A: ablative

6. Therefore you do not have a new form to learn. However, you will have to learn to distinguish between the ------ plural and the -------- plural.

A: dative
ablative

7-16. Echo your teacher as he says that somebody gives something to another person or persons. Write the dative on the right or left hand side of your Answer Pad, corresponding to the picture your teacher describes.

24-52

343. "Estne ille vir stultus an sapiēns?"
"-------."

R: Stultus.

344. V------ b---- -- p-------- ; ph--------
n---- v-----.

345. Now for a new use of the infinitive. So far the infinitives that you have seen all occurred in the {--------} construction.

A: {-s- s- est}

346. It is easy to hold a boar = F----- e---
ap--- t-----.

R: Facile est
aprum tenēre.

347. ★ ○ • ○ • *dēbēre*

348. Echo your teacher as he says in Latin, "The judge owes money." J----- p--------
d----. ★ ○ • ○ •

Cōnf: Jūdex pecūniam
dēbet.

349. Echo your teacher as he says in Latin, "The judge ought to condemn the guilty person."
J----- n-------- d------- d----. ★ ○ • ○ •

Cōnf: Jūdex nocentem damnāre dēbet.

21-2

7. ★ ○ • ○ • _____ juvenis vīnum dat.

Cōnf: Ducibus juvenis vīnum dat.

R: Ducibus

8. ★ ○ • ○ • _____ aeger pecūniam dat.

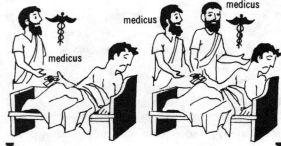

Cōnf: Medicō aeger pecūniam dat.

R: Medicō

9. ★ ○ • ○ • _____ vir pictūram dat.

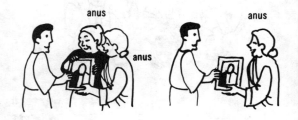

Cōnf: Anuī vir pictūram dat.

R: Anuī

---

339. Pretend that you are present when this obnoxious creature is showing off. All the questions refer to a *false philosopher.* "Habetne ille vir barbam et pallium?" "_____."

R: Habet.

340. "Quae signa philosophī possidet ille vir stultus?" "_____."

R: Barbam et pallium.

341. Now your teacher is asking you directly what *you* see. "Vidēsne signa philosophī?" "_____."

R: Videō.

342. "Vidēsne philosophum vērum?" "_____."

R: Nōn videō.

21-3

10. ★ ○ • ○ • _____ auctor opus dat.

Cōnf: Fēminīs auctor opus dat.

R: Fēminīs

11. ★ ○ • ○ • _____ homō rānās dat.

Cōnf: Vīperīs homō rānās dat.

R: Vīperīs

12. ★ ○ • ○ • _____ juvenis vīnum dat.

Cōnf: Ducī juvenis vīnum dat.

R: Ducī

24-50

335. This Basic Sentence comes from a story in Latin about a group of men who are approached by someone wearing the **pallium** and sporting a beard. This fellow makes a great show of his philosophical learning without really saying anything. One of the bystanders says:

Videō barbam et pallium; philosophum nōndum videō.

This is a perfect squelch.

He said, "I s--- the b----- and --- do --- n--- --- ph----------."

A: I see the beard and the cloak; I do not see the philosopher.

336. Copy in your Notebook.

337. This means that while the man dresses like a philosopher and has a beard like a philosopher, he doesn't ____ like a philosopher.

A: talk (act, seem, etc.)

338. ★ ○ • ○ •

Singular	Plural
hoc signum	haec signa
hoc signum	haec signa
hōc signō	hīs signīs
huic signō	hīs signīs
hujus signī	hōrum signōrum

Echo the paradigm of the Latin phrase that means "This sign," first the singular, then the plural.

21-4

13. ★ ○ • ○ • _____ auctor opus dat.

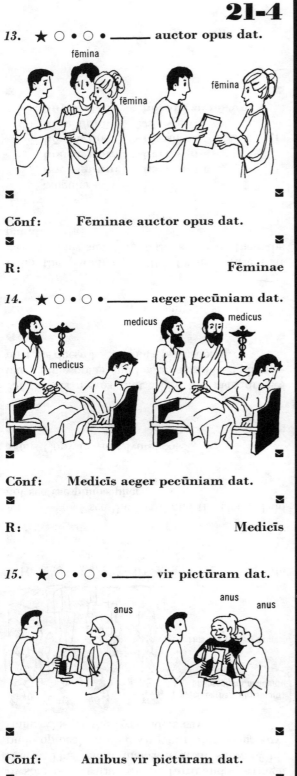

Cōnf: Fēminae auctor opus dat.

R: Fēminae

14. ★ ○ • ○ • _____ aeger pecūniam dat.

Cōnf: Medicīs aeger pecūniam dat.

R: Medicīs

15. ★ ○ • ○ • _____ vir pictūram dat.

Cōnf: Anibus vir pictūram dat.

R: Anibus

---

330. Write this entire Basic Sentence. ★ ○ ○
V_____ b_____ p_____; ph_____
n_____ v_____.

R: Videō barbam et pallium; philosophum nōndum videō.

331. "Quid significat haec vōx 'pallium'?
Pallium est vestis *Graeca* quam philosophī
habent. Barba est ūnum signum philosophī; pallium est secundum signum philosophī. Quota in pictūrā vir habet pallium?"

"_____."

R: Quārta in pictūrā vir habet pallium.

332. The new adjective *Graecus, -a, -um*
used in the last frame meant "_____."

A: Greek.

333. Videō barbam et pallium = _____.

A: I see a cloak and a beard.

334. In other words, the man sees someone who
has the outward s___s of a _____.

A: signs of a philosopher.

21-5

16. ★ ○ • ○ • _____ jūdex effigiem dat.

◪

Cōnf: Sapientibus jūdex effigiem dat.
◪

R: Sapientibus

17-26. Now describe these pictures. Say the whole sentence, and write the word which shows *to whom* (singular or plural) the person gives something.

17. _____ v__ p_____ dat.

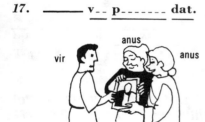

◪

R: Anibus vir pictūram dat.

18. _____ aeg__ p_____ dat.

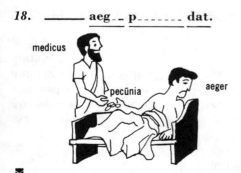

◪

R: Medicō aeger pecūniam dat.

---

326. "Habēsne tū barbam?" "_____."
◪

R: Barbam habeō. (?)
Barbam nōn habeō. (?)

Here for the first time are two answers, but for you, only one is correct. To check, run your hand over your face. If you feel whiskers, **Barbam habeō** is correct; if there are no whiskers, then **Barbam nōn habeō** is right.

327. Beards varied in fashion with the Romans, just as they do with us, but at the time when this Basic Sentence was written, most Romans were clean shaven. The Greeks, however, often wore beards, particularly the philosophers. Since the majority of the philosophers in Rome were Greeks, the beard became the sign of a _____.

A: philosopher.

328. Write down what your teacher says.
★ ○ ○ B_____ s_____ ph_____.
◪

R: Barba est signum philosophī.

329. The sentence you just wrote means that a _____ is the _____ a _____.
◪

A: a beard is the sign of a philosopher.

21-6

19. _____ auc___ op__ dat.

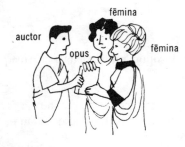

R: Fēminīs auctor opus dat.

20. _____ j_____ v____ dat.

R: Ducī juvenis vīnum dat.

21. _____ h___ r____ dat.

R: Vīperīs homō rānās dat.

22. _____ j____ ef_____ dat.

R: Sapientibus jūdex effigiem dat.

24-47

321. The expression "**Fēmina**" significat "**mulier**." means that the word **fēmina** _____ [In your own words]

A: means the same thing as the word **mulier**. [We use the nominative case here in English because we are talking about "**mulier**" as a word, not as a form].

322. "Quid significat mulier?" "Mulier" s_____ f_____."

R: "Mulier" significat 'fēmina.'

323. Videō barbam et pallium; philoso- phum nōndum videō. (103) √ ★ ○ •

324. V ○ ○ ★ b____ et p_____; ph_____ n____ v____.

R: Videō barbam et pallium; philosophum nōndum videō.

325. Quid significat haec vōx "*barba*"? Barba est pars faciēī et habet multōs capillōs. Vir, nōn fēmina, barbam habet. "Quotā in pictūrā vidēs hominem qui barbam habet?" "_____ in p_____ vid___ hom____ qui b_____ habet."

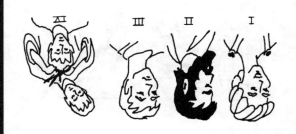

R: Secundā in pictūrā ego videō hominem qui barbam habet.

21-7

23. ____ a_____ o___ dat.

R: Fēminae auctor opus dat.

24. ____ a____ p_____ dat.

R: Medicīs aeger pecūniam dat.

25. ____ v__ p_____ dat.

R: Anuī vir pictūram dat.

26. ____ j_____ v____ dat.

R: Ducibus juvenis vīnum dat.

24-46

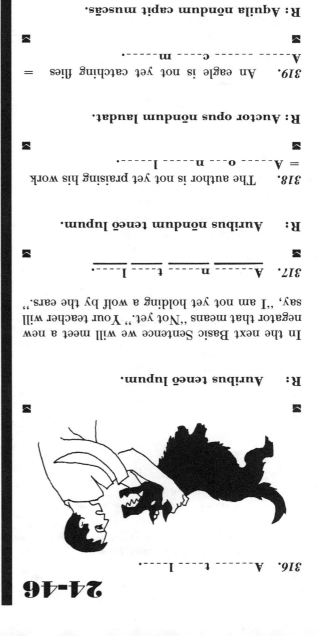

316. A____ t____ l_____.

R: Auribus teneō lupum.

In the next Basic Sentence we will meet a new negator that means "Not yet." Your teacher will say, "I am not yet holding a wolf by the ears."

317. A____ n____ t____ l_____.

R: Auribus nōndum teneō lupum.

318. A_____ o____ n___ l_____. = The author is not yet praising his work

R: Auctor opus nōndum laudat.

319. An eagle is not yet catching flies = A_____ _____ c____ m_____.

R: Aquila nōndum capit muscās.

320. In line with our earlier promise, we will do more and more explaining of the meaning of new words in Latin. To do this, we will make frequent use of words for "mean." The first word we will use is easy because it has an English derivative. The word is **significāre**, and the English derivative is "_____y."

A: signify.

21-8

27-35. Echo the paradigm of these sample nouns of the five declensions, first the singular, then the plural. Learn them thoroughly, since you will use them in the next sequence.

27. ★ ○ •
   First Declension
musca	muscae
muscam	muscās
muscā	muscīs
muscae	muscīs

28. ★ ○ •
   Second Declension
   (nom sg in Ø)
aeger	aegrī
aegrum	aegrōs
aegrō	aegrīs
aegrō	aegrīs

29. ★ ○ •
   Second Declension
   (nom sg in -s)
agnus	agnī
agnum	agnōs
agnō	agnīs
agnō	agnīs

30. ★ ○ •
   Second Declension
   (neuter)
vitium	vitia
vitium	vitia
vitiō	vitiīs
vitiō	vitiīs

31. ★ ○ •
   Third Declension
   (nom sg in -s)
nāvis	nāvēs
nāvem	nāvēs
nāve	nāvibus
nāvī	nāvibus

24-45

308. **Auribus teneō lupum.** (102) ✓ ★ ○ •

309. [Do not look at the previous frame.]
★ ○ ─── ─── ─── ─── ───

R: **Auribus teneō lupum.**

310. Auribus teneō lupum = ─ ──── a ──── the ─── (102).

A: I hold a wolf by the ears.

311. Copy in your Notebook.

312. This means that the person is in ─────── [In your own words]
───────────────────

A: a situation which he cannot control.

Quaestiōnēs et Respōnsa

313. "Cujus aurēs hic vir tenet?" "─────."

R: **Lupī.**

314. "Quae membra lupī tenet hic vir?" "─────."

R: **Aurēs.**

315. "Quibus membrīs vir aurēs lupī tenet?" "M─────."

R: **Manibus.**

21-9

32. ★ ○ •

Third Declension
(nom sg in Ø)

mulier	mulierēs
mulierem	mulierēs
muliere	mulieribus
mulierī	mulieribus

33. ★ ○ •

Third Declension
(neuter)

corpus	corpora
corpus	corpora
corpore	corporibus
corporī	corporibus

34. ★ ○ •

Fourth Declension

flētus	flētūs
flētum	flētūs
flētū	flētibus
flētuī	flētibus

35. ★ ○ •

Fifth Declension

rēs	rēs
rem	rēs
rē	rēbus
reī	rēbus

36. The new dative plural form is *always* like the _____ _____ form.

A: ablative plural

37-46. Depending on how you feel *you* learn best, either say or write the paradigm of these same nine nouns. Note that the nouns are now in a different order. You must remember the declension of each. Be sure to check your answer carefully so that you will not learn the wrong one. Don't forget the macrons.

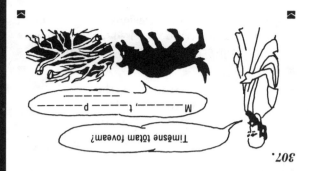

304. Vidēsne tōtam effigiem?
Minimē, v------ p------
R: Minimē, videō partem effigiēī.

305. Possidēsne tōtam vestem?
Minimē, pos------ p------
R: Minimē, possideō partem vestis.

306. Habēsne tōtum flōrem?
Minimē, h------ p------
R: Minimē, habeō partem flōris.

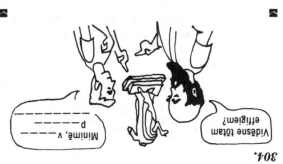

307. Timēsne tōtam foveam?
Minimē, t------ p------
R: Minimē, timeō partem foveae. (Surely not a very cautious wolf.)

37. **vitium** (Invenītur sub hāc līneā auxilium.)

Aux: This is a Second Declension neuter noun with the characteristic vowel **-o-**, which appears as **-o-**, however, in *only two* of these forms.

R:
vitium	vitia
vitium	vitia
vitiō	vitiīs
vitiō	vitiīs

38. **flētus** (Auxilium sub hāc līneā est.)

Aux: This is a Fourth Declension noun (the **-u** type): the **-u** appears in all forms except the last two.

R:
flētus	flētūs
flētum	flētūs
flētū	flētibus
flētuī	flētibus

39. **musca** (Hāc sub līneā est auxilium.)

Aux: This is an **-a-** type; **-a-** appears in all forms except the last two.

R:
musca	muscae
muscam	muscās
muscā	muscīs
muscae	muscīs

40. **agnus** (Invenītur hāc sub līneā auxilium.)

Aux: The characteristic vowel **-o-** of the Second Declension appears in three of the forms; in two forms it has changed to **-u-**; in three forms it has disappeared.

R:
agnus	agnī
agnum	agnōs
agnō	agnīs
agnō	agnīs

300. Say the singular paradigm of **effigiēs**.

R: effigiēs
effigiem
effigiē
effigiēī
effigiēī

301. Say the singular paradigm of **vestis**.

R: vestis
vestem
veste
vestī
vestis

302. Say the singular paradigm of **flōs**.

R: flōs
flōrem
flōre
flōrī
flōris

303-307. In the next five frames, your teacher will ask you if you are holding (seeing, etc.) *all of something*. You reply, "No, I am holding (seeing, etc.) *part of it*."

303.

Tenēsne tōtum arcum?

Minimē, t——ō partem arc——

R: Minimē, teneō partem arcūs.

41. aeger (Auxilium invenītur hāc sub līneā.)

Aux: This is also a Second Declension noun; except for the nominative, its forms are just like the **agnus** you have just given.

R: aeger   aegrī
       aegrum   aegrōs
       aegrō   aegrīs
       aegrō   aegrīs

42. nāvis (Hāc sub līneā invenītur auxilium.)

Aux: The characteristic vowel **-e-** or **-i-** of the Third Declension appears in every form.

R: nāvis   nāvēs
       nāvem   nāvēs
       nāve   nāvibus
       nāvī   nāvibus

[Did you mark all the macrons?]

43. mulier (Auxilium sub hāc līneā est.)

Aux: Except for the nominative, which ends in Ø, this is declined exactly like **nāvis**.

R: mulier   mulierēs
       mulierem   mulierēs
       muliere   mulieribus
       mulierī   mulieribus

44. rēs (Invenītur hāc sub līneā auxilium.)

Aux: The characteristic vowel of the Fifth Declension, **-ē-**, occurs in every form, although it is short before **-m** and the vowel **-ī**.

R: rēs   rēs
       rem   rēs
       rē   rēbus
       reī   rēbus

---

291. Manum lavō → -------- --------
∨ ★ ○ •

R: Egō manum lavō.

292. Flōris nōn pingō odōrem →--------
--------- ∨ ★ ○ •

R: Egō flōris
nōn pingō odōrem.

Before you begin the next sequence, echo the singular paradigms of the words which you will use.

293. ★ ○ •
effigiēs   fovea
effigiem   foveam
effigiē   foveā
effigiēī   foveae
effigiēī   foveae

294. ★ ○ •
295. ★ ○ •   *296.* ★ ○ •   *297.* ★ ○ •
arcus   vestis   flōs
arcum   vestem   flōrem
arcū   veste   flōre
arcuī   vestī   flōrī
arcūs   vestis   flōris

298. Say the singular paradigm of arcus.

R: arcus
        arcum
        arcū
        arcuī
        arcūs

299. Say the singular paradigm of fovea.

R: fovea
        foveam
        foveā
        foveae
        foveae

45. The only two Fifth Declension nouns which have the plural forms are **rēs** and ____.

A: diēs.

46. corpus (Sub hāc lineā quid invenītur? Auxilium.)

Aux. This is a neuter; the **-us** of the nominative-accusative changes to **-or** in all other forms.

R:
corpus	corpora
corpus	corpora
corpore	corporibus
corporī	corporibus

47. Your teacher will ask you three questions on each of the following three pictures. One of the three will be a **Quibus?** question, asking for a dative answer. **Quibus juvenis aquam dat?** = --------------------------------?

A: To whom is the young man giving water?

48. The dative plural forms which you will be expected to produce are all included in this list.
★ ○ • **fēminīs equīs agnīs medicīs vīnīs auctōribus mulieribus ducibus jūdicibus**

49. "Quid vir dōnat?" "_____."

R: Vestem.

50. "Quibus dōnat?" "_____."

R: Mulieribus.

283-292. Expand the next ten sentences with the missing subject, that is, by **egō** or **tū**.

∨ ★ ○ •
283. Omnibus hōris sapis ⟵ ---------

R: Tū omnibus hōris sapis.

∨ ★ ○ •
284. Omnibus miserīs noceō ⟵ --------

R: Egō omnibus miserīs noceō.

∨ ★ ○ •
285. Impōnō fīnem et rēbus honestīs ⟵

R: Egō impōnō fīnem et rēbus honestīs.

∨ ★ ○ •
286. Nōn cēnās sine aprō ⟵ ---------

R: Tū nōn cēnās sine aprō.

∨ ★ ○ •
287. Īnsidiās, nōn flētum, indicō ⟵

R: Egō īnsidiās, nōn flētum, indicō.

∨ ★ ○ •
288. Levēs capis animōs ⟵ ---------

R: Tū levēs capis animōs.

∨ ★ ○ •
289. Mediō flūmine quaeris aquam ⟵

R: Tū mediō flūmine quaeris aquam.

∨ ★ ○ •
290. Nōn semper aurem facilem habēs ⟵

R: Tū nōn semper aurem facilem habēs.

21-13

51. "Ā quō vestis dōnātur?" "_____."

R: Ā virō.

52. "Ā quō aqua equīs dōnātur?" "_____."

R: Ā juvene.

53. "Quid ā juvene equīs dōnātur?" "_____."

R: Aqua.

54. "Quibus aqua dōnātur?" "_____."

R: Equīs.

55. "Quibus dux cōnsilium dat?" "_____."

R: Auctōribus.

56. "Quid dux dat?" "_____."

R: Cōnsilium.

57. "Quōs dux auxiliō adjuvat?" "_____."

R: Auctōrēs.

24-40

274. Hilarem datōrem dīligis → ------- ∨ ★ ○ •

R: Tū hilarem datōrem dīligis.

A: You love a cheerful giver.

275. Hilarem datōrem dīligis = ----------

276. Vēritātem aperiō → ------ ∨ ★ ○ •

R: Ego vēritātem aperiō.

277. Vēritātem aperiō = ----------

A: I disclose the truth.

278. Nōn cēnō sine aprō → ------ ∨ ★ ○ •

R: Ego nōn cēnō sine aprō.

279. Nōn cēnō sine aprō = ----------

A: I do not dine without a boar.

280. Īnsidiās, nōn flētum, indicās → ------ ∨ ★ ○ •

R: Tū īnsidiās, nōn flētum, indicās.

281. Nōn capis mūrem → ------ ∨ ★ ○ •

R: Tū nōn capis mūrem.

282. Nōn capis mūrem = ----------

A: You do not catch mice.

58. Now for an echelon sentence, in which we add a word at a time to the beginning of the Latin sentence. He gives money = **Pec_____ d___.**

R: Pecūniam dat.

59. He gives money to the authors = **Auct_____ p_____ d___.**

R: Auctōribus pecūniam dat.

60. He gives money to the authors twice = **B__ a_____ p_____ d___.**

R: Bis auctōribus pecūniam dat.

61. The king gives money to the authors twice = **R__ b__ a_____ p_____ d___.**

R: Rēx bis auctōribus pecūniam dat.

62. Here is another echelon sentence. The philosopher (blanks) advice = **Phil_____ cōn_____.**

R: Philosophus cōnsilium.

63. The philosopher gives advice = **D__ ph_____ c_____.**

R: Dat philosophus cōnsilium.

64. The philosopher gives advice to kings = **R_____ d__ ph_____ c_____.**

R: Rēgibus dat philosophus cōnsilium.

65. The philosopher gives advice to kings quickly = **C_____ r_____ d__ ph_____ c_____.**

R: Celeriter rēgibus dat philosophus cōnsilium.

266-270. We will now give you the paradigms of all four classes of verbs so that you can see how much alike they are. You are not expected to *learn* them now, but merely echo. Note that there are two types of Third Conjugation verbs.

266. ★ ○ •
First
lavō
lavās
lavat

267. ★ ○ •
Second
teneō
tenēs
tenet

268. ★ ○ •
Third
quaerō
quaeris
quaerit

269. ★ ○ •
Third
capiō
capis
capit

270. ★ ○ •
Fourth
audiō
audīs
audit

271. In all these verbs, the signal for First Person is _____, the signal for Second Person is _____, and the signal for Third Person is _____.

A: -ō
-s
-t.

272. Notice that in **lavō** and **quaerō** the characteristic vowel has _____ed.

A: disappeared.

273. To recognize which *person* a verb is, you have only to _____
[In your own words]

A: observe whether the signal is -ō, -s, or -t.

274-282. We will now give you five Basic Sentences without any subjects, in which the Third Person verb has been changed to the First or Second Person. Expand at the beginning of the sentence with the predictable subject (**egō** or **tū**). We will occasionally ask you to translate.

21-15

66. Echo your teacher as he describes this picture. ★ ○ • ○ • **Mulier proxima virīs est.**

67. An *approximate* answer is one that is *near* the exact answer. **Mulier proxima virīs est** = The ___ is ___ the ___.

A: The woman is near the men.

68. You will remember that the adjective
    m&f   n
similis, simile patterns with the ___ case.

A: dative

69. It makes little sense to say that someone is near unless you know who or what he is near to.
             m   f   n
The adjective **proximus, proxima, proximum** also ___ ___ ___ ___ ___.

A: patterns with the dative case.

70. Under "Facts About Latin" add "and **proximus**" to **similis**.

71-78. Describe the following pictures, on the model of **Mulier proxima virīs est**.

71. Agnī pr___ī t___īs sunt.

R: **Agnī proximī taurīs sunt.**

---

259. Saccum teneō = ___.
A: I am holding the sack.

260. Saccum tenēs = ___.
A: You are holding the sack.

261. Saccum tenet = ___.
A: He (she, it) is holding the sack.

262. Using **tenēre** as a model, say the singular paradigm of **vidēre**. ∧ ★ ○ •
R: videō
   vidēs
   videt

263. Say the singular paradigm of **habēre**. ∧ ★ ○ •
R: habeō
   habēs
   habet

264. Say the singular paradigm of **possidēre**. ∧ ★ ○ •
R: possideō
   possidēs
   possidet

265. Say the singular paradigm of **timēre**. ∧ ★ ○ •
R: timeō
   timēs
   timet

21-16

72. R__a pr____a m___īs est.

R: Rāna proxima muscīs est.

73. C____ pr____ī l__ibus sunt.

R: Canēs proximī leōnibus sunt.

74. E____ pr____us s___ae est.

R: Equus proximus sīmiae est.

75. As___ pr____ī qu____ s____.

R: Asinī proximī quercuī sunt.

24-37

251. Fortūnam timeō → ----------------
✓ ★ ○ •
R: Ego Fortūnam timeō.

252. Umbram habēs → ----------------
✓ ★ ○ •
R: Tū umbram habēs.

253. Multīs nōn placeō → ----------------
✓ ★ ○ •
R: Ego multīs nōn placeō.

254. Fortūnam timēs → ----------------
✓ ★ ○ •
R: Tū Fortūnam timēs.

255. Rēgnum possideō → ----------------
✓ ★ ○ •
R: Ego rēgnum possideō.

256. Īrātum video → ----------------
✓ ★ ○ •
R: Ego īrātum video.

257. Rēgnum possidēs → ----------------
✓ ★ ○ •
R: Tū rēgnum possidēs.

258. Echo the singular paradigm of tenēre.
★ ○ •
teneō
tenēs
tenet

21-17

76. Op__ pr____um auc____ e__.

R: Opus proximum auctōrī est.

77. Ap__ ____ī an____ s____.

R: Aprī proximī anibus sunt.

78. M____ ____a fa__ē e__.

R: Musca proxima faciēī est.

[In the last frame, if you were wondering, the vowel of the Fifth Declension is long in the dative singular if it follows the vowel **-i-**, short otherwise. Thus we have **reī**, but **diēī**.]

79. Anim____a _____a ef_____ s____.

R: Animālia proxima effigiēī sunt.

24-36

In this sequence five Basic Sentences (or parts of them) will appear, with the verb transformed to either the First Person ("I") or the Second Person ("You"). You are to expand with the proper subject. Here is how you do it. The only possible subject for a verb form in **-ō** is the personal pronoun **egō**. The only possible subject for a verb form in **-s** is the personal pronoun **tū**.

245. Therefore, if you see **Rēgnum possideō**, you expand it to ___ **rēgnum possideō**.

R: Egō rēgnum possideō.

246. If you see **Rēgnum possidēs**, you expand it to ___ **rēgnum possidēs**.

R: Tū rēgnum possidēs.

247. Remember that the Latin **tū** differs from English "you," because **tū** refers to _____.

A: only one person.

248-257. Here is the sequence: expand with **Egō** ("I") if the verb ends in **-ō**, with **Tū** ("you") if the verb ends in **-s**.

248. Umbram habeō ← — — — — — — — — — — — ∨ ★ ○ •

R: Egō umbram habeō.

249. Īrātum vidēs ← — — — — — — — — — — — ∨ ★ ○ •

R: Tū īrātum vidēs.

250. Multīs nōn placēs ← — — — — — — — — — ∨ ★ ○ •

R: Tū multīs nōn placēs.

21-18

80. L_____ _____i el_____ s___.

R: Leōnēs proximī elephantō sunt.

81. Fl_____ _____m ac___ e___.

R: Flūmen proximum aciēī est.

82. P_____ _____a gr_____ e___.

R: Porticus proxima gradibus est.

83. Here is a new point of structure. You have already learned that the most common type of Latin sentence is the {-s -m -t} like **Vēritātem diēs aperit,** which contains a tr_____ verb whose complement is in the _____ case.

A: transitive
accusative

24-35

238. "Tenēsne saccum?" "_____ s_____."

R: Egō saccum teneō.

239. "Possidēsne instrūmentum?" "_____ in_____."

R: Egō instrūmentum possideō.

240-244. Your teacher will ask you if he is doing certain things. Tell him that he is.

240. "Timeōne medicōs ēloquentēs?" "Tū m_____ ēl_____ t_____ ēs."

R: Tū medicōs ēloquentēs timēs.

241. "Tenēone aprōs?" "Tū ap_____ t_____ ēs."

R: Tū aprōs tenēs.

242. "Moveōne saccōs?" "_____ s_____ m_____."

R: Tū saccōs movēs.

243. "Habeōne pedēs magnōs?" "_____ _____ _____."

R: Tū pedēs magnōs habēs.

244. "Taceōne sub jūdice?" "_____."

R: Tū sub jūdice tacēs.

84. You already know, however, that not all verbs take their complement in the accusative case. For example, the verb **est**, in a sentence like **Īra furor brevis est,** takes its complement in the _____ case.

A: nominative

85. Another verb which takes its complement in the nominative case is the word which means "seems."

The judge seems just = J____ j____s v___tur.

A: **Jūdex jūstus vidētur.**

86. To say "Fortune rules life," you have learned to use an {-s -m -t} kernel and say F_____ v____ r_____.

A: **Fortūna vītam regit.**

87. But there is another way to express almost exactly the same thought. Your teacher will now use a new verb **(imperat)**, which is a synonym of **regit**, but whose complement is in the *dative* case.

★ ○ • ○ • F_____ v____ im_____.

Cōnf: **Fortūna vītae imperat.**

88. Write what you have just echoed. _____

R: **Fortūna vītae imperat.**

89. There is a slight difference in meaning between **regit** and **imperat**. **Imperat** means to give an order to someone; if this order is expressed, it is put in the accusative case. **Rēgīna pecūniam imperat** = The _____ is _____ing some _____.

A: The queen is ordering some money.

90. Rēgīna ducī imperat = The _____ is _____ing the _____.

A: The queen is ordering the leader.

233.

Magister: Magnōs pedēs habēs

Discipulus: m ____ p ____ h ____

R: **Tū quoque magnōs pedēs habēs.**

234.

Magister: Saccōs nōn movēs.

Discipulus: s ____ n ____ m ____

R: **Tū quoque saccōs nōn movēs.**

235-239. Your teacher will ask you if you are doing certain things. You are to reply that you are.

235. "Timēsne vulpem?" "Egō v____ m t____eō."

R: Egō vulpem timeō.

236. "Habēsne longās aurēs?" "I____ l____ h____."

R: Egō longās aurēs habeō.

237. "Vidēsne leōnem?" "I____ l____."

R: Egō leōnem videō.

91. It is apparent that ordering the money and ordering the leader are quite different. She gives the order *to* the ------.

A: leader.

92. But *what* she orders is some ------.

A: money.

93. If we combine these two sentences, then **Rēgīna ducī pecūniam imperat** means that the queen is ------------------------------.

A: ordering money from the leader (or giving an order to the leader for money).

94. In the sentence **Rēgīna ducī pecūniam imperat** the word **imperat** (like **dat, reddit,** and **indicat**) takes both a ------ ob---t and an -------- ------.

A: direct object indirect object.

95. But **imperat** is often used in the sense of "command," and in this sense it is a synonym of the Latin verb r---t.

A: regit.

96-111. Echo your teacher as he says that these various people command other people, changing **regit** (or **regunt**) plus the *accusative* to **imperat** (or **imperant**) plus the *dative*.

96. Fāta orbem rēgunt → F--- orb- imper----. ★ ○ • ○ •

Cōnf: Fāta orbī imperant.

97. Rēgīna jūdicēs regit → R----- j-----bus imp----. ★ ○ • ○ •

Cōnf: Rēgīna jūdicibus imperat.

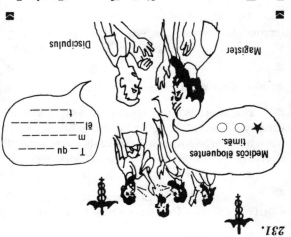

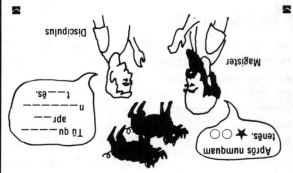

98. Virī equōs regunt → V___ equ___ imp_____. ★ ○ • ○ •

Cōnf: Virī equīs imperant.

99. Medicī aegrōs regunt → ___ ___ imp_____. ★ ○ • ○ •

Cōnf: Medicī aegrīs imperant.

100. Rēgēs ducēs regunt → _____. ★ ○ • ○ •

Cōnf: Rēgēs ducibus imperant.

101. Fortūna vītās regit → _____. ★ ○ • ○ •

Cōnf: Fortūna vītīs imperat.

102. Senex anum regit → _____. ★ ○ • ○ •

Cōnf: Senex anuī imperat.

103. Ducēs aciem regunt → _____. ★ ○ • ○ •

Cōnf: Ducēs aciēī imperant.

104-111. Make these same changes yourself.

104. Virī equōs regunt → V___ ___īs imperant.

R: Virī equīs imperant.

105. Fāta orbem regunt → F___ ___ī im_____.

R: Fāta orbī imperant.

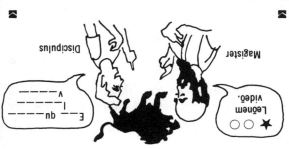

226. R: Egō quoque leōnem videō.

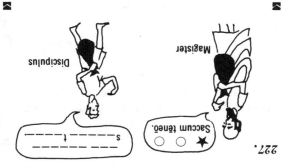

227. R: Egō quoque saccum teneō.

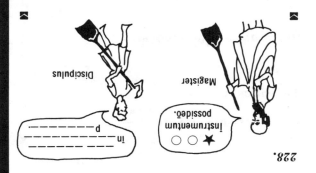

228. R: Egō quoque instrūmentum possideō.

229. When small boys have an argument, it frequently takes this form: "You're a liar!" "So are you!" "You're crazy!" "So are you!" This type of reply (which does not require much wit or skill) is called the "tū quoque" type of argument. Note that we did not put the macron on the first word, because "tū quoque" is in this sentence ---- (an English/a Latin) expression.

A: an English

21-22

106. Rēgēs ducēs regunt → R_____ _____ibus _____.

R: Rēgēs ducibus imperant.

107. Ducēs aciem regunt → _____ _____ī _____.

R: Ducēs aciēī imperant.

108. Senex anum regit → _____ _____ _____.

R: Senex anuī imperat.

109. Rēgīna jūdicēs regit → _____.

R: Rēgīna jūdicibus imperat.

110. Fortūna vītās regit → _____.

R: Fortūna vītīs imperat.

111. Medicī aegrōs regunt → _____.

R: Medicī aegrīs imperant.

112. In Basic Sentence 37 **Religiō deōs colit, superstitiō violat,** we translated the verb **colit** as "_____s."

A: honors.

113. Echo your teacher as he expresses about the same thought, that religion serves the gods. ★ ○ • ○ • **Religiō dīs servit.**

114. As you can see from this example, the verb **servit** has its complement *not* in the accusative case but in the _____ case.

A: dative

24-31

221. We call the form **timeō** the "First Person," and **timet** the "Third Person." The form **timēs** is called the "_____ Person."

A: Second

222. Echo a new intensifier. ★ ○ • ○ • **quoque** ("also").

223-228. In the following sequence your teacher (**Magister**) will be performing different actions which he will describe. You are to take the part of the student (**Discipulus**). When your teacher says what he is doing, you are to answer enthusiastically that you are doing it too. You, the student (**Discipulus**), do this by repeating what he says, but expanding it with "**Ego** **quoque**" ("I too").

223.

R: **Ego quoque vulpem timeō.**

A: I too fear the fox.

224. **Ego quoque vulpem timeō** = _____.

225.

R: **Ego quoque longās aurēs habeō.**

21-23

115. There are not very many of these verbs that take their complement in the dative case, but the ones that do exist are common. The two that you know are _____ and _____.

A: imperat   servit.

116. Echo your teacher as he transforms these sentences with **colit** (and **colunt**) to **servit** (and **serviunt**). In doing so he must transform the _____ case into the _____ case.

A: accusative   dative

117. Homō Fāta colit → H___ F__īs serv___. ★ ○ • ○ •

Cōnf: Homō Fātīs servit.

118. Anus īnfantēs colit → A___ īn_____ s_____. ★ ○ • ○ •

Cōnf: Anus īnfantibus servit.

119. Superstitiō deōs nōn colit → _____ ___ ___ s_____. ★ ○ • ○ •

Cōnf: Superstitiō dīs nōn servit.

120. Medicī artem colunt → _____. ★ ○ • ○ •

Cōnf: Medicī artī serviunt.

121. Sapientēs vēritātem colunt → _____ _____. ★ ○ • ○ •

Cōnf: Sapientēs vēritātī serviunt.

122. Avārī pecūniam colunt → _____. ★ ○ • ○ •

Cōnf: Avārī pecūniae serviunt.

24-30

213. Multīs nōn placeō = _____.

A: I do not please many people.

214. Echo a new technical term. ★ ○ • ○ •

p e r s o n a l   p r o n o u n

215. The words "you" and "I" are called "personal pronouns." In English the difference between "I hold" and "You hold" is not any change in the *verb*, but a change in the *personal pronouns* "___" and "___."

A: I   you.

216. In Latin the difference between **teneō** and **tenet** is _____ [In your own words]

A: a change in the form of the verb.

217. However, Latin does have personal pronouns, which it uses for *emphasis*. ★ ○ • ○ • **ego** ("I")   **tū** ("you")

218. Echo your teacher as he emphasizes the subject when he says in Latin, "*I* please many people." ★ ○ • ○ •

Cōnf: **Ego multīs placeō.**

219. Echo your teacher as he says in Latin, "*You* (one person) please many people." ★ ○ • ○ •

Cōnf: **Tū multīs placēs.**

220. Echo the paradigm of **timēre**. ★ ○ •

timeō
timēs
timet

21-24

123. Ducēs rēgīnam colunt → _____.
★ ○ • ○ •

Cōnf: Ducēs rēgīnae serviunt.

124. Juvenis anūs colit → _____.
★ ○ • ○ •

Cōnf: Juvenis anibus servit.

125-131. Make these same changes yourself.

125. Avārī pecūniam colunt → A_____-__ae ___viunt.

R: Avārī pecūniae serviunt.

126. Superstitiō deōs nōn colit → S____ _____īs ___ _____it.

R: Superstitiō dīs nōn servit.

127. Anus īnfantēs colit → ____ _____ibus _____.

R: Anus īnfantibus servit.

128. Medicī artem colunt → _____.

R: Medicī artī serviunt.

129. Sapientēs vēritātem colunt → _____ _____.

R: Sapientēs vēritātī serviunt.

130. Juvenis anūs colit → _____.

R: Juvenis anibus servit.

24-29

204. Umbram habet = _____.
A: He (she, it) casts a shadow.

205. Fortūnam timet = _____.
A: He (she, it) fears Fortune.

206. Rēgnum possideō = _____.
A: I possess a kingdom.

207. Lēgem nōn videō = _____.
A: I do not see the law.

208. Umbram habēs = _____.
A: You (one person) cast a shadow.

209. Multīs nōn placet = _____.
A: He (she, it) does not please many people.

210. Rēgnum possidēs = _____.
A: You (one person) possess a kingdom.

211. Fortūnam timēs = _____.
A: You fear Fortune.

212. Lēgem nōn videt = _____.
A: He does not see the law.

21-25

131. Ducēs rēgīnam colunt → _____.

R: Ducēs rēgīnae serviunt.

132. We will now read a Basic Sentence which contains both **imperat** and **servit**. You therefore expect that the complements of these verbs will be in the _____ case.

A: dative

133. ★ ○ • ○ • *Artēs serviunt vītae, sapientia imperat.* (73)

134. ★ ○ ○ A____ s_____ v____, s_____ imp___t.

A: *Artēs serviunt vītae, sapientia imperat.*

135. Which of these statements is true about this Basic Sentence?
1) The first kernel is complete but not the second.
2) The second kernel is complete but not the first.
3) Both kernels are complete.
4) Neither kernel is complete.

A: 1) The first kernel is complete but not the second.

136. Expand as indicated: **Artēs serviunt vītae, sapientia imperat** _____.

A: vītae.

137. We have met **ars** before, both in the sense "___" and as "sc_____."

A: art science.

24-28

195. Give the meaning of the following sentences. Remember that the signal **-ō** on the verb means "- am doing such-and-such."

A: I

196. The signal **-s** on the verb means "--- (_____) are doing such-and-such."

A: You (one person)

197. The signal **-t** on the verb means "---, --- or --- is doing such-and-such."

A: He, she, or it

198. **Rēgnum possidet** = _____

A: He (she, it) possesses a kingdom.

199. Although "I possess" is two words in English, the corresponding Latin expression consists of ___ word(s).

A: one

200. **Umbram habeō** = _____

A: I cast a shadow.

201. **Multīs nōn placēs** = _____

A: You (one person) do not please many people.

202. **Fortūnam timeō** = _____

A: I fear Fortune.

203. **Lēgem nōn vidēs** = _____

A: You (one person) do not see the law.

21-26

138. In this sentence the word **artēs** has the meaning of "education." We use "arts" in this sense today when we speak of the "liberal arts" in a college, the kind of course which most of you will eventually take. "Liberal" here comes from the Latin word **līber** meaning "free man," so that liberal arts colleges are places that offer an education that a ____ man (as opposed to a slave) should have.

A: free

139. A person who wishes to become a mechanic studies mechanical ___s.

A: arts.

140. In our Basic Sentence, the contrast is between **artēs**, which is *education* that can be learned by almost anyone, and **sapientia**, which is *wisdom* that can be acquired only by the few. The author, Seneca, is saying that the education which we acquire is useful to us, but more than this, that the quality which tells us how to act is _____.

A: wisdom.

141. Artēs serviunt vītae, sapientia imperat = _____.

A: Education serves life, (but) wisdom commands it.

142. Copy in your Notebook.

143. Echo the singular paradigm of the question word. ★ ○ •

quis?   quid?
quem?   quid?
quō?   quō?
cui?   cui?

---

187. He will repeat what he said. Write. ★ ○ •
____ ____ ____.

R: **Agnum pede tenēs.**

188. What he said was, "___ ___ing ___ are ___ing ___ a ___ the ___."

A: You are holding a lamb by the foot.

189. To change "*I am* holding" to "*You are* holding," we change the signal -**ō** to ____.

A: -s.

190. In Latin the word **tū** means "You-one-person." In English the word "You" can refer to one ____ or ____ ___ ____.

A: one person   more than one person.

191. Echo the paradigm of **tenēre** in the singular. ★ ○ • •

teneō   ("I am holding.")
tenēs   ("You-one-person are holding.")
tenet   ("He [she, it] is holding.")

192. The characteristic vowel of **tenēre** is -ē-. This *long* vowel becomes *short* in the forms ____, ____, and ____, but remains long in the forms ____ and ____.

A: teneō, tenet, tenent, and tenentur. tenēs and tenētur.

193. Pronounce the word "conjugation," and check. √ ★ ○ •

VCh: "con-jew-gāy-shun"

194. We will begin with the conjugation to which **tenēre** belongs, whose characteristic vowel is ____. [With the macron.]

A: -ē-.

21-27

Quaestiōnēs et Respōnsa

144. "Quae rēs vītam nostram adjuvant?"
"_____."

R: Artēs.

145. "Quid vītam nostram regit?"
"_____."

R: Sapientia.

146. "Cui artēs serviunt?" "_____."

R: _____ Vītae.

147. "Quō vīta nostra regitur?" "_____."

R: _____ Sapientiā.

148. Here is another Basic Sentence which contains the verb **servit**. In addition to a subject, you will expect that **servit** will have a _____ in the _____ case.

A: _____ complement
   dative

149. Echo the word that means "free."
★ ○ • ○ •   m   f   n
         līber, lībera, līberum

150. The small letters over the adjectives remind you that _____. [In your own words]

A: _____ there are three different genders.

151. Echo the kernel of a Basic Sentence.
★ ○ • ○ • **Nēmō līber est.**

152. This is an { __ __ ___ } type of sentence.

A: _____ {-s -s est}

24-26

In this Unit you will discover how to say, "I am holding a lamb" and "You are holding a lamb."

182. Listen to your teacher tell you (you are the one on the right) what he is doing.

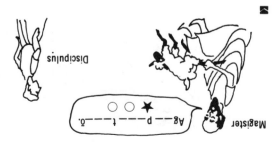

Cōnf: **Agnum pede teneō.**

183. He will repeat what he said. Write what he says he is doing. ★ ○ ○ _____ _____ _____.

R: **Agnum pede teneō.**

184. What he said was, "_____ am _____ing a _____ the _____."

A: I am holding a lamb by the foot.

185. To change from "He is holding" to "I am holding," we change the signal -t of tenet to _____ the signal _____.

A: -ō.

186. Remember that you are the student on the right (even though you may not think that it looks much like you). Listen to your teacher tell you what you are doing.

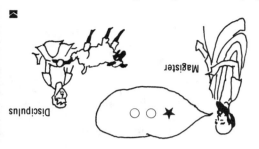

Cōnf: **Agnum pede tenēs.**

21-28

153. Nēmō līber est = _____ __ ____.

A: Nobody is free.

154. ★ ○ ○ N___ l____ ____.

A: Nēmō līber est.

155. We have been using the technical term "modify" for some time now. Perhaps you wonder what connection this has with the word "modify" which you use in ordinary life. When you say that you have "modified" your plans, you mean that you have ch_____ your plans.

A: changed

156. The technical word "modify" also means "change." A modifier _____s in some way the idea of the word it goes with.

A: changes

157. It is a disturbing thought to say **Nēmō līber est,** "Nobody is free." But you will find that our Basic Sentence does not say that *no* one is free; the **nēmō** will be "m_____ed" and only *certain* people are not free.

A: modified

158. Echo the complete Basic Sentence with its modifier. ★ ○ • ○ • **Nēmō līber est, quī corporī servit.** (74)

159. ★ ○ ○ Nēmō līber est, _____.

R: Nēmō līber est, quī corporī servit. [Did you mark the five long vowels?]

24-25

174. "Pereuntne hominēs jūstē an in-jūstē?" "_____."

R: Jūstē.

175. "Sī mors nōn est poena, quid est?" "_____."

R: Lēx.

176-179. Echo the four Basic Sentences which contain an infinitive.

176. R. ____m ____t ★ ○ • ○ •

Cōnf: **Rēs est magna tacēre.** (98)

177. D. ____l ____s ____d ★ ○ • ○ •
____ am

Cōnf: **Difficile est longum subitō dēpōnere amōrem.** (99)

178. N. ____ qu ____m ____d ____p____ ★ ○ • ○ •

Cōnf: **Nātūram quidem mūtāre difficile est.** (100)

179. Om ____ m ____ d ____ l ____ n ____
p____ p____ • ○ • ○ ★

Cōnf: **Omnia mors poscit: lēx est, nōn poena, perīre.** (101)

180. Echo words for "Teacher" and "Student": ★ ○ • ○ • **Magister Discipulus**

181. So far, all the verbs we have had have been describing the actions of somebody else, and not what you or I may be doing. In the sentence **Magister aprum tenet,** the subject is not you or I, but is a _____.

A: teacher.

21-29

160. This Basic Sentence says that no one is free who is a ----- to his ----.

A: slave to his body.

161. Copy in your Notebook.

162. This saying is by Seneca, the St____ philosopher.

A: Stoic

163. Say the Basic Sentence which says that education serves life but wisdom commands it.
Ar___ ser_____ v____, sap_____ imp_____.
√ ★ ○ •

Cōnf: **Artēs serviunt vītae, sapientia imperat.**

164. Write the Basic Sentence which says that no one is free who is a slave to his body. N___ l____ ___, q__ c_____ s_____.

R: **Nēmō līber est, quī corporī servit.**

165. ★ ○ • ○ • *Dīs proximus ille est quem ratiō, nōn īra, movet.* (75)

166. ★ ○ ○ D__ pr_____ ___ ___ qu__ r____, n__ ___, m____.

R: **Dīs proximus ille est quem ratiō, nōn īra, movet.** [Remember, there are four macrons.]

167. The structure of this sentence is {__ __ ___}.

A: {-s -s est}.

165. "Ā quō omnia poscuntur?" "——————."

R: Ā ———— morte.

166. "Cujus sub rēgnō sunt omnia?" "——————."

R: **Mortis sub rēgnō.**

167. "Cui omnia serviunt?" "——————."

R: **Mortī.**

168. "Pereuntne omnēs hominēs?" "——————."

R: **Pereunt.**

169. "Suntne hominēs mortālēs an immortālēs?" "——————."

R: **Mortālēs.**

170. In this last frame, there was a new word made up of the prefix **in-** plus the adjective **mortālis**. The prefix **in-** means "———."

A: not.

171. The new word was not spelled *immortā-lis, however, but ———.

A: **immortālis.**

172. In other words, before the sound **m**, the prefix **in-** changes to ———.

A: **im-**

173. "Quibus imperat mors?" "Om———."

R: **Omnibus.**

21-30

168. The {-s -s est} kernel is "___ ___ ___."

A: Proximus ille est.

169. Proximus ille est = ___ ___ __ ___

A: That one (or "he") is near.

170. In this Basic Sentence **ratiō** means "reason" in the sense of "sound judgment." **Quem ratiō movet** = W___ r_____ m___s.

A: Whom reason moves.

171. Dīs proximus ille est quem ratiō movet = _____

A: He is near the gods whom reason moves.

172. Pronounce and check. √ ★ ○ • **Dīs proximus ille est quem ratiō, nōn īra, movet.**

173. This sentence means, "_____."

A: He is near the gods whom reason, not anger, moves.

174. Copy in your Notebook.

Quaestiōnēs et Respōnsa

175. "Quō sapiēns movētur?" "_____."

R: Ratiōne.

176. "Quis ratiōne movētur?" "_____."

R: Sapiēns.

24-23

157. The last clause means, "_____ (and) _____."

A: To die is a law and not a punishment.

158. Copy in your Notebook (both clauses).

159. This means that the conditions under which you were born are that you eventually have to ___.

A: die.

160. Therefore you shouldn't feel that you are unjustly treated because you must die. This is a ___ of life and not a special _____ which is visited upon you personally.

A: law   punishment

Quaestiōnēs et Respōnsa

161-169. In the following questions we are treating death as a personal noun, since it demands things of people.

161. "Quanta mors poscit?" "_____."

R: Omnia.

162. "Quanta ā morte poscuntur?" "_____."

R: Omnia.

163. In illā sententiā, "Quanta mors poscit?", "quanta" est cāsūs ____īvī.

R: accūsātīvī.

164. In hāc sententiā, "Quanta ā morte poscuntur?", "quanta" est cāsūs ____īvī.

R: nōminātīvī.

21-31

177. "Quō sapiēns nōn movētur?"
"_____."

R: Īrā.

178. "Quibus similis est quem ratiō, nōn īra, movet?" "_____."

R: Dīs.

179. The next question on this Basic Sentence will use a new Latin word whose meaning should be clear from its resemblance to English. "Quibuscum comparātur sapiēns?" "C__ d___."

R: Cum dīs.

180. Quibuscum comparātur sapiēns? means, "_ _ _ _ _ _ _ _ _ _ _ _ _ _ _ _ _?"

A: With whom is a wise man compared?

181. "Estne ratiō vitium an virtūs?"
"_____."

R: Virtūs.

182. "Estne īra vitium an virtūs?"
"_____."

R: Vitium.

183. "Estne īra virtūs?" "Minimē, īra _____ est."

R: vitium

184. "Quālem virum ratiō indicat?"
"Sap_____."

R: Sapientem.

185. "Quālem virum īra indicat?"
"St_____."

R: Stultum.

---

149. The verb poscere means "demand."
Mors omnia poscit = _____

A: Death demands all things.

150. We met perīre in the Basic Sentence Vēritās numquam _____

A: perit.

151. Perīre is the _____ of the irregular verb perit.

A: infinitive

152. The structure of Lēx est perīre is similar to that of Difficile est perīre, except that the adjective difficile has been replaced by the noun ____

A: lēx.

153. However, we can translate difficile est perīre by another English structure, that is, "To ___ is _____."

A: To die is difficult.

154. Lēx est perīre = To ___ is a ____.

A: To die is a law.

155. Expand: Lēx est perīre, nōn poena
p____.

R: Lēx est perīre, nōn poena est perīre.

156. Nōn poena est perīre = To __ __ __ __ _____.

A: To die is not a punishment.

21-32

186. Say the Basic Sentence which states that he is close to the gods whom reason, not anger, moves. D__ prox____ il__ ___ qu__ rat__, n__ ___, mov___.

R: Dīs proximus ille est quem ratiō, nōn īra, movet.

187. ★ ○ • ○ • *Ingrātus ūnus omnibus miserīs nocet.* (76)

188. **Nocet** is another verb which, like **servit** and **imperat**, takes its complement not in the accusative case but in the _____ case.

A: dative

189. The three verbs you now know which take their complement in the dative case are **noc__, ser___,** and **imp_____**.

A: **nocet   servit   imperat.**

190. **Nocet** is a synonym of **laedit.** You will remember the Basic Sentence **Absentem laedit, cum ēbriō quī lītigat,** which means, "_____ _____."

A: Who quarrels with a drunken person harms an absent person.

191. Substitute the synonym **nocet** which patterns with the dative. Pronounce and check. **Absent_ _____, cum ēbriō quī lītigat.** ✓ ★ ○ •

R: **Absentī nocet, cum ēbriō quī lītigat.**

192. You have had the adjectives **nocēns** and **innocēns** meaning "_____" and "_____."

A: guilty   innocent.

193. The adjective **nocēns** is actually the _____ participle of the verb **nocet**.

A: present

---

140. The form **omnia** is _____ number and _____ gender.

A: plural   neuter

141. The form **omnia** could be either _____ or _____ case.

A: nominative   accusative

142. If **omnia** modifies a noun, draw an arrow connecting it with the noun it modifies; if it does not modify any noun, say so. **Omnia mors poscit; lēx est, nōn poena, perīre.**

A: It doesn't modify any noun.

143. Since **omnia** does not modify any noun, it is used as a ____ itself.

A: noun

144. **Omnia** = ___ th_____ (as subject or object).

A: All things

145. **Mors** is the {__} of the kernel.

A: {s-}

146. Since **mors** is the {s-}, then the ambiguous form **omnia** must be the {__}.

A: {-m}.

147. From now on, whenever we talk about a verb (as here) we will use the _____ form of the verb.

A: infinitive

148. **Poscere** is an unknown word. **Omnia mors poscit** = _____.

A: Death blanks all things.

21-33

	m	f	n
194.	★ ○ • ○ •	miser, misera, miserum	

195. **Miser** is the part of speech called an _____.

A: adjective.

196. The forms **miser** and **miserum** belong to the _____ Declension.

A: Second

197. The form **misera** belongs to the _____ Declension.

A: First

198. The word **miser** has the English derivatives "misery" and "miserable." As an adjective the word **miser** means "_____le."

A: miserable.

199. Used as a noun the word **miser** means "_____."

A: miserable person.

200. ★ ○ ○ In_____ ūn__ om_____ m_____ n_____

R: **Ingrātus ūnus omnibus miserīs nocet.**

201. This sentence means that ___ _____ _____ _____ ___ _____.

A: one ungrateful person harms all miserable people.

202. Copy in your Notebook.

21-34

203. This sentence means that if a wealthy person helps someone who is in trouble and the person he helps turns out to be ungrateful, then this rich person_____ [In your own words]

A: _____ may never help any one else again.

Quaestiōnēs et Respōnsa

[Remember: your answer must be in the same case as the question word.]

204. "Quibus nocet ūnus ingrātus?"
"_____ _____."

R: Omnibus miserīs.

205. "Quis omnibus miserīs nocet?"
"_____ _____."

R: Ūnus ingrātus.

206. "Quōs laedit ingrātus ūnus?" "_____
_____."

R: _____ Omnēs miserōs.

207. "Ā quō omnēs miserī laeduntur?"
"_____ _____ _____."

R: Ab ingrātō ūnō.

208. "Quī ab ingrātō ūnō laeduntur?"
"_____ _____."

R: Omnēs miserī.

209. Say the Basic Sentence which states that one ungrateful person harms all unhappy people.
In_____ ū___ om_____ mis____ noc___.
✓ ★ ○ •

R: Ingrātus ūnus omnibus miserīs nocet.

---

124. There are several English derivatives of **mūtāre**. Sometimes in nature the offspring will change very much from the parent type. Biologists call this change a "mutation." A "mutant" is an organism which has so ch---ed.

A: changed.

125. Nātūram quidem mūtāre difficile est = _____.

A: It is difficult to change nature, anyway.

126. Copy in your Notebook.

Quaestiōnēs et Respōnsa

127. "Quid difficile est?" "_____ ____."

R: Nātūram quidem mūtāre.

128. "Quāle est nātūram mūtāre?" "_____ ____."

R: Difficile est.

129. ★ ○ • **difficultās** difficultātēs
difficultātem difficultātēs
difficultāte difficultātibus
difficultātī difficultātibus
difficultātis difficultātum

130. "Quid magnā difficultāte mūtātur?"
"_____."

R: Nātūra.

131. The word **difficultās** is a new word made up of familiar parts. The prefix is _____.

A: dis- (or dif-).

21-35

210. We will have a sequence in which your teacher will transform the transitive verb **laedit** to the special verb **nocet**. We call **nocet** a "special verb" because _ [In your own words]

A: _ _ _ _ _ _ _ _ _ it takes its complement in the dative case and not in the accusative case as most verbs do.

211. Lupī agnōs laedunt → L_ _ _ _ agn_ _ _ noc_ _ _ _. ★ ○ • ○ •

Cōnf: Lupī agnīs nocent.

212. Vīnum ēbriōs laedit → V_ _ _ _ ēbr_ _ _ n_ _ _ _ _. ★ ○ • ○ •

Cōnf: Vīnum ēbriīs nocet.

213. Elephantī aciem laedunt → _ _ _ _ _ _ _ _ _ _ _ _ _ _ _ _ _ _. ★ ○ • ○ •

Cōnf: Elephantī aciēī nocent.

214. Juvenēs effigiem laedunt → _. ★ ○ • ○ •

Cōnf: Juvenēs effigiēī nocent.

215. Pedēs vīperās laedunt → _ _ _ _ _ _ _ _ _ _ _ _. ★ ○ • ○ •

Cōnf: Pedēs vīperīs nocent.

216. Venēnum omnēs laedit → _ _ _ _ _ _ _ _ _ _ _ _ _ _ _ _. ★ ○ • ○ •

Cōnf: Venēnum omnibus nocet.

118-119. Expand these Basic Sentences so as to emphasize the italicized word by means of the new intensifier.

118. *Aquila* nōn capit muscās → A_ _ _ _ _ qu_ _ _ c_ _ _ m_ _ _ _ _.

R: *Aquila* quidem nōn capit muscās.

119. Fortēs *Fortūna* adjuvat → F_ _ _ _ _ F_ _ _ _ _ qu_ _ _ ad_ _ _ _ _.

R: Fortēs *Fortūna* quidem adjuvat.

120. *Nātūram quidem mūtāre difficile est.* (100) ∧ ★ ○ •

121. [Keep the previous frame covered.] ★ ○ ○
N_ _ _ _ _ _ _ _ qu_ _ _ _ m_ _ _ _ _ d_ _ _ _ _ _ _ _ _.

R: *Nātūram quidem mūtāre difficile est.*

122. The new word **mūtāre** is the form called an "_ _ _ _ _ _."

A: infinitive.

123. The word which is being emphasized in this Basic Sentence is the unknown word "_ _ _ _ _."

A: **Nātūram**. (It has an English derivative.)

111. Echo the paradigm of **puella** ("girl").
★ ○ •

Cōnf: puella   puellae
      puellam   puellās
      puellae   puellīs
      puellae   puellīs
      puellā   puellīs

112. The man is giving flowers to a girl = V-- fl----- p----- d--.

R: **Vir flōrēs puellae dat.**

113. Your teacher will now expand this sentence and emphasize the word **vir** by adding the intensifier **quidem**. ★ ○ • ○ • V--- qu---- fl----- p----- d--.

Cōnf: **Vir quidem flōrēs puellae dat.**

114. The intensifier **quidem** comes ---- (before/after) the word it emphasizes.

A: after

115. In English we might show the meaning of **quidem** by putting in the word "anyway," and raising the pitch of the word that is emphasized. Listen to your teacher translate **Vir quidem flōrēs puellae dat**. ★ ○

VCh: The *man*, anyway, is giving flowers to a girl.

116. Shift the emphasis by putting **quidem** in the position which will say, "The man is giving *flowers*, anyway, to a girl." V-- fl----- p----- d--.

R: **Vir flōrēs quidem puellae dat.**

117. The man is giving flowers to a *girl*, anyway = ------------------------------.

A: **Vir flōrēs puellae quidem dat.**

---

217. Mūrēs anūs laedunt → ....
★ ○ • ○ •

Cōnf: **Mūrēs anibus nocent.**

218. Malī mōrēs lēgēs laedunt → ....
.... ★ ○ • ○ •

Cōnf: **Malī mōrēs lēgibus nocent.**

219. Sīmiae arcum laedunt → ....
★ ○ • ○ •

Cōnf: **Sīmiae arcuī nocent.**

220. Lacrimae faciem laedunt → ....
.... ★ ○ • ○ •

Cōnf: **Lacrimae faciēī nocent.**

221-230. Now produce this same transformation yourself, changing **laedit** (or **laedunt**) to **nocet** (or **nocent**), then check with the tape. Remember to make the change in case from accusative to dative.

221. Mūrēs anūs laedunt → M----- ---ibus n------t. ✓ ★ ○ •

R: **Mūrēs anibus nocent.**

222. Juvenēs effigiem laedunt → J------ ef------ n------. ✓ ★ ○ •

R: **Juvenēs effigiēī nocent.**

223. Sīmiae arcum laedunt → S----- ar--- n------. ✓ ★ ○ •

R: **Sīmiae arcuī nocent.**

224. Elephantī aciem laedunt → El_____ ac____ n_____. ✓ ★ ○ •

R: Elephantī aciēī nocent.

225. Vīnum ēbriōs laedit → V____ ēb____ n_____. ✓ ★ ○ •

R: Vīnum ēbriīs nocet.

226. Malī mōrēs lēgēs laedunt → M___ m____ l_____ n_____. ✓ ★ ○ •

R: Malī mōrēs lēgibus nocent.

227. Lacrimae faciem laedunt → L_____ f_____ n_____. ✓ ★ ○ •

R: Lacrimae faciēī nocent.

228. Venēnum omnēs laedit → V_____ om____ n_____. ✓ ★ ○ •

R: Venēnum omnibus nocet.

229. Lupī agnōs laedunt → L___ ag___ n_____. ✓ ★ ○ •

R: Lupī agnīs nocent.

230. Pedēs vīperās laedunt → P____ v____ n_____. ✓ ★ ○ •

R: Pedēs vīperīs nocent.

Echo the 14 infinitives which you have learned, conjugation by conjugation.

103. ★ ○ • First Conjugation   104. ★ ○ • Second Conjugation
curāre   adjuvāre   possidēre   tacēre
laudāre   necāre   vidēre

105. ★ ○ • Third Conjugation   106. ★ ○ • Fourth Conjugation
capere   pingere   aperīre   audīre
sapere   dēpōnere   custōdīre

Now for another new Basic Sentence.

You have already learned two "intensifiers," a part of speech which emphasizes the words that it patterns with. Add the missing intensifiers to these two familiar Basic Sentences.

107. ____ capillus ūnus habet umbram suam.

R: Etiam

108. Impōnit fīnem sapiēns ____ rēbus honestīs.

R: et

109. Etiam and et come ____ (before/after) the words they emphasize.

A: before

110. Echo the paradigm of flōs ("flower"). ★ ○ •

Conj: flōs   flōrēs
        flōrem   flōrēs
        flōre   flōribus
        flōrī   flōribus
        flōris   flōrum

21-38

231. You now know three verbs that take their complement in the dative case. This Basic Sentence uses two of them. **Art__ serviu__ vīt__, sapien____ impera__.** (73)

R: **Artēs serviunt vītae, sapientia imperat.**

232. **Nēm_ līb__ est quī corp___ serv___.**

R: **Nēmō līber est quī corporī servit.**

233. **Ingrāt__ ūn__ omn____ miser__ n_____.**

R: **Ingrātus ūnus omnibus miserīs nocet.**

234. The three verbs that you have just seen in the Basic Sentences which take their complement in the dative case are the verbs **im_____, n____ and s_____.**

A: **imperat, nocet servit.**

235. Echo your teacher as he says, "One donkey pleases another." ★ ○ • ○ • **As____ as___ pl_____.**

Cōnf: **Asinus asinō placet.**

236. Cover the last frame and write what you have just echoed. _____ _____ _____.

R: **Asinus asinō placet.**

---

96. "Quid juvenis in memoriā tenet?" "L__ a_____."

R: Longum amōrem.

97. "Cum longus amor perit, manetne memoria puellae?" "_____."

R: Manet.

98. "Quid manet cum longus amor perit?" "M_____ p_____."

R: Memoria puellae.

99. "Quid nōn sine difficultāte perit?" "L____ a____."

R: Longus amor.

100. The different classes of nouns are called the five d_____s.

A: declensions.

101. Echo a new technical term. ★ ○ • ○ • **conjugation**

VCh: "con-jew-gāy-shun"

102. The characteristic vowel of a verb shows what "conjugation" a verb belongs to. **Tenēre** and **cūrāre** have different characteristic vowels. They therefore belong to different _____s.

A: **conjugations.**

237. The word **placet** is another verb which, like **imperat**, **servit**, and **nocet**, _____.

A: _____ takes its complement in the dative case.

238-242. Using the sentence **Asinus asinō placet** as a model, describe the following pictures.

238. √ ★ ○ • P_____ p____ pl____.

R: Piscis piscī placet.

239. √ ★ ○ • S____ _____ pl____.

R: Sīmia sīmiae placet.

240. √ ★ ○ • V_____ _____ _____t.

R: Vīpera vīperae placet.

---

89. The neuter ablative singular form **subitō** however, we can best translate by an English adverb, "s____ly."

A: suddenly

90. In this sentence, **longus amor** means "longstanding love affair." **Difficile est longum subitō dēpōnere amōrem** = _____.

A: It is difficult to put aside suddenly a longstanding love affair.

91. Copy in your Notebook.

92. √ ★ ○ •

longus amor   longī amōrēs
longum amōrem   longōs amōrēs
longō amōre   longīs amōribus
longō amōrī   longīs amōribus
longī amōris   longōrum amōrum

[Repeat as many times as necessary to learn the paradigm.]

Quaestiōnēs et Respōnsa

(The answers may sometimes be found in earlier questions. If you forget, you may, of course, look back.)

93. "Manetne an perit memoria longī amōris?" "_____."

R: Manet.

94. "Quantī amōris manet memoria?" "L____."

R: Longī.

95. "Tenetne in memoriā juvenis longum amōrem?" "_____."

R: Tenet.

21-40

241. √ ★ ○ • An__ ____ _____.

R: Anus anuī placet.

242. √ ★ ○ • Eq__ ____ _____.

R: Equus equō placet.

243. Let's transform these to the plural and say that donkeys please other donkeys, etc. Remember that if the singular dative is **-ae** or **-ō**, as in **sīmiae** and **equō**, the dative plural is **-īs**, as in **sīmiīs** and **equīs**, whereas if the dative is in **-ī** as in **anuī** and **piscī**, then the dative plural ends in _____.

A: -bus.

244. A__ī a__īs pl__ent.

R: Asinī asinīs placent.

---

82. **Pōnere** means "_____." [From now on we will use the infinitive form in talking about verbs.]

A: place

83. The prefix **dē-** in the verb **dēfluere** meant "d____."

A: down.

84. In this sentence, however, the prefix **dē-** has the meaning of "aside." **Difficile est dēpōnere amōrem** therefore means that _____.

A: it is difficult to put aside love.

85. ○ ★ ○ D___ ___ l___ s___ am____ d___.

86. **Longus** and **subitus** are both adjectives. If **longus** modifies any noun in the sentence, draw an arrow connecting it with the noun it modifies; if it does not modify any noun (and is used as a noun itself), then say so. **Difficile est longum subitō dēpōnere amōrem.**

R: **Difficile est longum subitō dēpōnere amōrem.**

87. **Subitus** is an adjective meaning "sudden." If it modifies any noun in the sentence, draw an arrow connecting it with the noun it modifies; if it does not modify any noun (and is used as a noun itself), then say so. **Difficile est longum subitō dēpōnere amōrem.**

A: **Difficile est longum subitō dēpōnere amōrem.**

88. The noun is **subitum-ī** and means "sudden occurrence." It is _____ gender.

A: neuter

21-41

245. S_____ s_____s pl__ent.

R: Sīmiae sīmiīs placent.

246. V_____ v_____ pl_____.

R: Vīperae vīperīs placent.

247. P_____ p___ibus pl_____.

R: Piscēs piscibus placent.

21-42

248. An__ an____ pl_____.

R: Anūs anibus placent.

249. Eq__ _____ _____.

R: Equī equīs placent.

250. In the next Basic Sentence is another verb which takes its complement in the dative case, like the verbs s_____, i_____, n____, and pl_____.

A: servit   imperat   nocet   placet.

251. In English we use the word "marry" in three different ways: the groom marries the _____.

A: bride.

252. The bride marries the _____.

A: groom.

253. And the minister marries both the _____ and the _____.

A: bride groom.

24-11

68. Also, in difficilis the -a- in facilis becomes the vowel -_-.

A: -i-.

69. An English derivative of difficilis is the adjective "_____ lt."

A: difficult.

70-74. Echo your teacher as he says that these various tasks are difficult to do.

70. ★ ● ○ ● ○ • Difficile est taurum morsū necāre.

71. ★ ● ○ ● ○ • Difficil_ est aprum manibus tenēre.

Cōnf: Difficile est aprum manibus tenēre.

72. ★ ● ○ ● ○ • Difficil_ ___ flōris imāgi- nem pinge__

Cōnf: Difficile est flōris imāgi- nem pingere.

73. ★ ● ○ ● ○ • D_____ vōcēs canum aud____

74. ★ ● ○ ● ○ • Difficile est vōcēs canum audīre.

Cōnf: Difficile est vōcēs canum audīre.

A: It is difficult to hear the dogs' voices.

75-78. Make this same transformation your- self, and when you are told that a snake kills a bull by biting say that it is difficult to kill a bull by biting. [It depends on who is doing the biting.]

21-43

254. In Latin there are different words for the groom's part in the ceremony and the bride's part. Echo your teacher as he says that Titus is marrying Laecania. ★ ○ • ○ • [Remember to listen to the long vowels.] T____ L_____ d____.

Cōnf: Titus Laecāniam dūcit.

255. Cover the last frame and write what you just echoed. [Don't forget the macrons.] ____ ____ ____ .

R: Titus Laecāniam dūcit.

256. In Basic Sentence 45, **Dūcunt volentem Fāta, nōlentem trahunt,** the word **dūcunt** meant "_____."

A: guide.

257. Earlier you learned that **Vir asinum dūcit** means, "_____."

A: The man leads the donkey.

258. Now you learn that **Vir fēminam dūcit** means that the ___ is _____ing the _____.

A: man is marrying the woman.

259. **Vir fēminam dūcit** means that the man is leading the woman into m_____ge.

A: marriage. (**Vir fēminam dūcit** could also mean that the man is guiding the woman; if the author does not want ambiguity he can insert the Latin words **in mātrimōnium** meaning "into marriage.")

60. Write the Basic Sentence again. R: ____ m___ t_____ .

R: Rēs est magna tacēre.

Quaestiōnēs et Respōnsa

61. "Quanta rēs est tacēre?" "_____."

R: Magna.

62. "Quid est magna rēs?" "_____."

R: Tacēre.

63. "Quantum est tacēre?" "_____ m ____ ."

R: Magnum est.

[In answering the following, remember the original poem: Maron insisted upon reciting the poem in public, that is, in "publishing" his works, even though he was sick.]

64. "Quid agit sapiēns auctor cum aeger est, tacetne an recitat?" "_____."

R: Tacet.

65. "Quid agit stultus auctor Marōn cum aeger est?" "_____."

R: Recitat.

66. "Qualis est auctor qui cum aeger est recitat?" "_____."

R: Stultus.

67. The adjective **difficilis, difficile** is an antonym of **facilis, facile**. The prefix **dis-** (as in English "dissimilar," meaning "not similar"), but before the **-f-** of **facilis,** the **-s-** of **dis-** becomes the sound ____.

A: -f-.

21-44

260. Echo your teacher as he says that Laecania (a girl) is marrying Titus. ★ ○ ● ○ ●
L‾‾‾‾‾‾ T‾‾‾ n‾‾‾‾‾.

Conf: Laecānia Titō nūbit.

261. Cover the last frame and write what you just echoed. ‾‾‾‾‾‾ ‾‾‾‾‾ ‾‾‾‾‾.

R: Laecānia Titō nūbit.

262. The verb **nūbit** takes its complement in the ‾‾‾‾‾‾ case.

A: dative

263. Describe the picture by writing that Titus is marrying Laecania, and Laecania is marrying Titus. [This sentence contains five macrons.]
T‾‾‾‾ L‾‾‾‾‾‾‾‾ d‾‾‾‾ et L‾‾‾‾‾‾‾‾ T‾‾‾ n‾‾‾‾.

R: Titus Laecāniam dūcit et Laecānia Titō nūbit.

264. **Dūcit** and **nūbit** are not synonyms, because **dūcit** is used of the ‾‾‾ and **nūbit** is used of the ‾‾‾‾‾.

A: man
woman.

---

54. We must therefore find a translation of **rēs magna** that fits both Maron's observation about how important it is for him to publish his poetry by reciting it and Martial's comment that when he has a fever he should rest. Maron says, "It's ‾‾‾‾‾‾‾‾ for me to give this recitation," and Martial replies, "It is ‾‾‾‾‾‾‾‾‾ for you to ‾‾‾‾."

A: important
be
silent.

55. A second point about the sentence: The Latin verb is one word (**tacēre**), while the English verb phrase that translates it consists of ‾‾‾ words.

A: two

56. In the English phrase "be silent," the word "silent" is the part of speech called an ‾‾‾‾‾‾‾‾‾.

A: adjective.

57. And the English word "be" is a ‾‾‾‾‾.

A: verb.

58. You may wonder why the structure of Latin and English seem to be becoming less and less similar. The answer is that although language systems may resemble each other at some points, they are d‾‾‾‾‾‾‾nt systems.

A: different

59. At the beginning we picked out the structures (and sentences) which offered *as few problems as possible*. Now that you have accepted the fact that Latin does not work like English, we are introducing structures which show the ‾‾‾‾‾‾‾‾‾s between the two systems.

A: differences

21-45

265. When the adjective **multī** is used as a noun it means ____ p___le.

A: many people.

266. ★ ○ • ○ • *Mulier quae multīs nūbit multīs nōn placet.* (77)

267. ★ ○ ○ M_____ qu__ m_____ n____ m_____ n__ p_____.

R: Mulier quae multīs nūbit multīs nōn placet. [Did you mark all four macrons?]

268. The kernel of this sentence is _____ _____.

A: Mulier multīs placet.

269. The modifier of the subject **mulier** is _____.

A: quae multīs nūbit.

270. The kernel with the negator added (**mulier multīs nōn placet**) means that a _____n't _____ ____ _____.

A: woman doesn't please many persons.

271. But what kind of a woman doesn't please many people? Write the sentence. **Mulier qu__ mul___ n___t multīs nōn placet.**

R: Mulier quae multīs nūbit multīs nōn placet.

---

50. Notice how we are gradually getting into structures that are more and more unlike English. For **Vēritātem diēs aperit**, we could give almost word for word; the only difference in the English translation was the addition of the noun marker "___" before the word "truth."

A: the ("Time discloses the truth.)

51. It might pay us to examine some of the differences between **Rēs est magna tacēre** and "It is important to be silent." We might have chosen to translate the Latin by "The big thing is to be silent," which would have corresponded more closely to the _____ structure.

A: Latin

52. There are two reasons for preferring "It is important" to "The big thing is." This line is taken from a poem by Martial. Which translation sounds more appropriate in a poem? _____

A: It is a matter of opinion: I think most people would say that "The big thing is" is too informal to use in translating a poem.

53. The second reason is the context in which the line occurs. Here is a translation of the whole poem. (Note: the recitation of a poem was the Roman way of publication.)

"Maron, you recite your poetry when you're sick; you recite it when you have malaria. This is excusable only if you can't sweat out the fever in any other way." "But my recitation is **rēs magna**," Maron says. "You're wrong. When the fever burns your body, **rēs est magna tacēre, Marōn**." The reason that Martial uses the expression **rēs magna** is that Maron _____ [In your own words]

A: has just used it.

24-8

21-46

272. The woman who does not please many people is the woman who ------s---- -------.

A: marries many people.

273. This Basic Sentence is by P--------
S------. √ ★ ○ •

Cōnf: Publilius Syrus.

274. Publilius Syrus says that a woman who has been married many times is ---- (popular/unpopular).

A: unpopular.

275. You would think that the fact that she was able to attract so many men would prove that she was popular; but if she had really been someone that people liked she would have ----
------------------------------------.
[In your own words]

A: been able to hold on to her first husband.

276. Give the Latin for, "The woman who marries many people does not please many people." Say, check, and write. Muli--- qu---
mult--- nūb--- mult--- --- pl-----. √ ★ ○ •

R: Mulier quae multīs nūbit multīs nōn placet.

277. Copy in your Notebook.

278. Write in "Facts About Latin": The dative is used as the complement of the special verbs **imperat, nocet, nūbit, placet, servit**.

279. Here is the last Basic Sentence of this Unit. When you met the verb **pōnit** before, it meant "pl---s."

A: places.

24-7

45. "Nēmō omnibus hōris sapit." "R---
m--- om----- h------ s---e---." √ ★ ○ •

R: Rēs magna est omnibus hōris sapere.

In this Unit we will continue to have you first pronounce (and check) the new Basic Sentence and then write from dictation.

46. Rēs est magna tacēre. (98) √ ★ ○ •
[Take care not to look back at this frame.]

47. R--- ---m--- t---
------- √ ★ ○ •

R: Rēs est magna tacēre.

48. Although there is an unknown word in the sentence, you know that this means that ----------
[Auxilium sub lineā inveniētur.]
Aux: For the unknown word substitute "something" (or "somebody") or "blanks."

A: it is important to blank.

49. A "tacit" agreement is one which is not mentioned, but is understood. Tacēre is an antonym of verba dīcere. Therefore Rēs est magna tacēre means that ----------
[Auxilium sub lineā.]

Aux ---- ---- to be s----nt.

A: It is important to be silent.

280. Verbs with prefixes are called "compound" verbs. Verbs without prefixes are called "simple verbs." **Dēfluit** is a ____ (compound/simple) verb.

A: compound

281. Vir pedem pōnit = The man ____s his f____.

A: The man places his foot.

282. You know that the prefix **in-** means "not" (as in **incertus**). There is a different prefix **in-** which means "on." ★ ○ • ○ • **Vir pedem inpōnit.**

283. This means that the man ____s his ____ on something.

A: places foot

284. Echo again. ★ ○ • ○ • **Vir pedem impōnit.**

285. Notice that before **pōnit** the n in **in-** is pronounced _____.

A: m.

286. The word is *spelled* either **inpōnit** or **impōnit**, but it is pronounced **impōnit**. Pronounce **impōnit**. √ ★ ○ •

287. In this course we will spell the word **impōnit** to help you pronounce it correctly. But you must remember that the prefix in **impōnit** is not **im-** but _____.

A: in-.

288. Pōnit is a _____ verb, while impōnit is a _____ verb.

A: simple compound

---

37. This means that it is _____

A: important to help the brave.

38. ★ ○ • ○ • Rēs magna est lēgem vidēre.

39. ★ ○ • ○ • R__ m____ est omnibus hōris sapere.

Conf: Rēs magna est omnibus hōris sapere.

40. ★ ○ • ○ • R__ m____ est pecūniam custōdī___

Conf: Rēs magna est pecūniam custōdīre.

Say that these things are important.

41. "Elephantus mūrem capit." "Rēs m____ est m____ c____ere." √ ★ ○ •

R: Rēs magna est mūrem capere.

42. "Vēritātem diēs aperit." "R__ m____ v____ a____ire." √ ★ ○ •

R: Rēs magna est vēritātem aperīre.

43. "Auctor opus laudat." "R__ m____ o__ l____āre." √ ★ ○ •

R: Rēs magna est opus laudāre.

44. "Fortēs Fortūna adjuvat." "R__ m____ f____ ad____āre." √ ★ ○ •

R: Rēs magna est fortēs adjuvāre.

289. Echo your teacher as he describes this picture. ★ ○ • ○ • **Vir vīperae pedem impōnit.**

290. *What* the person places on the snake (his foot in this example) in Latin is in the _____ case. The animal *on which* he places his foot is in the _____ case.

A: accusative
    dative

291. Copy in "Facts About Latin": The dative case is used with compound verbs like **impōnit**.

Using **Vir vīperae pedem impōnit** as a model, describe the following pictures of a very clumsy man.

292. V__ m____ _____.

R: **Vir mūrī pedem impōnit.**

293. V__ r____ _____.

R: **Vir rānae pedem impōnit.**

---

29. Which are the special verbs like "can," and "must," which can fill the slot before "buy" in this new list?

A: may; had better (not much used in writing); will; does; should

30. To summarize, the "buy" form is found ____ (with only a few special verbs/with almost any verb that is not one of the special verbs).

A: with only a few special verbs (and phrases).

31. The "to buy" form, on the other hand, may occur after ------------------------------------

A: almost any verb that is not one of the special verbs.

The Latin infinitive is used with *only a few* verbs and phrases. Here is another phrase similar to the **Facile est mūrem capere** construction. Echo your teacher as he says that these things are important to do.

32. ★ ○ • ○ • **Rēs magna est mūrem capere.**

33. ★ ○ • ○ • **Rēs magna est vēritātem aperīre.**

34. ★ ○ • ○ • **Rēs magna est opus laudāre.**

35. ★ ○ • ○ • **Rēs magna est rēgnum possidēre.**

36. ★ ○ • ○ • **Rēs magna est fortēs adjuvāre.**

294. Notice that in this picture he has his feet on two things. V__ p_____ ___ēs _____.

R: Vir piscibus pedēs impōnit.

295. V__ gr_____ _____ _____.

R: Vir gradibus pedēs impōnit.

296. Notice the difference. Here the man is putting his *hand* on an animal. V__ ___ m___ _____.

R: Vir asinō manum impōnit.

297. ___ c___ m____ _____.

R: Vir canī manum impōnit.

21-50

298. Now he is using both his hands and placing them on two animals. ___ aq_____ m___ūs _____.

R: Vir aquilīs manūs impōnit.

299. ___ p_____ _____ _____.

R: Vir piscibus manūs impōnit.

300. In **Etiam capillus ūnus habet umbram suam** the word **etiam** is an intensifier meaning "____."

A: even.

301. There is also an intensifier **et**. **Vir et ūnum piscem nōn capit** = The man doesn't catch ____ one fish.

A: even

302. How can you tell **et** the connector (as in **Vir piscem et rānam capit**) which means "___" and the intensifier (as in **Piscis et rānam nōn capit**) which means "e___"?

A: and
even?

---

16. In the forms **cūrat/cūratur/cūrāre/cūrantur/cūrantur,** the infinitive is the form ____.

A: cūrāre.

17. **Cápere** is the _____ of the verb capit.

A: infinitive

18. Contrasting the forms **aperīre, cápere, possídere,** and **laudāre,** you can see that the signal for the infinitive is {---}.

A: {-re}.

19. Looking again at the forms **aperīre, cápere, laudāre,** and **possidēre,** you can see the characteristic vowel of the different classes of verbs. How many *different* vowels come just before the signal -re? (1/2/3/4/5)

A: 4

20. [Look back for this frame.] These four vowels are ___, ___, ___, and ___.

A: ā e ī ē.

21. There are therefore ____ different classes of verbs.

A: four

Say that all of these things are easy to do: (Answer first, and *then* check.)

22. "Elephantus capit mūrem." "Facil___ est m___ere m____."

R: Facile est capere mūrem.

23. "Mēns rēgnum possidet." "F____ est rēg___ p_____ere."

R: Facile est rēgnum possidēre.

303. The answer is that if the *et* comes between *equal* things, then *et* is the _____ and means "____."

📧

A: connector and.

304. If *et* comes between *unequal* things, it is the _____ and means "____."

📧

A: intensifier even.

305. Vir piscem et rānam capit = _____
_____.

📧

A: The man catches a fish and a frog.

306. Vir piscem et rānam nōn capit = _____
_____.

📧

A: The man doesn't catch a fish and a frog.

307. Piscis et rānam nōn capit = _____
_____.

📧

A: The fish doesn't catch even a frog.

308. Rāna et piscis nōn capiuntur = _____
_____.

📧

A: The frog and the fish are not caught.

309. Rāna et piscem capit = _____
_____.

📧

A: The frog catches even a fish.

310. Echo the paradigm of a new word.
★ ○ • ○ • fīnis

📧

Cōnf:	fīnis	fīnēs
	fīnem	fīnēs
	fīne	fīnibus
	fīnī	fīnibus

8-10. Your teacher seems to be cynical today. Echo him as he observes that all of these things are easy.

8. ★ ○ • ○ • "Elephantus capit mūrem."
"Facile est cāpeRE mūrem."

9. ★ ○ • ○ • "Auctor opus laudat."
"Facile est opus laudāRE."

10. ★ ○ • ○ • "Mēns rēgnum possidet."
"Facile est rēgnum possidēRE."

📧

11. These last four sentences are all {-s -s est} sentences, but while one of the {-s}'s is the neuter adjective *facile*, the other {-s} is a new form of the part of speech called a ____.

📧

A: verb.

12. Comparing the sentences Facile est respōnsum and Facile est opus laudāre, you can see that the verb form laudāre can be substituted for the word _____.

📧

A: respōnsum.

13. Respōnsum is the part of speech called a ____.

📧

A: noun.

14. Just as the forms laudāns and laudātus were adjectives of the verb, so the new form laudāre is the ____ of the verb.

📧

A: noun.

15. Echo a new technical term. ★ ○ • ○ • infinitive

📧

A: VCh: "inn-fīn-nit-tive"

Laudāre is the infinitive of the verb which has the forms laudat/laudant/laudātur/laudantur.

21-52

311. At the end of a motion picture you frequently see the title FINIS. This title means that it is the ___ of the picture.

A: end

312. ★ ○ • ○ • *Impōnit fīnem sapiēns et rēbus honestīs.* (78)

313. The dative in this sentence is _____.

A. *rēbus honestīs.*

314. In this sentence *et* is the part of speech called an _____.

A: intensifier.

315. ★ ○ ○ Im_____ f____ s_____ __ r____ h_____. [Remember that there are 5 macrons.]

R: *Impōnit fīnem sapiēns et rēbus honestīs.*

316. *Honestae rēs* here means "honorable endeavors." The whole sentence means that the ____ _____ puts a _____ to ____ _____ _____.

A: wise person puts a limit to even honorable endeavors.

317. Copy in your Notebook.

UNIT TWENTY-FOUR

We now turn to the verb system. Although the Latin verb has more forms than the Latin noun, the verb system itself is simpler. For example, there are very few variant forms.

1. If you look in your Notebook at the nouns you can observe that there is not one case, singular or plural, which does not have two or more _____ _____.

A: variant forms.

2. Latin verbs have ____ (few/many) variant forms.

A: few

First you will find out how many classes of verbs there are.

3. We will explain why the vowel before the -*tur* in *capitur* is a _____ vowel, while the vowel before the -*tur* in *audītur* is a _____ vowel.

A: short
long

4. Here is a familiar construction. *Facile est respōnsum.* This means, "The _____ is _____."

A: The answer is easy.

5. *Facile est opus* = _____.

A: The work is easy.

6. Tell your teacher that time discloses the truth. V_____ d____ ap____.

A: *Vēritātem diēs aperit.*

7. Echo him as he says scornfully that it is easy to disclose the truth. ★ ○ • ○ • *Facile est vēritātem aperīre.* [Repeat until you have learned the expression.]

318. Pronounce the author's name in English. Juvenal √ ★ ○ •

VCh: "jéw-vuh-null"

319. The Greeks and Romans believed one should avoid excesses such as too much eating or drinking. Juvenal says that we should avoid excess even _____.

A: in honorable endeavors.

Quaestiōnēs et Respōnsa

320. "Quis fīnem et rēbus honestīs impōnit?" "_____."

R: Sapiēns.

321. "Quid impōnit sapiēns et rēbus honestīs?" "_____."

R: Fīnem.

322. "Quālibus rēbus impōnit fīnem sapiēns?" "_____ _____."

R: Rēbus honestīs.

323. "Estne sapiēns intemperāns?" "_____."

R: Nōn est.

324. "Quālēs rēs sapiēns nōn intemperanter colit?" "Et _____ _____."

R: Et honestās rēs.

TEST INFORMATION

You will be asked new questions on Basic Sentences, both new and review, but you will not be asked to produce any genitive plurals which you have not practiced in this Unit.

*Remember that the asterisk in this list means a *new* meaning for a familiar word.

A new connector: **atque** (198)

A new combination of familiar words: **nōn numquam** (225)

Adjectives: **hūmānus-a-um** (111-114)
mortuus-a-um (188)
praeteritus-a-um (83-89)
sēcūrus-a-um (60-62)
jūcundus-a-um (75-80)
praesēns (86-88)
plūrālis, plūrāle (48-52)
vīvus-a-um (189)
mortālis, mortāle (216-218)

21-54

325. Imp____ fī____ s_____ et rē____ hon-
n_____. √ ★ ○ •

R: Impōnit fīnem sapiēns et rēbus honestīs. (78)

326. In such a sentence as **Agnus et lupus stant** you know that **et** is a connector because the nominative **agnus** on one side of **et** is balanced by the word _____ on the other side.

A: lupus

327. Et is a connector when _____.

A: it connects equal things.

328. In the sentence **Impōnit fīnem sapiēns et rēbus honestīs,** on one side of **et** is **impōnit fīnem sapiēns** and on the other side is _____ _____.

A: rēbus honestīs.

329. Therefore in this sentence the word **et** ____ (does/does not) connect equal things.

A: does not

330. In this sentence **et** is not a connector but an _____ meaning "____."

A: intensifier   even.

VOCABULARY INVENTORY

Verbs: sentit (127)

Nouns: domina-ae, f (109)
memoria-ae, f (77)
*rēs, rei, f (111)
malum-i, n (78)
numerus-i, m (49-53)
terra-ae, f (55)

315. N____ m____ om____ h____ s_____. (96)

316-318. Say the Basic Sentences which convey these thoughts.

316. Omnēs virtūtēs sub rēgnō Jūstitiae sunt. J____ om____ ___ d____ et r_____ v_____. (97)

R: Jūstitia omnium est domina et rēgina virtūtum.

317. Fortūna hominibus imperat. R____ h_____ d_____ F_____. (92)

R: Rērum hūmānārum domina Fortūna.

318. Jūstus jūdex nostrōrum operum orbis est. S_____ j_____ or____ t_____. (90)

R: Sēcūrus jūdicat orbis terrārum.

23-47

331. You know that **et** here is the intensifier and not the connector because it _____.

A: _____ does not connect equal things.

332-341. In the following sentences, echo your teacher as he transforms the ambiguous dative or ablative words from plural to singular.

          plural   singular
332. Vir taurīs timet → _____
★ ○ • ○ •

Cōnf: Vir taurō timet.

333. Medicus vīnum fēminīs dat → _____ _____ ★ ○ • ○ •

Cōnf: Medicus vīnum fēminae dat.

334. Amīcus in rēbus incertīs cernitur → _____ ★ ○ • ○ •

Cōnf: Amīcus in rē incertā cernitur.

335. Fortibus magna dī cūrant → _____ _____ ★ ○ • ○ •

Cōnf: Fortī magna dī cūrant.

336. Mors omnibus imperat → _____
★ ○ • ○ •

Cōnf: Mors omnī imperat.

337. Sub jūdicibus līs est → _____
★ ○ • ○ •

Cōnf: Sub jūdice līs est.

---

312. Gr___ i___ r___ e___ s_____. (93)

R: Gravis īra rēgum est semper.

313. V_____ m_____ in m_____ v_____ e_____ p_____. (94)

R: Vīta mortuōrum in memoriā vīvōrum est posita.

314. M_____ r_____ au_____ at_____ oc_____. (95)

R: Multae rēgum aurēs atque oculī.

21-56

338. Nāvēs in flūminibus sunt → .... ★○•○•

▰ ▰

Cōnf: Nāvēs in flūmine sunt.

339. Cēnat sine aprīs convīva → .... ★○•○•

▰ ▰

Cōnf: Cēnat sine aprō convīva.

340. Mors īnfantibus fēlīx → .... ★○•○•

▰ ▰

Cōnf: Mors īnfantī fēlīx.

341. Aqua asinīs placet → .... ★○•○•

▰ ▰

Cōnf: Aqua asinō placet.

341-351. Change these same sentences from plural to singular yourself. [If you have any doubt about the meaning of these sentences which you have transformed, get some assistance.]

342. Mors omnibus imperat → ....

▰ ▰

R: Mors omnī imperat.

343. Vir taurīs timet → ....

▰ ▰

R: Vir taurō timet.

344. Amīcus in rēbus incertīs cernitur → ....

▰ ▰

R: Amīcus in rē incertā cernitur.

345. Medicus vīnum fēminīs dat → ....

▰ ▰

R: Medicus vīnum fēminae dat.

SUMMARY

23-45

308. In this Unit you learned the last bit of the Latin noun system, the form that is called the ....

▰ ▰

A: genitive plural.

309. You learned to discriminate between rhyming forms which are actually different cases. For example, you now know that the form **equum** is .... case and .... number, while **canum**, which has the same last syllable (namely, **-um**), is .... case and .... number.

▰ ▰

A: accusative   singular
   genitive   plural

▰ ▰

310. The signal on **equum** is ---, while the signal on **canum** is ---.

▰ ▰

A: -m-   -um.

▰ ▰

311-315. You learned eight new Basic Sentences. First say the Basic Sentences which these pictures illustrate; review first if you wish.

311. J------ m------ e--- pr--------- m------- (91)

R: Jūcunda memoria est praeteritōrum malōrum.

▰ ▰

21-57

346. Fortibus magna dī cūrant → _____ _____.

R: Fortī magna dī cūrant.

347. Sub jūdicibus līs est → _____.

R: Sub jūdice līs est.

348. Nāvēs in flūminibus sunt → _____ _____.

R: Nāvēs in flūmine sunt.

349. Cēnat sine aprīs convīva → _____ _____.

R: Cēnat sine aprō convīva.

350. Mors īnfantibus fēlīx → _____.

R: Mors īnfantī fēlīx.

351. Aqua asinīs placet → _____.

R: Aqua asinō placet.

352. The dative and ablative plural are *always* alike; there are *no* exceptions. The question naturally arises: How do we tell them apart? The answer is: by c_____.

A: context.

353. The form **fēminīs** could be either dative or ablative. The only use of the ablative with personal nouns which you have had (so far) has been with prepositions. Therefore, if you see **fēminīs** without a preposition, you know that (for now) it must be the _____ case.

A: dative

23-44

301. Which accusative plurals have the variant of length of vowel and -s?

A: **similās, lupōs, virōs, canēs, leōnēs, manūs, rēs, diēs**

302. Which accusative plurals have the variant -a?

A: **rēgna, genera**

303. The dative and ablative plurals are *always* al____.

A: alike.

304. Which dative-ablative forms have the variant -īs?

A: **similīs, lupīs, virīs, rēgnīs**

305. Which dative-ablative forms have the variant -bus?

A: **canibus, leōnibus, generibus, manibus, rēbus, diēbus**

306. Which genitive plurals have the variant -rum?

A: **similārum, lupōrum, virōrum, rēgnōrum, rērum, diērum,** (and not **generum**)

307. Which genitive plurals have the variant -um?

A: **canum, leōnum, generum, manuum**

For those of you who elected to do this section, we hope you enjoyed it and that it made the system a little clearer. If it makes you feel any better, the Latin noun system is a *very* complicated one.

21-58

354. You have had five Latin verbs which take the dative as their complement. These verbs are:
im_____ s_____ pl_____ no___ nū___

A: imperat servit placet nocet nūbit

355. If you see the combination **fēminīs placet**, you know that **fēminīs** must be _____ case.

A: dative

356. **Fēminīs** is dative because it is the _____ of **placet**.

A: complement

357. You also know that when you have the verbs **indicat, dōnat, dat, reddit,** and **impōnit**, you usually have included in the sentence both the _____ case and the _____ case.

A: accusative   dative

358. Therefore if you find **hominibus** in the environment of **dat**, you realize that **hominibus** is the _____ case.

A: dative

359. Bearing these facts in mind, change this ambiguous dative or ablative from the plural to singular.
plural: **Canibus vir aquam dat.**
singular: _____ **vir aquam dat.**

R: Canī

360. You knew that the personal noun **canibus** was dative because it was the _____ of the verb ___.

A: indirect object
     dat.

---

292. Which ablative singulars have the variant ∅ plus length of the characteristic vowel?

A: simiā, lupō, virō, rēgnō, manū, rē, diē

293. Which ablative singulars have the variant ∅ *without* length of the vowel?

A: cane, leōne, genere

294. Remembering that the combination **ai** is written **ae**, tell which dative singulars have the variant -ī?

A: simiae, canī, leōnī, generī, manuī, reī, diēī

295. Which dative singulars have the ambiguous form which is like the ablative singular?

A: lupō, virō, rēgnō

296. Which genitive singulars have the variant -ī?

A: simiae, lupī, virī, rēgnī, reī, diēī

297. Which genitive singulars have the variant -s?

A: canis, leōnis, generis, manūs (Note that **manūs** has a long **u**.)

298. Now for the *plural*. Which nominative plurals have the variant -ī?

A: simiae, lupī, virī

299. Which nominative plurals have the variant of length of vowel and -s?

A: canēs, leōnēs, manūs, rēs, diēs

300. Which nominative plurals have the variant -a?

A: rēgna, genera

23-43

21-59

361. Change the ambiguous dative or ablative word from plural to singular.

plural: **Crūdēlis lacrimīs pāscitur, nōn frangitur.**
singular: **Crūdēlis _____ pāscitur, nōn frangitur.**

◼ ◼

R: **lacrimā**

362. Change the ambiguous dative or ablative word from plural to singular.

plural: **Titus vīnum convīvīs dat.**
singular: **Titus vīnum _____ dat.**

◼ ◼

R: **convīvae**

363. You knew that **convīvīs** was _____ because _____.

◼ ◼

A: dative it was the indirect object of **dat**.

364. Change the ambiguous dative or ablative word from plural to singular.

plural: **Inopibus beneficium bis dat quī dat celeriter.**
singular: **_____ beneficium bis dat quī dat celeriter.**

◼ ◼

R: **Inopī**

365. You knew that **inopibus** was dative because _____.

◼ ◼

A: it was the indirect object of **dat**.

366. Change the ambiguous dative or ablative words from plural to singular.

plural: **In omnibus rēbus vincit imitātiōnem vēritās.**
singular: **In _____ _____ vincit imitātiōnem vēritās.**

◼ ◼

R: **omnī rē**

23-42

285. **Mēns rēgnum bona possidet.** (28) "Cui similis est philosophus?" "R____."

◼

R: **Rēgī.**

286. **Ars longa, vīta brevis.** (52) "Quōrum vīta brevis est?" "H____."

◼

R: **Hominum.**

287-307. One of the interesting things about the Latin noun system is that there is not a *single case*, either in the singular or plural, which does not have two or more variant signals. Those who are interested in seeing what the system is may proceed with this sequence. Those who are not may go directly to the Summary. There will be nothing from this sequence on the Unit Test. Some people find that this kind of talk about the language helps them; others find it only confusing. Take your choice.

287. Turn to the pages in your Notebook where you have the noun paradigms. In the nominative singular, which forms have the variant **-s**?

◼

A: **lupus, canis, manus, rēs, diēs** (*not* **genus**).

◼ ◼

288. Which nominative singulars have the variant Ø?

◼

A: **sīmia, vir, leō, genus**

◼ ◼

289. Which nominative singulars have the variant **-m**?

◼

A: **rēgnum**

◼ ◼

290. Which accusative singulars have the variant **-m**?

◼

A: **sīmiam, lupum, virum, rēgnum, canem, leōnem, manum, rem, diem**

◼ ◼

291. Which accusative singulars have the variant Ø?

◼

A: **genus**

◼ ◼

21-60

367. The phrase **in omnibus rēbus** is ablative, as you can tell, because ――――――.

A: of the word **in**, which is a preposition.

SUMMARY

368. The main point upon which you worked in this Unit was the ―― ――.

A: dative plural.

369. The difficult part about the dative plural is ――――――――――.

A: it is *always* identical with the ablative plural.

370. You learned eight new verbs. The five which take their complement in the dative are im＿＿, pl＿＿, no＿＿, nū＿＿, and s＿＿＿.

A: **imperat, placet, nocet, nūbit,** servit.

371. You learned a new adjective, which like **similis**, nearly always patterns with the dative case. This word, which means "near," is pro＿＿＿.

A: **proximus.**

372-380. You learned the declension of the following nouns: **musca, aeger, agnus, vitium, nāvis, mulier, corpus, flētus,** and **rēs**.

372. Write [or say] the paradigm of **nāvis**.

R: nāvis   nāvēs
     nāvem   nāvēs
     nāve   nāvibus
     nāvī   nāvibus

[Be sure you are working in the most efficient way.]

---

278. Religiō deōs colit, superstitiō violat. (37) "Quibus nocet superstitiō?" "――――."

R: Dīs (vel Deīs).

[Both forms are acceptable, although **Dīs** is more common.]

279-286. This last sequence will be just a bit different from the other three. In it you will answer not with a word in the Basic Sentence but with some word which gives a sensible answer to the question. Here are the words which will furnish reasonable answers.

279. ★ ○ •
   sapiēns   sapientēs
   sapientem   sapientēs
   sapiente   sapientibus
   sapientī   sapientibus
   sapientis   sapientium

280. ★ ○ •
   mulier   mulierēs
   mulierem   mulierēs
   muliere   mulieribus
   mulierī   mulieribus
   mulieris   mulierum

281. ★ ○ •   **282.** ★ ○ •
   rēx   rēgēs   homō   hominēs
   rēgem   rēgēs   hominem   hominēs
   rēge   rēgibus   homine   hominibus
   rēgī   rēgibus   hominī   hominibus
   rēgis   rēgum   hominis   hominum

283. Sapientia vīnō obumbrātur. (27) "Quālibus hominibus vīnum nocet?" "Etiam ――――."

R: Etiam sapientibus.

284. Vulpēs vult fraudem, lupus agnum, fēmina laudem. (15) "Cui laus placet?" "Mul――."

R: Mulierī.

21-61

373. Write [or say] the paradigm of **corpus**.

R:
corpus	corpora
corpus	corpora
corpore	corporibus
corporī	corporibus

374. Write [or say] the paradigm of **aeger**.

R:
aeger	aegrī
aegrum	aegrōs
aegrō	aegrīs
aegrō	aegrīs

375. Write [or say] the paradigm of **rēs**.

R:
rēs	rēs
rem	rēs
rē	rēbus
reī	rēbus

376. Write [or say] the paradigm of **vitium**.

R:
vitium	vitia
vitium	vitia
vitiō	vitiīs
vitiō	vitiīs

377. Write [or say] the paradigm of **musca**.

R:
musca	muscae
muscam	muscās
muscā	muscīs
muscae	muscīs

378. Write [or say] the paradigm of **mulier**.

R:
mulier	mulierēs
mulierem	mulierēs
muliere	mulieribus
mulierī	mulieribus

---

270. Impōnit fīnem sapiēns et rēbus honestīs. (78) "Quōrum fīnem cognōscit sapiēns?" "‗‗‗‗‗."

R: Rērum honestārum.

271. ★ ○ •
musca	muscae	Deus	dī
muscam	muscās	Deum	deōs
muscā	muscīs	Deō	dīs
muscae	muscīs	Deō	dīs

272. ★ ○ •
| musca | muscae | Dei | deōrum |

273. ★ ○ •
crūdēlis	crūdēlēs
crūdēlem	crūdēlēs
crūdēlī	crūdēlibus
crūdēlī	crūdēlibus
crūdēlī	crūdēlium

("cruel person")

274. ★ ○ •
rēs hūmāna	rēs hūmānae
rem hūmānam	rēs hūmānās
rē hūmānā	rēbus hūmānīs
rei hūmānae	rēbus hūmānīs
reī hūmānae	rērum hūmānārum

275. Aquila nōn capit muscās. (36) "Quōrum mortem nōn vult aquila?" "‗‗‗‗‗."

R: Muscārum.

276. Rērum hūmānārum domina Fortūna. (92) "Quālibus rēbus imperat Fortūna?" "‗‗‗‗‗."

R: Rēbus hūmānīs.

277. Crūdēlis lacrimīs pāscitur, nōn frangitur. (39) "Cui lacrimae placent?" "‗‗‗‗‗."

R: Crūdēlī.

379. Write [or say] the paradigm of **flētus**.

R: flētus   flētūs
    flētum   flētūs
    flētū   flētibus
    flētuī   flētibus

380. Write [or say] the paradigm of **agnus**.

R: agnus   agnī
    agnum   agnōs
    agnō   agnīs
    agnō   agnīs

381-386. You learned six new Basic Sentences.

381. Education serves our life (but) wisdom commands it = A____ s_____ v____, s_____ i_____.

R: Artēs serviunt vītae, sapientia imperat. (73)

382. N___ l____ e__, quī c_____ s_____.

R: Nēmō līber est, quī corporī servit. (74)

383. He is near the gods whom reason, (and) not anger moves = D__ pr_____ il__ e__ qu__ r____, n__ ī__, m_____.

R: Dīs proximus ille est quem ratiō, nōn īra, movet. (75)

---

262. Nōn semper aurem facilem habet Fēlicitās. (10) "Cujus aurēs nōn semper dicta nostra audiunt?" "_____."

R: Fēlicitātis.

263. ★ ○ •

mūs   mūrēs   asinī   asinōrum
mūrem   mūrēs   asinōs   asinōrum
mūre   mūribus   asinō   asinīs
mūrī   mūribus   asinō   asinīs
mūris   mūrum   asinī   asinōrum

264. ★ ○ •

265. ★ ○ •

fortis   fortēs
fortem   fortēs
fortī   fortibus
fortī   fortibus
fortis   fortium

("brave person")

266. ★ ○ •

rēs honesta   rēs honestae
rem honestam   rēs honestās
rē honestā   rēbus honestīs
reī honestae   rēbus honestīs
reī honestae   rērum honestārum

267. Elephantus nōn capit mūrem. (5) "Quōrum animālium nōn sunt elephantī captōrēs?" "_____."

R: Mūrum.

268. Fortūna fortēs metuit, ignāvōs premit. (41) "Quibus servit Fortūna?" "_____."

R: Fortibus.

269. Ex auribus cognōscitur asinus. (43) "Cujus aurēs stultitiam indicant?" "_____."

R: Asinī.

384. One ungrateful person harms all miserable persons = In_____ ū___ om_____ m_____ n_____.

R: Ingrātus ūnus omnibus miserīs nocet. (76)

385. M_____ qu__ m_____ n____, m_____ n__ pl____.

R: Mulier quae multīs nūbit, multīs nōn placet. (77)

386. Im_____ f____ s_____ __ r____ h_____.

R: Impōnit fīnem sapiēns et rēbus honestīs. (78)

If there are any of these Basic Sentences which you do not know, study them *now*.

VOCABULARY INVENTORY

(Remember that the asterisk means a new meaning for a familiar word.)

Nouns: **fīnis** (310) *****ars** (137) *****ratiō** (170)
  *****rēs** (316)

---

255. ★ ○ •

senex	senēs	fātum	Fāta
senem	senēs	fātum	Fāta
sene	senibus	fātō	Fātīs
senī	senibus	fātō	Fātīs
senis	senum	fātī	Fātōrum

256. ★ ○ •

257. ★ ○ •

fēlīcitās	fēlīcitātēs
fēlīcitātem	fēlīcitātēs
fēlīcitāte	fēlīcitātibus
fēlīcitātī	fēlīcitātibus
fēlīcitātis	fēlīcitātum

258. ★ ○ •

fēmina	fēminae
fēminam	fēminās
fēminā	fēminīs
fēminae	fēminīs
fēminae	fēminārum

[If you have learned the noun system, a single echo will be enough practice. If you have not learned the nouns, *this* is the time to do it.]

259. Mors īnfantī fēlīx, juvenī acerba, nimis sēra senī. (71) "Quibus hominibus est mors nimis sēra?" "_____."

R: Senibus.

260. Dūcunt volentem Fāta, nōlentem trahunt. (45) "Quōrum sub rēgnō sunt omnēs, volentēs et nōlentēs?" "_____."

R: Fātōrum.

261. Malō in cōnsiliō fēminae vincunt virōs. (38) "Quōrum cōnsilium malum est?" "_____."

R: Fēminārum.

21-64

Verbs: *colit (112)   movet (170)
        comparat (180) nocet (189)
        *dūcit (258)   nūbit (266)
        imperat (87)   placet (235)
        impōnit (287)   servit (113)

Adjectives: miser, misera, miserum (194)
            proximus-a-um (69)
            honestus-a-um (316)
            līber, lībera, līberum (149)

Intensifier: et (301)

TEST INFORMATION

You will be asked to write paradigms different from the nine you practiced in this Unit. However, they will be nouns whose forms you have practiced in drills in this lesson. In any event, as far as the paradigm goes, the new form, dative plural, is *always* like the ablative plural.

You will be asked to do drills similar to but not identical with those you did in this Unit. However, you will not be asked to produce any form which you have not practiced in some way.

23-37

250. Quī rēgī nōn placet magnō in perīc'lō est. Gr...... ī...... r...... s.......

R: **Gravis īra rēgum est semper.** (93)

251. Fortūna vītam mortālium regit. R...... h........ d...... F........

R: **Rērum hūmānārum domina Fortūna.** (92)

252. Placet memoria perīc'lōrum quae praeterita sunt. J........ m........ ---pr...........m.........

R: **Jūcunda memoria est praeteritōrum malōrum.** (91)

253. Orbis jūstus jūdex est. S........ j........ or...... t...........

R: **Sēcūrus jūdicat orbis terrārum.** (90)

254-278. We will end this Unit with a review of Basic Sentences which will give you practice on the forms of nouns and adjectives. These will be in sequences of five. First we will ask you to echo the paradigm of the nouns which you will use in the answers. Then we will ask you one question on each of four Basic Sentences.

254. In this sequence, answer with a word which occurs in the Basic Sentence. Be sure to answer with a word in the same ----- and ----- as the question word.

A: ----- number case

[Review the question word **Quis?**, **Quid?** in your Reference Notebook if you are not sure of the forms.]

UNIT TWENTY-TWO

22-1

1. Latin has an adjective which emphasizes the noun it modifies. Echo your teacher as he says that it's the woman herself. ★ ○ • ○ • _ _ t f _ _ _ _ _ ip _ _ _.

Cōnf: Est fēmina ipsa.

2. Echo as he says that it is the bull itself. ★ ○ • ○ • _ _ t t _ _ _ _ _ i _ _ e.

Cōnf: Est taurus ipse.

3. Echo as he says that it is the family itself. ★ ○ • ○ • _ _ t g _ _ _ _ i _ _ _ m.

Cōnf: Est genus ipsum.

4. Echo the nominative forms of this word.
                m   f   n
    ★ ○ • ○ •   ipse   ipsa   ipsum

5. Most of the forms of this word are like **bonus, bona, bonum**. The irregular form in the nominative singular is _____.

A: ipse.

6. In the sentence **Fēmina ipsam pictūram videt**, the word **ipsam** modifies the word _____.

A: pictūram.

7. **Fēmina ipsam pictūram videt** = _____ _____.

A: The woman sees the picture itself.

8. We might have said in English, "The woman sees the *picture*." We put extra stress on the word "picture" to show that in Latin the word **pictūram** was modified by _____.

A: ipsam.

23-36

243. ★ ○ • ○ • M_ _ _ _ r_ _ _ _ _ au_ _ at_ _ oc_ _ _. (95)

Cōnf: Multae rēgum aurēs atque oculī.

244. ★ ○ • ○ • N_ _ m_ _ _ _ _ _ om_ _ _ _ _ h_ _ _ s_ _ _ _. (96)

Cōnf: Nēmō mortālium omnibus hōris sapit.

245. ★ ○ • ○ • J_ _ _ _ _ _ _ om_ _ _ _ d_ _ _ _ _ r_ _ _ _ v_ _ _ _ _ _ _. (97)

Cōnf: Jūstitia omnium est domina et rēgīna virtūtum.

246-252. From the last eight Basic Sentences which we have had, produce the one which most nearly fits the thought of these statements. Review in your Notebook first if you like.

246. **Bonus est quī jūstē agit.** J_ _ _ _ _ _ _ om_ _ _ est d_ _ _ _ e_ _ r_ _ _ _ _ v_ _ _ _ _ _ _.

R: **Jūstitia est domina et rēgīna virtūtum.** (97)

247. **Multī sunt quī omnia quae vident et audiunt rēgī suō dīcunt.** M_ _ _ _ _ r_ _ _ _ a_ _ _ _ at_ _ oc_ _ _.

R: **Multae rēgum aurēs atque oculī.** (95)

248. (**Pereunt** is the irregular plural of **perit**.) **Fortēs nōn rē vērā pereunt, sī memoria manet.** V_ _ _ _ m_ _ _ _ _ _ _ _ _ _ v_ _ _ _ _ _ _ p_ _ _ _ _ _.

R: **Vīta mortuōrum in memoriā vīvōrum est posita.** (94)

249. **Etiam sapiēns nōn numquam stultus est.** N_ _ _ _ m_ _ _ _ _ _ _ _ _ _ om_ _ _ _ _ h_ _ _ s_ _ _ _.

R: **Nēmō mortālium omnibus hōris sapit.** (96)

22-2

9. We will now take up the *last* of the Latin cases. Ask your teacher whether this is the woman herself; he will answer that it isn't the woman herself but a picture of a woman. Echo him. "**Estne fēmina ipsa?**" ★ ○ • ○ • "**Nōn est fē____ ip__ s__ p_____ f____ae.**"

Cōnf: Nōn est fēmina ipsa sed pictūra fēminae.

10. Now you answer in the same way. "**Estne sīmia ipsa?**" "**Nōn est s_____ a s__ p_____ s___ae.**" √ ★ ○ • [Say aloud first; *then* check.]

R: Nōn est sīmia ipsa sed pictūra sīmiae.

11. "**Estne taurus ipse?**" ★ ○ • ○ • "**N__ ____ t_____ ___e s__ p_____ t___ī.**"

R: Nōn est taurus ipse sed pictūra taurī.

23-35

Quaestiōnēs et Respōnsa

236. "Quis omnēs virtūtēs regit?" "_____."

R: Jūstitia.

237. "Ā quō omnēs virtūtēs reguntur?" "_____."

R: Ā Jūstitiā.

238. "Cujus sub rēgnō sunt omnēs virtūtēs?" "_____."

R: Jūstitiae sub rēgnō.

239. "Quibus imperat jūstitia?" "_____."

R: Omnibus virtūtibus.

240. "Cui serviunt omnēs virtūtēs?" "_____."

R: Jūstitiae.

241. Justice is the mistress and queen of all the virtues = Jūst____ om_____ ○ • V_____ dom____ = rēg___ vir_____.

R: Jūstitia omnium est domina et rēgīna virtūtum.

242-245. Here is a quick review on the last four Basic Sentences by echoing them. If you need more study, turn to your Notebook.

242. ★ ○ • ○ • V_____ m_____ in m_____ (94) p_____ v_____.

Cōnf: Vīta mortuōrum in memoriā vīvōrum est posita.

22-3

12. "Estne agnus ipse?" "Nōn est ag___ ipse sed p_____ ag_ī." √ ★ ○ •

R: Nōn est agnus ipse sed pictūra agnī.

13. "Estne leō ipse?" ★ ○ • ○ • "N__ ___ l__ ___ e s__ p_____ l___is."

R: Nōn est leō ipse sed pictūra leōnis.

14. "Estne īnfāns?" "N__ ___ īn____ ___e s__ p_____ īn____is." √ ★ ○ •

R: Nōn est īnfāns ipse sed pictūra īnfantis.

---

228. Jūstitia omnium est domina et rēgīna virtūtum. √ ★ ○ • (97)

229. J ○ ○ ★ ○ ○ ____ om____ d___ ___ r____ v____.

R: Jūstitia omnium est domina et rēgīna virtūtum.

230. There is an adjective in this sentence. If it modifies a noun, then draw an arrow from it to the noun it modifies. If there is no noun for it to modify, then say what this adjective means when used as a noun.

R: Jūstitia omnium est domina et rēgīna virtūtum.

231. "Cujus cāsūs et cujus numerī est 'omnium virtūtum'?"

R: "Omnium virtū-tum" est cāsūs genitīvī et numerī plūrālis.

232. You know that the word jūstus means "just"; then the noun jūstitia must mean _____.

A: justice.

233. Jūstitia omnium est domina et rēgīna virtūtum = the _____ ___ of ___ the _____s.

A: Justice is the mistress and queen of all the virtues.

234. Copy in your Notebook.

235. This means that _____ [In your own words]

A: doing the just thing is the best of all the virtues.

22-4

15. "Estne quercus ipsa?" ★ ○ • ○ • "_ _ _
_ _ _ _ _ _ _ _ _ _ _ _ _ _ _ ūs."

R: Nōn est quercus ipsa sed pictūra quercūs.

16. "Estne anus ipsa?" "N_ _ e_ _ _ _ _ _ _
_ _ _ p_ _ _ _ _ _ _ūs." √ ★ ○ •

R: Nōn est anus ipsa sed pictūra anūs.

17. "Estne effigiēs ipsa?" ★ ○ • ○ • "_ _ _
_ _ _ _ _ _ _ _ _ _ _ _ _ _ _ ēī."

R: Nōn est effigiēs ipsa sed pictūra effigiēī.

23-33

221. Nēmō mortālium omnibus hōrīs
sapit = _ _ _ _ _ _ _ _ _ _ _ at _ _ _ _ _ _ _ _ _ _ _.

A: No mortal is wise at all hours.

Quaestiōnēs et Respōnsa

222. "Quālem hominem facit vīnum ex sapiente?" "St_ _ _ _ _ h_ _ _ _ _ _."

R: Stultum hominem.

223. "Sapitne semper philosophus?" "_ _ _ _ _ _ _ _ _ _."

R: Nōn semper sapit.

224. "Quam virtūtem nōn semper possidet philosophus?" "_ _ _ _ _ _ _ _ _ _ _."

R: Sapientiam.

225. The combination nōn numquam ("not never") means "some_ _ _ _ _s."

A: sometimes.

226. "Quod vitium nōn numquam possidet etiam sapiēns?" "St_ _ _ _ _ _ _ _ _."

R: Stultitiam.

227. N_ _ ★ √ ○ • (96) mor_ _ _ _ omn_ _ _ _ h_ _ _ _ sap_ _ _.

R: Nēmō mortālium omnibus hōrīs sapit.

18. "Estne faciēs ipsa?" "N__ __t _____ ____ ___ _____ ___ēī."

R: Nōn est faciēs ipsa sed pictūra faciēī.

19-28. Go through this sequence again, saying that it isn't the person (animal, etc.) itself but a picture.

19. "Estne īnfāns ipse?" "Nōn est īnfāns ipse sed pictūra _____is."

R: Nōn est īnfāns ipse sed pictūra īnfantis.

20. "Estne quercus ipsa?" "N__ est qu___ ___a sed p_____ _____ūs."

R: Nōn est quercus ipsa sed pictūra quercūs.

---

214. Homō sub rēgnō fātī est → H___ s__ r____ F____. ∨ ★ ○ •

R: Homō sub rēgnō Fātōrum est.

215. Perīc'lum taurī magnum est → ∨ ★ ○ • p___ t_, m____

R: Perīc'lum taurōrum magnum est.

216. Nēmō mortālium omnibus hōris sapit. ∨ ★ ○ • (96)

217. ★ ○ ○ N___ m_____ o_____ h___ ____.

R: Nēmō mortālium omnibus hōris sapit.

218. Cujus cāsūs et cujus numerī est "mortālium"?

R: "Mortālium" est cāsūs genitīvī et numerī plūrālis.

219. We are constantly getting more and more structures which sound strange if translated into nearest corresponding English construction. Nēmō mortālium might be translated as "N__ of m___als."

A: Nobody of mortals.

220. But it sounds much better to translate it by "No m_____."

A: mortal.

21. "Estne fēmina ipsa?" "N__ __t f_____
 ___ s__ p_____ _____ae."

R: Nōn est fēmina ipsa sed pictūra fēminae.

22. "Estne agnus ipse?" "___ ___ ag___
 ___ s__ _____ ___ī."

R: Nōn est agnus
ipse sed pictūra agnī.

23. "Estne leō ipse?" "___ ___ ___ ___
 _____ ____is."

R: Nōn est leō ipse sed
pictūra leōnis.

Change the italicized genitives from singular to plural.

R: Multae rēgum aurēs atque oculī.

208. M__ ___ V ★ ○ • (95)
 r___ a___ a___ o_____.

209. Vīta *hominis* brevis est → V___
 h_____ br___ e___ V ★ ○ •
R: Vīta
hominum brevis est.

210. Laus *ducis* blanda est → L___ d___
 bl___st. V ★ ○ •
R: Laus ducum
blanda est.

211. Īra *puellae* gravis est → Ī___ p_____
 gr___ V ★ ○ •
R: Īra puellārum
gravis est.

212. Hōrae *diēī* longae sunt → H____
 d___ l___s__ V ★ ○ •
R: Hōrae
diērum longae sunt.

213. Mors *senis* sēra est → M___ s____
 s____ V ★ ○ •
R: Mors senum
sēra est.

199. Its most common use is to connect two words which are the same part of speech. In this sentence atque connects two ____s.

A: nouns.

200. M____ ○ ○ ★ r____ a____ a____ : ____

R: Multae rēgum aurēs atque oculī.

201. Vōx "rēgum" hāc in sententiā est cāsūs ____, ____ numerī ____.

R: genitīvī plūrālis.

202. Multae rēgum aurēs atque oculī = M____ s____ s of ____s.

A: Many are the eyes and ears of kings.

203. Copy in your Notebook.

204. This means that ____ [In your own words]

A: there are always plenty of people ready to tell kings what they see and hear.

Quaestiōnēs et Respōnsa

205. "Quī habent multōs oculōs atque aurēs?" "____."

R: Rēgēs.

206. "Ā quibus multa cernuntur atque audiuntur?" "____."

R: Ā rēgibus.

207. "Quibus multae rēs dīcuntur?" "____."

R: Rēgibus.

---

24. "Estne taurus ipse?" "____ ī."

R: Nōn est taurus ipse sed pictūra taurī.

25. "Estne effigiēs ipsa?" "____ ēī."

R: Nōn est effigiēs ipsa sed pictūra effigiēī.

26. "Estne sīmia ipsa?" "____ ae."

R: Nōn est sīmia ipsa sed pictūra sīmiae.

22-8

27. "Estne lacus ipse?" "_____ūs."

R: Nōn est lacus ipse sed pictūra lacūs.

28. "Estne faciēs ipsa?" "_____ēī."

R: Nōn est faciēs ipsa sed pictūra faciēī.

29. Echo a new technical term. ★ ○ • ○ •
Genitive case

VCh: "jénn-nit-tiv"

30. Echo these examples of the genitive case, singular number, representing the five declensions. ★ ○ •

I	II	III	IV	V
fēminae	taurī	īnfantis	quercūs	effigiēī

31. Echo these other examples of the genitive case. ★ ○ •

I	II	III	IV	V
sīmiae	agnī	leōnis	lacūs	faciēī

23-29

Quaestiōnēs et Respōnsa

193. "Quōs vīvī in memoriā tenent?"

R: Mortuōs.

194. "In quō est posita vīta mortuōrum?"

R: In memoriā vīvōrum.

195. "Ā quibus fortēs mortuī laudantur?"

R: Ā vīvīs.

196. V____ ★ ○ • (94)
mort____ mem____ vīv____ pos____

R: Vīta mortuōrum in memoriā vīvōrum est posita.

197. Multae rēgum aurēs atque oculī. ★ ○ • (95)

198. Like *et*, the new word *atque* is a connective and serves to connect ____ things.

A: equal

32. The chief use of the genitive case is to show that one noun modifies another noun. In the sentence **Est pictūra īnfantis,** the genitive noun _____ modifies the noun _____.

A: īnfantis   pictūra.

33. Under "Facts About Latin," copy the following: In **Latin: Level One** the only use of the genitive case is to have one noun modify another.

34. You will remember that when the word **similis** occurs in Latin, it almost always patterns with a noun in the dative case, to show what the person or thing is l___.

A: like.

35. In this same way, when we use the word "part" as in "This is part," we would almost always want to ask the question, "Part of wh__?"

A: Part of what?

36. Echo your teacher as he asks you if the foot is the whole frog. ★ ○ • ○ • "___ne p__ t___ r___?"

Cōnf: Estne pēs tōta rāna?

37. From the Latin adjective **tōtus, tōta, tōtum** we have an English derivative, as in the sentence, "He wrote down the ___al amount of the bill."

A: total

---

185. *Vita mortuōrum in memoriā vīvōrum est posita.* (94) ∨ ★ ○ •

186. ∨ ○ ○ ★ m ___ ___ m ___ ___ . v ___ ___ p ___ ___

R: *Vita mortuōrum in memoriā vīvōrum est posita.*

187. "Quae vōcēs hāc in sententiā sunt cāsūs genitīvī?" "_____ et _____."

R: *Mortuōrum et vīvōrum.*

188. The adjective **mortuus** is connected with the word **mors. Mortuus** means "d___."

A: dead.

189. **Mortuus** and **vīvus** are adjectives and antonyms. *Vīta mortuōrum in memoriā vīvōrum est posita* = ___ l___ ___ ___ ___ ___ d ___ ___ m ___ ___ ___ ___ .

A: The life of the dead is placed in the memory of the living.

190. Copy in your Notebook.

191. This means that _____. [In your own words]

192. Although **vīvus** and **mortuus** are adjectives, in this sentence they were _____. [In your own words]

A: people who die continue to live because their loved ones remember them.

A: used as nouns.

38. Ask your teacher the same Latin question, "Is the foot the whole frog?" "___ne p__ t___ r___?" ✓ ★ ○ •

Cōnf: Estne pēs tōta rāna?

39. Write down his answer. ★ ○ ○ "M___ē, p__ est pars r____."

R: Minimē, pēs est pars rānae.

40-43. Answer these questions in the same way; it is not the whole thing but only part of it.

40. "Estne manus tōtus elephantus?" "M_____; m____ ___ p___ _____ī."

R: Minimē; manus est pars elephantī.

41. "Estne angulus tōtus orbis?" "M_____; an_____ ___ p___ ___is."

R: Minimē; angulus est pars orbis.

---

179. "In quō est maximum perīc'lum?" "_____."

R: In īrā rēgum.

180. G____ī_ r__ e__ s____ ✓ ★ ○ •

181-184. Echo the four Basic Sentences which you have had in this Unit so far.

R: Gravis īra rēgum est semper. [According to the instructions, you should have said, checked, and written.]

181. ★ ○ • S____ j___ or___ t____. (90)

Cōnf: Sēcūrus jūdicat orbis terrārum.

182. ★ ○ • J___ m___ ___ pr___ ___rd _____m _____. (91)

Cōnf: Jūcunda memoria est praeteritōrum malōrum.

183. ★ ○ • R___ h___ d___ F___ ____. (92)

Cōnf: Rērum hūmānārum domina Fortūna.

184. ★ ○ • Gr__ ī_ r___ ___ s_____. (93)

Cōnf: Gravis īra rēgum est semper.

42. "Estne gradus tōta porticus?" "____; _____ ___ p___ ____ūs."

R: Minimē; gradus est pars porticūs.

43. "Estne hōra tōta diēs?" "_____ _____ēī."

R: Minimē; hōra est pars diēī.

44. The new word **hōra** must mean "h____."

A: hour.

45. Echo the singular paradigm of the question word. ★ ○ • ○ •

m&f	n
quis?	quid?
quem?	quid?
quō?	quō?
cui?	cui?
cujus?	cujus?

46. Add the dative and genitive cases to the paradigm of **Quis?** in your Notebook.

47. Answer your teacher as he asks whose ears are short. "Cujus aurēs brevēs sunt?" "____ae aurēs brevēs sunt." √ ★ ○ •

R: Sīmiae aurēs brevēs sunt.

---

171. Can **gravis** therefore modify **īra**? ____ (Yes/No).

A: Yes

(It could also modify a genitive that has not yet appeared, but we will help you out by telling you that **gravis** does modify **īra**.)

172. However, there is an ambiguity. **Gravis īra** can be subject of any one of the sentence types we have had, with **gravis** modifying **īra** directly. On the other hand, **gravis** could be one of the {-s}'s in an {-s = est} kernel. In an {-s-m-t} kernel **gravis īra** would mean, "S____ a____ s____ ____."

A: Serious anger blanks somebody.

173. If **gravis** were one of the {-s}'s in an {-s = est} kernel then **gravis īra** would mean, "____ ____."

A: Anger is serious.

174. **Gravis īra rēgum est** = ____ ____ ____ ____.

A: Anger of kings is serious.

175. **Gravis īra rēgum est semper** = ____ ____ ____.

A: The anger of kings is always serious.

176. Copy in your Notebook.

Quaestiōnēs et Respōnsa

177. "Quantō in perīculō est quī rēgibus nōn placet?" "____ ____."

R: Magnō in perīculō.

178. "Quōrum īram omnēs timent?" "____ ____."

R: Rēgum īram.

22-12

48-50. In this sequence we will ask you questions on three pictures, all of which require as an answer a genitive of the First Declension noun like **sīmiae**.

48. "Cujus oculī magnī sunt?" "R____ oculī magnī sunt."

R: Rānae
oculī magnī sunt.

49. "Cujus forma brevis est?" "Pue____ f____ br____ est."

R: Puellae
forma brevis est.

50. "Cujus vīnum acerbum est?" "Con-v____ _____ _____ ___."

R: Convīvae vīnum acerbum est.

---

164. *Gravis īra rēgum est semper.* ✓ ○ ★ •

165. ★ ○ ○ G_____ ī__ r___ s_____ .

R: *Gravis īra rēgum est semper.*

166. "Quae vōx hāc in sententiā est cāsūs genitīvī et numerī plūrālis?" "_____."

R: Rēgum.

167. Echo the paradigm of *gravis*. ★ ○ ●

m & f	m & f	n	n
gravis	grave	gravēs	gravia
gravem	grave	gravēs	gravia
gravī	gravī	gravibus	gravibus
gravī	gravī	gravibus	gravibus
gravis	gravis	gravium	gravium

168. *Gravis* can be either _____ case, _____ number, or _____ .

A: nominative or genitive singular

169. In order to tell whether *gravis* is nominative or genitive case we must _____ [In your own words]

A: wait for the noun it modifies.

170. Is *īra* a nominative singular (like **sīmia**) or a nominative-accusative plural (like **Fāta**)?

A: It is nominative singular (like **sīmia**).

(93)

23-25

22-13

51-53. These three questions require a Second Declension noun like **taurī** as an answer.

51. "Cujus dentēs ferōcēs sunt?" "L___
___ ___ ___."

R: Lupī
dentēs ferōcēs sunt.

52. "Cujus vīta in perīc'lō est?" "Eq___
___ ___ ___ ___."

R: Equī
vīta in perīc'lō est.

53. "Cujus aurēs longae sunt?" "As___
___ ___ ___?"

R: Asinī
aurēs longae sunt.

28-24

158. "Cui haec aciēs bene servit?" "___
___."

R: Reī
pūblicae.

159. ★ ○ • IV

irāta anus   irātae anūs
irātam anum   irātae anuī
irātā anū   irātārum anuum
irātīs anibus irātīs anibus
              irātae anūs

160. ★ ○ • III

anus   inopēs
anum   inopem
anūs   inope
anuī   inopibus
anū   inopibus
              inopum

161. "Quibuscum lītigat hic inops?" "___
___ ___."

(irāta anus, inops, irāta anus)

R: Cum
irātīs anibus.

162. "Quālēs anūs sunt?" "___
___."

R: Irātae anūs
sunt.

163. "Cui anūs īram suam indicant?" "___
___."

R: Inopī.

22-14

54-59. These questions require a Third Declension noun like **leōnis**.

54. Cujus auxiliō = By wh--- h---?

A: By whose help?

55. "Cujus auxiliō agnus ex foveā servātur?" "Ju_____."

R: Juvenis auxiliō agnus servātur.

56. Juvenis is an ambiguous form; it could be _____ singular or _____ singular.

A: nominative   genitive

57. In the sentence **Juvenis auxiliō agnus servātur**, the form **juvenis** is _____ case.

A: genitive

58. "Cujus vōcem fēmina timet?" "Mū___ _____ _____ _____."

R: Mūris vōcem fēmina timet.

23-23

151. "Quae animālia hāc in pictūrā celeriter saliunt?" "_____."

R: Rānae.

152. "Ā quō rānae salientēs cernuntur?" "_____."

R: Ā sene.

153. "Quōrum saltūs senex aspicit?" "_____."

R: Rānārum.

154. ★ ○ • ∨   **155.** ★ ○ • ∨

aciēs (no plural)	rēs pūblica
aciem	rem pūblicam
aciē	rē pūblicā
aciēī	reī pūblicae
aciēī	reī pūblicae

156. "Quid omnēs laudant?" "_____."

R: Aciem.

157. "Cui rēs pūblica glōriam dat?" "_____."

R: Aciēī.

59. "Cujus aquam equus bibit?" "Fon___
___ ___ ___."

R: Fontis
aquam equus bibit.

60-62. These questions require a Fourth Declension noun like **lacūs**.

60. "Cujus auxiliō vir īnfantem lavat?"
"A___ ___ ___ ___."

R: Anūs auxiliō vir īnfantem lavat. [If you have ever washed a baby, you know how helpful an old woman can be.]

61. "Cujus auxiliō mūs tenētur?" "Ma___
___ ___ ___."

R: Manūs
auxiliō mūs tenētur.

---

142. "Quōrum corpora in umbrā quercuum sunt?" "___."

R: Taurōrum.

143. "Quōrum umbra taurīs grāta est?" "___."

R: Quercuum.

144. ✱ ○ • III   **145.** ✱ ○ • I

jūdex	jūdicēs	ira	irae
jūdicem	jūdicēs	iram	irās
jūdice	jūdicibus	irā	irīs
jūdicī	jūdicibus	irae	irīs
jūdicis	jūdicum	irae	irārum

146. "Quōrum ira magna est?" "___."

R: Jūdicum.

147. "Quibus fūr nōn placet?" "___."

R: Jūdicibus.

148. "Cujus exemplum jūdicēs nōn laudant?" "___."

R: Fūris.

149. ✱ ○ • I   **150.** ✱ ○ • III

rāna	rānae	senex	senēs
rānam	rānās	senem	senēs
rānā	rānīs	sene	senibus
rānae	rānīs	senī	senibus
rānae	rānārum	senis	senum

22-16

62. "Cujus auxiliō musca canem irrītat?"
"Mors_____ _____ _____ ____ _____"

R: Morsūs auxiliō musca canem irrītat.

63-68. These questions require a Fifth Declension noun like **faciēī**.

63. "Cujus auxiliō dux adjuvātur?" "Aci___
_____ ___ _____"

R: Aciēī
auxiliō dux adjuvātur.

64. "Cujus aspectū fūr invenītur?" "Di___
_____ ___ _____"

R: Diēī
aspectū fūr invenītur.

23-21

136. "Quibus gloria magna accidit?"
"D_____"

R: Ducibus.

137. "Ā quibus duces trahuntur in victōria?" "_____ _____"

R: Ab equīs.

138. "Quōrum victōria ab omnibus laudātur?" "_____ _____"

R: Ducum victōria.

139. ✱ ○ • II   **140.** ✱ ○ • IV

taurus taurī	quercus quercūs
taurum taurōs	quercum quercūs
taurī taurōrum	quercūs quercuum
taurō taurīs	quercuī quercibus
taurō taurīs	quercū quercibus

141. "Quibus umbra quercuum placet?"
"_____"

R: Taurīs.

65. This means that the th___ is f___d by the ap_____ce of the dayl___t.

A: thief is found by the appearance of the daylight.

66. "Cujus gravitāte premitur servus?" "Ef_____ _____ _____ _____."

R: **Effigieī gravitāte premitur servus.**

67. Remember that the servants of the Romans were not free persons but sl___s.

A: slaves.

68. The last Latin sentence said that the sl___ is cr___ed by the w_____ of the _____.

A: slave is crushed by the weight of the statue.

69-72. Now you will not be told what declension the nouns belong to.

69. "Cujus formam vir aspicit?" "_____ _____ ___ _____."

R: **Effigieī formam vir aspicit.**

---

129. ★ ○ • V

    effigiēs (no plural)
    effigiem
    effigiē
    effigiēī
    effigiēī

130. ★ ○ •

vir ēloquēns   virī ēloquentēs
virum ēloquentem   virōs ēloquentēs
virō ēloquentī   virīs ēloquentibus
virō ēloquentī   virīs ēloquentibus
virī ēloquentis   virōrum ēloquentium

131. "Quid vir ēloquēns laudat?" "_____."

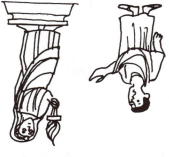

R: **Effigiem.**

132. "Cui vir ēloquēns laudem dat?" "_____."

R: **Effigieī.**

133. "Quālī ā virō effigiēs laudātur?" "_____."

R: **Ēloquentī ā virō.**

134. ★ ○ • III   **135.** ★ ○ • II

dux   ducēs   equus   equī
ducem   ducēs   equum   equōs
duce   ducibus   equō   equīs
ducī   ducibus   equō   equīs
ducis   ducum   equī   equōrum

22-18

70. "Cujus in umbrā taurī stant?" "_____."

R: Quercūs in umbrā taurī stant.

71. "Cujus pedēs magnī sunt?" "_____."

R: Elephantī pedēs magnī sunt.

72. "Cujus ex oculīs dēfluunt lacrimae?" "_____."

R: Īnfantis ex oculīs dēfluunt lacrimae. [If you did not understand the meaning of any of these frames, get some assistance.]

23-19

124. ★ ○ • I

puella	puellae
puellās	puellam
puellīs	puellā
puellīs	puellae
puellae	puellārum

125. ★ ○ • III

flōs	flōrēs
flōrem	flōrēs
flōre	flōribus
flōrī	flōrum
flōris	

126. "Quibus odor flōrum placet?" "P_____."

R: Puellīs.

127. "Quōrum odōrem sentiunt puellae?" "_____ odōrem sentiunt puellae."

[Auxilium invenītur hāc sub līneā.]

Aux: The past participle of *sentīt* is *sēnsus*. *Sentīt* means "feels, senses, smells."

R: Flōrum odōrem sentiunt puellae.

128. "Quās rēs puellae manibus tenent?" "_____."

R: Flōrēs. [If you had trouble answering these three questions, study the paradigms more carefully before going to the pictures.]

22-19

73. In Latin dictionaries it is customary to give both the nominative and genitive cases of nouns. This should remind you of the entire singular paradigm. For example, when you see the word for "truth" listed as **"Vēritās, vēritātis"** you should realize that this is a short way of saying:

	nom	**vēritās**
	acc	---------
	abl	--------
	dat	--------
	gen	**vēritātis**

A:
vēritās
vēritātem
vēritāte
vēritātī
vēritātis

74. The genitive singular of the Second Declension ends in **-ī**. Therefore, when you see **perīc'lum, perīc'lī,** you know that this word belongs to the ____ (1/2/3/4/5) Declension.

A: 2d

75. Pēs, pedis belongs to the ____ (1/2/3/4/5) Declension.

A: 3d

76. Poena, poenae belongs to the ____ (1/2/3/4/5) Declension.

A: 1st

77. Orbis, orbis belongs to the _____.

A: 3d Declension.

78. Oculus, oculī belongs to the _____.

A: 2d Declension.

79. Lacus, lacūs belongs to the _____.

A: 4th Declension.

23-18

116. "Quibus Fortūna imperat?" "_____."

R: Hominibus.

117. "Cui hominēs serviunt?" "_____."

R: Fortūnae.

118-123. Echo the last three Basic Sentences:

118. ✷ • ○ S------ j------ or-- t------.

Conf: Sēcūrus jūdicat orbis terrārum. (90)

119. This means, "_____."

A: The world makes its judgement with security.

120. ✷ • ○ J------ m ------ j ------ m --- pr-- --- m ---------.

Conf: Jūcunda memoria est praeteritōrum malōrum. (91)

121. This means, "_____."

A: Pleasant is the memory of past evils.

122. ✷ • ○ R------ h------ d----- F------.

Conf: Rērum hūmānārum domina Fortūna. (92)

123. This means, "_____."

A: Fortune is the mistress of human affairs.

124-163. The next sequence will consist of eight pictures. You will be asked three questions on each picture. You will first be given a paradigm review of the words which you will use in answering the questions.

80. **Agnus, agnī** belongs to the _____.

A: 2d Declension.

81. **Effigiēs, effigiēī** belongs to the _____.

A: 5th Declension.

82. It is also customary in lists of words to add the gender, using the abbreviations "m," "f," and "n." The dictionary entry for the Latin word for "pitfall" is **fovea, foveae,** f. This means that **fovea** is a _____ Declension noun and _____ gender.

A: First   feminine

83. The listing **cōnsilium, cōnsiliī,** n means that this word belongs to the _____ Declension and is _____ gender.

A: Second
   neuter

84. The genitive form is sometimes abbreviated. The entry **factum-ī,** n means that the genitive of **factum** is _____.

A: **factī.**

85. If you saw the listing **animus-ī,** m. you would know that **animus** is _____ Declension and _____ gender.

A: Second
   masculine

86-90. Echo the singular paradigm of the following nouns representing the five declensions. [Most of you will want to repeat the paradigm several times after echoing.]

86. **rāna-ae,** f (First Declension) ★ ○ •
   rāna
   rānam
   rānā
   rānae
   rānae

108. "**Dominus**" est vir quī servōs possidet. "**Domina**" est fē____ quae servōs possidet.

R: **fēmina**

109. Since a **dominus** is a "m__-er," the feminine form **domina** must mean a "m____ess."

A: master
   mistress

110. This sentence is a {_____} type. [**Auxilium sub hāc līneā est.**]

Aux: Note the two nominatives and no verb.

A: {-s -s est}

111. The adjective **hūmānus** has an obvious English derivative; in this sentence the word **rēs** can be translated as "affairs." The sentence therefore means that _____ is the _____.

A: Fortune is the mistress of human affairs.

112. Copy in your Notebook.

Quaestiōnēs et Respōnsa

113. "**Quālēs rēs regit Fortūna?**" "_____."

R: **Rēs hūmānās.**

114. [In answering this, remember that **hūmānus** is an adjective connected with the word **homō.**] "**Quōs regit Fortūna?**" "_____."

R: **Hominēs.**

115. "**Cujus sub rēgnō sunt omnēs hominēs?**" "_____."

R: **Fortūnae sub rēgnō.**

22-21

87. elephantus-ī, m (Second Declension) ★ ○ •

    elephantus
    elephantum
    elephantō
    elephantō
    elephantī

88. īnfāns, īnfantis, m (Third Declension) ★ ○ •

    īnfāns
    īnfantem
    īnfante
    īnfantī
    īnfantis

[Remember that the **-a-** is long before **-ns**, short before **-nt**.]

89. quercus-ūs, f (Fourth Declension) (In Latin, all trees are feminine gender) ★ ○ •

    quercus
    quercum
    quercū
    quercuī
    quercūs

90. effigiēs-ēī, f (Fifth Declension) ★ ○ •

    effigiēs
    effigiem
    effigiē
    effigiēī
    effigiēī

91-95. Write [or say] the singular paradigm of these same nouns.

91. rāna-ae, f (First Declension) _____

R: rāna
        rānam
        rānā
        rānae
        rānae

23-16

100. Sī mulierēs flent, quārum lacrimae sunt? M_____ l_____ s_____. ∨ ★ ○ •

R: Mulierum lacrimae sunt.

101. Sī auctōrēs opera scrībunt quōrum opera sunt? A_____ o_____ s_____. ∨ ★ ○ •

R: Auctōrum opera sunt.

102. Sī Fāta hominem adjuvant, quārum auxiliō homō adjuvātur? F_____ rum a_____ h_____ ad_____. ∨ ★ ○ •

R: Fātōrum auxiliō homō adjuvātur.

103. Sī fēminae male cōgitant, quārum cōnsilium malum est? F_____ rum c_____ m_____. ∨ ★ ○ •

R: Fēminārum cōnsilium malum est.

104. Sī quercūs agnōs obumbrant, quōrum umbrae agnīs grātae sunt? Qu_____ um u_____ ag_____ gr_____ s_____. ∨ ★ ○ •

R: Quercuum umbrae agnīs grātae sunt.

105. Rērum hūmānārum domina Fortūna. (92) ∨ ★ ○ •

106. ★ ○ ○ R_____ h_____ d_____ F_____.

R: Rērum hūmānārum domina Fortūna.

107. "Quae vōcēs hāc in sententiā sunt cāsūs genitīvī, numerī plūrālis?" "_____ et _____."

R: Rērum hūmānārum.

22-22

92. **elephantus-ī,** m (Second Declension) [Say or write.]

———

R: elephantus
      elephantum
      elephantō
      elephantō
      elephantī

93. **īnfāns, īnfantis,** m (Third Declension)

———

R: īnfāns
      īnfantem
      īnfante
      īnfantī
      īnfantis

94. **quercus-ūs,** f (Fourth Declension) [Say or write.]

———

R: quercus
      quercum
      quercū
      quercuī
      quercūs

95. **effigiēs-ēī,** f (Fifth Declension)

———

R: effigiēs
      effigiem
      effigiē
      effigiēī
      effigiēī

[In the last sequence, you were given your choice of saying or writing the answers. We did this because we wish people to work in the way which is most efficient and quickest for them. The question which you should face now is this: did you really learn the paradigms? Here follows a testing sequence which will show you whether you learned or not.]

23-15

100-104. In this sequence you will be asked questions like, "If women weep, whose tears are they?" to which you reply, "They are women's tears."

R: **Ē**loquentium dictīs jūdex irrītātur.

99. "Quōrum dictīs jūdex irrītātur?" "Ēl_____ d_____ j_____ ir_____."

R: **Ī**nfantium flētūs audiunt mulierēs.

98. "Quōrum flētūs audiunt mulierēs?" "Īnf_____ fl_____ au_____ m_____."

R: **A**rcuum auxiliō virī leōnem vincunt.

97. "Quōrum auxiliō virī leōnem vincunt?" "Arc_____ a_____ v_____ l_____ v_____."

22-23

96-100. Write the following forms.

96. Dative singular of **rāna**: _____

R: rānae

97. Genitive singular of **elephantus**: _____

R: elephantī

98. Ablative singular of **īnfāns**: _____

R: īnfante

99. Dative singular of **quercus**: _____

R: quercuī

100. Genitive singular of **effigiēs**: _____

R: effigiēī

101. In this sequence you will be asked silly questions, like, "If the baby cries, whose tears are they?" Well, they are obviously the ____'s tears.

A: baby's

102. "Sī īnfāns plōrat, cujus lacrimae sunt?" "_____ is l_____ s___."

R: Īnfantis lacrimae sunt.

103. The word which means "if" is _____.

A: sī.

104. "Sī aciēs vincit, cujus victōria est?" "___ēī v_____ __t."

R: Aciēī victōria est.

105. "Sī agnus perit, cujus mors est?" "___ī m___ __t."

R: Agnī mors est.

---

94. "Quōrum aurēs magnae sunt?" "E____ ____ m____ s____."

R: Elephantōrum aurēs magnae sunt.

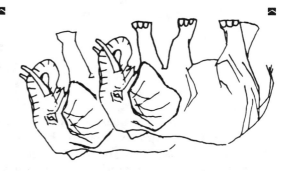

95. "Quōrum morsibus necātur taurus?" "V____ m_____ n____ t____."

R: Vīperārum morsibus necātur taurus.

96-99. This sequence will be like the last except that it will practice the genitive plural of nouns of the Third and Fourth Declensions. All the answers will have the signal -um. We will put in the characteristic vowel -i- if it occurs in any Third Declension word.

96. "Quōrum pictūram pingit juvenis?" "An____ p_____ j_____."

R: Annuum pictūram pingit juvenis.

22-24

106. "Sī effigiēs frangitur, cujus frāctūra est?" "_____ ēī _____."

R: Effigiēī frāctūra est.

107. "Sī mūs mordet, cujus morsus est?" "___is m_____ ___."

R: Mūris morsus est.

108. "Sī rēgīna adjuvat, cujus auxilium est?" "_____ae au_____ ___."

R: Rēgīnae auxilium est.

109. "Sī anus quaerit, cujus quaestiō est?" "__ūs _____ ___."

R: Anūs quaestiō est.

110. "Sī quercus obumbrat, cujus umbra est?" "_____ūs _____ ___."

R: Quercūs umbra est.

111. "Sī fēmina bene cōgitat, cujus cōnsilium bonum est?" "_____ae _____ _____ ___."

R: Fēminae cōnsilium bonum est.

112. "Sī vir lītigat, cujus līs est?" "___ī ___ ___."

R: Virī līs est.

113. Now answer the questions without the help which was given to you before. First, echo the genitive forms which you will use. ★ ○ •
rēgīnae, fēminae, virī, agnī, mūris, īnfantis, anūs, quercūs, effigiēī, aciēī.

23-13

90. _____ f_____ m_____ pr_____ m_____

R: Jūcunda memoria est praeteritōrum malōrum.

91-95. We will now return to practice on the forms of the genitive plural of the First and Second Declensions. All the answers will have the signal -rum.

91. "Quōrum vōcēs audit anus?" "R_____ v___ au___ a___."

R: Rānārum vōcēs audit anus.

92. "Quōrum saltūs cernunt fēminae?" "E_____ s_____ c_____ f_____."

R: Equōrum saltūs cernunt fēminae.

93. "Quōrum cōnsilium stultum est?" "S_____ c_____ s_____ e_____."

R: Simiārum cōnsilium stultum est.

22-25

114. "Cujus victōria est?" "Ac___ v_____ __t."

R: Aciēī victōria est.

115. "Cujus morsus est?" "Mū___ m_____ ___."

R: Mūris morsus est.

116. "Cujus quaestiō est?" "An___ _____ ___."

R: Anūs quaestiō est.

117. "Cujus lacrimae sunt?" "Īn_____ _____ ____."

R: Īnfantis lacrimae sunt.

118. "Cujus līs est?" "V___ ___ ___."

R: Virī līs est.

119. "Cujus umbra est?" "Qu_____ _____ ___."

R: Quercūs umbra est.

120. "Cujus auxilium est?" "Rēg____ _____ ___."

R: Rēgīnae auxilium est.

121. "Cujus frāctūra est?" "Ef_____ ____- ____ ___."

R: Effigiēī frāctūra est.

---

83. Jūcunda memoria est praeteritōrum malōrum = ------ p--- ------ --- -- ---- p--- [Auxilium hāc sub līneā inveniētur.]

Aux: You can guess praeteritōrum if you consider that you can't remember *present* evils or *future* evils.

A: Pleasant is the memory of past evils.

84. Copy in your Notebook.

85. This means that when our difficulties are over ---------------------------------- [In your own words]

A: it is pleasant to remember them.

Quaestiōnēs et Respōnsa

86. "Quālia perīc'la jūcunda sunt, praesentia an praeterita?" "----------." [Auxilium illum invenītur sub hāc līneā.]

Aux: Praesēns is an adjective; it has an obvious English derivative.

R: Praeterita.

87. "Quālia perīc'la acerba sunt, praesentia an praeterita?" "----------."

R: Praeterita.

88. Praesēns is an adjective of the ----- Declension.

A: Third

R: Praesentia.

89. From the form praeteritōrum you can tell that the nominative forms of this adjective are ------, ------, ------.

R: m f n praeteritus praeterita praeteritum.

22-26

122. "Cujus mors est?" "Ag__ ____ ___."

R: Agnī mors est.

123. "Cujus cōnsilium bonum est?" "Fēm____ _____ _____ ___."

R: Fēminae cōnsilium bonum est.

124. ★ ○ • ○ • *Avārus ipse miseriae causa est suae.* (79)

125. There are two new words. If you change the **-a** of one of them you have an English word which has the same meaning as this Latin word from which it is derived. The Latin word c____ means "_____" in English.

A: causa cause

126. From now on we will explain the meaning of new words more and more in Latin. In the next frame your teacher will read an explanation of the new word **miseria**. The new verb **oppōnitur** means "is opposed to" in the sense of "is the opposite of," "is an antonym of," and it patterns with the dative case. For example, the statement **Fraus vēritātī oppōnitur** means that the word "_____" is ____ed to "_____."

A: trickery opposed truth.

127. Listen to your teacher explain the new word. ★ ○ "Miser" est homō quī nōn est fēlīx. Homō miser hominī fēlīcī oppōnitur. Homō fēlīx possidet virtūtem quae "fēlīcitās" dīcitur. Homō miser vitium habet quod "miseria" dīcitur. *Miseria fēlīcitātī oppōnitur.*

128. The word **miseria** seems to mean "m_____."

A: misery (unhappiness, etc.).

---

76. "Quotus homō jūcundus est?" "_____."

R: Prīmus homō jūcundus est.

77. The English derivative of **memoria** is "_____."

A: memory.

78. In this sentence the word **malōrum** is used as a noun meaning "ev____."

A: evils.

79. "Cujus cāsūs est haec vōx 'malōrum' et cujus numerī?" "Est cāsūs _____ et numerī _____."

R: genitīvī plūrālis.

80. Jūcunda memoria est malōrum = Pl__nt -- the _____-s.

A: Pleasant is the memory of evils.

81. This sounds ridiculous until we remember that there is a modifier of the word _____.

A: malōrum.

82. We have frequently reminded you that one of your tasks in learning Latin is to be able to work out the meaning of new words from the _____.

A: context.

22-27

129. In "Facts About Latin" add **oppōnit** to the list of compound verbs which pattern with the dative.

130. ★ ○ ○ A_____ i___ m_____ c____ e___ s____. (79)

R: Avārus ipse miseriae causa est suae.

131. This sentence means that a _____ _____ is h_____ the _____ __ his own _____.

A: greedy person is himself the cause of his own misery.

132. ★ ○ •
miseria
miseriam
miseriā
miseriae
miseriae

Quaestiōnēs et Respōnsa

133. "Quis est causa miseriae suae?" "_____."

R: Avārus ipse.

134. "Estne avārus miser an fēlīx?" "_____."

R: Miser.

135. "Quod vitium reddit hominem miserum?" "_____."

R: Avāritia.

23-10

71. The world makes its judgment with security = S_____ jū___ or___ t_____. ✓ ★ ○ •

R: Sēcurus jūdicat orbis terrārum. [The symbols meant that you should first say the Basic Sentence, then check with the tape, and finally write it. Did you do all these?]

72. *Jūcunda est praeteritōrum malōrum.* (91) • ○ ★ ✓ [Keep this frame covered when doing the next frame.]

73. ✓ ★ ○ ○ J___ ○ ○ m_____ pr___ ___ m_____.

R: Jūcunda memoria est praeteritōrum malōrum.

74. "Quae vōcēs hāc in sententiā sunt cāsūs genitīvī et numerī plūrālis?" "_____."

R: Praeteritōrum malōrum.

75. Homō jūcundus est homo qui est blandus vel hilaris. Homō jūcundō oppōnitur hominī ac___ō.

R: acerbō.

22-28

136. Echo the paradigm of a new adjective that means "each." ★ ○ •

	m	f	n
	quisque	quaeque	quodque
	quemque	quamque	quodque
	quōque	quāque	quōque
	cuique	cuique	cuique
	cujusque	cujusque	cujusque

137. When **quisque** is used as a noun, it means "each p_____."

A: person.

138. ★ ○ • ○ • *Exemplum Deī quisque est in imāgine parvā.* (80)

139. Echo the singular paradigm of **exemplum**. ★ ○ •

Cōnf: exemplum
       exemplum
       exemplō
       exemplō
       exemplī

140. In the Basic Sentence **Exemplum Deī quisque est in imāgine parvā,** the new noun **exemplum-ī,** n is _____ case.

A: nominative

141. We have an {_ _ _ _ _} type of sentence.

A: {-s -s est}

142. Since there is no masculine nominative noun for **quisque** to modify, it must mean "_____ _____."

A: each person.

143. Listen to the sentence and write down just the {-s -s est} kernel. ★ ○ ○ _____ _____ _____.

R: Exemplum quisque est.

---

65. **Sēcūrus jūdicat orbis terrārum** = ___ ___s ___ ___ ___.

A: The world makes its judgment with security.

66. This means that the _____ of the _____ can be tr___ed.

A: judgment of the world can be trusted.

67. These words were written by St. Augustine, prominent Christian churchman of the 5th Century. The meaning is that whatever the collective judgment of mankind has almost universally approved for many years must be _____.

A: right.

68. Observe that he is speaking about *judgment* and not about factual knowledge. This saying has a particular application to the study of Latin. Since the works which you will read in the Western World for 2000 years, you can have confidence that the study of Latin _____.

A: is worthwhile.

Quaestiōnēs et Respōnsa

69. "Quid sēcūrē jūdicat?" "_____."

R: Orbis terrārum.

70. "Quāliter jūdicat orbis terrārum?" "_____."

R: Sēcūrē. [Did you remember to put the three macrons in?]

22-29

144. This means that ____ _____ is an _____.

▼

A: each person is an example.

145. ★ ○ ○ Ex_____ D__ qu_____ ___ in im_____ p____.

▼

R: **Exemplum Deī quisque est in imāgine parvā.** [Do you have the three long vowels marked?]

146. The Basic Sentence means that ____ _____ __ __ _____ of ___ in a _____ _____. [There are two new words in this sentence. See if you can figure out what they must mean.]

▼

A: each person is an example of God in a small image.

147. Copy in your Notebook.

▼

148. ★ ○ • ("small image")
    parva imāgō
    parvam imāginem
    parvā imāgine
    parvae imāginī
    parvae imāginis

▼

149. **Imāgō** belongs to the ____ (1/2/3/4/5) Declension, while the feminine adjective **parva** belongs to the ____ (1/2/3/4/5) Declension.

▼

A: 3d
    1st

150. Latin adjectives ____ (have to be/do not have to be) in the same declension as the noun they modify.

▼

A: do not have to be

151. Latin adjectives *must* be the same _____, _____, and ____ as the noun they modify.

▼

A: number
gender   case

59. As you proceed further, you will discover increasingly that turning Latin into English is not simply a matter of replacing the Latin structure by the nearest English equivalent. If you do this, the English translation will *almost always* sound awkward. At the beginning, we purposely chose sentences where this one-to-one substitution (Latin subject becomes English subject, etc.) was possible, but from now on you will find that you frequently have to use a different English structure. In the sentence **Sēcūrus jūdicat orbis terrārum**, the word **sēcūrus** is an _____ and it modifies _____.

▲

A: adjective   orbis.

60. Try this one-for-one substitution and see how awkward the English sounds. **Sēcūrus jūdicat orbis terrārum** = The s_____ w_____ j_____ s.

▲

A: The secure world judges.

61. Now let us improve "The secure world judges." It would sound much better in English to have the idea of security modify the verb, perhaps by an adverb: "The world judges _____ly."

▲

A: securely.

62. Or we might make a prepositional phrase out of it and say that the world judges "w____ s_____y."

▲

A: with security.

63. **Sēcūrus jūdicat orbis terrārum** means that ___ _____ s_____ _____ s_____y.

▲

A: the world judges with security.

64. This still has an awkward sound, and it seems to improve if changed from "The world judges," to "The world m___ s its j_____nt."

▲

A: makes its judgment.

152. In the phrase **parva imāgō,** the adjective and noun belong to ____ (the same declension/different declensions).

A: different declensions.

153. However, **parva** and **imāgō** are the same _____, _____, and ____.

A: number, gender case.

Quaestiōnēs et Respōnsa

154. "Quid est homō in imāgine parvā?" "_____ _____."

R: Exemplum Deī.

155. "Cujus est homō exemplum?" "_____."

R: Deī.

156. "Cui similis est homō in imāgine parvā?" "_____."

R: Deō.

157. "Quōcum homō comparātur?" "_____ _____."

R: Cum Deō.

158. "Quanta imāgō Deī est homō?" "_____ _____."

R: Parva imāgō.

159-178. Echo the following paradigms of ten sample nouns of the five declensions and then add the dative and genitive to the forms in your Notebook.

159. ★ ○ • First Declension
  sīmia
  sīmiam
  sīmiā
  sīmiae
  sīmiae

52. Quae vōx hāc in sententiā est cāsūs genitīvī et numerī plūrālis? = What w___ in _____ is ____ and _____ ?

A: What word in this sentence is genitive case and plural number?

53. "Quae vōx hāc in sententiā est cāsūs genitīvī et numerī plūrālis?" "_____."

R: Terrārum.

54. "Aquatic" animals are those that live in the water; "terrestrial" animals are those that live on the l____.

A: land.

55. The new Latin word **terra** means "l____."

A: land.

56. The English derivative of the new word **secūrus** is "_____."

A: secure.

57. The first meaning that you learned for **orbis** was "circle," but in the sentence **Fāta regunt orbem; certā stant omnia lēge** you discovered that **orbis** also meant "_____."

A: world.

58. However, the full Latin expression for the "world" appears in this Basic Sentence; it is a two-word phrase, ____ t_____.

A: orbis terrārum.

22-31

160. Now copy it; leave room for the plural to be added later.

161. ★ ○ • **Second Declension (nom sg in -s)**
    lupus
    lupum
    lupō
    lupō
    lupī

162. Copy.

163. ★ ○ • **Second Declension (nom sg in ∅)**
    vir
    virum
    virō
    virō
    virī

164. Copy.

165. ★ ○ • **Second Declension Neuter**
    rēgnum
    rēgnum
    rēgnō
    rēgnō
    rēgnī

166. Copy.

167. ★ ○ • **Third Declension (nom sg in -s)**
    canis
    canem
    cane
    canī
    canis

168. Copy.

---

35. ★ ○ • V
    diēs   diēs
    diem   diēs
    diē   diēbus
    diēī   diēbus
    diēī   diērum

[That's the whole noun system. Doesn't look too bad, does it?]

36-45. Now copy the plurals in your Notebook under "Forms."

46. Sēcūrus jūdicat orbis terrārum. (90)

47. ★ ○ ○ S‾‾‾‾ j‾‾‾‾‾ or t‾‾‾‾‾‾.

R: Sēcūrus jūdicat orbis terrārum. [For a while, you will pronounce each Basic Sentence, then write it.]

48. The English derivative of plūrālis is "‾‾‾‾‾‾."

A: plural.

49. The English derivative of numerus is "n‾‾‾ber."

A: number.

50. Like cāsūs genitīvī, the phrase numerī plūrālis is ‾‾‾‾‾‾‾‾ case.

A: genitive

51. Quae vōx est numerī plūrālis? = ‾‾‾‾ w‾‾‾‾‾ is n‾‾‾er?

A: What word is plural number?

22-32

169. ★ ○ • Third Declension (nom sg in Ø)
      leō
      leōnem
      leōne
      leōnī
      leōnis

170. Copy.

171. ★ ○ • Third Declension Neuter
      genus
      genus
      genere
      generī
      generis

172. Copy.

173. ★ ○ • Fourth Declension
      manus
      manum
      manū
      manuī
      manūs

174. Copy.

175. ★ ○ • Fifth Declension (Characteristic vowel *short* in dative and genitive)
      rēs
      rem
      rē
      reī
      reī

176. Copy.

177. ★ ○ • Fifth Declension (Characteristic vowel *long* in dative and genitive)
      diēs
      diem
      diē
      diēī
      diēī

178. Copy.

---

29. ★ ○ • II N
    rēgnum   rēgna
    rēgnum   rēgna
    rēgnō   rēgnīs
    rēgnō   rēgnīs
    rēgnī   rēgnōrum

30. ★ ○ • III
    canis   canēs
    canem   canēs
    cane   canibus
    canī   canibus
    canis   canum

31. ★ ○ • III
    leō   leōnēs
    leōnem   leōnēs
    leōne   leōnibus
    leōnī   leōnibus
    leōnis   leōnum

32. ★ ○ • III N
    genus   genera
    genus   genera
    genere   generibus
    generī   generibus
    generis   generum

33. ★ ○ • IV
    manus   manūs
    manum   manūs
    manū   manibus
    manuī   manibus
    manūs   manuum

34. ★ ○ • V
    rēs   rēs
    rem   rēs
    rē   rēbus
    reī   rēbus
    reī   rērum

22-33

179. Looking at the paradigms of the two Fifth Declension nouns, you will notice that the **-e-** is long when it follows the vowel **-i-** as in **diēī**, but in the form **reī**, the **-e-** is a _____ vowel.

A: short

180. The rule therefore is that in Fifth Declension nouns like **aciēs** and **effigiēs**, the **-e-** is ____ (short/long) after the **-i-**.

A: long (as in **effigiēī**)

181. In words like **rēs** and **spēs**, which have no **-i-**, the **-e-** in the dative and genitive is ____ (short/long).

A: short (as in **speī**).

182. ★ ○ • ○ •
Lingua malī pars pessima servī. (81)

183. Chorus with your teacher as he explains a new word. ★ ◉ *"Lingua est pars corporis. Auribus hominēs audiunt, linguā dīcunt, manū scrībunt, pedibus currunt. Quotō in orbe est lingua?"*

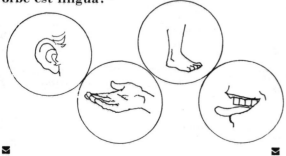

184. "_____."

R: Quārtō in orbe est lingua.

---

22. *Causa rērum* = _____.

A: The cause of the things blanks.

23. *Lingua servōrum* = _____.

A: The tongue of slaves blanks.

24. *Index fūrem* = _____.

A: The betrayer blanks the thief.

25. *Finis nāvium* = _____.

A: The end of the ships blanks.

26-34. Echo representative nouns of the five declensions.

26. ★ ○ • I

simia	simiae
simiam	simiās
simiā	simiīs
simiae	simiīs
simiae	simiārum

27. ★ ○ • II

lupus	lupī
lupum	lupōs
lupō	lupīs
lupō	lupīs
lupī	lupōrum

28. ★ ○ • II

vir	virī
virum	virōs
virō	virīs
virō	virīs
virī	virōrum

22-34

185. Homō in hāc pictūrā nōn est līber sed *dominō* servit. Est homō ēmptus, cui pecūnia prō opere suō nōn datur. Hic vir dīcitur "s___us."

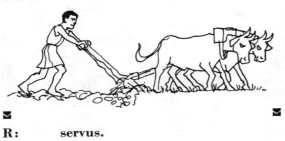

R: servus.

186. Quī servit dīcitur "servus." Quī imperat dīcitur "dom__us."

R: dominus.

187. *Servus* means "_____," while *dominus* is his "_____."

A: slave
     master.

188. An "optimist" is one who expects that the best is going to happen. A "pessimist," on the other hand, expects that the w____ is going to happen.

A: worst

189. ★ ○ ○
L_____ m___ p___ p_____ s____.

R: Lingua malī pars pessima servī.

190. In your answer pad, connect the adjectives with the nouns they modify. If they do not modify nouns, say so.
Lingua malī pars pessima servī.

A: Lingua malī pars pessima servī.

191. This is an {__ __ ___} type of sentence with the {___} omitted.

A: {-s -s est}
        {est}

---

14. Īra hominum = _____.
A: Anger of human beings (men) blanks.
Anger blanks a human being (man).

15. Rēgīna virtūtum = _____.
A: Queen of virtues blanks.
The queen blanks virtue.

16. Glōria vītam = _____.
A: Glory blanks life.

17. Pictūra vultum = _____.
A: The picture blanks the face.

18. Ēloquentia anuum = _____.
A: The eloquence of old ladies blanks.

19. Gradus porticuum = _____.
A: The step of the covered walks blanks.

20. Umbra quercuum = _____.
A: Shade of the oak trees blanks.

21. Frāctūra arcum = _____.
A: The breaking blanks the bow.

16-25. Try these without the advantage of being able to see both forms at once.

22-35

192. Lingua malī pars pessima servī =
The _____ is the _____ ____ of a ___ _____.

⌄

A: The tongue is the worst part of a bad slave.

193. Copy in your Notebook.

⌄

Quaestiōnēs et Respōnsa

194. "Quālis servus est quī nimis dīcit?"
"M____."

⌄

R: Malus.

195. "Cujus lingua dominō nocet?" "____
_____."

⌄

R: Malī
servī.

196. "Quāliter servit dominō suō servus
quī nimis dīcit, bene an male?" "____."

⌄

R: Male.

197. "Cui nocet servus quī nimis dīcit?"
"Dom___ suō."

⌄

R: Dominō suō.

198. Write the sentence. L_____ m___ p___
pes____ se___.

⌄

R: Lingua malī pars
pessima servī. [If you had any trouble, learn
the Basic Sentence *now*.]

199. ★ ○ • ○ • *Malitia ipsa maximam
partem venēnī suī bibit.* (82) [If you feel that
you know the meaning go to frame 207. Otherwise continue with the program.]

⌄

200. Malitia est vitium quod possidet
homō malus. "Malitia" oppōnitur v____ūtī.

⌄

R: virtūtī.

---

7. There is just one difficulty, and we will practice on that right now. The forms **equum** (accusative singular) and **canum** (genitive plural) have the same last two letters. The -um of **equum** is the ch------- v---- plus the ending ---

⌄

A: characteristic vowel
-m-.

⌄

8. However, in **canum**, the characteristic vowel is missing, and the signal is ---.

⌄

A: -um-.

9-13. Let us practice some of these contrasts like **equum** (acc sg) and **canum** (gen pl), using the word "blanks" to furnish a slot for the English subjects and objects.

9. Mors leōnem = the ----- s----- ---

⌄

A: Death blanks the lion.

⌄

10. "Cujus cāsus est 'leōnem'?" "Leōnem ___ --- ------."

⌄

R: "Leō-
nem" est cāsūs accūsatīvī.

⌄

11. Mors leōnum = ------ --- --- -----
------s.

⌄

A: Death of the lions blanks.

⌄

12. "Cujus cāsus est 'leōnum'?" "Leōnum ___ --- ------."

⌄

R: "Leō-
num" est cāsūs genitīvī.

⌄

13. Give the meaning of these pairs:
Pars fēminam = --------------------
Pars fēminārum = --------------------

⌄

A: Part blanks the woman.
Part of the women blanks.

22-36

201. From the English word "minimum" you can guess that the Latin adjective **minimus, minima, minimum** means "sm___est."

A: smallest.

202. From the English word "maximum" you can guess that the Latin adjective **maximus, maxima, maximum** means "_____."

A: largest.

203. **Malitia ipsa maximam partem venēnī suī bibit** = M__ice its___ ___s the _____ p___ of its ___ _____.

A: Malice itself drinks the largest part of its own poison.

204. Copy in your Notebook.

205. The sentence means that a person who hates other people hurts _____.

A: himself more than anyone else.

206. "Malice" is derived from the Latin word _____.

A: **malitia**.

Quaestiōnēs et Respōnsa

207. "Quantam partem venēnī suī bibit malitia?" "_____ p_____."

R: Maximam partem.

208. "Quō malitia laeditur?" "V_____ suō."

R: Venēnō suō.

UNIT TWENTY-THREE

23-1

This Unit marks a milestone in your Latin course. When you complete it, you will have learned the entire noun system, which is the major portion of the structure of the Latin language. And there is further good news: the last form, the genitive plural, is the easiest of all the noun forms. Here are sample genitive plurals from the five declensions.

1. ★ ○ ● ○ ●

1st	2d	3d	4th	5th
aquārum	equōrum	canum	manuum	diērum

2. In the First, Second, and Fifth Declension the signal for the genitive plural is _____ -rum.

A: -rum.

3. In the Third and Fourth Declensions the signal for genitive plural is _____ -um.

A: -um.

4. The characteristic vowel appears in all the declensions except the _____ Declension.

A: Third

5. You will discover, however, that most adjectives of the Third Declension (and a few nouns) have the characteristic vowel -i before the signal -um. For example, the form **crūdēlium** is the _____ of **crūdēlis**.

A: genitive plural

6. Here is the complete declension of a Third Declension noun. ★ ○ ●

homō	hominēs
hominem	hominēs
homine	hominibus
hominī	hominibus
hominis	hominum

22-37

209. "Quid agit malitia?" "M_____ p_____ v_____ s__ b_____."

R: Maximam partem venēnī suī bibit.

210. "Sī homō malus miser est, quid est causa miseriae suae?" "_____."

R: Malitia.

211. "Adjuvāturne an laeditur homō malus malitiā suā?" "_____."

R: Laeditur.

212. "Quō homō malus maximē laeditur?" "M_____ s__." [Auxilium sub hāc līneā est.]

Aux: The new word **maximē** means "mostly"; **quō** does not modify **homō** but means "By what?"

R: Malitiā suā.

213. Write the sentence. M_____ ip__ m_____ p_____ v_____ s__ b_____.

R: Malitia ipsa maximam partem venēnī suī bibit.

214. ★ ○ • ○ • Mors lupī agnīs vīta. (83)

215. ★ ○ ○ M___ l___ ag___ v___.

R: Mors lupī agnīs vīta.

TEST INFORMATION

You will be asked to do only paradigms taken from the 26 which you practiced in this Unit, and then only in the singular. You are responsible for **quisque**, but not yet for the different forms of **hic**.

The tasks will be similar to those which you did in the program, but, except for the paradigms, they will not be taken from frames in the Unit. However, you will be asked to give the genitive only of forms which you have practiced in this Unit.

Verbs: **accidit** (276) **oppōnit** (126) **pingit** (229)

Adverb: **maximē** (212)

Subordinating Conjunction: **sī** (103)

One new phrase: **rēs pūblica** (322)

You are now ready for the test for Unit Twenty-two. Review the new words first if you need to.

216. Expand this partial pattern to make it complete. **Mors lupī _ _ _ agnīs vīta.**

R: est

217. The kernel of the sentence is ____ (est) ____.

A: **Mors (est) vīta.**

218. In **Mors lupī agnīs vīta**, the word **lupī** is _____ case and _____ number, while the word **agnīs** is _____ case and _____ number.

A: genitive   singular
   dative   plural

219. **Mors lupī agnīs vīta** = The ____ __ the ____ __ ____ ___ the _____.

A: The death of the wolf is life for the lambs.

220. Copy in your Notebook.

221. **Mors lupī agnīs vīta** means that _____.
[In your own words]

A: what may be a misfortune for one person will be a blessing for someone else.

Quaestiōnēs et Respōnsa

222. "Quae animālia adjuvat lupī mors?"
"_____."

R: Agnōs.

223. "Quibus mors lupī grāta est?"
"_____."

R: Agnīs.

364. Avāritia hominem miserum reddit.

Av____ ip__ m_____ c____ _t s____.

R: Avārus ipse miseriae causa est suae.

VOCABULARY INVENTORY

Nouns: [From now on we will list nouns with nominative, genitive, and gender.]

cāsus-ūs, m (241)
causa-ae, f (125)
cultus-ūs, m (338)
*diēs, diēī, m&f (64)
dominus-ī, m (186)
exemplum-ī, n (139)
firmāmentum-ī, n (320)
flōs, flōris, m (229)
glōria-ae, f (280)
hōra-ae, f (44)
imāgō, imāginis, f (148)
index, indicis, m&f (303)
īnstrūmentum-ī, n (319)
lingua-ae, f (183)
miseria-ae, f (128)
odor, odōris, m (229)
*ōrātiō, ōrātiōnis, f (340)
pars, partis, f (39)
sententia-ae, f (275)
servus-ī, m (66)
*vōx, vōcis, f (241)
vultus-ūs, m (302)

Adjectives:

ablātīvus-a-um (251)
accūsātīvus-a-um (250)
datīvus-a-um (252)
genitīvus-a-um (253)
ipse, ipsa, ipsum (4)
maximus-a-um (202)
minimus-a-um (201)
nōminātīvus-a-um (249)
pessimus-a-um (189)
quisque, quaeque, quodque (136)
tōtus-a-um (37)

224. "Ā quibus animālibus agnī saepe laeduntur?" "_ _____."

R: Ā lupīs.

225. "Quid placet agnīs omnibus?" "M___ l___."

R: Mors lupī.

226. "Cum lupus perit, quī hilarēs sunt?" "____."

R: Agnī.

227. "Quālēs sunt agnī cum lupus perit?" "_____."

R: Hilarēs.

228. Say the Basic Sentence described by this picture. M___ l___ a____ v___.

R: Mors lupī agnīs vīta.

229. ★ ○ • ○ • *Quī pingit flōrem flōris nōn pingit odōrem.* (84)

Now write the Basic Sentence which expresses about the same thought as the Latin sentence.

338. Religiō vēra rem pūblicam adjuvat.
R: V___ r__ f___ t___ p_____.
R: Religiō vēra est firmāmentum reī pūblicae.

339. Ōrātiō animum hominis colit. Ō___ c___ an___ t.
R: Ōrātiō cultus animī est.

360. Homō vultū suō indicātur. V_____ in___ an___.
R: Vultus index animī.

361. Homō celeriter perit. V___ h___ br___ t.
R: Vīta hominis brevis est.

362. Homō malus verbīs suīs maximē laeditur. M____ ip__ m____ p____ v___ s__ b____.
R: Malitia ipsa maximam partem venēnī suī bibit.

363. Homō parvulus similis Deō magnō est. Ex____ D__ qu___ t in im____ p____.
R: Exemplum Deī quisque est in imāgine parva.

22-40

230. The subject of this sentence is not one word but _____ words.

A: three

231. The subject is the clause ___ _____ _____.

A: Quī pingit flōrem.

232. ★ ○ ○ Q__ p_____ fl____ fl____ n___ p_____ o_____.

R: Quī pingit flōrem flōris nōn pingit odōrem. [Five macrons!]

233. Quī pingit flōrem flōris nōn pingit odōrem = Who _____s the _____ doesn't _____ the _____'s ____. [There are three new words in this sentence. But if you look at the picture you ought to be able to guess the meaning.]

A: Who paints the flower doesn't paint the flower's odor.

234. Copy in your Notebook.

235. This sentence means that if you have had some wonderful experience it is impossible for you to _____. [In your own words]

A: completely describe it.

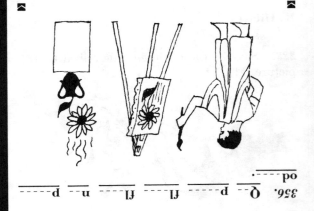

22-41

Quaestiōnēs et Respōnsa

236. "Utra rēs habet odōrem, flōs ipse an pictūra flōris?" "_____."

R: Flōs ipse.

237. "Cujus odōrem nēmō pingit?" "_____ od____."

R: Flōris odōrem.

238. "Hāc in pictūrā quid juvenis pingit?" "_____."

R: Flōrem.

239. "Quid nōn pingit?" "_____ _____."

R: Flōris odōrem.

240. Review Sentences 79-84 in your Notebook.

241. Echo your teacher as he says in Latin "What case is this word 'virum'?" ★ ○ • ○ •
C____ c____ __t h___ v__ "v____"?

Cōnf: Cujus cāsūs est haec vōx "virum"? [In doing the next frame, be sure not to look at this frame.]

242. Listen again and write. C____ c____ ___ h___ v__ "_____"? ★ ○ •

R: Cujus cāsūs est haec vōx "virum"?

243. Ask your teacher this same question. "C____ c_____ ___ ___ ___ '____'"? √ ★ ○ •

Cōnf: Cujus cāsūs est haec vōx "virum"?

244. Write his answer. ★ ○ ○ " 'V____' ___ c____ ac_____."

R: "Virum" est cāsūs accūsātīvī.

R: Lingua malī pars pessima servī. (81)

334. L__ m__ p__ s_____.

[Review first which are illustrated by pictures. [Review first in your Notebook if you like.]

A: modifies another noun.

333. The main use of the genitive case is to show that one noun _____.

A: genitive

332. In this Unit you learned a new case called the _____ case.

SUMMARY

R: Cāsūs genitīvī.

351. "Cujus cāsūs est haec vōx 'animī'" in 'Ōrātiō cultus animī est'?" "_____."

R: Animum.

350. "Quid ōrātiō colit?" "_____."

R: Cultū animī.

349. "Quō ōrātor redditur?" "_____."

245. Notice that the noun **cāsūs** is ‒‒‒‒‒‒‒‒ case.

A: genitive

246. The reason the Romans used the genitive was that they didn't consider **virum** the *whole* accusative case; it was simply a ‒‒‒‒ of the accusative case.

A: part (example, etc.)

247. Haec vōx "virum" nōn est tōtus cāsus accūsātīvus sed est pars c‒‒‒‒ ac‒‒‒‒‒‒‒‒.

R: cāsus accūsātīvī.

248. Echo the nominative form of the names of the Latin cases. ★ ○ • ○ • **cāsus nōminātīvus, cāsus accūsātīvus, cāsus ablātīvus, cāsus datīvus, cāsus genitīvus.**

249-253. Echo as your teacher describes each case of the paradigm of the word **rēs**.

249. ★ ○ • "**Rēs**" est cāsūs nōmināt‒‒‒‒.

Cōnf: nōminātīvī.

250. ★ ○ • "**Rem**" est cās‒‒ accūs‒‒‒‒‒.

Cōnf: cāsūs accūsātīvī.

251. ★ ○ • "**Rē**" est c‒‒‒‒ abl‒‒‒‒‒‒.

Cōnf: cāsūs ablātīvī.

Quaestiōnēs et Respōnsa

346. "Quid animum hominis colit?" "‒‒‒‒‒‒‒."

R: Ōrātiō.

347. "Quō animus hominis colitur?" "‒‒‒‒‒‒‒."

R: Ōrātiōne.

348. "Quid ōrātōrem reddit?" "C‒‒‒‒‒ a‒‒‒‒."

R: Cultus animī.

---

342. Ōrātiō cultus animī est = ‒‒‒‒‒‒‒‒‒‒‒‒‒‒‒‒‒‒.

A: Oratory is the cultivation of the mind.

343. You may now copy this in your Notebook.

344. ★ ○ • Fourth Declension cultus
cultum
cultū
cultuī
cultūs

345. ★ ○ • Third Declension ōrātiō
ōrātiōnem
ōrātiōne
ōrātiōnī
ōrātiōnis

22-43

252. ★ ○ • "Reī" est c____ d____.

Cōnf: cāsūs datīvī.

253. ★ ○ • "Reī" est c____ g____.

Cōnf: cāsūs genitīvī.

254-269. In this sequence we will ask you for the case of one of the nouns in each of sixteen Basic Sentences. [Reply aloud, of course.]

254. **Exemplum Deī quisque est in imāgine parvā.** (80) "Cujus cāsūs est 'imāgine'?" "Est cāsūs _____vī."

R: Est cāsūs ablātīvī.

255. **Dīs proximus ille est quem ratiō, nōn īra, movet.** (75) "Cujus cāsūs est 'dīs'?" "Est c____ _____."

R: Est cāsūs datīvī.

256. **Quī pingit flōrem flōris nōn pingit odōrem.** (84) "Cujus cāsūs est 'flōris'?" "___ _____ _____."

R: Est cāsūs genitīvī.

257. **Artēs serviunt vītae, sapientia imperat.** (73) "Cujus cāsūs est 'vītae'?" "____ _____."

R: Est cāsūs datīvī.

258. **Malitia ipsa maximam partem venēnī suī bibit.** (82) "Cujus cāsūs est 'venēnī'?" "_____."

R: Est cāsūs genitīvī.

337. ★ ○ ○ O____ c____ a____ ____.

R: **Ōrātiō cultus animī est.**

338. **Cultus** is a Fourth Declension noun formed on the past participle stem of the verb **colō**; in this sentence it means "_____tion."

A: cultivation.

339. You have met the word **ōrātiō** in Basic Sentence 34: H____ s____ v____ bl____ or____.

A: **Habet suum venēnum blanda ōrātiō.**

340. You are familiar by now with the fact that words have different meanings according to the context. The best procedure is to try the old meaning, being always ready to find a new one if the old one doesn't make sense. Let's do that now: **Ōrātiō cultus animī est** = _____ _____.

A: Speech is the cultivation of the mind. [Do not copy this in your Notebook.]

341. This requires a little more explanation. To a Roman, **ōrātiō**, the art of speaking in public, was the sum total of a man's education, which would permit him to participate in the public and private affairs of his time. It meant not only the ability to present ideas in forceful fashion but also the education which would give him the experience to conceive worthwhile ideas to present. Perhaps the best we can do is to use the English word "oratory," keeping in mind that it means in talking about the Romans not only _____ but also _____ [In your own words]

A: the art of speaking education in general.

22-44

259. Avārus ipse miseriae causa est suae. (79) "Cujus cāsūs est 'ipse'?" "——————."

R: —————— Est cāsūs nōminātīvī.

260. Inopī beneficium bis dat quī dat celeriter. (70) "Cujus cāsūs est 'inopī'?" "——————."

R: Est cāsūs datīvī.

261. Impōnit fīnem sapiēns et rēbus honestīs. (78) "Cujus cāsūs est 'rēbus'?" "——————."

R: Est cāsūs datīvī.

262. Deō, Rēgī, Patriae. (72) "Cujus cāsūs est 'patriae'?" "——————."

R: —————— Est cāsūs datīvī.

263. Lingua malī pars pessima servī. (81) "Cujus cāsūs est 'servī'?" "——————."

R: —————— Est cāsūs genitīvī.

264. Mors īnfantī fēlīx, juvenī acerba, nimis sēra senī. (71) "Cujus cāsūs est 'senī'?" "——————."

R: —————— Est cāsūs datīvī.

265. Nēmō līber est quī corporī servit. (74) "Cujus cāsūs est 'nēmō'?" "——————."

R: —————— Est cāsūs nōminātīvī.

266. Mors lupī agnīs vīta. (83) "Cujus cāsūs est 'lupī'?" "——————."

R: —————— Est cāsūs genitīvī.

22-53

330. "Nocetne an servit reī pūblicae superstitio?" "——————."

R: Nocet.

331. "Quid agit superstitio?" "R—— p—— n——."

R: Reī pūblicae nocet.

332. "In hāc sententiā 'Religiō vēra est firmāmentum reī pūblicae,' cujus cāsūs est haec vōx 'reī,' datīvī an genitīvī?" "——————."

R: Cāsūs genitīvī.

333. "Cui servit religiō vēra?" "——————."

R: Reī pūblicae.

334. "In illō respōnsō 'Reī pūblicae nocet,' cujus cāsūs est haec vōx 'reī'?" "——————."

R: Cāsūs datīvī.

335. Write Basic Sentence 88. R—— v—— firm—— r—— pūb——.

R: Religiō vēra est firmāmentum reī pūblicae.

336. ★ ○ ● ○ *Ōrātiō* cultus animī est. (68)

22-45

267. Ingrātus ūnus omnibus miserīs nocet. (76) "Cujus cāsūs est 'miserīs'?" "_____."

R: Est cāsūs datīvī.

268. Mulier quae multīs nūbit multīs nōn placet. (77) "Cujus cāsūs est 'multīs'?" "_____."

R: Est cāsūs datīvī.

269. Asinus asinō, sūs suī pulcher. (69) "Cujus cāsūs est 'asinō'?" "_____."

R: Est cāsūs datīvī.

We will now take up five new Basic Sentences.

270. ★ ○ • ○ • *Vīta hominis brevis est.* (85)

271. ★ ○ ○ V___ h_____ br____ ___.

R: Vīta hominis brevis est.

272. This means that the _____.

A: life of man is short.

273. Copy in your Notebook.

274. ★ ○ • homō
 hominem
 homine
 hominī
 hominis

---

322. However, since the word "republic" refers today to a particular form of government, we will translate *rēs pūblica* in this Basic Sentence as the "st____."

A: state.

323. • ○ ★ rēs pūblica
 rem pūblicam
 rē pūblicā
 reī pūblicae
 reī pūblicae

324. **Religiō vēra est firmāmentum reī pūblicae** = --- _____ is the _____ of the state.

A: True religion is the foundation of the state.

325. Copy in your Notebook.

Quaestiōnēs et Respōnsa

326. "Quālis religiō rem pūblicam custōdit?" "_____."

R: Vēra religiō.

327. "Quālī religiōne rēs pūblica custōditur?" "_____."

R: Vērā religiōne.

328. "Cujus est religiō vēra maxima pars?" "R--- p---____."

R: Reī pūblicae.

329. "Quō rēs pūblica custōdītur?" "_____."

R: Vērā religiōne.

275. "Hāc in sententiā vōx 'vīta' est cāsūs nōminātīvī." The word vōx in this sentence must mean "w___," and the word sententia must mean "s____ce."

A: word
         sentence.

276. "Quae vōx hāc in sententiā (Vīta hominis brevis est) est cāsūs genitīvī?" "_____."

R: Hominis.

Quaestiōnēs et Respōnsa

An accident is something that happens unexpectedly. The Latin verb **accidit** means "happen"; it takes its complement in the dative case.

277. "Cui mors accidit?" "H_____."

R: Hominī.

278. "Cujus vīta nōn longa est?" "_____."

R: Hominis.

279. Write Basic Sentence 85. Vī__ hom____ br____ ___.

R: Vīta hominis brevis est.

280. ★ ○ • ○ • *Glōria umbra virtūtis est.* (86)

314. "Cujus cāsūs est 'animī'?" "_____."

R: Cāsūs genitīvī.

315. Write Basic Sentence 87. Vul___ in___ an___.

R: Vultus index animī.

316. ● ○ ★ ● ○ • *Religiō vēra est firmāmentum reī pūblicae.* (88)

317. ★ ○ ○ R___ v___ ___ f___ ___ r___ p___.

R: Religiō vēra est firmāmentum reī pūblicae.

318. The unknown word **firmāmentum** must be a _____ noun of the _____ Declension. [Auxilium sub hāc līneā]

Aux: Remember what type of sentence this is.

A: neuter   second

319. The ending **-mentum** indicates a noun which does something, like the word **instrūmentum**. **Firmāmentum** is the thing which makes something f___.

A: firm.

320. The meaning of **firmāmentum** in this sentence is found_____.

A: foundation.

321. The expression **rēs pūblica** always occurs in this order and in fact is sometimes written as one word, like this: **rēspūblica**. In this form it is easier to see that the English derivative is the word "r___c____."

A: republic.

281. ★ ○ ○ Gl____ u____ v_____ ___.

R: Glōria umbra virtūtis est.

282. This means, "___ry is the _____ __ _____."

A: Glory is the shadow of virtue.

283. Copy in your Notebook.

284. This means that if a person is truly good, fame will follow him just as surely as his _____ follows him.

A: shadow

285. In other words, just as you cannot catch your own shadow so you cannot catch fame, but if you live a virtuous life fame will _____ you like your shadow.

A: follow

Quaestiōnēs et Respōnsa

286. "Cujus umbra est glōria?" "_____."

R: Virtūtis.

287. "Quaeritne glōria virum bonum an malum?" "_____."

R: Bonum.

288. "Quālem virum glōria quaerit?" "_____ _____."

R: Bonum virum.

289. "Quālī hominī glōria accidit?" "_____ _____."

R: Bonō hominī.

304. The finger that we point with is called in English the _____ finger.

A: index

305. Vultus index animī. ∨ ★ ○ •

306. This means that the ____ __ ___ betr__r __ ___ ____.

A: face is the betrayer of the mind.

307. Copy in your Notebook.

308. This means that _____.
[In your own words]

309. ★ ○ • vultus
vultum
vultū
vultuī
vultūs

A: our face reveals our thoughts.

310. "Quō animus indicātur?" "V_____."

R: Vultū.

311. "Quid vultū indicātur?" "_____."

R: Animus.

312. "Cujus auxiliō animus indicātur?" "V____ a_____."

R: Vultūs auxiliō.

313. "Quid mentem hominis indicat?"

R: Vultus.

22-48

290. "Quid possidet bonus homō?" "Gl_____."

R: Glōriam.

291. "Quālī hominī glōria proxima est?" "____ _____."

R: Bonō hominī.

292. "Quōcum comparātur glōria?" "___ u_____."

R: Cum umbrā.

293. "Cui glōria similis est?" "_____."

R: Umbrae.

294. "Cujus cāsūs est 'virtūtis'?" "_____ _____."

R: Cāsūs genitīvī.

295. Gl____ um___ vir_____ ___. (86)

R: Glōria umbra virtūtis est.

296. ★ ○ • ○ • *Vultus index animī.* (87)

297. ★ ○ ○ V____ i____ _____.

R: Vultus index animī.

22-49

298. This is an {_____} type of sentence.

A: {-s -s est}

299. Write your teacher's description of this picture. ★ ○ ○ V_____ h_____ f_____ bl_____.

R: Vultus hujus fēminae blandus est.

300. Hujus must be the _____ case of the adjective hic, haec, hoc.

A: genitive

301. Write your teacher's description of this picture. ★ ○ ○ V_____ h_____ f_____ ac_____.

R: Vultus hujus fēminae acerbus est.

302. The word vultus refers to the expr_____ on the f____.

A: expression on the face.

303. The word index, indicis, m or f, is connected with the verb _____.

A: indicat.

To continue the program, turn your book around and begin work on column 22-49.

Artes Latinae
by Waldo Sweet

Published by Bolchazy-Carducci Publishers, Inc.,
Originally published by
Encyclopaedia Brittanica Educational Corporation

CD-ROM Format

Each disk is the equivalent of Books 1 & 2 and the cassettes in the traditional format.

CD-ROM package includes the following materials:
✦ Manual   ✦ Graded Reader   ✦ TM Graded Reader
✦ Reference Notebook   ✦ Unit Test Booklet   ✦ Unit Test Guide

Level 1 CD-ROM features three pronunciations
Level 2 CD-ROM features two pronunciations
(Continental/Ecclesiastical will be available in an upgrade)

CD-ROM Requirements

IBM or Compatible   VGA Monitor
2X CD-ROM Drive or better 1 MB Space on Hard Drive
16-bit Sound Capabilities in Windows   Windows 3.1 or later (Incl. Windows-95)

Level I Disk Package:, #0105

#295-6, Additional *Reference Notebook*
  (consumable)
#293-X, Additional *Unit Test booklet*
  (consumable)
#294-8, Additional *Graded Reader*
  (Lectiones Primae)
#311-1, *Level I Disk* alone

Level II Disk Package: #0205

#303-0, Additional *Reference Notebook*
  (consumable)
#301-4, Additional *Unit Test booklet*
  (consumable)
#302-2, Additional *Graded Reader*
  (Lectiones Seccundae)
#312-X, *Level II Disk* alone

Also Available...

Filmstrips:
  #389-8, Basic Sentences & Structures (set of 5)
  #390-1, Roma Antiqua (set of 5 with guide)
  #391-X, Roma: Urbs et Orbis (set of 5 with guide)
  Filmstrip viewer available

Bolchazy-Carducci Publishers, Inc.
1000 Brown St., Unit 101
Wauconda, IL 60084

847/526-4344; *Fax:* 847/526-2867

E-mail: latin@bolchazy.com
Website: http://www.bolchazy.com

This is as practical and easy to use as any language program I have ever encountered.
  John A. Jackson
  International Congress on Medieval Studies Conferee